D0725397

Urban Problems in Sociological Perspective

Fourth Edition

Thomas R. Shannon
Radford University

Nancy Kleniewski
Bridgewater State College

William M. Cross
Illinois College

WAVELAND
PRESS, INC.

Long Grove, Illinois

For information about this book, contact:
  Waveland Press, Inc.
  4180 IL Route 83, Suite 101
  Long Grove, IL 60047-9580
  (847) 634-0081
  info@waveland.com
  www.waveland.com

10-digit ISBN 1-57766-195-8
13-digit ISBN 978-1-57766-195-5

Printed in the United States of America

10 9 8 7 6 5 4

Contents

Preface

The fourth edition of this book remains faithful to the goal of the previous editions to provide a text for urban sociology students that is concise, clearly written, and theoretically balanced. We continue to believe that clarity and brevity can be achieved without unduly sacrificing intellectual rigor. This book continues to be heavily oriented to the sociological analysis of contemporary urban problems. At the same time we seek to put those problems clearly within the context of urban history and sociological theory. We also devote more time than most texts to what we hope is even-handed evaluation of social policy. The first chapters provide an overview of U.S. urban history and an introduction to the major theoretical traditions in urban sociology. Most of the rest of the book examines specific contemporary urban problems and trends. A chapter on urban conditions outside the United States continues to provide a comparative framework for thinking about urban conditions in this country.

In the short time that has elapsed since the third edition, much has changed on the urban landscape. Even a short list of these changes makes clear that our revision work had to be fairly extensive. Immigration has changed the ethnic mix of cities in an increasingly dramatic way. Urban migration flows in the Third World appear to be shifting away from "primate" cities. Most of the former Soviet empire has joined the ranks of the partially industrialized countries of the Third World. The welfare system has been completely changed, but poverty persists as a problem of low-wage workers. Urban sprawl continues to create ever larger, lower density metropolitan areas. Central cities continue to struggle with economic decline. The emerging role of the United States in a global economy continues to be a factor in changing U.S. urban conditions.

As a consequence, almost every part of the third edition required some updating or revision. Chapter 2 on recent urban trends obviously required the most revision. However, we tried to retain, as much as possible, the topical organization of the previous edition and to avoid significant changes in the length of chapters. Users of the previous edition will not see large, obvious changes. Rather, careful reading will reveal a substantial reworking and updating of the treatment of topics and new data.

Thomas R. Shannon
Nancy Kleniewski
William M. Cross

1

Origins of the Urban Crisis

1

To understand the problems of contemporary urban areas requires that we first review the historical origins of urban America. To a very significant degree, the present dilemmas urban areas face can be traced to the past.

The United States offers one of the most dramatic examples of transformation by means of urbanization and industrialization. Politically, it moved from a colonial to a global power. Economically, it moved from being a collector and exporter of raw materials to being the world's largest producer of industrial goods. Systematically, America moved from being a peripheral entity tied to a European core to establishing itself as the center of the modern world system (Abu-Lughod, 1991:80).

In the period from 1609 to 1830, the nation moved from colonization to decolonization. The Revolutionary War focused on the distrust of central government. Yet to defend the new land, a central government emerged, albeit grudgingly. By 1830, an urban system came into existence that would dominate the nation for the rest of the century. Its elements included small-scale industrialization, immigration from Europe, slums paralleling those found in European manufacturing towns, and an entrepreneurial model dominated by promoters and land speculators. During the mid-1800s industrial capitalism came to dominate. The industrial core depended heavily on European migration and on the development of the Midwest. Chicago came to play a dominant role in connecting the financial headquarters of New York with the expanding frontier, while simultaneously emerging as a great industrial center (Abu-Lughod, 1991:80–87, 92, 95).

During the period between the Civil War and World War I, there was a drastic reorganization of the socioeconomic and political systems of the nation. This reorganization included the shift to capital-intensive industrial production dependent on steam power; an increase in the scale of commerce and industry characterized by professional management separated from ownership and accompanied by an increase in conflict between labor and management; and an increased involvement of government in financing infrastructure, regulating the economy, and assuming responsibility for planning, education, and welfare. Government was called on to provide infrastructures needed by business and industry, as well as urban services desired by the upper class. There was a strong emphasis on law and order (Abu-Lughod, 1991:96–100).

Following the lead of the railroads, which organized nationally and obtained great amounts of subsidies from the federal government, businesses and corporations joined forces with the government. They too obtained protection of their property, much needed infrastructure, and the benefits of fire and police departments. Class segregation occurred as a result of improved transportation, which functioned in such a way as to segregate housing (Abu-Lughod, 1991:104–8).

THE RISE OF THE INDUSTRIAL CITY

The last half of the nineteenth century saw the transformation of American cities in the North and Northeast into a new kind of city: the industrial city. This new kind of city was the creation of a fundamentally different kind of technology and system for organizing production: factory-based industrial production.

At the roots of this new system were certain basic technological innovations. Improved agricultural techniques and the introduction of agricultural machinery meant that each farmer could now produce much more than before. This, in turn, meant that farmers could produce much more than their families could consume. Farmers could sell this surplus production and use the cash to buy consumer goods and machinery. For society as a whole, this development had two important results. First, there was a growing market for finished manufactured goods. Second, there now were more workers available in the economy to engage in nonagricultural production (the farmers' surplus was available to feed them). These nonagricultural workers, in turn, could be employed to operate the new steam-powered factories to produce more finished goods.

The rapid development of industrial machinery and the application of steam power to production increased the output of each worker immensely. This decreased the cost (relative to people's incomes) of the goods produced. The availability of cheaper manufactured goods stimulated consumption, increased the standard of living, and launched a period of rapid, long-term economic growth. Manufacturing grew rapidly as a result.

Steam power for railroads, river boats, and ships meant that raw materials could be moved relatively inexpensively to central factories. Goods produced in one place could be shipped long distances economically. Thus, a single large manufacturer could produce goods for a national or international market.

In short, this Industrial Revolution created a system of large-scale factory production. These factories required the concentration of large numbers of workers in one place. In turn, until the early twentieth century, these large factories tended to cluster together in just a few cities.[1] The industrial city was born.

Reasons for Industrial Concentration

Why did the factories cluster together in cities? A number of factors favored the cities as places to locate industry.

For one thing, reliance on steam power encouraged industrial concentration. Steam is produced most efficiently in large boilers and cannot be piped long distances. Factories and their power supply needed to be close together, and it often made sense for several factories to share a common steam plant. Steam was produced from coal, and the only efficient ways to move coal were by railroad, ship, or barge. Hence, factories had to be located along rail lines or rivers, or near port areas.

Limited transportation technology meant that workers had to live close to where they worked. Only the more affluent could afford to travel by train or carriage every day. Even after the introduction of the electric trolley in the latter part of the century, regular commuting by working-class people was expensive and avoided when possible. As late as the turn of the century, the average commuting distance for workers in New York City was only two blocks (Palen, 1987:71). This created pressures to build working-class housing within walking distance of the factory district. Very quickly, densely packed multiple-story tenement buildings sprang up around the industrial districts. Once a large number of workers were concentrated in a particular city and industrial district, additional industry was attracted, anxious to take advantage of the existing pool of readily accessible (and already experienced) industrial workers.

Movement of bulky raw materials and finished goods also required that factories cluster immediately around railroad switching facilities and dock areas. Once goods left the railroad car, they became very difficult and expensive to move: street transportation was by horse-drawn wagon and handcart.

Moreover, as the early sociologist Charles Horton Cooley pointed out, industry was usually attracted to certain points along the transportation system. These points he called *breaks in transportation*. These are places where goods must be moved from one vehicle to another (lake boat to train, train to train, train to ship, etc.). This entails labor costs. It is cheaper to process goods at transportation breaks because one has to pay the labor costs whether or not anything is done to the raw materials or merchandise. Storage facilities are often required at such transportation breaks, and other facilities such as banks and brokerage houses must be present since ownership often changes hands at these points. This further enhances the attractiveness of building factories at these breaks (Cooley, 1930:17–19). Thus, the city of Chicago grew into a major industrial center partly because it was where the railroad lines came together from the Northwest (lumber and cattle), Midwest (agricultural products), and Southwest (cattle, grain, and coal from central Illinois). At the same time, lumber, grain, and iron ore and other minerals came down the lake by boat. Chicago became home for the production of steel, agricultural machinery, wholesale merchandising, food processing ("hog butcher for the world"), and that great mail-order house for rural America, Sears Roebuck.

To some extent, success and growth tended to bring further success and growth to the already large cities. Larger cities provided a place to locate a factory where there was an easily accessible, very large market.

In addition, the existing large cities had the advantage of already having an infrastructure of services such as water supplies, warehouses, switching facilities, docks, raw materials suppliers, municipal services, and skilled repairmen. It was cheaper to use these already existing services than to create them from scratch at a different location (Wallace, 1980:44). Corporate offices, in an era of slow communications and transportation, needed both to be near their factories and to be adjacent to other corporate headquarters and to such services as financial institutions, legal offices, and courts (Palen, 1987:73). Finally, some areas were better able to capitalize on their local advantages because of the organization and skill of their business and political leaders. These "growth entrepreneurs" mobilized local resources and governmental connections to provide incentives to business for locating in their cities (Molotch, 1988). For example, there was competition between eastern cities to get state subsidies for canal building in the 1830s and 1840s.

Consequences of Concentration

These centralizing forces meant that a large proportion of all industry located in cities and that a few cities grew very large. The last half of the nineteenth century was a period in which much of the urban population came to be concentrated in a few large urban areas.

Within these urban areas, most of the population lived inside the city limits of one municipal government. This was because urban growth in the nineteenth century was characterized by the process of *annexation*. In most states, cities had the right to incorporate surrounding areas (including other independent towns) into the city as it spread out from the center. For instance, in 1854, Philadelphia swallowed twenty-eight cities, towns, and boroughs in a single year (Kotler, 1969). This process was enhanced in the late 1800s by the introduction of the horse-drawn cart and then, at the end of the century, the electric streetcar. Streetcars expanded the potential space of the city and made possible the outward expansion of the city. Growth proceeded outward along the streetcar lines and allowed convenient commuting as far as twelve miles from the downtown areas. Where streetcar lines crossed, these "breaks" in the transportation system encouraged the creation of small, neighborhood business districts. Gradually, the space between the streetcar lines filled in (Hawley, 1971:92).

A convenient (if somewhat arbitrary) date to designate as the zenith of the industrial city is 1920. In that year, the census found 51 percent of the population living in cities and towns (see table 1.1). In a statistical sense, U.S. society had become a predominately urban society. Moreover, despite the fact that movement of industry to suburban areas had already begun, central cities still clearly dominated the urban landscape. There were three cities with more than a million in population and nine with between half a million and a million (U.S. Census Bureau, 1973).

Table 1.1
Percent Population Urban, Urban Population Size, and
Total Population Size, United States, 1790–1998 (Selected Years)

Year	Percent Urban	Urban Population (in millions)	Total Population (in millions)
1790	5	.2	4
1840	11	2	17
1890	35	22	63
1920	51	55	107
1940	57	75	133
1960	70	126	181
1980	75	167	226
1990	77.5	193	249
1998	80.1	216.51	270.3

SOURCE: U.S. Census Bureau.

What was the industrial city like? There was an extremely compact and crowded downtown district. The attraction of this downtown area was simple. It was centrally located, and transit lines radiated out from it like spokes on a wheel. This made it the single most accessible point in the city. Offices clustered together to make possible easy communication by means of messenger and face-to-face contact. Office workers could commute in on the transit lines. Stores and places of entertainment catering to a mass market could be reached by the most people with the least inconvenience by locating in the downtown district. Intercity transportation was by train, and massive passenger terminals were usually located near the edge of the business district. The fact that, once downtown, people had to walk required that the downtown be very compact. All this meant that competition for space in the downtown district was intense and the price of land very high. In 1930, street frontage on Wall Street sold for $100,000 a foot. Thus, the downtown location was practical only for business enterprises, and only for those businesses that had the greatest need for accessibility to large numbers of customers or workers. Banks, hotels, department stores, luxury shops, corporate headquarters, legal firms, other business professionals, and the like crowded together within easy walking distance of one another. The premium on space and the need to be close meant that the invention of the elevator and steel girder building quickly led to taller and taller "skyscrapers." These buildings made it possible to jam very large numbers of people together with rapid access to one another by elevator.

Factories, warehouses, and residential housing—activities which required large amounts of space—could not afford to locate in the central downtowns. Rather, they located, depending on their transportation needs and ability to pay, in different parts of the city. Each part of the city tended to specialize in a particular type of land use.

Adjacent to the downtown was usually a district of railroad switching yards, warehouses, factories, and slums. The factories needed to be close to the railroads, warehouse facilities, and each other. Workers in these facilities needed to be close to their work, and they could not pay much for either transportation or housing. The result was densely packed working-class housing districts mixed in with and adjacent to the factory district. Multiple-story tenements housed huge numbers of people under conditions of appalling squalor and crowding. Families of six to eight people crowded into one, two, or three rooms, often with no plumbing facilities (or with the bathroom down the hall and shared by several families). There were dangerous, poorly vented coal stoves for heat, few or no windows for light and ventilation, and inadequate fire escapes. The danger of fire, desperate cold in the winter and suffocating heat in the summer, ghastly sanitation and hygiene problems, and disease were part of the shared experience for many in the urban lower classes in the late 1800s and early 1900s. At the end of the nineteenth century in New York, urban reformers of the day considered it a major victory to require that newly built tenements at least have windows facing into air shafts for ventilation and metal fire escapes outside the building. Overall densities of these areas were higher than at any other point in our urban history. In 1894, one district on the West Side of Chicago was three times more crowded than the most crowded portions of Tokyo or Calcutta. In some neighborhoods, density reached 900 people per acre (Mayer and Wade, 1969:256).

As one moved beyond the working-class districts, the quality of the residential areas improved. However, limited transportation still required that people be fairly close to their places of work: streetcars were very slow. Competition for land close to the center meant that land costs were high. Hence, by modern suburban standards, the housing was still densely packed. Apartment buildings, row houses, and two-family houses were the order of the day for most of the better-off skilled workers and average middle-class families of the period. In this regard, it should be remembered that the average purchasing power of even these more affluent workers was much lower than it is today. Hence, what a middle-class standard of living implied for such things as housing and basic comforts was much different than now.

Those neighborhoods of large Victorian clapboard houses and tree-lined streets which seem to be the popular image of the urban past were really preserves for a small portion of the population: the affluent, upper middle classes composed of successful professionals, independent successful businessmen, and the new class of corporate managers. Even in these areas, the premium on land in the city often meant relatively large houses crowded together on small lots.

By 1920, in many cities, the upper middle classes and the upper classes also had begun settling in suburban towns outside the city limits. Many of these communities had started out as independent rural towns in which wealthy people in the nineteenth century had built summer homes. Gradually these summer residences were converted into year-round homes. Early commuting to the city was made possible by the availability of rail passenger service. Later, the streetcar lines were extended beyond the city limits to create inter-urban trolley systems that actually ran cross-country between cities. (At one time, it was possible to travel between New York and Boston by streetcar.) These streetcar systems further spurred suburban growth. By 1920, most large cities had suburban "bedroom" communities from which people commuted to the central business district. By and large, these were fairly prestigious enclaves of affluent residents, such as Evanston, just north of Chicago (Wilson and Schulz, 1978:1190–91; Jackson, 1985:113–15, 120–22, 256; Warner, 1962:20–29, 43–45).

The early twentieth century also saw another movement that was an indication of the future directions of urban development. Industries began locating (still on rail lines, of course) outside the city in industrial "satellite" towns. Up until 1900, industrial employment had increased most rapidly in the central cities. But between 1899 and 1909, industrial employment in cities grew by about 40 percent, while in areas surrounding the cities such employment increased by 98 percent (Gordon, 1977:74). Thus, for example, the newly formed giant of the steel industry, United States Steel, built a whole industrial city outside of Chicago and named it after the chairman of the board of directors, Judge Gary (creating Gary, Indiana).

A very significant fact about this development of affluent suburban communities and industrial satellites in the early twentieth century was that it did not, as it had in the past, lead to annexation by the central cities. The great wave of annexation in the nineteenth century crested with the consolidation of the city of Brooklyn into New York in 1898. The pace of annexation abruptly slowed in the early 1900s. Of the twenty largest cities, thirteen had stopped expanding by 1910 (Gordon, 1977:77). Partly this was the result of ethnic and class hostilities. The "WASPs" (white, Anglo-Saxon Protestants) of the suburbs feared and disliked what they saw as the corrupt, lower-class, immigrant-dominated political "machines" which had come to power in the central cities (Banfield and Wilson, 1966:37–44). The new suburbanites also did not want to pay taxes for services which went to the lower classes, and wanted to control the quality and type of services in their neighborhoods (such as schools). Large corporations had fled the central cities partly to escape taxes, the lower-class dominated city government, and the unions. They also wanted to locate in communities in which they had more political control. Hence, they also resisted annexation. Rural-dominated legislatures, also fearing the political power of the growing cities, were understandably sympathetic to the fears of these groups and quickly created legal barriers to annexation (Gluck and Meister, 1979:133).

These trends, however, seemed only distant dark clouds on the horizon in 1920. For all their poverty, coal-polluted air, political corruption, and squalid slums, the great industrial cities of the early 1900s were vibrant economic, cultural, and social centers of an optimistic and rapidly growing new industrial society. They were massive symbols of one of the most fundamental social and economic transformations in human history. Not surprisingly, they quickly became the focus of scholars from a new academic discipline, itself an outgrowth and response to this transformation: sociology.

THE HUMAN ECOLOGY OF THE INDUSTRIAL CITY

One of the major concerns of the early urban sociologists was to search for uniformities in the patterns of physical development in these new industrial cities. Underlying this search was the assumption that the physical structure of the new cities reflected certain basic social and economic structures and processes in industrial societies. This perspective for studying cities came to be known as the *human-ecology approach* in sociology. This approach asked two key questions about cities: (1) do cities all tend to develop some common general physical form, and (2) what accounts for this common form?

Concentric-Zone Theory

The most famous theory to develop out of the human-ecology approach was the one developed at the University of Chicago in the 1920s by Ernest Burgess and Robert Park (Burgess, 1924). Their basic concern was to develop a generalized model of how, as cities grow, land-use patterns change. Their model was based on several general principles which they saw governing the process of urban growth.

Invasion and Succession

Burgess and Park were looking at cities in which urban growth had been very rapid. Hence, they saw a pattern of rapid outward expansion as cities spread out from their original centers to accommodate more people and economic activities. This outward growth from a common center meant that land that was originally used for one purpose frequently was converted to other purposes as the city expanded. Thus, for example, residential areas that had originally clustered around the small commercial areas of a city would be torn down to accommodate factories and rail yards. Later, downtown expansion would replace the warehouses and factories with stores and office buildings. Since growth was outward, the general process was one in which activities in the center would expand outward into adjacent areas which, in turn, would expand outward into areas next to them. This was labeled the process of *invasion and succession.* Inner areas (such as the downtown) were constantly expanding and invading the areas further out, replacing one land use with another.

Competition and Segregation

Burgess and Park noted that cities tended to consist of a set of homogeneous land-use areas. Factories would cluster together in one area, middle-class homes in another, and slums in another. This, they argued, was because different areas of the city had different degrees of attractiveness. Most critical in determining attractiveness was accessibility. Generally, this meant that locations in the center of the city were the most attractive. Each kind of land use competed with other kinds to obtain the most attractive location. This drove up the value of the land in the center. Only those activities which could use the land very intensively and pay its high cost could locate in the center. As one moved away from the center, the value of land declined and less intensive kinds of land-use activities could afford to locate there (e.g., factories and housing). Thus, each land use tended to find the location it could afford, and those activities which could not afford a central location had to place themselves further out. The results were areas of homogeneous land use Burgess and Park called *natural areas* because they were the result of the natural processes of free-market competition, rather than the result of zoning or government planning. Because each land-use area tended to attract people of certain occupations and classes, they also tended to be homogeneous in terms of their demographic characteristics.

Structural Results: Concentric Zones

The resulting general pattern of land use, claimed Burgess and Park, was a set of concentric zones of homogeneous land-use areas. In their most general formulation, they suggested five such zones (see figure 1.1).

Zone 1 was the *central business district* (CBD). This zone was where large mass-merchandise stores, luxury shops, theaters, hotels, banks, central offices, and professional services centered. Surrounding the outside edge of the zone were warehouses, wholesale markets, and railroad stations.

Zone 2 was called the *zone in transition.* It contained railroad yards, the old main factory district, and the most decayed and densely packed lower-class slum housing. Burgess and Park called it the zone in transition because, at the time they were writing, central business districts were rapidly expanding into ("invading") this zone. Slums

Figure 1.1
The Concentric Zone Theory

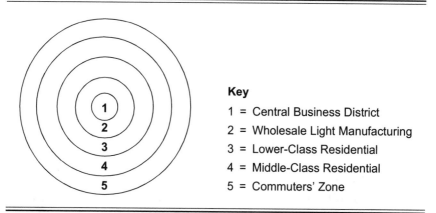

Key

1 = Central Business District

2 = Wholesale Light Manufacturing

3 = Lower-Class Residential

4 = Middle-Class Residential

5 = Commuters' Zone

SOURCE: Chauncey D. Harris and Edward L. Ullman, "The Nature of Cities," *The Annals of the American Academy of Political and Social Science* 242 (November 1945), pp. 7–17, adapted.

could afford to be located so close to the center because, even if the rents were low, the high density meant that the actual income produced from each building was high. Also, the area attracted land speculators who bought property there in anticipation that future CBD expansion would make it more valuable in the future.

Zone 3 was called the *zone of workingmen's homes.* This was where the more affluent working-class families lived. At least in Chicago, this area consisted mostly of smaller apartment buildings and two-family houses.

Zone 4 was the *zone of better residences.* Essentially a middle-class residential area, it consisted (in Chicago in the 1920s) of simple single-family homes combined with modest-sized, good quality apartment buildings, and some residential hotels. The latter type of structure suggested the beginnings of invasion from Zone 3.

Zone 5 was designated the *commuter zone.* It included the early suburbs we discussed previously and functioned as a residential "dormitory" for upper middle-class and upper-class workers, most of whom commuted by transit (and even by car in the 1920s) to the CBD.

Evaluation

How accurate a picture of the industrial city was the Burgess and Park theory? Numerous criticisms have been leveled at the theory. We need only note them here. Certainly, the picture painted of the city was oversimplified and overgeneralized. Real cities of the time only crudely approximated the kind of structure Burgess and Park hypothesized. Land use was never as regular and homogeneous as the theory suggested. Moreover, the theory never did apply to all cities everywhere. At best, it applied to large, North American cities with significant concentrations of industry, which were built mostly after 1860 and before 1920. Thus, the less industrialized cities of the South in 1920, cities like Los Angeles (which grew later), European cities, and cities like New York and Boston (with special topography and economic functions) fit the concentric pattern very poorly or not at all. However, in a crude way, Burgess and Park captured some general tendencies of a type of city which housed a large portion of the North American urban population at the time (Schnore, 1972; Smith, 1970; Haggerty, 1971). Decayed and surrounded by suburban sprawls, these monuments to early industrialization continue to dot the urban landscape.

Sector Theory

Given its crudity, it is not surprising the Burgess-Park formulation provoked not only criticism but attempts to modify it or refute it by proposing alternative models.

One such attempt was the modification suggested in the late 1930s by Homer Hoyt (1939). Based on the study of rental costs in different areas of 142 cities, Hoyt rejected the notion that "natural areas" always tended to form continuous rings around the center. Hoyt discovered what he felt was a much different pattern from that of concentric rings. He concluded that "high-rent" areas were more likely to form pie-shaped sectors which extended out from the CBD (see figure 1.2). These areas, according to Hoyt's *sector theory*, tended to extend out along existing transportation routes and favored areas away from industrial districts with such scenic attractions as high ground or shorelines with good views. In general, they tended to be protected from other land uses by barriers or buffers of medium-rent housing. Hoyt also pointed out that industrial districts tended to be arranged along transportation lines or in dock districts, rather than forming concentric zones.

Hoyt's theory really is not a full theory, but rather a set of descriptive generalizations drawn from empirical observations. Nor (as the figure indicates) is it a total rejection of either the processes or the patterns suggested by Burgess and Park.

Multiple-Nuclei Theory

A much more ambitious attempt to develop a completely different theory came in the 1940s when the geographers C. D. Harris and E. L. Ullman suggested the *multiple-nuclei theory* (1945). They rejected the notion that cities had just one center from which they simply expanded outward. Rather, they believed that cities had several different centers (nuclei). Each center specialized in a different activity, such as finance, government, wholesaling, or warehousing (see figure 1.3). These differ-

Figure 1.2
The Sector Theory

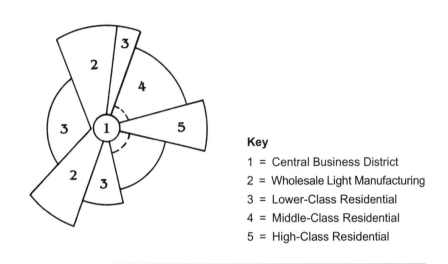

Key

1 = Central Business District

2 = Wholesale Light Manufacturing

3 = Lower-Class Residential

4 = Middle-Class Residential

5 = High-Class Residential

SOURCE: Chauncey D. Harris and Edward L. Ullman, "The Nature of Cities," *The Annals of the American Academy of Political and Social Science* 242 (November 1945), pp. 7–17, adapted.

ent centers may have sprung up at about the same time, or they may have originally started in some common center and later separated from that center. Thus, for example, manufacturing originally started near the downtown in Chicago. However, it eventually scattered to subcenters, such as the concentration of the steel industry in the southeast part of the city.

Harris and Ullman were skeptical about the possibility that one general model of city structure could do justice to the tremendous diversity found in actual city structures. They felt that different historical influences in each city's development tended to give it its own unique physical structure. However, they felt that four factors influenced the development of homogeneous land-use areas:

(1) Certain activities require specialized facilities and cluster together to share these facilities. Thus, retail stores will tend to locate together near transportation facilities.

(2) Similar activities will tend to group together because they benefit from being close to one another. For example, a new car dealership will often locate near existing dealers, since people looking for cars already come there.

Figure 1.3
The Multiple-Nuclei Theory

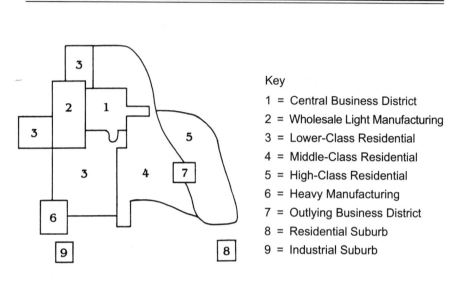

Key

1 = Central Business District
2 = Wholesale Light Manufacturing
3 = Lower-Class Residential
4 = Middle-Class Residential
5 = High-Class Residential
6 = Heavy Manufacturing
7 = Outlying Business District
8 = Residential Suburb
9 = Industrial Suburb

SOURCE: Chauncey D. Harris and Edward L. Ullman, "The Nature of Cities," *The Annals of the American Academy of Political and Social Science* 242 (November 1945), pp. 7–17, adapted.

(3) Certain dissimilar activities may be harmed by being close to one another. Obviously, heavy industry and expensive housing will not be close together because the land is too expensive for the industry, and industry will make the area less attractive for high-status residential use.

(4) Certain activities, such as warehousing, must avoid downtown locations because land costs are too high and there is no economic advantage to locating in the CBD.

Multiple-nuclei theory does not logically exclude the possibility that some cities may develop patterns that approximate concentric zones at some point in their development. Thus, it is not really a total rejection of Burgess and Park's description of cities like Chicago in the 1920s. It does have the advantage of applying more generally to all cities of the period (e.g., New York) and correcting the excessive emphasis on the CBD in concentric-zone theory.

Social Area Analysis

Social area analysis is an attempt to describe land use in cities by concentrating on the social characteristics of urban populations. Social rank, family status and housing, and race and ethnicity were the traits considered. Shevky and Bell (1955:18) examined census tract data in order to learn how census tracts shared these characteristics. An area where a high percentage of residents had these traits was designated a social area. Several combinations emerged. In San Francisco, people in some districts had low social rank (measured by social class) and family status (measured by extent of mother's employment), but high ethnic status. These residents tended to be lower class, and also had large families in multiple housing, along with clear ethnic or racial characteristics. In other sections of the city, people were low on family status and ethnicity, but high in social rank. Shevky and Bell emphasized that urban residents regarded these social characteristics as very important.

Factorial Ecology

Factorial ecology put computers to use in the analysis of urban social characteristics. All characteristics were analyzed, not only the three looked at in social area analysis. All traits were compared to see which ones were related. Those found to be associated were then used to describe a city's land-use patterns. The original choice in social area analysis of social rank, family status, and race or ethnicity were given substantial support. Berry and Rees (1969) emphasized that all earlier land-use theories (concentric zone, sector, and multiple nuclei) were partially correct and that factorial ecology brought them together under one umbrella. Census data patterns, as sorted out by computer, suggested that family status was best described by the concentric-zone model; social rank by sector theory; and race and ethnicity by multiple-nuclei theory.

CITIES IN TRANSITION: 1920–1945

Viewed from the perspective of the early twenty-first century, the industrial city was a transitory phenomenon. The very forces that rapidly created it just as quickly replaced it with new urban forms. In the 1920s, the direction of the change urban areas were to undergo was already apparent.

Early industrialization had been a force for concentrating large numbers of people in relatively compact, very densely settled cities. As industrial society matured, the process began to be reversed. Most of the twentieth century was characterized by the growing decentralization of urban areas and accompanying decreases in density.

By the 1920s that process was in full swing. While the old industrial cities were still the predominant urban form and the place where most metropolitan residents still lived, rapid out-movement of population and industry was underway. For the first time, suburban population growth outstripped that of the central cities (Wallace, 1980:79).

As the suburbs grew in the 1920s, the nature of the suburbs began to change. For one thing, they were no longer located solely on the commuter railroad and streetcar lines. The number of cars in the United States increased from nine million in 1920 to twenty-six million in 1930 (Wilson and Schulz, 1978:191). This greater flexibility in the transportation system allowed the development of suburban housing away from transit lines and farther out from the city limits. (However, suburban development was still hampered by the slow expansion of the paved highway system outside the cities, and this remained a barrier to suburban development for the next few decades.)

The 1920s also saw the further "democratization" of the suburbs. More and more average middle-class people could afford to live in the suburbs. For middle-class people at least, the 1920s was a period of prosperity. The cheap, mass-produced car was within their financial reach. (The cost of a Model T was less than a thousand dollars.) The 1920s also saw the appearance of the first housing subdivisions, providing modest single-family houses at affordable prices.

The result was a brief suburban building boom in the last half of the decade. In the absence of building codes and zoning requirements, suburban real-estate speculators and contractors hurriedly mapped out subdivisions and developed commercial strips along the highways. This created the first suburban "sprawl" of scattered, haphazard land use. It finally also led to the first large suburban shopping center (Country Club Plaza in Kansas City).

The Great Depression of the 1930s brought an abrupt end to this suburban boom. Purchasing power fell abruptly, and with industrial production drastically reduced, expansion of industrial plants outside the cities virtually ceased. Real-estate speculators went bankrupt, and the new housing market collapsed. For the first half of the decade, American cities were in a state of virtual suspended animation (despite the completion of a few spectacular projects such as Rockefeller Center and the Golden Gate Bridge). The modest and uneven economic recovery toward the end of the decade did little to change the picture immediately. Some small-scale suburban construction resumed. A few of the early urban expressways were opened (such as the West Side Highway in New York), and extensive planning to create more was underway. Even this modest recovery in urban and suburban growth was cut short by World War II. The war-time economy boomed, but shortages of building materials and labor prevented any construction not directly related to war production (Wilson and Schulz, 1978:191–92).

AT THE CROSSROADS:
THE INDUSTRIAL CITY IN 1945

At the end of the war in 1945, the effect of fifteen years of economic stagnation followed by war meant that the great industrial cities and their modest surrounding suburbs had changed little from 1930. Central cities were still the dominant places of residence and employment. Central business districts were still the major centers for commercial, retail, professional, and office activities. But beneath the appearance of stability, pent-up forces for long-term change and a host of accumulating central-city problems had set the stage for another period of rapid change in American urban areas (Hawley, 1950).

Both the residential areas and the factories in the industrial districts of the large industrial cities were getting old. The problem was compounded by the fifteen years in which little new housing had been built, and old factories had not been replaced or modernized. As a result, there was a tremendous need to repair, modernize, or replace the physical structures of the cities.

The growing reliance on the automobile and the failure to build highways at a rate to accommodate the increasing traffic in the previous decades meant that urban streets and highways were congested, slow-moving, and often in bad repair. Cities were being strangled by the automobile. The fact that public transit had been allowed to decay (see chapter 5) added further to the transportation problem. Gasoline rationing during the war had led to a temporary resurgence in transit use, but with the end of rationing, urban residents abandoned the aging and inadequate transit systems in droves in favor of the more convenient transportation that the car (despite congestion) seemed to offer.

In most cities, most of the large tracts of open land were gone. Both in industrial districts and residential areas, the remaining open land was in relatively small parcels and very expensive. Construction of housing, for example, was mostly limited to the construction of single homes on widely scattered open lots or the construction of higher density housing (e.g., apartments) on land cleared of lower density, older housing (an expensive proposition).

The current crisis in our cities tends to obscure the fact that the cities of the past were also centers of severe social and economic problems which made major portions of these cities unattractive places to live and work. For example, according to the 1950 census, one-fifth of "low-income"[2] urban residents renting housing lacked complete plumbing facilities, and an equal proportion lived in overcrowded housing (deLeeuw et al., 1976:122). Thus, poverty, slums, high crime rates, and spreading urban decay affected many urban neighborhoods. Ethnic group hostility—not just between African Americans and whites, but between the various white ethnic groups—was considered a serious urban problem. In short, cities were plagued by major social problems and, just as importantly, were seen as places where those problems were concentrated.

The period immediately after 1945 was characterized by a severe housing shortage. Little new housing had been constructed in the previous fifteen years. Meanwhile, marriages, which had been postponed by war and the Depression, occurred at a rapid rate as veterans returned home. The large group of babies born during the 1920s (when the birth rate was fairly high) was reaching the age of marriage. These young families began to have children at a very rapid rate (the "baby boom"). The result was a tremendous increase in the number of growing young families in need of housing. The existing stock of housing in the cities did not even begin to meet their needs.

SUBURBANIZATION AND THE RISE OF MEGALOPOLIS: 1945–1970

The aforementioned problems combined with rapid economic growth and a continuation of the process of economic decentralization that had begun earlier. The result was a period of massive, rapid suburbanization of population and economic activity after 1945. As a consequence, by 1970, the basic nature of our urban areas had been transformed. Along with this transformation came the conditions which underlie the contemporary "urban crisis."

The Process of Suburbanization

As we have learned, suburbanization prior to 1945 had consisted of industrial satellite communities and middle- and upper-class residential communities from which workers commuted to the central city. The initial wave of suburbanization after 1945 was a continuation of this pattern. The open fields around the cities were quickly being filled with subdivisions of single-family homes to provide housing for young, increasingly affluent and mostly middle-class office workers.

However, it quickly became apparent that this suburbanization was different from the past. For one thing, it was on a much vaster scale than before. Forty million people in the United States were living in metropolitan areas outside of central cities in 1950. By 1960 that figure reached sixty million, and by 1970 it had reached seventy-six million. Instead of the suburbs being a fringe of settlements around a central city, central cities rapidly became islands in a sea of suburbs. For the country as a whole, central cities grew slowly, and many cities began to actually decline in population size. By 1970, more metropolitan residents lived in the suburbs than lived in central cities. Thus, after 1945, urban growth was essentially suburban growth (see table 1.2).

The size of this suburban growth also reflected another trend: suburban residents gradually became a much more diverse group in terms of socioeconomic background. Instead of just being middle- and upper-class enclaves, the suburbs also became home for a substantial portion of the (white) working class and even lower class. Popular stereotypes to the contrary, the "typical" suburbanite was no longer always a middle-class office

Table 1.2
Population by Residence: United States, 1970–1990

Residence	Population (millions)			Percentage Change		Percent
	1970	1980	1990	1970–80	1980–90	1990
MSAs*	155.9	172.5	192.7	10.6	11.7	77.5
Central Cities	72.2	72.8	77.8	0.9	7.0	31.2
Outside Central Cities	83.7	99.6	114.8	19.0	15.3	46.2
Nonmetropolitan Areas	47.3	54.1	55.9	15.1	14.4	22.4
U.S. Population	203.4	226.5	248.7	11.4	9.8	100.0

*Metropolitan Statistical Area

SOURCE: U.S. Census Bureau, *Statistical Abstract*, 1995:38, 43.

worker or professional (Palen, 1987: 183). He or she was, however, almost exclusively white (an issue to which we will return in a later chapter).

The changing class composition of the suburbs was reflected in another change in the nature of the suburbs: mass produced housing. Early suburbs, even when they contained subdivisions constructed by the same building contractor, consisted of mostly custom-built housing which was constructed one house at a time "on order" for a particular family. After 1945, it became more and more common to build large numbers of fairly standardized units (hundreds at a time) and then sell them. These mass-produced subdivisions helped open up the suburbs to a wider range of income groups.

The new suburbanites were also more dependent on their cars than those in the past. Suburbs were now much less likely to be tied to mass-transit lines. In part this reflected another, even more significant, change. Fewer and fewer suburban residents were commuters to the CBD of the central city (Palen, 1987:184). This was the result of the massive movement of employment to the suburbs and the wider range of workers residing in the suburbs.

This brings us to a fundamental point to be made about post-1945 suburbanization. Suburbanization of residence was only one part of the process. Equally significant was the suburbanization of most (but not all) kinds of economic activities. An increasing portion of industrial employment moved to the suburbs during this period, resuming a trend interrupted by the Depression. Retail activities in the central business districts of the central cities grew little after 1945. Instead, most of the very substantial growth in retail activity occurred at the scattered suburban shopping centers and malls that sprang up to serve the growing suburban population. Similarly, services and service professionals followed their customers to the suburbs. The result was that the whole focus of economic activity and employment growth moved to the suburbs. Hence, by 1970, the average suburban resident worked (and, of course, shopped) in the suburbs as well. Census figures show that by 1970, a full 72 percent of the suburban residents in the fifteen largest metropolitan areas were also employed in the suburbs (Palen, 1987:184).

The resulting pattern of urban settlement was, by 1970, quite different from that which existed in 1945. Urban areas were no longer dominated by a compact central city, but by low-density suburban sprawls covering large areas. The basic pattern of land use was a multiple nuclei of specialized land uses similar to that suggested by Harris and Ullman. In part because of the independent zoning power of suburban governments and the desire of suburban residents to live in homogeneous communities, each suburb tended to specialize in a particular land use. Thus, some suburbs specialized in middle-class residential use. Others were primarily upper-middle or upper class. Still others combined working-class housing districts with industrial parks and strips of commercial development along major highways. In other words, the basic pattern was a great diversity of land uses across the metropolitan area, but homogeneity of land use within each particular community.

Moreover, most research suggests that each suburb tended to maintain considerable continuity over time in terms of the social status of its residents relative to other suburbs. This tendency, called *suburban persistence,* meant, for example, that a suburb which started out as middle-class residential tended to maintain its basic character for decades. More recent research, however, suggests that such persistence may not be universal in all metropolitan areas—especially rapidly growing ones. Other researchers have detected a gradual evolution of suburban status rankings when they employ different measurements than earlier researchers. Certainly, over the very long term, an aging housing stock will create conditions favorable to urban decay and status declines even in relatively affluent suburbs (Farley, 1964; Guest, 1978; Logan and Schneider, 1981; Stahura, 1979).

Suburbs came to cover vast land areas surrounding the cities not just because of the large number of people who moved into them, but also because of low-density land use. Single-family residential areas with each house on a substantial lot meant much lower residential densities than in the central cities. Low-rise shopping malls, single-story factories, and low-rise office complexes, all surrounded by massive parking lots, further reduced density. Finally, suburban development was characterized by what is called *leapfrogging.* Rather than always locating housing and economic activities on the open land closest to the central city, suburban developers frequently jumped over this closer-in, often more expensive, land and located in the relatively more open areas farther out. The result was a substantial amount of land left undeveloped between existing built-up areas.

Hence, suburban development consumed very large areas of land to accommodate people and activities that were once accommodated in much more compact and dense central cities. The resulting urban areas were massive in their territorial scope.

This scattered, spread-out pattern of land use was also one in which there was no one single center of industrial, retail, commercial, or office activities. Some workers and (fewer) shoppers in the suburbs continued to head downtown to the old CBD. However, the majority of suburban residents by 1970 were headed to a multitude of specialized subcenters scattered throughout the metropolitan area, and they frequently were traveling very long distances to do so. As we will see (in chapter 6), this pattern of multiple destinations has important implications for urban transportation.

Thus, the popular stereotype of the suburbs as a homogeneous sea of middle-class "bedroom communities" had less and less validity after 1945. The suburbs had a diverse mix of working-class, middle-class, and upper-class residential areas and substantial but scattered concentrations of industrial commercial activities. The suburbs had matured from mere "bedrooms" of central cities to complex systems of residence, work, shopping, and entertainment. In other words, to a very large degree, the suburbs had become the new form of urban development in the United States.

Muller (1981:162–67) noted the emergence of important multiuse centers in suburbia which encompassed virtually all the facilities found formerly only in the downtown areas of central cities. These areas are in effect suburban mini-cities, and are built around large regional shopping malls. Conveniently adjacent are a large number of such diverse activities as manufacturing plants, warehouses, hotels and motels, apartments, restaurants, and cultural and religious centers. A number of these suburban centers have become very specialized, providing such services as year-round convention centers. The development of such mini-cities has resulted in a number of increasingly complex traffic problems, including the clogging of roads and highways that is getting increasingly worse in suburban areas.

As the suburbs spread outward from the central cities, something else happened. In those areas where the existing central cities were close together, their suburbs eventually grew into each other. This process of metropolitan areas linking up to one another to create large areas of continuous metropolitan land use is known as *conurbanization*. Huge urban strips of low-density suburban sprawl linked nearby central cities to create "supermetropolitan areas." The most spectacular example of this phenomenon was on the Eastern seaboard. With some gaps, a massive metropolitan strip was created linking urban areas between Boston and Washington, D.C. Sometimes nicknamed "Boswash" or the "Eastern Metropolitan Strip," geographer Jean Gottman

(1964) christened this new form of urban development *megalopolis*. Based on the trends of the 1950s, many demographers and geographers expected (or feared) that the eventual consequences might be the creation of even larger systems of linked urban sprawls. Such systems would form continuous urban environments covering thousands of square miles. (Imagine driving all day and never being out of sight of subdivisions, shopping centers, and the "golden arches" of McDonald's.)

The Causes of Suburbanization

What set off this massive suburbanization? The causes are complex and interrelated. However, for present purposes it is possible to distinguish between two general groups of factors: (1) factors contributing to the suburbanization of residence and (2) factors contributing to the suburbanization of industry. Obviously, in reality, these factors were closely related and mutually reinforcing.

Suburbanization of Residence

As we have seen, suburbanization began in the context of rapid family formation, continuing urbanization of the population, and the baby boom. At the same time, there was an extreme shortage of housing in the cities. Obviously, people had to be provided with new housing of some kind, somewhere. What is not so obvious is why the particular housing pattern of suburban, low-density, single-family housing emerged in the United States. Other urban societies also grew after 1945, but the pattern of urban growth was not identical to that of the United States. In other words, the question is not why did American urban areas grow, but why suburbs? Suburbs developed the way they did in the United States not because of the workings of some inevitable, universal natural laws, but because of the convergence of certain particular factors that favored one form of urban development instead of another.

Government housing policy was one such factor. There was some government construction of new housing for the urban poor (see chapter 5). But the basic thrust of government housing policy was to subsidize construction of private housing for the middle class and the more affluent sections of the working class. This is known as the *trickle-down* approach to housing policy. The basic idea is to encourage the creation of new housing for the more affluent. As these groups move into new housing, they abandon their older neighborhoods. These older neighborhoods then become available and affordable to less affluent working-class people. In turn, as these working-class neighborhoods become older and newer neighborhoods open up to working-class people, they become progressively less attractive and even less affluent people move in. Finally, physical deterioration sets in, and the neighborhood becomes a lower-class slum. In this way, each neighborhood houses successively lower-class individuals over time. Housing gradually "trickles down" to the poor (Downs, 1973).

Thus, after World War II, the federal government tried to create more housing for everybody primarily by subsidizing the more affluent sections of the population. Put these people into new housing, the thinking went, and the less affluent could "inherit" the housing that the more affluent abandoned. The basic mechanism for this policy was the FHA (Federal Housing Administration) and VA (Veterans Administration) mortgage-loan guarantee programs. Through these programs, people could obtain private mortgage loans with very low down payments, low interest rates, and long payback periods. Financial institutions were willing to make these loans because there was very little risk to them. If the person failed to pay the mortgage, the federal government would repay the loan.

This program represented a massive effort to subsidize primarily suburban housing. This was because, first of all, eligibility requirements for the program meant that a family had to at least be affluent working class to qualify for a loan guarantee. In addition, the program was oriented toward the purchase of single-family dwellings. Given land availability and the need for new housing, such housing had to be constructed in suburban areas. Various FHA and VA restrictions also made it easier to get loans on new housing rather than on old housing in the cities. In fact, there is evidence that internal procedures at the FHA essentially excluded a large portion of central cities from participation in the loan guarantee program (Larsen and Nikkel, 1979:241–46).

The other critical role government played in suburbanization was in the area of transportation policy. Federal subsidy of the urban expressway system (and failure to assist mass transit in the cities) encouraged car use and made suburban commuting convenient. At the same time, car ownership became almost universal. The result was that most workers could afford to be much more flexible about where they lived and how far they could travel to get to work (see chapter 6).

The economics of housing construction also favored suburban development. The loan guarantee program created a huge potential market of home buyers. Hence, contractors could build large numbers of houses "on speculation" with the assurance that there would be buyers for the completed homes. Standardized mass production of identical houses cut construction costs. Large tracts of land in outlying areas could be obtained at low cost per house lot. Building code restrictions were often less stringent outside of the city. This cut costs even further. Overall, then, builders could offer more house for less money in the suburbs and, thereby, attract buyers more readily.

The two decades following World War II were also a time of steadily rising average purchasing power. After deducting the effects of a modest rate of inflation, the average family doubled its real buying power during that period. Housing costs increased more slowly than average income (deLeeuw et al., 1976:136). This, combined with government loan programs, increased the percentage of the population that could afford to buy a new home.

There also was an undeniably strong public preference for suburban residence. Partly this preference can be seen as a continuation of the American cultural tradition that tends to idolize small-town life and view cities as immoral, impersonal, lonely places. (We will return to this issue of traditional "anti-urban bias" in chapter 3.) In addition, many observers in the 1950s felt that the move to the suburbs reflected, in part, the status appeal of the suburbs (Whyte, 1956). Most people at the time perceived the suburbs as middle- and upper-class preserves. Hence, to move to the suburbs could be seen as a means of asserting one's middle-class status. It symbolized having "made it" in society. This was especially true for the children of working-class parents for whom moving to the suburbs could be seen as proof positive of successful upward mobility and an achievement of the "American dream." (For the generations that have grown up in the suburbs and that tend to either take suburban life for granted or be critical of it, such a view of the suburbs may seem somewhat curious. But for many of the people who made the move to the suburbs in the 1950s, with their memories of fifteen years of economic depression and war, that "little house in the suburbs" represented real personal achievement.)

Two decades of sociological research on why people preferred the suburbs, however, point to another factor that overshadows the rest. Studies of suburbanites during the period revealed a strong concern for a lifestyle that emphasized nuclear family relationships, joint family activities around the home, and rearing children. Most suburbanites also displayed what sociologists call a strong "local" orientation: the primary focus was on things immediately related to family life such as neighborhood quality, schools, and local community problems (Fava, 1975; Bell, 1958). This general orientation toward life has come to be known as *familism*. And, familism appears to have reached something of a peak in the 1950s and early 1960s. (Remember this was also the time of the baby boom.) Thus, the choice of suburban residence during the period can be seen partially as a result of this familism. As late as the early 1960s, studies of why people moved to the suburbs indicated that, for most people, the move represented an attempt to provide for family needs, especially those of children (Wilson and Schulz, 1978:200). The suburbs were perceived as a good place to raise children.

Most popular accounts of the movement to the suburbs have emphasized another, essentially negative, motivation. This motivation is usually summed up in the term "white flight." In this view, middle- and working-class whites moved to the suburbs to flee the growing problems of the central cities: urban decay, high taxes, poor schools and city services, high crime rates, and very importantly, the growing African-American population in the central cities. However, this popular view turns out to have exaggerated the extent to which suburban-ization represented a "flight" from the problems of the central cities. Most of the available evidence suggests that white flight was a rela-tively minor factor in suburbanization—though it played some role that probably varied from city to city, time to time, and family to fam-ily. Rather, it appears that the positive attractions of the suburbs and the simple fact that the suburbs were where the newer, affordable housing was to be found were of primary importance in the growth of the suburbs after 1945 (Marshall, 1979).

Finally, as a simple practical matter, suburban residence became more attractive because, increasingly, that was where the jobs were. We now need to turn to the issue of why that became true.

Suburbanization of Industry

As we have seen, suburbanization of industry really began earlier in the 1900s. The process was interrupted in the 1930s, but resumed at a rapid pace after 1945. A number of factors were involved.

Changing energy technology substantially increased flexibility in the choice of plant locations. Instead of relying on coal-fired plants, increasingly, industry turned to oil, natural gas, and electricity. Hence, industrial plants no longer needed to be located near rail lines or docks.

By the 1950s, major changes also were taking place in terms of the kind of industrial activity that dominated the economy. Most earlier industrial growth had emphasized the production of heavy manufac-tured goods (e.g., steel, machinery, automobiles). These industrial plants required bulky raw materials, and the resulting products were often large and heavy. Railroads were the preferred and generally nec-essary method to move these raw materials and finished products. Post-1945 industrial development began to move in the direction of lighter "high-technology" products such as electronic equipment. These could just as easily or more easily be moved by truck. Again, this freed industry from railroad dependence.

Industry could take advantage of truck transportation because trucks were becoming larger and faster, and truck fuel was cheap. Also, the highway system (including the Interstate System in the 1960s), both within and between urban areas, steadily improved as the result of a massive government highway-building program.

Industry also increasingly needed large tracts of land on which to build factories. Single-story factories were more efficient than the old multiple-story factories in the central cities. Employees were more likely to commute to work by car and needed a place to park. Little open land was available in the old city industrial districts, and what was available was expensive. It was also likely to be heavily taxed by city government. Suburban locations, in contrast, offered ample, rela-tively cheap, and lightly taxed land on which to locate.

With almost universal car ownership, factories also no longer needed to locate near working-class residential districts or on mass-transit lines. Industry could count on workers being able to commute longer distances by automobile.

In addition, industry wanted to escape the power of highly unionized workers who were demanding higher wages and restrictions on the authority of management. In many cities, this union power was augmented by the fact that the unions had become politically powerful in city government. The suburbs offered a much more congenial environment from the corporate point of view. Workers, even when they belonged to a union, tended to live in more dispersed locations and were, consequently, less likely to be active in union activities. The new union locals in the suburbs were more likely to be composed of younger workers who lacked the militant union traditions of the older workers in the city. Politically, the unions had much less power in the suburbs (Gordon, 1977:76–79).

As residential suburbanization continued, location in the suburbs was also more attractive because that was where the workers, especially the more skilled white workers, lived. And to some extent, like white families, industry began to move to the suburbs in the 1960s to avoid what they saw as the problems of the deteriorating, increasingly African-American central cities.

The suburban transformation of the American city has been intensified and accelerated in recent years by the globalization of economic activities, according to Peter Muller. He points to the rapidly expanding international role of suburban business complexes in large metropolitan areas. This trend has sobering implications for central cities as their CBDs confront the fact that additional economic activities no longer need to be located there (Muller, 1997:44–58).

THE DECLINE OF THE OLD CENTRAL CITIES

The opposite side of the coin of suburban growth was stagnation and decline of the large central cities—especially those in the Northeast and North Central regions. The problems of decline were intensified by the simultaneous influx of the rural poor. By the late 1960s, this combination of trends had produced the conditions that are a major concern of this book: a set of severe economic, social, and political problems in the central cities.

Economic Decline of the Central Cities

As we have seen, even prior to the 1920s, central cities were growing more slowly economically than the surrounding suburban areas. Following World War II, that slower rate of growth began changing into a pattern of stagnation, and by the late 1960s, absolute declines were being recorded in overall economic activity in many of the major central cities in the North. (We will talk about the South in the next chapter.) However, the overall decline was an uneven one. Some kinds of activities declined much more than others. For simplicity, the present discussion will be limited to three general areas of economic activity: industrial, retail, and administrative activities.

Industrial Activity

The most dramatic aspect of central-city decline was in the area of industrial activity and employment. In 1920 about nine out of every ten industrial workers in metropolitan areas were employed in central cities. By the late 1960s, only about six out of ten were employed there (Fremon, 1970). In the large industrial cities of the North, these changes generally translated into absolute declines in manufacturing employment (Hughes, 1974).

Moreover, the type of industrial employment lost and the type retained made the trend even more ominous. Industries that stayed in the central city were often stagnant or declining, remaining for the simple reason that they did not need to expand. Even when a factory in a more dynamic industry stayed, the plant was likely to be old and inefficient. Hence, its long-term prospects for continued operation were poor. The new, rapidly growing, high-technology industries which had the best economic prospects tended to choose suburban locations. Industry that required skilled workers was more likely to leave. This tendency was reflected, for example, in statistics that compared average wages of workers leaving central cities and workers remaining or entering, which revealed a consistent tendency for central-city workers to be less well paid (Gorham and Glazer, 1976:20).

In short, central-city industry became more and more characterized by old, inefficient factories, employing less skilled, less well-paid workers, in the more "marginal," stagnant, or declining industries. By the 1960s, it was clear that central cities were rapidly losing their dominant position as industrial centers. Further industrial decline appeared likely.

Retail Activity

Overall, the percentage of the total sales in metropolitan areas accounted for by CBD stores steadily declined. In some cities, this meant absolute declines in retail sales volume and the closing of major retail stores. In other cities, it meant that the CBD simply failed to grow, and all retail sales growth occurred in the suburbs. In all metropolitan areas, it meant that the CBD was no longer the dominant center of retail activity. Hardest hit were the mass merchandising stores catering to middle-income customers and dependent on high sales volume (e.g., department stores, furniture stores). Smaller stores and stores serving the needs of the lower class were more likely to survive because of the high percentage of these people residing in cities. Luxury shops were also more likely to survive because of the continued presence of well-paid office workers in the CBD (Palen, 1987:250–52).

Administrative Activity

The one relatively bright spot in the central city economy was the continued importance of the CBD as a location of administrative offices for both government and private industry. While there was some significant suburbanization of office activities by the late 1960s, in general, finance, management, and control activities were much less likely to decentralize to suburban locations. Top executives frequently felt the need for face-to-face contact with executives of other businesses. Professional services were more available and convenient in the CBD. Access to government offices and officials was often important in business administration. Hence, there was a continued tendency for most bank headquarters, major law firms, advertising agencies, and corporate headquarters to stay downtown. Office operations that were more self-contained (e.g., insurance companies), however, often did move to the suburbs (Palen, 1987:252–53).

This helped some cities more than others. Such cities as New York, Chicago, San Francisco, and Atlanta were major centers for corporate administration. These cities experienced major expansions in office-building construction in the 1960s. Other cities, whose economic base was more dependent on industry and downtown retail activity, were much less fortunate.

Influx of the Rural Poor

Just as the central cities began to experience economic stagnation and decline, they also experienced a major in-movement of new residents. These new residents were primarily poor, unskilled migrants from rural areas of the South. Most of them were African Americans, but a significant minority came from rural Appalachia. The total number of people involved was quite impressive. Between 1950 and 1970, the total African-American population in central cities grew from 6.6 million to 13.1 million. Or, put another way, in 1910, nine out of ten African Americans lived in the South, and 73 percent were rural residents. By 1980, only about half the African-American population lived in the South (Palen, 1987:222). African Americans are more concentrated both in large cities and metropolitan areas than are Caucasians. More than half of all African Americans in the United States live in central cities, and about 35 percent live in suburban areas (U.S. Census Bureau, 2000e).

For rural, southern African Americans, this movement to northern central cities was a continuation of a trend begun around 1910 but interrupted by the Depression. The single most important reason for the movement was that employment opportunities in southern agriculture steadily declined during most of the 1900s. Mechanization of production and the changing nature of agriculture in the South were eliminating the need for agricultural laborers and sharecroppers and making survival of the small, independent African-American farmer more and more difficult. The southern urban economy was unable to absorb all of these surplus workers because of the extremely late industrialization of the South. Rapid urban industrial growth only began in the 1940s, and it was not until the 1970s that this growth finally could provide employment for all the available workers. The end result was that the only places the displaced rural poor could go was to the northern cities. There, the majority could at least survive by working as unskilled laborers in industry and service occupations. And there was at least some hope for eventual economic advance. In this respect, African Americans resembled the European immigrants who had come before them to American cities. (Immigration was severely restricted after 1920.) The difference was that African Americans came at a time when the period of economic growth in the cities was coming to an end. And, of course, African Americans faced special social barriers that were much more difficult to overcome than the social barriers faced by the immigrants. (We will explore the nature of these barriers in chapter 4.)

Appalachian migration was also partially a response to the increasing difficulty of surviving on small subsistence farms. However, the big push to the cities really came with the rapid decline of employment in the coal industry after World War II and the absence of significant industrial growth in the region until the 1960s (Brown, 1972:130–44).

The Industrial City in Crisis

The result of these changes was that by 1970, instead of simply talking about "urban problems," more and more observers began raising the alarm in regard to an "urban crisis." At the root of their concerns were certain basic trends in the old industrial central cities in the North.

Most of the larger central cities in the North were experiencing declines in population size. They declined despite the influx of the rural poor because of the rapid suburbanization of younger, white, middle- and working-class families. Economic decline had reached the point where the absolute number of job opportunities in a majority of large central cities was decreasing. Moreover, the best-paid and most highly skilled kinds of jobs were increasingly being moved to the suburbs. In short, there were fewer jobs and poorer jobs available in the central cities. Continued industrial decline was making the situation progressively worse.

The result of these trends was that central-city populations were composed of increasing proportions of poor people, minorities, and the elderly. Low-wage workers and the very poor stayed behind in the cities while the more affluent left for the suburbs. These poor were joined by additional poor people from the rural South. Young families left the cities while the elderly (especially the poor elderly) stayed. Whites left for the suburbs, while a growing African-American population remained concentrated almost exclusively in the cities.

In turn, these trends formed the basis for a number of specific problems that we will examine in later chapters: neighborhood deterioration, government financial difficulties, racial hostilities and discrimination, increasing transportation costs, deteriorating conditions in schools, rising crime, and much, much more. We will explore the connection between these problems as we proceed. For now, we need merely to note that central cities had become enmeshed in a complex web of serious problems. Underlying this situation, as we have seen in this chapter, were deep-seated, long-term changes in technology, the economy, and the basic spatial organization of urban life—changes that made these problems extremely difficult to treat.

Recent Developments

Despite the persistence of these problems, the decline of industrial cities is not intractable. Reardon (1997) points to East St. Louis, Illinois, as an example of urban recovery. Between 1980–1996, East St. Louis lost 30 percent of its population—a mass exodus of the workers and consumers needed to improve its economy (U.S. Department of Housing and Urban Development, 1999). However, the city has now stabilized and is presently experiencing a modest economic growth. How can this be explained? While the selection of an effective mayor committed to good government and reform was important, there was also a very significant contribution in the form of state and federal resources. These investments enabled the city to avoid bankruptcy, restore basic municipal services, and to improve living conditions in several significant ways. For example, a committee appointed by the Illinois Board of Higher Education has implemented reforms in the East St. Louis schools that have resulted in cleaner schools, more school supplies, and more classroom teachers. A task force set up by the governor of Illinois has developed innovative approaches to alcohol and drug abuse intervention and treatment programs, and has helped establish a database on alcohol- and drug-related crimes to better direct law enforcement efforts. Over 500 units of public housing have been rehabilitated, and unemployed youth have received instruction in building-trade skills as they help build affordable housing. The Metrolink (light rail system) has made it possible for residents to commute to St. Louis for employment. In addition, the federal government has assisted the city with its flooding problem by helping to develop a new storm sewer system. A recent survey of residents indicates a great rise in residents' satisfaction with municipal services. Moreover, crime is down and residential housing investment has increased (Reardon, 1997). This success story highlights the critical contribution of state and federal governments to the stabilization of smaller industrial cities devastated by suburbanization, deindustrialization, and globalization in the post-World War II period (Reardon, 1997:234–247).

Warf and Holly have traced the recent renewal of Cleveland, Ohio. This city underwent massive deindustrialization in the 1970s and 1980s, but has transformed itself into a producer of high-tech services and a cultural center. These authors see Cleveland's renewal from the perspective of its changing competitive position in the face of national and global trends. They note, however, that although the metropolitan area is predominantly white collar and heavily suburbanized, the problems of the inner-city ghetto persist (Warf and Holly, 1997:208–221).

EVALUATION

In this chapter, we have traced the development of urban areas in the United States from their beginnings, pointing out that contemporary urban conditions are the outgrowth of a very long historical process. The lesson should be clear: urban problems are not isolated events which spring out of nowhere. They have their origins in a complex chain of events growing out of the very forces that have shaped the basic nature of our society. In a very real sense, the same technological forces and methods of social and economic organization that brought prosperity, national power, and the "Big Mac" helped create slums and urban decay. Just how they did so will be explored in more detail in later chapters.

The consequences of rapid urbanization and the subsequent urban "crisis" can be viewed in terms of several policy options. Public officials claim that an urban social policy operates for the general welfare. In actuality, urban social policy is seen more accurately in terms of political economy. The power of businesses and corporations is used primarily for profit. This goal may be attained by giving it priority in either the long or short run. Social policy can be enlightened as well as efficient, can be lean but at the same time not mean. Urban social policy and social policy in general can be strengthened greatly if it fosters meaning for the masses of people, the poor as well as the relatively well-off and rich.

MAIN POINTS

1. The United States offers one of the most dramatic examples of transformation by means of urbanization and industrialization. From 1609 to 1830, the nation moved from colonization to decolonization. During the mid-1800s industrial capitalism came to dominate. The years between the Civil War and World War I saw a drastic reorganization of the socioeconomic and political systems of the country.

2. Rapid urbanization in the nineteenth century was the outgrowth of industrialization. Industrialization resulted in the concentration of workers and factories in cities because of the reliance on steam power, rail transportation, the need for workers to live very near the factories, the effect of breaks in transportation, and the need for factories to be near large urban markets and to use urban services.

3. Industrial cities were large (because of annexation), geographically compact, and very densely populated. There tended to be one large central business district that dominated retail activity and housed central offices, recreational and cultural activities, and government offices. Compact industrial districts were surrounded by large, very crowded, and squalid working-class slums. Even middle-class residential areas were relatively dense and close to the central business district. By the 1920s, residential suburbs for the more affluent and industrial satellite cities had developed.

4. The "human-ecology" approach to studying cities tried to develop a theory about the nature of the physical structure of the industrial city and the causes of that structure. Three main theories were developed: concentric-zone, sector, and multiple-nuclei theory. Social area analysis attempted to describe urban land use by concentrating on the social characteristics of the population, while factorial ecology used computers to analyze and associate social traits, which were then used to describe a city's land-use patterns.

5. Rapid suburbanization in the 1920s gave way to a fifteen-year period of relative stagnation in urban areas caused by the Depression and World War II.

6. By 1945, North American urban areas were facing a number of severe problems: physical aging, transportation and congestion problems, high land costs and lack of land to build on, concentrated social and economic problems, and a housing shortage.

7. Between 1945 and 1970, urban areas in the North experienced a period of explosive suburbanization. The suburbs were transformed from residential enclaves for the affluent to sprawling, low-density urban areas which contained a wide range of different land uses: industrial, commercial, and residential. By 1970, most suburban residents also worked in the suburbs. The suburbs were the focus of most economic growth during the period. Conurbanization created massive urban sprawls connecting metropolitan areas together into a type of urban system called a "megalopolis."

8. Residential suburbanization was the result of a number of factors: government housing policy, government transportation policy, car ownership, the economics of housing construction, rising purchasing power, and public preference for suburban residence.

9. Suburbanization of industry was the result of changing energy technology, changes in industrial production, changes in transportation technology, the need for large tracts of land for factories, the desire to avoid city taxes, the attempt to escape the strong worker unions in the cities, the desire to avoid city problems, and the need for a skilled work force.

10. The result was economic stagnation and then the decline of the central cities. At the same time, the large central cities of the North experienced an influx of the rural poor, mostly from the South.

KEY TERMS

Annexation The process by which cities have added surrounding areas to their legal jurisdiction. The condition under which it occurs is governed by state law.

Breaks in Transportation Points along the transportation system where goods must be moved from one vehicle to another.

Central Business District or **CBD** The central retail shopping area and dominant commercial district of a city.

Competition and Segregation Basic ecological processes in concentric-zone theory by which economic activities compete for the most attractive locations in a city and end up segregated in different areas of the city based on their need and ability to afford different locations.

Concentric-Zone Theory The ecological theory set forth by Burgess and Park which suggests that the basic pattern of land use in cities resembles concentric circles of homogeneous land-use areas.

Conurbanization The process by which metropolitan areas grow outward until they merge with other metropolitan areas.

Factorial Ecology The application of computer technology to the analysis of the social characteristics of an urban population.

Familism The cultural orientation associated with post-1945 suburban life which emphasizes the importance of family life and child rearing.

Human-Ecology Approach The study of community structure through the analysis of the spatial and temporal distribution of persons and groups, and the factors associated with changes in these distributive patterns.

Invasion and Succession The process in concentric-zone theory by which land use in one zone is gradually replaced by that of the next innermost zone as a city grows.

Leapfrogging The process by which, in suburban areas after 1945, new residential and commercial activities tended to jump over existing, partially built-up suburban areas to locate farther away from the central city. The result was that open areas were often left between various built-up areas in the suburbs.

Megalopolis The structure of urban land use which results from large-scale conurbanization; a "supermetropolis."

Metropolitan Area A contiguous territorial unit economically and socially integrated around a large city or metropolis.

Multiple-Nuclei Theory The theory of human ecology which claims that cities develop a number of specialized centers rather than growing out from a central downtown, and that urban land use, while homogeneous, is affected by a number of factors unique to each urban area.

Natural Areas According to Burgess and Park, these were areas of homogeneous land use that resulted from natural free-market processes, rather than from zoning or government planning.

Sector Theory The theory of human ecology which claims that urban land use resembles pie-shaped sectors of homogeneous land-use areas.

Social Area Analysis The description of urban land use in terms of the social characteristics of the population.

Suburban Persistence The tendency of suburban communities to maintain their original pattern of land use over long periods of time.

Trickle-down Approach Housing policy that encourages the creation of new housing for the more affluent, with the result that the housing they abandon "trickles down" to the less affluent.

SUGGESTED READING

Feagin, Joe R., and Robert Parker. 1990. *Building American Cities: The Urban Real Estate Game*. 2d ed. Englewood Cliffs, NJ: Prentice Hall.

Gans, Herbert J. 1991. *People, Plans, and Policies: Essays on Poverty, Racism, and Other National Urban Problems*. New York: Columbia University/Russell Sage Foundation. A collection of essays by one of sociology's most engaging thinkers. Gans links theory and social policy as he confronts a host of contemporary problems.

Glaab, Charles, and Theodore Brown. 1967. *A History of Urban America*. New York: Macmillan. A discussion of North American urban growth prior to 1920.

Gordon, David. 1977. "Class Struggle and the Stages of American Urban Development." In *The Rise of the Sunbelt Cities*, edited by D. Perry and A. Watkins. Beverly Hills: Sage Publications. A brief analysis of the development of cities in different regions of the United States from a neo-Marxian perspective. The first part of the article relates to the discussion in this chapter.

Harris, Chauncey D., and Edward L. Ullman. 1945. "The Nature of Cities." *Annals of the American Academy of Political and Social Science* 242:7–17. The classic summary of the early theories of human ecology.

Kling, Rob, Spencer Olin, and Mark Poster. 1991. *Postsuburban California: The Transformation of Orange County Since World War II.* Berkeley: University of California Press. This historical case study of Orange County, which spreads south from Los Angeles and whose population has grown tenfold since 1945, explores the social changes that accompany a growth boom.

McKelvey, Blake. 1968. *The Emergence of Metropolitan America 1915–1966.* New Brunswick, NJ: Rutgers University. A major review of the development of North American urban areas in the first two-thirds of the twentieth century.

Muller, Peter O. 1981. *Contemporary Suburban America.* Englewood Cliffs, NJ: Prentice Hall. A clear and thorough summary of the details and nature of suburban development.

Palen, J. John. 1995. *The Suburbs.* New York: McGraw-Hill. This book provides an updated description and analysis of suburban development, with relevant use of contemporary census data.

Thernstrom, Stephan, and Richard Sennet, eds. 1969. *Nineteenth-Century Cities: Essays in the New Urban History.* New Haven: Yale University Press. A collection of essays that attempts to dispel many myths about life and conditions in early North American cities.

ENDNOTES

[1] Not all factories did so locate, however. Some industries located in small communities. The result was the creation of "mill towns" or "company towns" dominated by a single large factory. The state of Ohio, for instance, is still dotted with small and medium-sized factory towns.

[2] These were families with less than $3,000 a year income in 1950. Given income levels in that year, people in this group were not just the poor, they included a large number of working-class people.

Patterns of Regional and Metropolitan Growth

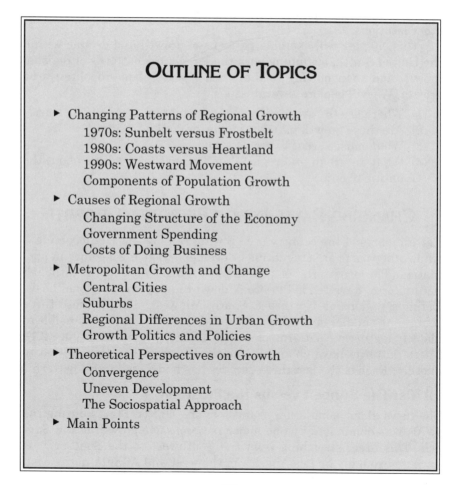

OUTLINE OF TOPICS

▶ Changing Patterns of Regional Growth
    1970s: Sunbelt versus Frostbelt
    1980s: Coasts versus Heartland
    1990s: Westward Movement
    Components of Population Growth
▶ Causes of Regional Growth
    Changing Structure of the Economy
    Government Spending
    Costs of Doing Business
▶ Metropolitan Growth and Change
    Central Cities
    Suburbs
    Regional Differences in Urban Growth
    Growth Politics and Policies
▶ Theoretical Perspectives on Growth
    Convergence
    Uneven Development
    The Sociospatial Approach
▶ Main Points

$\mathbf{A}$ll cities and urban areas are not alike, even within a single country such as the United States. Cities vary on a number of dimensions. This chapter will focus on the different patterns of population growth found in urban areas, and particularly on the relationship of growth to the cities in different regions of the United States. Whether a city's population is growing, shrinking, or stable has an enormous effect on the inhabitants. A community's growth rate affects the quality of life for the residents of that area.

Growth in population is often tied to economic growth. An overall expansion of business and industry provides jobs that attract new residents who in turn consume products and services, contributing to increased expansion of business. The opposite is also true: companies' closing or downsizing contributes to an overall shrinking of the local economy and a decline in population as residents leave to seek jobs in other locations.

This chapter will examine patterns of growth and decline within the United States, beginning with the large-scale patterns of regional growth and then moving to the smaller scale of metropolitan area growth. We will explore several issues:

(1) Where are the areas of the most population growth? The least?
(2) Are these growth patterns stable, or do they change?
(3) What causes areas to grow?
(4) What do urban and regional growth patterns tell us about the nature of cities?

CHANGING PATTERNS OF REGIONAL GROWTH

Certain parts of the country are growing rapidly—in fact, booming— while other parts are stagnating or even experiencing declines in population. These patterns of population growth and decline, although not uniform, have tended to break down roughly on a regional basis. Defining regions as Northeast, South, Midwest (each of these three containing smaller subregions), Mountain, and Pacific, it is possible to identify distinctive patterns of growth in each region (see figure 2.1). These patterns have changed dramatically from one time period to another. Each of the last three decades has had a distinctive pattern.

1970s: The Sunbelt versus the Frostbelt

The news about population changes in the United States during the 1970s was dominated by one major fact: massive growth of the *Sunbelt*. This area, stretching from the Southwest to the Southeast, is anchored roughly by Los Angeles in the west and Atlanta in the east. Although the growth of this area had begun well before 1970, it became more dramatic during the decade as growth of other areas

Figure 2.1
Regions of the United States

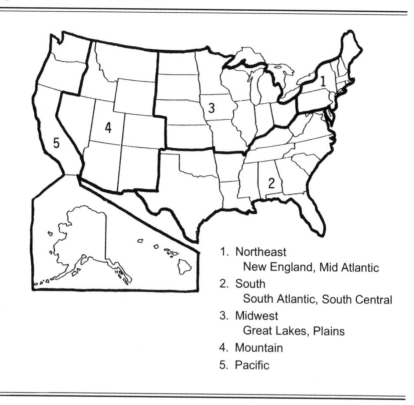

1. Northeast
   New England, Mid Atlantic
2. South
   South Atlantic, South Central
3. Midwest
   Great Lakes, Plains
4. Mountain
5. Pacific

slowed. In second place for growth during the 1970s were the Mountain states, those located between the Pacific states and the Plains. The Mountain states actually had a faster growth rate than the Sunbelt, due to the fact that the populations living in them were substantially smaller than the populations of the Sunbelt states. The Sunbelt states, then, grew more in absolute numbers, while the Mountain states added larger percentages of their population.

Both the Sunbelt and the Mountain states shared characteristic growth patterns that differentiated them from the other parts of the country. The chief difference was that their growth was much less centralized than growth in other areas. While the large metropolitan areas such as Atlanta, Denver, and Dallas grew, even in their central cities, an enormous proportion of the growth occurred outside of metropolitan areas. Some was *exurban* growth; that is, existing suburban growth that happened to cross over the border of the metropolitan area and into an adjacent county. Much of the growth, however, was in smaller metropolitan areas and, most strikingly, in nonmetropolitan areas (small towns and rural areas) far from cities. These types of communities, which had been experiencing population declines for decades, were responsible for the remarkably dispersed nature of Sunbelt and Mountain growth (Berry and Dahlman, 1978).

Although the Sunbelt and Mountain states were growing rapidly, the northern states were not. Throughout the 1970s, the states in the Northeast and Midwest (with the exception of northern New England) grew very slowly, or in a few cases, actually lost population. In contrast with the Sunbelt, these states were quickly dubbed the "Frostbelt." However, their slow or negligible growth rates were not attributable solely to their cooler climates. (Nor, as we shall see, was the majority of Sunbelt growth due to the sunny climate.)

The Frostbelt states of the Northeast and Midwest consisted of two kinds of areas: the highly industrialized sections bordering the Atlantic Ocean and Great Lakes and the rural agricultural sections from the plains to central Ohio. From 1900 to the 1960s, the industrial areas' cities had acted as urban magnets, growing steadily from internal population growth, migration from rural areas, and foreign immigration. During the 1970s, few migrants entered the region, and declining birth rates added to the stagnation of population growth.

Despite their overall patterns of growth, however, both the Sunbelt and the Frostbelt experienced uneven growth within their regions. While some areas were shrinking rapidly, some were maintaining a steady population, and others were growing. Although these very different small-scale patterns added up to a larger pattern of slow growth for the Frostbelt and rapid growth for the Sunbelt, it would be wrong to conclude that no northern areas were growing in population and that the entire South was booming.

1980s: Coasts versus Heartland

In the early 1980s, the patterns of regional growth and decline were similar to those of the 1970s. Gradually, however, a new growth pattern complicated the Sunbelt-Frostbelt dichotomy. In the mid- and late 1980s, the fastest growing areas of the country were on the Atlantic and Pacific coasts, and population growth was no longer as heavily concentrated in the South. In fact, four of the seven states that lost population between 1987 and 1988 were Sunbelt or Mountain states (*Population Today*, 1989). During this period, the coasts were the overwhelming destination of people moving out of state. Of the sixteen states that received the largest number of new residents, twelve were coastal states.

Conversely, the states with the least population growth in the 1980s were those in the center of the country, often called the *Heartland*. This area, encompassing a band from Wyoming in the west to

Pennsylvania in the east and from Minnesota in the north to Mississippi in the south, showed the lowest rates of population growth *(Population Today,* 1989).

1990s: Westward Movement

Patterns of growth shifted again in the 1990s. As shown in figure 2.2, the fastest growing states during the decade were the Mountain states, particularly Nevada, Arizona, Colorado, Utah, and Idaho. Between 1990 and 2000, their rates of population growth ranged from 8.9 percent in Wyoming to a whopping 66.3 percent in Nevada. Compare those figures with the average growth rate for all states, 13.1 percent (U.S. Census Bureau, 2000d).

Besides the Mountain states, two other regions had growth rates above the national average: the Pacific Coast and the South. The regions with the slowest growth in the 1990s were the Northeast and the Midwest. Compared with the 1980s, the Midwest experienced somewhat more growth; the Northeast, on the other hand, experienced less growth.

California provides an insight into the complicated business of measuring growth trends. During the 1990s, population growth in California slowed considerably from its rapid increase in the 1980s. Between 1990 and 1994, California went from being number five among the states in growth rates to being number nineteen. Although its growth slowed, however, it surely did not stop. Even with a lower growth *rate* than eighteen other states, California still had a larger population increase in *absolute* numbers than any other state (Byerly, 1995). The reason for this seeming discrepancy is that California has the largest population of any state. If a state with a small population and one with a large population each have an increase of 100 residents, that increase represents a smaller percent in the large state than it does in the small one. So when you examine growth figures it is important to know whether growth is being reported in actual numbers of people or in percent increases.

Components of Population Growth

Population growth is difficult to predict accurately. According to demographers (sociologists who specialize in studying populations), population changes are made up of three components: migration, natural increase, and immigration. Each of these factors is independent of the others.

Migration includes both those people moving into an area (say, a state or region) and those moving out. *Net migration,* or the overall impact of these moves on the population total, is obtained by subtracting the number of people moving out of an area from the number moving into the area. (If more people move out than move in, the state or region will have negative net migration, or out-migration.) The chang-

Figure 2.2
Population Growth Rates, 1990 to 2000, by State

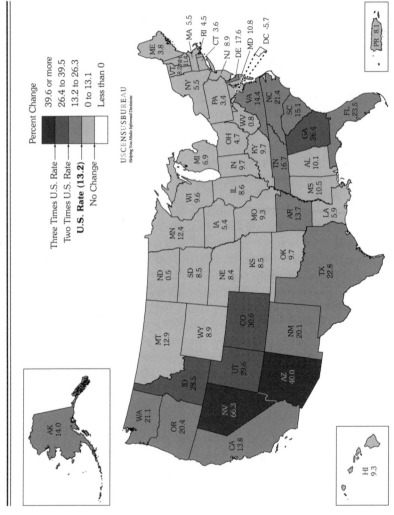

Percent Change

Three Times U.S. Rate → 39.6 or more
Two Times U.S. Rate → 26.4 to 39.5
13.2 to 26.3
U.S. Rate (13.2) → 0 to 13.1
No Change → Less than 0

US CENSUS BUREAU
Helping You Make Informed Decisions

ME 3.8
NH 1.1
MA 5.5
RI 4.5
CT 3.6
NJ 8.9
DE 17.6
MD 10.8
DC -5.7
VT 9.2
NY 5.5
PA 3.4
WV 0.8
VA 14.4
NC 21.4
SC 15.1
FL 23.5
GA 26.4
AL 10.1
MS 10.5
LA 5.9
OH 4.7
KY 9.7
TN 16.7
MI 6.9
IN 9.7
IL 8.6
WI 9.6
IA 5.4
MO 9.3
AR 13.7
MN 12.4
ND 0.5
SD 8.5
NE 8.4
KS 8.5
OK 9.7
TX 22.8
MT 12.9
WY 8.9
CO 30.6
NM 20.1
ID 28.5
UT 29.6
AZ 40.0
WA 21.1
OR 20.4
NV 66.3
CA 13.8

AK 14.0

HI 9.3

PR 8.1

ing population balance among regions is partly a product of the changing balance between in- and out-migration. Between 1990 and 1994, the South experienced the highest rate of net migration whereas the Northeast experienced substantial net out-migration (Byerly and Deardorff, 1995).

The second component of population change, natural increase, is the excess of births over deaths. Many factors, such as socioeconomic conditions and age of the population, influence both the birth rate and death rate. In the 1990s, the Pacific states, the Mountain states, and the state of Texas consistently had birth rates higher than the national average (U.S. Census Bureau, 2000d). The relatively young age of the people living in those states contributes to their high rates of natural increase. As a result, we would expect significant population growth in those states to continue through natural increase alone, regardless of the impact of in-migration.

Immigrants from outside the United States also add to population growth. In the most recent year for which data are available, 1997, some 798,000 immigrants entered the United States (U.S. Immigration and Naturalization Service, 1999). Immigrants do not settle in equal numbers throughout the country; rather, they tend to cluster in specific areas. These are overwhelmingly urban areas, especially the metropolitan areas in which the largest cities are located. In recent years, 95 percent of immigrants to the United States have settled in urban areas, the vast majority in five cities: New York, Los Angeles, Miami, Chicago, and Washington, D.C. (U.S. Immigration and Naturalization Service, 1999). In chapter 4 we will discuss in more detail the kinds of communities formed by immigrants from various countries.

In addition to the legal immigrants, the population is also increased by illegal immigrants. Obviously, we do not have reliable figures on illegal immigration, but it is estimated to be about 300,000 people per year. This is a net figure, including not only the many people who enter the country but also those who leave, voluntarily or involuntarily, each year. Further estimates tell us that approximately one-third of those living here illegally are Mexican citizens (Rumbaut, 1996). Although we have little data on the regional distribution of illegal immigrants, they appear to be concentrated most heavily in the South and West.

Taking all of these factors (migration, natural increase, and immigration) into account, we can more easily understand why population shifts are difficult to predict. One factor often offsets another, and all of the factors may change over time. Take California, for example. We saw that its rate of growth slowed considerably during the early 1990s, yet at the same time it had a high rate of immigration from abroad. When compared with other states, California also had a relatively high rate of natural increase. Just one factor accounted for California's slow rate of growth in the early 1990s: net out-migration. The proportion of California residents leaving the state grew each year from 1990 to 1994, and in 1994 California's out-migration rate was the highest in the nation (Byerly, 1995). By 1997, however, out-migration from California had slowed so much that it was balanced by migration into the state, so that overall, California's growth rate for the 1990s was just about the national average: 13.8 percent for California versus 13.1 percent for all states (U.S. Census Bureau, 2000d).

CAUSES OF REGIONAL GROWTH

What accounts for these regional shifts and changing patterns of urban development? The obvious answer, at least for most of this growth, is that the overall pattern of economic growth and development in the United States has been changing. The potential significance of this change cannot be overstated. It means that urban problems must be seen in the context of more widely based regional growth and decline. It also becomes necessary to distinguish between the urban problems of different areas of the country. Simply put, some urban problems are specific to declining areas and others to growing areas.

The reasons behind the regional shifts are complex and still not entirely understood. A number of explanations, some of them contradictory, have been advanced. We will begin by looking at individual factors that influence regional development. Later in the chapter we will examine general theories of regional development that encompass more than single-factor explanations.

Changing Structure of the Economy

The economy of the United States, like all capitalist economies, is constantly changing. Throughout our history, these economic changes have often had major consequences for regional growth and decline. In the nineteenth century, for example, the rural, agricultural-based South lost its economic and political dominance as the North gained economic power through large-scale industrialization. Population grew in the North's industrial regions and stagnated in the South.

The changes in regional population we have seen over the past three decades are the result of economic trends that have been going on at least since the late 1940s. One of these is a shift in the kinds of products and services being produced in the United States. Manufacturing employment has declined overall, and within the manufacturing sector, certain kinds of products have replaced others. The largest employment declines have been in the so-called heavy industries such as the production of steel and autos, as well as in certain labor-intensive industries such as the production of clothing and shoes. Growth areas of the economy have included new industries such as high-tech manufacturing (e.g., computer components) and the service sector (e.g., health care, accounting, banking, and hotels). In addition to these long-term trends, there are shorter cycles of economic change in certain industries; for example, energy production, in which growth can speed up or slow down abruptly as conditions in the world market change.

How have these economic changes affected regional growth and decline? The key fact to note is that many industries are concentrated in certain geographic locations. When changes occur within an industry that is geographically concentrated, the economic change has a major impact on the region.

In the 1970s, the high-technology economy was located disproportionately in the southern and western states, where new industries such as the semiconductor industry in California's Silicon Valley were growing. The growth of the high-tech sector helped to drive population growth in that area. In the 1980s, high-tech manufacturing and such related industries as research and development grew dramatically in the Northeast. The so-called Route 128 complex of computer-related companies linked by Boston's circumferential highway of the same name provided one anchor for New England's growth spurt in the 1980s, while California's boom continued. These two high-tech concentrations helped spur the bicoastal pattern of population growth in the 1980s. In the 1990s, the high-tech industries were no longer as closely related to manufacturing but were more software- and Internet-oriented, allowing them to disperse geographically. Concentrations of high-tech industries grew rapidly in Washington, Utah, Texas, and several other states. The movement of high-tech industries into the western and Mountain states helped spur population growth in those regions.

Innovative industries such as high technology are not the only growth-producing sectors of the economy. Changes in basic industries such as energy can also have a dramatic effect on regional growth patterns. When the Middle Eastern oil-producing nations formed a cartel (OPEC) in the early 1970s, oil prices soared on the world market. This price rise spurred investment in energy exploration in the United States, again disproportionately located in the Sunbelt and Mountain states (e.g., Texas, Oklahoma, Nevada, Colorado) as well as Alaska. The extremely rapid growth of these areas, however, was a temporary phenomenon. By the early 1980s, once energy prices had fallen, investors withdrew from the industry, employment opportunities dwindled, and the energy-producing areas began to lose population. The exodus from these areas is one factor in the slowdown of Sunbelt growth in the 1980s (Browne, 1989). Toward the end of the 1990s, the energy industry experienced a resurgence, which may lead to more investment and population growth in the South, Mountain, and western states in the present decade.

Another important type of economic change is the business cycle, or the ups and downs of economic expansions and recessions. When the national economy does badly, all regions do not suffer equally, and when the national economy does well, all regions do not prosper equally. Researchers have found that regional differences in economic recessions and recoveries are due to several factors, including the mix of industries in the region, prevailing wages, energy costs, and the availability of government services. Because these factors change over time, each national economic recovery has a different impact on each region. During the recovery of 1975–1978, for example, the South and West led the nation in economic growth, and during the economic recovery of 1982–1985 the two coasts led the nation in growth (Bradbury and Kodrzycki, 1992).

A final type of economic change, one that is increasing in importance, is the trend toward the *globalization of the economy*. No longer are economic conditions in different industries affected solely by events taking place in our own country. More and more, our economy is linked to those of other nations. One important manifestation of this trend is the emergence of multinational corporations. A multinational may have its headquarters in New York or London, its manufacturing plants in Mexico or Singapore, and its bookkeeping services in the Caribbean. Globalization of the economy has affected the regional growth patterns of the United States because some areas have become tightly integrated into international trade, banking, and manufacturing operations while others have not. California, for example, has become part of the Pacific Basin, trading with the expanding Asian nations. The Miami area is a major center for commerce and banking for Central and South America. Texas is the site of many border-straddling manufacturing operations, where corporations pair U.S. and Mexican plants to gain the advantages of both technical expertise and cheap labor. New York City has become one of the premier banking and finance centers of the new global economy. These areas have attracted investment, created jobs, and drawn new residents based on their changing roles in the national and international economy.

When areas grow and decline due to these changes in economic structure, the effects are fundamentally different from growth and decline due to the normal ups and downs of the business cycle (booms and recessions). Rather than cycles of expansion and contraction of the same industries within a region, we are seeing a pattern of *economic restructuring,* in which one set of industries is replaced by another. Restructuring has more long-term consequences for regional growth and decline than do the short-term changes of the business cycle.

Government Spending

The federal government plays a significant role in regional economic growth because federal expenditures have different effects on different parts of the country. We will first look at the role of public works expenditures and then examine the role of defense spending in shaping regional growth.

Between 1950 and 1970 the South received a very large share of the "pork-barrel" public works projects undertaken by the federal government. This was a reflection both of the traditionally depressed economic conditions in the region, which the federal government sought to correct, and the special political influence of the southern states in Congress. The seniority system in Congress (especially before some recent reforms) meant that senators and representatives with the longest service were appointed to the most powerful congressional committees and had the most say in where public works projects were undertaken. A very high proportion of these high-seniority members of Congress came from the South. The result was an influx of federal dollars for such things as power dams, harbor improvements, and river transportation systems. This helped to solve a major disadvantage of the South: it had a poor infrastructure (transportation, water, electricity), which made it difficult and expensive for industry to locate there.

Military expenditures played a significant role in the growth of the South's economy in past years, particularly as the location of a large number of military bases. As military spending has changed in nature, however, it has favored different regions of the country. During the 1980s the United States greatly increased the amount of military spending, particularly increasing the proportion going to high-tech weapons systems. Rather than benefiting the established (heavily southern) military bases and naval shipyards, these weapons contracts tended to go to a handful of defense-oriented technology companies: Lockheed, General Dynamics, Boeing, Grumman, and a few others. Military contracts also provided large amounts of money to the new computer-based research and design companies in California and New England.

The area that economist Ann Markusen calls the *Gunbelt* has received the lion's share of defense-related spending in recent years. The Gunbelt stretches ". . . along an arc from Alaska to Boston, sweeping down through Seattle, Silicon Valley, and Los Angeles in the West, across the more southerly Mountain and Plains states, through Texas and Florida, and up the Eastern seaboard through Newport News and Long Island to Massachusetts and Connecticut" (Markusen and Yudken, 1991:172). Economic research shows that government investment in defense industries attracts highly skilled workers in large numbers, contributing to the growth of the areas where defense contractors are concentrated (Ellis, Barff, and Markusen, 1993).

Because defense contracts are so large, their influence on the local economy can be enormous. As military spending rises and falls, so do the economies of the Gunbelt areas. In California, for example, military spending provided 14 percent of the state's economy in 1970 but only 8 percent in 1991, and the state's decline in high-tech employment was fueled by the layoffs in the aerospace industry in the late 1980s (Henderson, 1990). California's economic planners, realizing that the state's economy was highly dependent on defense-related employment, have attempted to diversify the economy. By the late 1990s, the state's economy had rebounded, not based on any one industry but on a mix of entertainment, high technology, business services, multimedia, and foreign trade (Gorov, 1997).

Government spending is not the only cause of regional growth, and reductions in government spending are not the only reason for regional decline. Federal projects, however, can be an important economic stimulus in two ways. First are the direct economic effects of federal dollars spent on salaries and purchases—for example, personnel and supplies for military bases. Second, federal spending provides important indirect economic effects through government contracts to private firms. These private contractors, in turn, hire or fire workers, buy more or fewer supplies, and so on, based on their ability to secure federal contracts. Thus, the private economy is heavily influenced by government spending.

Costs of Doing Business

Another cause of uneven growth between regions is differences in the costs of doing business. The reasons why businesses choose to locate in a particular area go well beyond calculations of cost. They include such factors as the availability of skilled labor, the proximity of suppliers and subcontractors, the locations of the markets for the products or services produced, and the level of services provided by local government. When these other factors are equal, however, the cost of doing business can be a deciding factor in establishing, enlarging, or moving an enterprise. Several of these cost factors have favored the South and the Mountain states for business location since the 1960s.

A low wage rate is one such advantage. The South and the Mountain states have traditionally had lower wages than the Northeast or Midwest states. In the past, this had little effect on the location of industry, since the Northeast and Midwest had other advantages (such as skilled workers and good infrastructure) that offset labor costs. Increasingly, however, employers (especially in manufacturing) are attempting to reduce labor costs. Thus, they are more often turning to the South and to Mountain states for their labor supply by locating new plants in those areas.

A related issue is regional differences in rates of unionization of workers. To employers, unionization in the North meant not only higher wages but also less ability to control the workplace as they wished. In the South and West, however, unions were weak, not only because of the lack of an industrial tradition, but also because of a more conservative political climate. Most states in the South, Pacific, and Mountain regions have long had "right-to-work" laws that make union organizing more difficult and reduce the effectiveness of the unions once they are formed. Several states have courted economic investment by advertising that businesses could avoid unions by locating in their area.

Tax policies also contribute to differences in regional investment and growth. There has been a persistent pattern of higher-than-average state and local taxes and expenditures in the Midwest, Pacific, and Northeast regions, but in the Sunbelt and certain Mountain states, taxes and expenditures have been lower than average. State and local governments in the Midwest, Pacific, and Northeast provide more services, employ more workers, and pay their workers more. Some of these areas also have slower-growing or declining tax bases from which to raise revenue (Bahl, 1984). Although there are many negative consequences of lower local taxes (the chief one being inferior services), the tax rate can be, on balance, a factor that affects business location and therefore population growth rates.

One of the paradoxes of the "costs of doing business" explanation for urban growth is that the cheaper costs in the South and Mountain regions may be due chiefly to the fact that those regions are less urbanized than the Northeast or Midwest. Because of investment since 1970, rural areas in the South are now the most highly industrialized of any rural areas in the nation. As more investment flows to these areas, they are becoming more urbanized, even if their form of urbanization is such low-density, sprawling areas as the Dallas-Fort Worth metroplex or the Raleigh-Durham-Chapel Hill triangle. With greater urbanization, the costs of doing business may continue to rise in the South and in the Mountain states. Later in the chapter we will see that theorists are debating whether the regions will become more alike in their patterns of economic growth and population growth.

METROPOLITAN GROWTH AND CHANGE

The economic and political factors that produce so much variation in regional growth also have an impact on both the size and the nature of communities within those regions. Overall, metropolitan areas have continued to grow steadily. Within metropolitan areas, however, central cities and suburbs have fared differently as a result of the changing economy.

Central Cities

One consequence of economic changes was that the larger central cities lost one set of functions and gained another. By 1970 it was clear that central cities were no longer going to be the location of the country's industrial activities. It was not clear, however, what would take the place of the departing manufacturing companies. During the 1970s, most of the nation's central cities lost population as residents migrated to suburbs and nonmetropolitan areas. These former "urban magnets" could no longer attract or hold population without the economic base of manufacturing that had given their residents a reason to locate there. Even in the growing Sunbelt area, the central cities were losing population or growing very slowly.

Since 1980 the impacts of the economic changes we have discussed began to be felt very strongly in U.S. cities, and the implications of the changes have varied from city to city. A handful of the largest cities, those most closely linked to the international networks of the global economy, have become world cities—centers for trade and finance and home to many multinational corporate headquarters. New York, Los Angeles, and Miami are usually considered in this category. Several other large cities, while not of world city status, have established themselves as economic centers for specific regions. Atlanta, Boston, Chicago, Denver, Houston, and San Francisco fill this role. Their economies revolve around the same functions as the world cities, namely, banking and finance, trade and commerce, and business services such as law, accounting, advertising, and real estate development (Sassen, 1990).

The changing nature of the economies of these central cities has caused profound changes in other aspects of urban life. The cities' occupational structures, for example, which formerly would have contained large proportions of skilled and unskilled manufacturing workers, are now dominated by service sector workers. Many of them are highly paid service workers such as attorneys, managers, and stockbrokers. A much larger number are clerical workers or relatively low-paid service workers such as janitors, health aides, and security guards.

With the growth of the downtown white-collar workforce in many cities, there has been an increase in *gentrification*. This is the movement of the gentry, or professional workers, into neighborhoods formerly dominated by poor or working-class households. Gentrification began in the 1970s and intensified in the 1980s, as urban workers found alternatives to suburban living in brownstones, condominiums, shingled Victorians, or former manufacturing lofts (Zukin, 1982). While most urban workers continued to look for housing in the suburbs, the white-collar labor force was so large that even a minority could produce a distinct trend such as gentrification. Gentrification was hailed as an "urban renaissance" by many city officials eager to have a large number of white, middle-class residents living in properties that were appreciating in value (and tax assessment). At the same time, gentrification was criticized for displacing working-class residents by raising housing costs (Cordova, 1991).

Changes in the urban economy have also prompted major changes in land use in these service-dominated central cities. Downtown business districts have expanded into areas that formerly housed factories, small businesses, and homes. In some cases, the older buildings are being demolished and replaced with new structures, but in many areas, the factories and warehouses are being refurbished as offices and shops to meet the space needs of the growing service sector. In Chicago, the growing downtown has threatened some areas of small manufacturing businesses because their proprietors cannot afford the high rents that service sector businesses can pay. Small manufacturing firms have tried to prevent this industrial displacement by enlisting the city's help in protecting certain areas as designated manufacturing zones (Ducharme, 1991).

What of the former industrial cities that have not become major world or regional centers? Many of these central cities have continued to decline in population. Detroit is one of the more extreme examples, having dropped in population from 1.2 million in 1980 to 970,000 in 1998 (U.S. Census Bureau, 1999a). Like several other deindustrializing cities, Detroit has tried to model itself on the world cities, providing new space for services, offices, tourism, and recreation. City officials have also attempted to retain a certain number of manufacturing jobs in the auto industry, and of course, the U.S. automakers are still headquartered in Detroit. But the Detroit metropolitan area contains "two Detroits," a declining central city surrounded by flourishing suburbs (Darden et al., 1987).

According to the U. S. Department of Housing and Urban Development (1999), "Too many cities are being left behind in the new economy" (p.14). The report begins with the good news that the economic boom during the 1990s spurred the growth of cities throughout the country. It goes on to point out, however, that while most central cities in the United States grew in population, 116 cities lost more than 5 percent of their population between 1980 and 1996. These shrinking cities tended to be small or mid-sized and to have higher rates of poverty and unemployment than the cities that were either growing or maintaining a stable population. Figure 2.3 shows the locations of these shrinking central cities. Their geographic concentration in the eastern half of the country, and particularly in the northeast quadrant, is striking.

Suburbs

Although metropolitan areas overall are growing, since 1960 the suburbs have been growing more rapidly than the central cities. By 1996, more than one and one-half times as many people lived in the suburbs as in the central cities within U.S. metropolitan areas (U.S. Department of Housing and Urban Development, 1999).

In some parts of the country (Southern California and Florida's east coast, for example), suburbs have begun to merge physically (although not legally/politically) with each other and with small nearby cities. The low-density sprawl and "leapfrogging" characteristic of suburban development undergoing rapid growth sometimes

Figure 2.3
Cities Losing 5% or More Population, 1980–1996

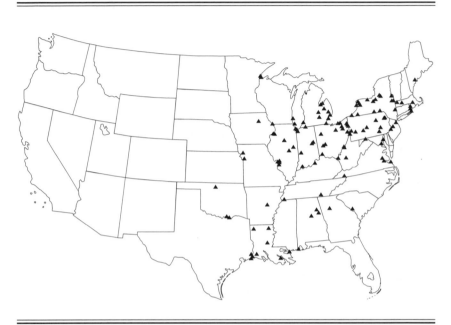

SOURCE: U.S. Department of Housing and Urban Development, 1999.

make it difficult to distinguish the boundaries between municipalities. They also make it less likely that suburban residents will travel to the central city for employment, shopping, and recreation. One area that has become in many ways a suburb independent of the city is Long Island. Formerly dominated by commuter suburbs and farms, it is rapidly industrializing. And its two counties, Nassau and Suffolk, by themselves (without New York City) rank among the ten most populous metropolitan areas in the United States.

During the 1970s and 1980s, it was common to think of suburban growth as a result of urban decline. The perception that suburban growth was fueled by residents fleeing the cities was supported by population statistics that showed central-city populations falling while suburbs grew. Since 1990, however, most central cities are growing, and even those cities that are losing population are losing it at a much slower rate than previously. Suburban growth is fueled as much by the economics of building and land as by the rejection of the city. In fact, some suburbs have become new cities in their own right, functionally independent of the central cities in their region. Joel Garreau (1991) has dubbed these "edge cities" since they are normally located on the outer boundary of a metropolitan area.

Regional Differences in Urban Growth

Why have some central cities grown while others have not? One reason, as we have seen, is that some cities have become world or regional business centers. Another factor has been the diffusion of the high-tech economy, which has fostered urban growth in many parts of the country. But there is a strong relationship between the region in which a city is located and its rate of growth.

Overall, central cities increased their population by 3.9 percent nationally between 1990 and 1998, but there was a substantial difference in the rate of urban growth from one region to another. The Mountain states led urban growth at 19.3 percent, followed by the West at 7.6 percent and the South at 5.3 percent. Cities of the Midwest lost an average of .3 percent, while cities of the Northeast lost an average of 2.5 percent (U.S. Census Bureau, 2000a). A complicating factor in this urban growth pattern is that cities in the South, Pacific, and Mountain regions regularly expand the boundaries of the central city to encompass growing suburbs whereas most cities of the Northeast and Midwest do not. Thus, the rapid growth of central cities in the South, Pacific, and Mountain states is partly due to the overall growth of the region and partly due to the political context that draws the suburbs into the central cities rather than leaving them as separate communities.

Growth Politics and Policies

How important is population growth for an area? How much growth is enough? What should government do about encouraging or regulating growth? These questions are increasingly being asked not only by academic researchers but by public officials and residents in both growing and declining areas. There is a certain logic within our economic system that says that economic growth is good—in fact, necessary. As a consequence (or sometimes a cause) of economic growth, population growth must therefore also be good. In fact, Logan and Molotch (1987) argue that cities in the United States were established precisely to promote economic growth. In their words, cities are "growth machines," generators of profits on investments. Typically, groups of business leaders, political officials, and media representatives—all of whom stand to benefit from growth in the area—promote growth. These groups publicize the benefits of growth, such as more jobs and increased tax revenues, and downplay the negative effects of growth, such as pollution and strains on public services. In Logan and Molotch's terms, these pro-growth groups remove the "value" aspect of growth—that is, they make growth seem natural—by avoiding questions about who really benefits from economic growth or what problems it generates (Logan and Molotch, 1987).

The city of Houston provides a vivid example of the problems that rapid, uncontrolled growth can produce. Houston was the fastest growing major city in the United States during the 1970s: the city added a thousand new residents every week. Unlike most northern cities, Houston was able to capture this new growth by annexing its suburbs as fast as they grew. Consequently, the city government was able to maintain its tax base and keep taxes low. Yet, despite its booming economy, problems began to accumulate. The highway system was overwhelmed by the increasing population. Rush-hour commuting times doubled between 1975 and 1980 as the expressway system steadily became more congested. The small, antiquated bus system was able to provide only minimal service to a small fraction of the total commuters. Built in a marshy area, with little control over land-development practices, the city experienced increasingly severe problems with annual flooding. City services were stretched to the breaking point as the city annexed more population. Houston's understaffed, poorly trained police force was unable to cope with the increased demand for police protection as the crime rate soared. The pro-growth forces in Houston, however, were able to circumvent attempts to control or manage growth. Indeed, the local "highly individualistic" business leaders united to fight the tax increases necessary to provide even the most minimal levels of public services (Feagin, 1988b).

In the 1980s, while Houston's population leveled off, Southern California experienced the growth problems that Houston had had during the previous decade: legendary traffic congestion, increased smog, overbuilding, strains on the sewer systems, and crowded schools. These problems generated a political movement of "slow growth" advocates who attempted to limit future development through legislation. Residents called for land-use controls and developer-financed schools and sewers in many Southern California communities. According to observers, local growth controls were the hottest political issue in California in the late 1980s (Salholz, Reese, and Buckley, 1988).

In the 1990s, growth became a political issue in the Pacific Northwest. Cities such as Seattle grew so rapidly that the same problems of congestion, pollution, and public service support that plagued California in the 1980s hit the Northwest in the 1990s. One response was to establish growth controls through planning. Portland, Oregon has a well-known policy of "smart growth" to prevent urban sprawl by limiting the amount of property that can be developed and preserving open space for the future. Some planners argue that suburban development throughout the country is now occurring so rapidly that many communities will be "built out" (meaning that no open space will remain) by 2015. Thus, demands for slow growth, preservation of open space, and building controls are popular in many rapidly growing areas. But what of the declining areas? Here the debate revolves not around whether growth is good or bad but around how to increase it. Should government be involved? At what level? And what actions should it take? These are questions that involve economic development policy.

A number of states and localities have tried to stimulate growth by establishing economic development policies. These include incentives to businesses such as low-interest loans, free or subsidized land, and tax abatements (reductions on local or state taxes for a certain length of time). As different states and cities compete to attract businesses, they tend to use the same incentives. Unfortunately, many businesses now expect these expensive incentives from local governments and play localities off against each other to try to increase the amounts. One attorney who challenged his state's business incentives termed them "self-imposed rape" (Greenwald, 1996).

Another strategy used by localities desiring increased investment and growth is the *enterprise zone* policy. Based on the assumption that government regulation was a deterrent to business, policy analysts suggested that certain areas be identified as enterprise zones and exempted from government regulations. Most states have adopted modified versions of enterprise zones: while retaining most government regulations, they relieve businesses of a substantial proportion of their state and local taxes for a specified period of time. Enterprise zone programs have had some success in attracting investors to targeted (often inner-city) areas, but the actual number of jobs generated by this investment has often been quite modest, especially when compared to the price paid by the cities and states in tax losses (Bendick and Rasmussen, 1986).

In 1994, the federal government began a grant program to assist "distressed" cities in boosting their economic and social resources. The program, which designates parts of cities as either *enterprise communities* or *empowerment zones*, helps local officials and residents to identify and build on local resources. The philosophy of these programs is not necessarily to attract businesses from outside to invest in an area (as the enterprise zones do) but to work with the residents already in the city to develop local businesses and such other economic and social needs as safe neighborhoods, revitalized housing, good schools, and after-school programs for children.

Policy debates for both the growing and declining areas can be reduced to a central issue: the role of government in regulating the economy. On one side stand those who say that uncontrolled investment produces much human suffering, dislocation, and destruction. On the other side are those who say that capitalist economies function best without regulation and produce more good than bad. This is a political debate, ultimately answering the question: "who benefits and who pays?"

THEORETICAL PERSPECTIVES ON GROWTH

How do we interpret these regional economic shifts? Does it mean that the northern urban areas are dying? Will regional urban growth equalize in the future? Is movement to the West and South just a temporary event, or does it represent a more fundamental change?

These are important issues because they will influence how we interpret the specific problems that both the growing and declining urban areas face. If, for example, the cities of the North are in for a period of sustained economic decline, then such problems as physical decay and unemployment are likely to get much worse or require very drastic measures to control. If they are likely to experience natural ups and downs, there is less need for immediate intervention to assist them.

In fact, there are no certain answers to the question of the actual meaning of these regional shifts. That uncertainty is increased by our inability to predict a highly uncertain economic future. At present, there are several ways to view these trends that seem plausible and that suggest different possible futures for urban areas in the various regions.

Convergence

One possibility is that the South and the Mountain states have just been "catching up" with the older urbanized regions of the country. According to this *convergence theory,* northern urban areas are not dying. Rather, there has just been a temporary shift of urban and economic growth to southern and western regions. At the moment, these areas offer cost advantages to industries which make them attractive places to locate. However, according to this view, those advantages will not last. As the new areas mature, they will become more and more like the older urban areas. Labor costs, standard of living, and the degree of unionization will increase. The physical structures (e.g., housing, factories, highways, and sewer systems) in these areas will age and require more maintenance and replacement, as they currently do in the North. As levels of education and income rise, people will expect more services from government. Urban decay will set in and repeat the pattern of decay that occurred in the North. Urban crime will become more serious. In response, government will have to do more and spend more. Tax levels will increase to resemble those in the North's urban areas. Once these new regions are no longer viewed as underdeveloped areas, the pattern of federal expenditures will shift away from them to provide assistance to declining areas in the North.

Over the long term, this view suggests, the urban areas of all regions will converge (become more similar). All areas will be roughly similar in terms of their attractiveness to industry. The growth rates of the South and West will slow, and those of the North will increase. What will emerge is a pattern of balanced growth across all regions of the country. Hence, the current patterns should be viewed as temporary trends and do not signify that the older urban areas will face steady decline at the expense of other regions of the country (Watkins and Perry, 1977).

Uneven Development

In contrast with the theory of long-term convergence, several analysts have proposed that, rather than long-term convergence of regions, what we can probably expect is continued uneven development of regions. While many theorists have written on this topic, we have chosen two examples to explain related but somewhat different views of the *uneven development* process.

In their book about the Sunbelt, Alfred Watkins and David Perry (1977) contend that regions grow or decline for long periods of time because they have certain features that attract specific kinds of economic activities. These features give them long-term advantages over other regions. During each period, these advantaged areas are able to increase their advantages and attractiveness. At the same time, less advantaged areas face continued obstacles to economic growth. In relative terms, "the rich get richer, and the poor get poorer."

Watkins and Perry argue that these periods of regional advantage correspond to different phases in the development of the economy. Thus, during the period in which heavy industry and manufacturing were the dynamic forces in the American economy, the Upper Midwest and Northeast were the favored regions. During this time, these regions were able to create a number of development barriers that had two results. First, they operated to prevent other regions from developing the economic activities in which the advantaged areas specialized. The other regions remained underdeveloped in terms of the sorts of industry prevalent in the Upper Midwest and Northeast regions. Thus, the South and the West failed to develop much in the way of heavy industry and mass-production facilities. Second, these barriers caused the advantaged areas to specialize more and more in what they did well. In the Midwest, for example, a complex, interlocking set of industries and production plants came into being, all related to and dependent upon the production of automobiles. In that sense, the successful regions became locked into certain types of economic activity (Watkins and Perry, 1977).

However, the economy did not stay the same. In the last few decades, the economy entered a phase in which a new group of dynamic industries appeared in such areas as military production, electronics, services, and leisure-oriented mass consumption. Watkins and Perry argue that the older industrial areas failed to develop in these new directions because they were trapped by the very barriers that protected their former advantages: the nature of their urban physical structures, transportation systems, labor force characteristics, and the like. Hence, it was the South and Mountain states that were able to take advantage of the new economic opportunities. They were not yet committed to and specialized in the older activities and were in a position to be flexible and innovative (Watkins and Perry, 1977).

From this point of view, western and southern development cannot be viewed as a process that will result in the long-term economic convergence of regions. Rather this development is a reflection of a new phase in the economy, one whose activity is highly concentrated in particular regions. Watkins and Perry consider the primary source of growth in the South and Mountain regions to be the emergence of new industries rather than the relocation of existing industries. Hence, rather than becoming just like the northern industrial areas, the new regions are developing in new directions and specializing in a different set of economic activities. Like the older industrial areas before them, they are in a position to create a set of developmental barriers which will assure that they continue to enjoy their initial advantages. The older industrial areas will, as a result, continue to stagnate, as long as the economy remains in this phase of development (Watkins and Perry, 1977).

Neil Smith (1984), while agreeing with Watkins and Perry on the prospects for continued uneven growth and development of regions, does not necessarily hold to their view that regional economic advantages are such long-term phenomena. Rather, he views growth and decline as a "see-saw" pattern of investment and disinvestment based on the nature of investment and profit within capitalist, market economies. Smith argues that, as economic conditions change, new opportunities for investment appear. As changes occur, investors not only channel their money into new investments but they also destroy, abandon, or write off their old investments—those which are no longer as profitable as the new investments. To Smith, the destruction of the old investment is an integral part of the investment process, since it prepares the way for new, more profitable investment to follow (Smith, 1984).

Like Watkins and Perry, Smith sees these investment patterns as occurring in cycles and as being concentrated in certain geographical areas. He agrees that investment flows into certain regions based on whether the conditions there are beneficial for the industries that happen to be growing at that time. Unlike Watkins and Perry, however, Smith does not see relatively long-term advantages accruing to one area over another. He stresses the change and variability of the investment process, noting that development of an area changes the very conditions that made it profitable in the first place. Land prices, for example, may be very low in an area in which no one wants to invest. If investors are attracted by the low cost of land, their investment, the companies they build, and the improvements they make help raise the price of the land to the point where it is no longer attractive. Eventually, before it will attract new investment again, the land prices (and the value of the buildings on the land) will have to be reduced (Smith, 1984).

Thus, the up-and-down movement of geographic areas, the see-saw pattern of investment, is a necessary part of the investment process, according to Smith. Some areas will have to grow, and some will have to stagnate or decline before they can grow again. This pattern occurs on three levels: between regions (such as Sunbelt and Frostbelt); within regions (such as growing suburbs and a declining central city within a single metropolitan area); and within cities (such as run-down and revitalized neighborhoods within the same city).

In our view, the theories of uneven development seem to explain patterns of regional growth and decline better than the convergence theory. Convergence theorists look at long periods of time (e.g., fifty years or more) and large geographic areas (e.g., the entire South) and identify an overall trend. This makes it appear as if the direction of the trend is linear (unchanging) and that the region is homogeneous. By examining shorter periods of time and smaller geographic areas, however, we find more and more variation and complexity, as noted by the theorists of uneven development. The process of investment and disinvestment thus does not appear to be smooth or linear, but proceeds jerkily, through many cycles.

The Sociospatial Approach

Both convergence theory and uneven development theory emphasize the role of economic factors as decisive in making a city grow. Sociologist Mark Gottdiener (1994) has proposed another way of looking at urban growth and at urban patterns in general. He calls this new approach sociospatial because it stresses the interaction between people and space.

The *sociospatial approach* begins with the fact that cities are part of a global system of capitalism—an economy—that produces certain patterns among cities. Then it adds the fact that government and political actors can change the result of economic (market) forces by enacting policies that channel urban development in particular ways. These two layers or dimensions are very similar to those used by the uneven development theorists.

The unique contribution of analysts who use the sociospatial approach is the symbolic dimension they add to their analysis of space. They see urban spaces not only as containers for people's actions but also as independent contributors to and shapers of those activities. The dual nature of urban space means that, as Winston Churchill once said, "We shape our buildings and afterwards our buildings shape us." Different locations have powerful symbolic meanings and identities for people.

Applied to urban and regional growth, the sociospatial approach identifies two types of factors, the push and pull factors, that contribute to a particular area's growth pattern. The push comes from the overall economy—the need for business to invest and make a profit by constructing buildings, which in large numbers produces growth. The pull comes from individuals' choices and involvement in buying and selling real estate. This pull factor combines two different impulses: people's desire to make money on property and their desire to live (or to locate their business) in a particular region for reasons other than economic ones (Gottdiener, 1994). The sociospatial approach holds that, to understand regional growth, we must understand not only the economies of different regions but also the meanings people attach to living or working in different regions.

MAIN POINTS

1. During the 1970s, the Sunbelt and Mountain states experienced population growth rates that were significantly higher than those of the rest of the country.
2. In the mid-1980s, Sunbelt growth slowed, and the growth rates of the East Coast and West Coast states accelerated. Growth in the "heartland" or central states, both northern and southern, remained slow.
3. During the 1990s, the highest rates of growth were in the Mountain states, the western (Pacific) states, and the Southeast.
4. Because of the complex nature of population changes—caused by natural increase, migration, and immigration—it is difficult to predict exactly where growth will be concentrated in the future.
5. Regional variation in growth rates is closely linked to variations in regional economic conditions. Industries of a certain type tend to be spatially concentrated; thus, their rapid growth or decline has a concentrated geographical impact.
6. Government spending has also had an impact on regional growth and decline. As political and federal spending priorities have changed, some states have benefited while others have been hurt.
7. Growth, decline, or change in the economy of a region affects the cities in that region. Many cities have lost their manufacturing functions; some have gained new economic roles as world cities or high-tech centers while others have continued to decline in population and employment.
8. An important political and social issue currently being debated is the government's role in promoting and/or controlling growth.

9. Three main theories have been developed to explain regional shifts. Convergence theory holds that, over the long run, the different regions will become more similar to each other. Uneven development theorists argue that growth and decline result from economic cycles, with decline being a necessary condition for future growth. The sociospatial approach argues that symbolic factors as well as economic and political factors drive growth.

KEY TERMS

Convergence Theory The notion that the economic attractiveness of the various regions of the country will tend to equalize over time and that relative rates of economic growth will equalize as a result.

Economic Restructuring A type of economic change in which one set of dominant industries is replaced by another set; contrast with cyclical change, in which the economy grows and contracts periodically without changing the mix of industries.

Enterprise Zone A policy that assumes government regulation is a deterrent to business and therefore suggests that targeted development areas be exempt from government regulations.

Gentrification The influx of upper-income residents into formerly lower-income neighborhoods.

Globalization of the Economy The trend for businesses in different countries to become increasingly interdependent.

Gunbelt Economist Ann Markusen's term for those areas of the country whose economies are heavily dependent on defense spending.

Heartland The section of the United States that encompasses the Midwest and South Central states.

Net Migration The total change in population in an area after the number of people who moved out is subtracted from the number who moved in.

Sociospatial Approach Theory of urban growth patterns that stresses the interaction between people and space.

Sunbelt The group of states in the southern part of the country from Arizona in the west to the Carolinas in the east.

Uneven Development Theory The notion that different areas have different growth trajectories and that these are not linear, but result in periods of decline as well as periods of growth.

SUGGESTED READING

Davis, Mike. 1992. *City of Quartz*. New York: Vintage Books. A fascinating account of the growth and current status of Los Angeles.

Feagin, Joe. 1988. *Free Enterprise City: Houston in Political and Economic Perspective*. New Brunswick: Rutgers University. A case study of the rise of Houston as a major city, showing how both free enterprise and government actions contributed to its growth.

Logan, John, and Harvey Molotch. 1987. *Urban Fortunes: The Political Economy of Place*. Berkeley: University of California Press. The most comprehensive treatment of the view that cities are machines for economic growth and that urban issues are largely struggles over growth.

U.S. Department of Housing and Urban Development. 2000. *The State of the Cities, 2000*. Washington, DC: U.S. Department of Housing and Urban Development. This free report contains a great deal of information about conditions in cities and metropolitan areas as well as urban policy. It is nontechnical and written for the general public.

3

The Nature of Urban Life
The Myth of the City

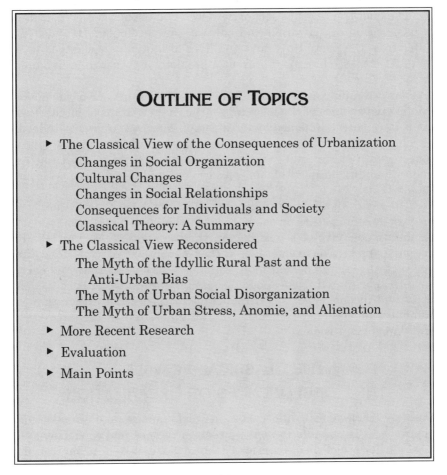

OUTLINE OF TOPICS

In the two previous chapters, we examined the factors that have shaped basic conditions in urban areas. We now turn to the central focus of this book: the specific problems faced by this urban society.

We are going to start with what is perhaps the most challenging and most important issue of all. Our concern in this chapter is with the general social, cultural and social psychological consequences of urbanization. Underlying this concern with the consequences of urbanization is recognition of a fundamental fact about urbanization—the industrialization and urbanization process of the last few centuries represents one of the great transformations in history. Only a few other periods of human social development rank with industrialization and urbanization in terms of their effect on society and individuals. What happened, in the short span of several generations, is that the basic nature of society changed. A new kind of society emerged.

The question is: what sort of new society has emerged? What kind of basic social organization and culture has developed? How does it differ from the past? How have the lives of individuals changed as a result? Do these changes represent a problem or threat to individuals or society?

The attempt to answer these questions represents one of the major intellectual themes of the last two centuries. Few areas of intellectual effort have been untouched by the attempt to provide answers. Indeed, sociology can fairly be said to have developed partly in response to the concern with these issues in the nineteenth century. Almost all the major "founding fathers" of modern sociology addressed these issues in their work.

The result of all this intellectual effort has been the creation of a large body of literature on the nature of urban life. Yet the complexity of the issues involved has meant that no definitive, universally accepted answers have emerged. Rather, as more research is done, the answers appear to be even more complex and elusive than the early writers appreciated. Hence, our discussion here must be both incomplete and inconclusive: an introduction to the issues rather than a summary of accepted conclusions. But that often is the case with really important issues.

THE CLASSICAL VIEW OF
THE CONSEQUENCES OF URBANIZATION

Despite tremendous differences in terminology and intellectual approach, it is possible to identify certain themes and conclusions in most earlier sociological theories of the consequences of urbanization. For want of a better term, we will call this the *classical view*. *To* lump all these theorists together in one unified approach is, of course, to do real violence to the diversity and richness of these theories. However, it is the only possible way to present a brief summary of early thinking about the consequences of urbanization.

Understanding the classical view is important for several reasons. For one thing, this approach dominated sociological thinking about urban society until fairly recently. In addition, most more recent work represents a reaction to and criticism of the classical approach. You really cannot understand this work unless you understand the approach being criticized. Finally, most sociologists still accept some elements of the classical view (with strong qualifications). As a result, many issues raised by the classical approach remain active sources of concern and research in urban sociology.

The group of theorists included in the classical approach reads like a veritable *Who's Who* in sociological theory. One of the most famous of the early pioneers of the classical approach was Ferdinand Tönnies. Tönnies (1957) described the shift to urban society as a shift from *gemeinschaft* (a community based on kinship ties) to *gesellschaft* (a society based on common practical interests). One of the major figures of French sociology, Émile Durkheim, suggested a distinction between small communities held together by ties of *mechanical solidarity* and modern urban societies held together by ties of *organic solidarity*. The former were ties based on shared ideas and common experiences. The latter were ties based on mutual dependence between people engaged in specialized tasks (Durkheim, 1947). At about the same time, the German sociologist Max Weber had suggested that the transition of urban society was a transition from "traditional" society to "rational" society (Bendix, 1960). An early social psychologist, Georg Simmel, suggested that urban life fundamentally affected the psychology of individuals (Wolff, 1950:409–24).

The themes suggested by these early European sociologists were picked up by the "Chicago School" of urban sociologists at the University of Chicago in the 1920s and 1930s. Most important in this group was a sociologist who was to shape sociological thinking about urban life for more than two decades, Louis Wirth. His summary article, "Urbanism as a Way of Life," represents the single most important statement of the classical view in sociology in the United States (Wirth, 1938:1–24). Soon afterward, anthropologist Robert Redfield further amplified the classical view's distinction between urban societies and previous societies by suggesting two general types of society: "folk" and "urban" (1947:293–308). More recently, the "structural functionalist" theorists (who dominated sociological theory in the 1950s and 1960s) such as Talcott Parsons (1969) and Neil Smelser (1967) incorporated many elements of the classical view into their analyses of industrialization and modernization.

At the heart of the basic perspective on urbanization shared by these theorists was the feeling that industrialization and urbanization were extraordinarily disruptive forces. They saw the emergence of urban society as a process in which a stable society of rural communities was shattered by the requirements of industrial production and the conditions of urban life. The basic characteristics of society—the nature of its social organization and culture—were transformed. At the level of individual social life, this was seen as causing major changes in the nature of people's social relationships. In turn, these changes were seen as creating major problems for individuals and society: social disorganization, psychological stress, anomie, and alienation. Figure 3.1 summarizes this basic model. We now turn to an examination of each of its elements.

Changes in Social Organization

Scale of Social Units

At the most basic level, classical theorists saw the transition from rural to urban society as a change in the size of the organizations and communities in which individuals participate. Rural society was characterized as one in which the individual's most important social ties were with small-scale social units: family, kin, and village. Most people lived out their lives within the confines of a small community of a few hundred people in which everybody knew everybody else. The basic unit of economic production was the family and kin group. Contact and involvement with what larger units existed (e.g., national government, centralized religious organizations) was limited, infrequent, and viewed with suspicion.

Figure 3.1
Basic Model of the Classical View of Urbanization

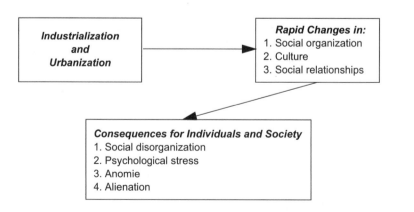

In contrast, the classical theorists pointed to the dominance of large-scale social units in modern urban society. People live in "communities" of thousands or millions of people, most of whom they do not know personally. They are aware of and their lives are constantly affected by events in the larger society. Most activities are carried out by very large, often society-wide, organizations: massive corporations and government agencies. Very importantly, people work in large organizations away from home and kin, rather than in small, kin-based work groups.

Social Complexity

Classical theorists characterized rural society as relatively simple in terms of its social organization. A major source of this simplicity was the nature of the *division of labor* (the division of tasks into separate work roles). Rural society was seen as having a simple division of labor. The basic tasks in rural society were such things as food production, handicraft manufacturing, and family service activities. Every family did most of these things themselves. There was only limited specialization of activities between families. Most people were engaged in agriculture, with only a few people in specialized trades or occupations. The specialization of roles which did exist consisted primarily of specialization within the kinship group based on age, sex, and family relationship.

On the other hand, urban society was characterized by classical theorists as one in which each member engages in some highly specialized task. The engineer designs, the assembly-line worker screws on door handles, and the sales representative sells the finished product. Hence, most activities involve the cooperation of large numbers of specialists who depend on each other. This is called a *complex division of labor*.

Bureaucratization

Beginning with Max Weber, a major theme of the classical view was that urban society is also a bureaucratic society. Very simply, large and complex organizations require a way to coordinate the activities of their members so that everyone in the organization does what is needed, when it is needed. Bureaucracy arose, according to the classical view, as a means to assure the coordination of the activities of members of large organizations. Centralized authority, formal rules and procedures, objective standards of evaluation, and the like make coordination of large numbers of specialists possible.

It also means that people work in, have services provided by, and have their lives regulated by large, impersonal organizations. This is in stark contrast, classical theorists said, to the smaller, kin-based organizations of rural society which operated more informally and personally.

Weakening of Kinship Ties

Perhaps the most critical change in social organization—according to the classical view—was the effect of urbanization on the family and kinship system. Classical theorists described traditional rural family relationships as an *extended kinship system*. In this system, people maintained close social ties not just with members of their *nuclear family* (husband, wife, and children) but also with large numbers of kin outside of the nuclear family. This extended kin system operated as the most important unit of social cooperation, the primary means of "social control" (the maintenance of conformity), and the central source of material and emotional security. Above all else, it was the basic unit of economic production. Kinship relationships were the basis of economic cooperation. In return for this cooperation, the family took care of most of the basic needs of its members: the care and training of children, assistance in times of sickness or need, recreational activities, care of the elderly, physical protection, work opportunities, all basic material needs, emotional support, and intimacy. Because family members were so dependent on their family relationships, the family had tremendous power over its members. Most aspects of an individual's life were regulated by obligations to kin. In a sense, one could not function or survive outside the web of one's kinship relationships. Hence, the individual's desires were subordinate to those of his or her kin. This control over family members was reflected in well-defined rules regulating behavior between kin, and there was a system of authority within the family in which the elder males made decisions binding on the rest of the family members. Thus, according to classical theorists, the family was the central institution of society and regulated most of the important aspects of community life.

All this changed, claimed these theorists, with industrialization and urbanization. The extended kinship system was shattered. It lost its function as a system of economic cooperation. People went to work as individuals in places away from their homes and kin. Government took over most of the responsibility for the education, protection, and basic security of individuals. As a result, the family lost its power over individuals: they were no longer dependent upon their extended family for most of their practical material needs. The move to the city also separated people geographically from their kin. Most of what was left of family relationships was concentrated in the nuclear family. Children still had to be cared for and socialized. In the absence of the assistance of extended kin, this burden fell more heavily on the nuclear family—especially the mother. Lacking the emotional support of extended kin and in the face of what classical theorists felt was the impersonality of urban life, nuclear family members were also much more dependent than before on each other for emotional intimacy. Intense emotional ties between parents and children, and an emphasis on romantic love between spouses, replaced the more pragmatic ties which bound family members in the past. Freedom from economic dependence on the family, weak kin ties, weakening traditional morals, and the increased emotional intensity in family relationships made the isolated nuclear family of the city much less stable than the rural extended family. The nuclear family was an "emotional pressure cooker" based on the unstable ties of romantic love. Divorce, family conflict, and general family instability were the result, said classical theorists.

Cultural Changes

Secularization and Rationality

The classical view of rural communities before industrialization was one in which the community was stabilized by a strongly held set of cultural beliefs and values. Theorists characterized this culture as one which emphasized the sacred and traditional. By an emphasis on the *sacred orientation*, they meant that rules of behavior and methods of doing things were justified and explained by reference to religious beliefs. The reasons for death, when to plant corn, the nature of the obligations between parents and children, and most other aspects of social life were based on religious conceptions of morality and the nature of reality. Moreover, it was seen as a stable belief system that was all the more influential because of its stability. Cultural beliefs and ways of life changed slowly and were revered partly because of this. The stable belief system provided people with a sense of continuity. This *traditional orientation* represented security; change represented a threat.

Industrialization and urbanization brought in their wake (or, according to Weber, were partly caused by) a shift in cultural orientation. The cultural emphasis shifted to *secular rationality*. Religious explanations and justifications were replaced by those based on science, empirical observation, logic, and systematic calculation. Beliefs were no longer accepted simply because they were divinely inspired or had "always" been believed true. Rather, they were accepted because they could be "proved" to be true by reason and observation.

Accompanying this change was a growing instability in belief systems. Today's truth could become tomorrow's falsehood—and it frequently did, as rapid advances occurred in science and technology. Traditional beliefs and the values supported by those beliefs were called into question. Instead of enjoying the continuity and security provided by tradition, individuals had to learn to adjust to a cultural world in constant change, where nothing was certain.

Heterogeneity and Organic Solidarity

According to most classical theorists, traditional rural communities were characterized by a high level of agreement among their members in terms of their cultural values and beliefs. Most people believed the same things, shared the same values, and perceived the world in the same way. This *cultural homogeneity* was a result of shared experiences, limited exposure to the "outside world," the religious basis of most cultural beliefs and values, and the strong hold of tradition. To disagree with the dominant beliefs and values of the community was to call into question something ordained by God, confirmed by everything people in the community had experienced, and sanctified by long tradition. Conformity was easy to monitor because the community was small: everyone knew everyone else's business. Hence, there were powerful pressures for the maintenance of cultural conformity and little tolerance for nonconformity. In turn, cultural homogeneity was a major source of community unity and prevented deviant behavior. In the terms used by Durkheim, cultural homogeneity maintained community *solidarity* (identification with and commitment to the community). Durkheim called this kind of community unity *mechanical solidarity.*

Durkheim, and the theorists who followed him, contrasted the high level of cultural agreement in the traditional community to the relative disunity of urban society. In the classical view, the tremendous diversity of urban society in terms of social classes, ethnic groups, religions, occupations, and the like assures that the beliefs and values of urban society will display *cultural heterogeneity:* great diversity and the lack of general consensus. As a result, argued Durkheim, cultural agreement is not as effective as a source of unity and a means of maintaining conformity. What holds society together then? Durkheim argued that the complex division of labor makes everyone dependent on everyone else for the things they need. People have to exchange or trade the things they make or do for the other things they need produced by others. The baker provides the butcher with bread in return for meat. In this sense, the "glue" that holds society together is the division of labor. What people agree on in urban society are not specific beliefs and values (they have to tolerate disagreement) but rules that regulate the process of exchange. Durkheim called this kind of community unity *organic solidarity.*

Changes in Social Relationships

Impersonality
In the classical view of the small community, social relationships were portrayed as close, emotional, intense, and personal. Everyone knew everyone else, and people interacted with each other based on this very complete knowledge of one another. In short, the majority of relationships were "primary" relationships based on long-term friendship and kinship ties.

In the classical view, this state of affairs in the small community contrasts sharply with the nature of most social relationships in urban society. According to classical theorists, it is simply impossible to spend the time to get to know most other people very well: the urban dweller interacts with too many different people. Consequently, people have to deal with one another based on their particular roles in the social situation (e.g., customer and clerk) following the general social rules deemed appropriate for that situation. There can be little concern about the personal characteristics of these role occupants. All people in a particular role are treated the same. Interaction is superficial, unemotional, and follows a set pattern. People are cold and calculating in their relationships: they interact with one another in order to achieve some specific goal. In short, urban social relationships are supposedly mostly impersonal and occur within the context of "secondary" groups, such as large organizations or small "task groups."

Segmental Social Relationships

Classical theorists portrayed rural community life as a "seamless web" in which the same individuals interacted with one another in different social contexts. The people who worked together were related by kinship, engaged in leisure activities together, lived in the same community, and participated in its affairs. These were *total social relationships*. This made for intense personal relationships in which people got to know most aspects of each other's personalities. It also made it very difficult to hide deviant behavior since each person knew so much about all the others. And it created a "sense of community."

In contrast, urban dwellers were portrayed as having *segmental social relationships*. Each person interacts with a different set of people in each social situation. The people you work with are not the same people who live in your neighborhood or with whom you spend your leisure time. This contributes to the superficiality and impersonality of urban social relationships and weakens the sense of common identity among urban dwellers. Thus, the urban social world was viewed by classical theorists as a set of compartments in which most of the people in one compartment (social situation) do not have any contact with people in the other compartments. Social life is fragmented.

Consequences for Individuals and Society

Classical theorists considered these changes in social organization, culture, and social relationships important because of the consequences they had for individuals and society. Classical theorists argued that the sort of society that had emerged was fundamentally and dangerously flawed. In their view, the problem of urban society was the nature of the society itself and what it did to the people living in cities.

The classical theorists, of course, did not deny that there were some positive consequences of urbanization. They acknowledged that the weakening of kin ties, the cultural diversity, the spirit of rational inquiry, and the quest for innovation created a climate of freedom and tolerance. Individuals were much freer to decide what to believe, what occupations to pursue, how to spend their leisure time, and what style of life to adopt. This freedom, they conceded, was augmented by improved material conditions for most people and greater opportunity for upward social mobility.

The problem, said classical theorists, was that these gains had been purchased at a high price. Rural communities had provided people with a stable, well-organized social environment, they argued. Life was predictable and the rules of behavior were clear. People knew what their social obligations were. There was a stable set of values and beliefs by which to set one's life goals and be evaluated by others. Close personal ties with others provided emotional security and a sense of identity and personal worth.

In contrast, the classical theorists argued, urban society was a disorganized and unstable social environment. The consequences for individuals were psychological stress, anomie, and alienation. The consequence for society was social disorganization.

Social Disorganization

The fundamental problem with urban society in the classical view was that the very conditions that brought freedom to the individual had "atomized" and "disorganized" society.

The close primary ties provided by the extended kinship system had decayed. This meant that the emotional support, intimacy, and security which these ties had provided were lacking in most of the social relationships experienced by urban dwellers. In their place, classical theorists saw only social relationships that were transitory, calculating, and impersonal. The nuclear family was also seen as being isolated from the support of extended kin in times of trouble or need. In addition, weakening of kin ties was viewed as having weakened a formerly important system of social control. Individuals no longer had to worry about conforming to the expectations of their kin.

These changes in kinship relationships were viewed as a problem because the new ways of performing the activities formerly performed by the extended family were considered to be only partially successful. The nuclear family tried to provide the missing emotional closeness. The result, said classical theorists, was to make family relationships too intense and increase family instability. Government agencies tried to provide economic and social assistance to families and individuals in trouble. However, many needs remained unmet. A bureaucratic system of criminal justice attempted to replace the informal social control of the family and community with formal social controls composed of laws, courts, and prisons. Still, urban communities were beset by high crime rates. In short, the decline of the family had left a social vacuum that urban society had yet to fill adequately.

Cultural heterogeneity was also seen as a force creating disorganization. Rapidly changing and often conflicting values resulted in the loss of clear, consistent guidelines for behavior. People were no longer certain what constituted acceptable behavior or appropriate life goals.

Further, classical theorists claimed that the individual no longer participated in a web of social relationships which they saw as constituting a "community." The pattern of assisting one's neighbors, informal community decision making, joint recreational activities, and the intimate knowledge of and concern for one's neighbors which supposedly characterized the small rural community was considered lacking in urban neighborhoods. In the classical view, the members of each nuclear family tried to care for themselves and were relatively unconcerned about the families living around them. People did not "get involved," and they "minded their own business." This further weakened social control and meant that families needing assistance either had to rely on themselves or turn to the government for help.

Psychological Stress

In the classical view, the psychological consequences of this sort of urban social environment were primarily negative. For instance, Georg Simmel in his famous article, "Metropolis and Mental Life," (Wolff, 1950) argued that the constantly changing social environment, the tremendous diversity of social experiences, and the large number of superficial, transitory social relationships in urban society caused nervous "overstimulation." As a defense against this overstimulation, Simmel believed that urban dwellers learned to be emotionally cold and calculating in their relationships with others. They avoided overstimulation, in addition, by simply learning not to respond to a large number of stimuli in the environment.

A more contemporary formulation similar to Simmel's analysis has been suggested by Stanley Milgram (1970). Milgram contended if people tried to become emotionally involved with all those with whom they had contact, the emotional demands of so many relationships would be more than they could handle. The result would be "emotional overload." As a strategy to avoid overload, Milgram argued that people develop interpersonal techniques that limit the amount of time and emotional involvement they devote to most social relationships. At the extreme, this may involve completely ignoring others, even when they are in distress and need assistance.

Perhaps the most extreme version of this view of urban life is that associated with the work of John B. Calhoun on the effect of high-density living (1960). Studying the behavior of overcrowded rat populations, Calhoun observed that the rats developed symptoms of extreme pathological behavior as population density increased. (Crowded rats tended, for example, to neglect their young, practice cannibalism, or become totally passive.) A number of subsequent observers have suggested that areas of very high densities in cities (e.g., slums) have the same kind of pathological effects on human beings (Hartley, 1972:76).

Anomie

Émile Durkheim (1951) coined the term *anomie* to refer to another psychological state that classical theorists also believed to be associated with urban social conditions. Anomie is a feeling of "normlessness." As a result of social disorganization and the cultural changes discussed in this section, the individual feels that there are no clear rules (norms) and values by which to evaluate his or her behavior. This uncertainty in regard to what constitutes socially and morally approved behavior creates feelings of anxiety and depression.

Alienation

Frequently referred to in conjunction with anomie, alienation was also viewed by classical theorists as a common response to urban life. The term has been defined in a number of different ways by various writers. For our purposes, a relatively simple definition will suffice to convey the general nature of the concept. Very simply, *alienation* refers to feelings of: (1) powerlessness, (2) meaninglessness, and (3) social isolation. Individuals have the feeling that they have no control over their lives or a particular social environment (such as work). Power is seen to be in the hands of distant or even unknown people and impersonal forces. Work and other daily activities are seen as meaningless routines with no clear purpose or ultimate justification to make them worthwhile. The person feels cut off from the people around her or him. Others are seen as uncaring or untrustworthy.

Alienation of various types was seen as an outgrowth of a number of conditions in urban society. For some theorists, the key problem was the bureaucratic nature of urban society. Most workers work in large, impersonal bureaucratic organizations in which power is centralized in the hands of distant managers. Work is controlled by rigid rules and frequently involves boring, routine tasks. Similarly, most other activities are bureaucratically controlled: education, public safety, government, and so on. Relationships, both in these organizations and in the city's neighborhoods, are superficial and impersonal. Other theorists argued that rationality, materialism, science, and technology create feelings of spiritual emptiness and meaninglessness. Still others blamed weak family ties for an increase in feelings of social isolation.

Behavioral Responses

The end result of social disorganization, psychological stress, anomie, and alienation is, according to classical theory, a severe problem for individuals who, in turn, create problems for society. The stressed, anomic, and alienated urbanite is likely to display any number of pathological responses: chronic depression, increased likelihood of committing suicide, increased risk of mental illness, cynicism and distrust in personal relationships, apathy and withdrawal from community and political affairs, alcoholism and drug addiction, aggression, criminality, and so on. The end result is that urban society is beset by a number of severe social problems: crime, other forms of deviant behavior, mental illness, broken families, low social participation, and political apathy.

Classical Theory: A Summary

Thus, classical theory, with its emphasis on the disruptive and disorganizing effects of the process of urbanization, paints a primarily negative picture of urban life. These theorists conceded that urbanization was accompanied by improved material conditions, greater intellectual rationality, and more freedom. But they saw these benefits from urbanization and industrialization as having been counterbalanced by costs to individuals and society. And they looked at the rural past almost with nostalgia: rural life, for all its poverty and ignorance, was portrayed as a stable, emotionally close community of strong family ties in which people had a sense of social place, continuity, personal importance, and meaning to their lives. Table 3.1 summarizes what has just been discussed.

Table 3.1
The Differences between Rural and Urban Society according to Classical Theories

Rural Society	Urban Society
Social Organization:	
Small social units	Large social units
Simple social organization	Complex social organization
Kin-based informal organization	Bureaucratic organizations
Strong extended kinship system	Weak, unstable nuclear family
Culture:	
Sacred and traditional	Secular and rational
Homogeneity and mechanical solidarity	Heterogeneity and organic solidarity
Social Relationships:	
Personal, emotionally based ("primary ties")	Impersonal ("secondary ties")
Total	Segmental
Consequences for Individuals and Society:	
Society well-organized	Social disorganization
Psychological security	Psychological stress
Little anomie	High anomie
Little alienation	High alienation

THE CLASSICAL VIEW RECONSIDERED

The classical view shaped sociological thinking about urban society during the first half of the twentieth century. Part of its persistence was due, no doubt, to the fact that it was consistent with popular perceptions of urban life (more about that in a moment). Yet, even at the height of its theoretical popularity, there were nagging doubts about the accuracy of the classical view's description of urban life. As more and more research evidence accumulated, those doubts developed into systematic criticisms of the classical view.

The basic thrust of most of these criticisms is not that the classical view was totally wrong. Many (but not all) of the changes in social organization and culture described by classical theories appear to be rough approximations of the actual changes which occurred, at least in Western societies. Rather, the heart of the criticism of classical theory revolves around the feeling that: (1) the picture of urban (and rural) life presented is incomplete, and (2) the classical view exaggerates the negative consequences of urban life.

These conclusions are based on a number of specific criticisms of the classical view, which we will briefly examine.

The Myth of the Idyllic Rural Past and the Anti-Urban Bias

Classical theory was based on a comparison between rural and urban society. In making that comparison, the classical theorists painted what we now realize to be an unrealistically rosy picture of life in the small, rural community. The result is that urban society looked bad in comparison. In fact, the classical view ignored or de-emphasized many of the problems of the rural community as well as presenting what we now know to be an idealized view of rural family life and rural social relationships.

In idealizing rural society, sociologists like Louis Wirth were really continuing in a cultural and intellectual tradition that has deep and enduring roots in American society. It is a tradition that stretches from Thomas Jefferson to contemporary television commercials. The most common label given this tradition is the *anti-urban bias*.

North Americans have traditionally felt a deep distrust of cities. Cities were seen as cold, impersonal places in which loneliness, crime, and immorality ran rampant. In contrast, the small community was seen as the repository of all virtues: honesty, strong family ties, neighborliness, hard work, and thrift (White and White, 1962). Even now, with over 80 percent of the population living in urban areas, most people in this country think that small communities are better places to live and raise families (Perrin, 1978; U.S. Census Bureau, 2000a).

In fact, these beliefs are based on a biased, nostalgic view of rural life. Rural society had its problems too.

Living Conditions

Living conditions in preindustrial communities were extremely harsh by modern standards. Most of the population worked at often brutally hard manual tasks and obtained a level of living which barely met their needs. The risk of fatal disease (especially for young children) was very high, and average life expectancy was low. The stereotype of the spacious white farmhouse neglects the large proportion of the rural population who lived in cabins, shacks, and even sod houses. By modern standards, a large percentage of the population lived under conditions of moderate to severe poverty.

Exploitation and Conflict

The idealized view of rural life has tended to emphasize the degree of harmony and cooperation in the rural community. But there was also a darker side to rural life. Rural life also had its share of "blood feuds," lynchings, slave abuse, and witch trials. The common image of the independent prosperous family farm neglects the large portion of the rural population in the United States who were exploited as bare subsistence tenant farmers, sharecroppers, migrant laborers, and just plain slaves. Even the farmer who owned his own land often lived in almost perpetual debt to town merchants and bankers. (The problem of indebtedness was a recurrent source of rural discontent during the nineteenth century in the United States.)

The Myth of the Rural Family

Perhaps no myth has died harder (even among sociologists) than the myth of the rural extended family system. The rural family system in North America (and Europe) was never as effective, stable, or close-knit as classical theorists seemed to believe. All the evidence is not in yet: this has been an area of active research, and considerable debate continues between scholars studying the history of the family. Enough evidence is in, however, to question the description of the family presented by classical theorists.

For instance, the proportion of "broken" families was almost as high in the nineteenth century as it is now. The rate of marital dissolution (loss of one spouse from the family) has stayed almost constant for a century. In the nineteenth century, the usual cause was the death of one spouse (Davis, 1975). (Now, the primary cause is divorce, but the result is the same.) Hence, children were almost as likely as now to grow up with one of their original parents absent for part of their childhood.

There is also considerable doubt about the actual strength of extended kin ties in the past. Many nuclear families were geographically separated from their kin as a result of the process of westward settlement. Even when they were not, the extent of closeness and cooperation between kin was probably not as great as the classical theorists thought. Indeed, it is highly questionable that the majority of families could actually be characterized as extended kinship systems. Some have suggested that a better term for what existed is the *modified extended family*. In this view, the basic unit of cooperation and emotional commitment was the nuclear family. However, that family also maintained significant, but less close, contacts with other kin (Gist and Fava, 1974:380). Other observers have argued the family system was basically a nuclear one, with the extent of contact with extended kin highly variable (Shorter, 1975).

Nor should we forget the status and treatment of women and children in the past. This was certainly one of the less attractive features of traditional family life. Children were often viewed simply as a source of labor to be exploited and abused. Women were burdened by heavy work obligations and frequent pregnancies (six to eight in the early nineteenth century). At the same time, their social and legal status was clearly that of second-class citizens, and male domination characterized both society and the family.

Parochialism and Intolerance

Classical theorists often tended to downplay how truly repressive the small community could be toward the expression of individuality. There was an extremely narrow range of acceptable behaviors and beliefs. Superstition and fear of innovation, suspicion of "outsiders," contempt and lack of understanding of intellectual endeavor, and the notion that anything different was necessarily wrong, all are frequently cited as characteristics of belief systems in the traditional rural community (Friedman, 1953). Treatment of those who failed to conform could be brutal and vicious.

The Myth of Urban Social Disorganization

Just as classical theorists tended to romanticize the small community, they exaggerated the degree to which urban society was disorganized and destructive of close personal ties between individuals. Several decades of research on urban social life reveal that urban society displays much less social disorganization than classical theorists thought. The same research reveals that individuals have worked out a number of strategies to maintain close personal ties with others.

Persistence of Kin Ties

There is substantial evidence that the urban family is not a weak, isolated nuclear one. Rather, the dominant tendency appears to be maintenance of something approximating a modified extended family system. This is not to say that family relationships are the same as in the past. Family members generally do not work together, but leave each other to go to separate jobs. Individuals are less compelled to depend on family for certain services and forms of assistance. Women are in a much better position to function in society independent of their family relationships. Children spend less time around their parents and live part of their lives in a separate social world of school and peer groups. In this sense, the family has less power over individuals because they are less dependent on it (Goode, 1963).

However, most people choose to maintain fairly strong emotional ties with their kin, spend leisure time with kin, and offer assistance to kin in time of need. And, it is worth noting, modern transportation and communication make this possible even for kin who are geographically distant from one another. A whole series of studies indicate that a majority of urban dwellers have regular and frequent contact with their kin. Very importantly, this contact is not limited to emotional ties and social occasions. Extended kin still remain an important source of services and assistance. Child care for a working mother, financial help, care of elderly parents, and the like are all important aspects of contemporary kinship relationships. The result is that both the nuclear family and extended kin remain important sources of emotional support and practical assistance under urban conditions (Applebaum and Chambliss, 1997; Coontz, 1992; Flanagan, 1995; Skolnick, 1992).

Some qualifications are in order, however. First, there appears to be considerable variation in the strength of kin ties in modern families. Some urban families maintain close relations and others do not. These differences reflect, in part, the particular preferences of individual families. In addition, research suggests that there are differences in kinship relationships based on such things as social class, ethnicity, religion, and region of the country. For instance, kin ties appear to be especially important in working-class, Catholic, "ethnic" neighborhoods (Gans, 1962; Fried, 1973). Second, nothing in what has been said should be construed to mean that urban families do not have problems. They do. Moreover, many of these problems can be traced to the conditions of modern life. The point being made here is that there is nothing uniquely disorganized about urban families that makes them fundamentally "weaker" than those of the past. Urbanization does not necessarily cause the family to break down.

Neighboring and Neighborhoods

Contrary to the classical view, another important source of informal and personal social relationships is the neighborhood. At the most casual level, this involves simple "neighboring." People know each other, provide modest mutual assistance, and may get together socially. In other urban neighborhoods, interaction may be more intense and/or organized. People may have a strong sense of identification with their neighborhood and select a large proportion of their friends from the neighborhood. Many neighborhoods are extensively organized in terms of community groups, social clubs, political organizations, and the like.

How much neighborhood interaction and organization exist varies from a lot to none at all. At one extreme, Jacqueline Zito (1974) describes a high-rise apartment complex with a large proportion of middle-class working couples in which there is very limited neighboring. At the other extreme, Herbert Gans' classic 1955 study of the West End of Boston describes a lower class Italian neighborhood that is an extremely well-organized community, with intense and extensive social relationships (Gans, 1962). Similarly, Gerald Suttles found very extensive social organizations within a Chicago slum (Suttles, 1968). More recent studies give support to these findings (Campbell, 1990; Wellman and Wortley, 1990). Min Zhou notes that immigrants settling in New York's Chinatown are able to obtain jobs as well as relatively inexpensive housing through networks that encompass not only the traditional kinship groups but also neighborhood and work contacts. These networks help new immigrants capitalize on opportunities to save money, start their own businesses, and plan for their children's futures (Zhou, 1992).

How extensive neighborhood ties become in any given neighborhood appears to depend on a number of factors. Physical arrangement can make neighboring easier or harder. In Boston's West End, Gans found that the close-together houses and apartments facing the street made the street the focus of social life in the summer. People sat out on their front porches and steps and it was easy to see each other, talk to one another, and visit informally (Gans, 1962). One summary of the research on neighboring suggests that neighboring generally increases as socioeconomic status decreases and proximity (physical closeness), homogeneity of the residents (social similarity), and dependency (need for assistance from others) increase (Wallace, 1980:254–66). Other specific factors that have been mentioned include gender, ethnicity, religion, occupation, family and kinship ties, leisure styles, and patterns of child rearing (Campbell and Lee, 1990; Hogan, Hao, and Parrish, 1990; Uehara, 1990).

The details of neighborhood research do not have to concern us here, however. The important point is to recognize that, for many people, ties with neighbors are an available source of personal, even intimate, social relationships. Urbanization does not necessarily result in disorganized neighborhoods, even among the poor.

Work-Based Ties

Urban residents may not choose to have close ties with their kin, and they may not have close relationships with their neighbors. That still does not mean that they are isolated in the urban social environment.

Work-based social relationships provide yet another means for the urbanite to establish close personal ties with others.

Much has been made of the supposed isolating and alienating effect of work in large-scale, bureaucratically administered organizations. And to be sure, research on work settings suggests that some kinds of modern work are alienating. Workers in certain kinds of mass production industries, where work is unskilled, repetitive, and closely supervised, are likely to experience work alienation (Blauner, 1964). However, a large proportion of the jobs available in urban society are not of that sort. Moreover, even in those relatively alienating work settings, almost a half century of sociological research suggests that workers often develop friendship ties with their coworkers. From the classic Hawthorne Study (Roethlisberger and Dickson, 1939) onward, industrial sociologists have found extensive networks of formal social relationships in most kinds of work organizations.

In some cases, work relationships are limited to the work setting. In other cases, work relationships form an important basis for establishing friendship relationships outside of work. In either case, these relationships again call into question the image of the urban dweller as someone who operates in a primarily impersonal social environment outside of his or her nuclear family relationships.

Membership in Voluntary Organizations

A final source of personal social relationships in an urban setting is widespread membership in various kinds of voluntary organizations. These are formally organized groups which exist to accomplish some specific goal and in which participation is optional on the part of the individual. Examples of such organizations range from the PTA, the Moose Lodge, and the local historical society to political party organizations, taxpayer groups, and professional organizations (like the American Medical Association). Traditionally, classical theorists (who acknowledged the prevalence of such organizations in urban society) viewed these groups as an attempt to compensate for the loss of close, primary ties in urban society and emphasized the formal, impersonal nature of these organizations. (People were seen as replacing "primary" ties with "secondary" ties.) More recently, voluntary group participation has come to be viewed as yet another strategy by which urban dwellers actually cultivate informal, personal ties. They participate in the organization not just because they support its formal goal, but because it provides opportunities to develop friendships and participate in social activities (Fischer, 1976).

As with other sources of close personal ties, different people rely on participation in voluntary associations to different degrees. Overall, Americans are more likely to be members of voluntary associations than are people in other nations (Curtis, Grabb, and Baer, 1992). Most studies suggest that such participation varies with social class: lower-class individuals are much less likely to join voluntary organizations than are middle- and upper-class individuals. About two-thirds of American adults say they belong to voluntary associations (Caplow et al., 1991). Putnam, however, found that there has been a sharp drop in organizational memberships of all kinds in the last twenty-five years. This decline holds for groups such as the Red Cross, the PTA, and social clubs such as the Elks and the Lions (Putnam, 1995).

The Myth of Urban Stress, Anomie, and Alienation

Attempts to demonstrate that urban life is uniquely stressful, anomic, or alienating have also resulted in findings which are, at best, ambiguous.

The research on this issue has encountered a number of problems. The attempt to assess the extent of such things as urban stress and alienation has been complicated by serious problems of definition and measurement. In addition, the classical view also implies an historical comparison which is hard to establish: the claim of the classical view is that people were happier and psychologically better off in the past. There simply is no direct way to test that claim now, after the fact. Certainly, just as strong an argument can be made that the opposite is the case. One intriguing survey compared levels of "happiness" and "life satisfaction" (with such things as work and family life) between advanced industrial societies and less technologically advanced societies. The results (based on samples in a total of seventy nations) indicated that people in urban industrial societies reported much higher levels of happiness and life satisfaction (Gallup, 1976–77).

Actual attempts to measure anomie and alienation have yielded findings that are complex and very hard to interpret. As a result, simple generalizations are difficult to make. Certainly, significant minorities of the population seem to display some sorts of alienation and anomie. One urban sociologist has suggested a range of 10 to 20 percent of the population are socially isolated and estimates that one-third of the population displays some sort of alienation (Butler, 1977:28). However, even if those estimates are remotely close to the truth, it suggests that the majority of the population is not isolated and alienated. Moreover, interpreting the sources of these feelings is even more hazardous. Melvin Seeman, for one, points out that there are several different kinds of alienation which appear to have different sources and are not closely related to one another. In short, people who experience one kind of alienation do not necessarily experience other kinds (Seeman, 1958). Consequently, sweeping statements about the generally alienating or anomic nature of urban society must be treated as, at best, gross oversimplifications of an extremely complex issue. Indeed, a number of evaluations of the available evidence reject the whole notion of a distinctively "urban" alienation and point to the continuing strength of close, personal social relationships. For example, research by Claude Fischer indicates that it is true that urban dwellers do feel untrusting toward and isolated from strangers and people unlike themselves. However, Fischer's findings suggest that these feelings do not result in general feelings of alienation because people maintain close, trusting ties with work associates, kin, and neighbors (Fischer, 1976, 1981; Kasarda and Janowitz, 1974; Berry, 1973; Fried, 1969; Wuthnow, 1994).

The available evidence also indicates that the general indictment of urban life as leading to undue stress and pathological behavior because of urban "crowding" needs to be heavily qualified and reformulated (Baldassare, 1978; Fischer, Baldassare, and Ofshe, 1975). The results strongly suggest that early statements of the dangers of living in high-density urban communities both exaggerated and misidentified the nature of the problem.

For one thing, it has proven necessary to distinguish between crowding and density. Density refers to general neighborhood or community conditions in terms of the number of people occupying a given land area (e.g., the number of people per square mile). Crowding refers to conditions within individual households: it is a measure of how many people share a given housing unit of a particular size and/or number of rooms.

Most of the research on the effect of general density has found that high densities have either no negative or only modest negative effects on behavior or mental health (Galle and Gove, 1978). Simply living in the higher density conditions of cities in comparison to rural areas does not seem to be a significant source of problems for human beings. It is also worth noting that, in any event, densities in urban areas in the United States declined very significantly during the 1900s (see chapters 1 and 2).

Research on residential crowding has yielded somewhat more mixed results. A number of researchers have concluded that living in a crowded household has only a very modest influence in creating physical, mental, or social pathologies. These researchers appear ready to dismiss crowding as a problem not meriting serious concern (Fischer et al., 1975). Others, such as Walter Gove, Michael Hughes, and Omer Galle, disagree with this conclusion. They argue that the number of persons per room does affect the number of social demands faced by a person and the person's perception of necessary privacy. They cite evidence that residential crowding, as a result of these primary effects, is associated with such things as physical and psychological withdrawal, poor planning behavior, poor social relationships in the home, poor child care, poor physical and mental health, and poor social relationships outside the home. Moreover, the independent effect of crowding on many of these problems appears to be as strong as other factors that are generally recognized as important influences on them, e.g., income (Gove, Hughes, and Galle, 1979).

However, even if crowding does have an effect, it cannot be the basis for a general criticism of contemporary urban life. The sort of crowding researchers have been investigating is greater than the norm for the urban population in the United States. In addition, like density, residential crowding steadily declined during the 1900s: the proportion of the population living in housing with more than one person per room has declined to the point where only a small minority live in such housing (see chapter 5).

Hence, the general charge that psychological damage is caused by urban life appears to be unfounded. That is not to deny that significant numbers of people experience stress and feelings of isolation, powerlessness, and the like under modern conditions. However, to place the primary or even the major blame on urbanization and urban social life is certainly premature and probably unjustified.

Anomie and alienation may have been characteristic of cities such as Chicago during periods of rapid urbanization in the early twentieth century. This disorganization was due largely to migration of large numbers of single males to the cities from Europe and the rural United States. However, there is no empirical support for theories associating psychological difficulties with urban living under current conditions (Lyon, 1987; Spates and Macionis, 1987; Poplin, 1979).

The issue of crowding and density currently can be seen in a somewhat different light as a concentration of poverty in neighborhoods characterized by violence. Massey (1996) cited in a recent address the findings of Elijah Anderson. Anderson discovered in his recent ethnographic fieldwork that a person living in such a neighborhood can increase the chances of survival by adopting a threatening demeanor and using violence selectively. As more people resort to violence, the violence level will rise in this setting. The relationship of violence to stress and alienation can be clearly seen in the increase in child and spousal abuse following deindustrialization and layoffs (Perucci et al., 1988; Rubin, 1994).

MORE RECENT RESEARCH

These criticisms of the classical view have led to research and theorizing about urban social relationships that attempt to specify how urbanites maintain close social ties. In his "subcultural theory," Fischer notes that cities do not necessarily have negative effects on their inhabitants. Size and density can be seen as providing the number of people sufficient for the development and existence of subcultures, whether they are conventional, unconventional, or deviant. Certain occupations and lifestyles can thus flourish, since enough people with similar interests and activities are present. Fischer concludes that the presence, intensity, and diversity of subcultures increase as the size and concentration of people in cities increase. Hence, the larger size and density of a city encourage development of highly organized subcultures, rather than the personal disorganization and loneliness expected by classical theorists (Fischer, 1976).

Harvey Choldin, summing up much of the recent research on neighborhoods, acknowledges that such factors as modern transportation and communication systems weaken neighborhood ties. However, local social life continues, though much of it is now voluntary and differentiated by demographic factors such as family life stage. For example, neighboring is higher in neighborhoods with large numbers of young children. Participation ranges from heavy involvement in local affairs, to more cosmopolitan, city-wide relationships. Some studies suggest that local uses of the neighborhood are of two types: instrumental uses and social psychological uses. Instrumental uses include such things as purchases at local stores and businesses and enrollment of children in schools. Social psychological uses are such activities as involvement in local groups and organizations and identification with and loyalty to the local community. One distinct factor encouraging local involvement is the feeling that the community is threatened with some problem outside itself, such as a proposed freeway that would destroy some or all local housing. Some have argued that "intense neighboring," involving very close relationships of people living in a relatively small geographical area, may well have declined with the emergence of the modern city. Several explanations can be advanced for this change. People moved more frequently. They communicated increasingly by phone with many besides their immediate neighbors. Friendship ties with coworkers increased in frequency. Neighboring came to be limited to homeowners, those with children, and people centered on family ties and contacts (Choldin, 1985:272–74, 287–96).

In their research, Wellman and Berkowitz studied neighborhoods in which there was little in the way of vital neighborhood activity. Evident, however, were a great number of community ties. Some of these provided strong support to people. These researchers concluded that the social networks they discovered were best described as "personal communities." Such communities consisted not in local ties, but rather in the way in which informal relationships tied people and families into bonds of friendship and assistance as well as mutual aid. The approach of Wellman and Berkowitz concentrates on the presence both of local ties between people, and also on the ties they have with those in the city and the metropolitan area. The concept of personal community thus enables us to see the whole picture, to take into account that people have both local and also area-wide bonds. The extent and detail of such relationships depend largely on one's social class and occupation. For example, those having higher class rank, such as accountants, lawyers, and engineers, tend to have much more extensive contacts across wider geographical areas. Generally speaking, ties provide identity and belonging, assistance and help, both generally as well as in advancing one's career (Wellman and Berkowitz, 1988:130–31, 134–35). This network approach, noting the continuity of social ties amidst great social and geographical mobility, is also affirmed by Hannerz. Fischer (1982) noted that social involvement varied with community size. In larger communities, people tend to associate more with nonkin, while the reverse holds true for those in smaller places (Hannerz, 1980:171–89, 200–201; Kim, 1981; Fischer, 1982; Marsden, 1987).

Perhaps a broader frame of reference can be seen that would include both the classical and revised interpretations. The global economy shapes and reshapes the local communities and context in which we live, as well as their societies. Urban sociology's agenda currently can be seen as the study of the local in the context of the global society (Flanagan, 1993:248–53; Gottdiener, 1994:144–45).

EVALUATION

Where does all this leave us? Were the classical theorists simply wrong? Yes and no. Much of what they said about the nature of the change from rural to urban society has some validity. Urban societies are complex, bureaucratic, secular, culturally heterogeneous, and so on. The basic structure of society and the nature of culture has changed in major ways—often in the ways the classical view suggests. Moreover, there are many social settings where the kind of social relationships described by classical theorists predominate: at the checkout counter of the grocery store, the police station, the state license-plate bureau, and the like.

What the classical view failed to recognize was the flexibility of human beings under conditions of rapid social change and their ability (and dogged determination) to maintain close personal relationships under modern urban conditions. The overwhelming majority of urban dwellers have developed a number of "coping strategies" to avoid the impersonality and social isolation which might otherwise result. Most urbanites have some source of intimate social ties: family, neighborhood, coworkers, or group memberships. The majority of people do not live out their lives in large-scale, impersonal social settings. Rather, they live their lives in much smaller and more personal social worlds, often worlds which they actively create or choose for themselves.

At the same time, the classical theorists tended to downplay the tremendous advantages urban life offered the individual. The improved material conditions, individual freedom, excitement, and diversity which the new cities offered were not just minor advantages of urban life. They were (and are) major attractions. The ultimate testimony to these attractions is to be found in the behavior of millions of individuals over the last two centuries who "voted with their feet": they left their rural communities and went to the city. The process continues today in Third World countries.

But we should be careful not to make the opposite mistake from that of the classical theorists, and deny that contemporary urban communities have problems. They certainly do. The remaining chapters of this book are concerned with some of those problems. Others are the more appropriate topics of another book or course. The purpose of this chapter has been to make sure that the tradition of the anti-urban bias would not distort the examination of those problems. Urban societies have flaws; so did the societies that preceded them. Rather than dreaming of a golden past of idyllic rural villages that never existed, we need to confront contemporary urban society as it is.

MAIN POINTS

1. Urbanization resulted in fundamental changes in the nature of society.
2. The classical view of the consequences of urbanization represented the attempt of early European and North American sociologists to evaluate the differences between rural and urban societies.
3. In the classical view, urbanization resulted in increased size of social units, increased social complexity, and the weakening of kinship ties. These changes in social organization were accompanied by major cultural changes: secularization, rationalization, cultural heterogeneity, and organic solidarity. Social relationships became more impersonal and segmented.
4. Classical theorists evaluated these changes primarily in negative terms. They felt that urbanization resulted in social disorganization, psychological stress, anomie, and alienation.
5. More recent research suggests that the classical view is only partly correct. The basic criticism is that the classical view provides an incomplete view of the nature of rural and urban society and exaggerates the negative characteristics of urban society.
6. This criticism of classical theory is based on a number of specific criticisms of claims made by classical theory.
7. One criticism is that classical theory presents too rosy a view of rural society. Rural society had a number of problems including poor living conditions, exploitation and conflict, parochialism,

and intolerance. In addition, the family system was not as effective, stable, or close-knit as it has been traditionally portrayed.

8. Another criticism of classical theory is that the extent of urban social disorganization is not as great as portrayed by classical theorists. Urbanites maintain stable, personal, and intimate relationships based on kin ties, neighboring, work-based friendships, and membership in voluntary organizations.

9. Finally, there is no clear proof that urban life is as stressful, anomic, or alienating as portrayed by classical theory.

10. Recent research notes that although traditional neighboring patterns have declined, informal relationships tie people into bonds of friendship and assistance.

KEY TERMS

Alienation   A feeling of powerlessness, meaninglessness, and social isolation.

Anomie   "Normlessness"—feeling that there are no clear social rules or goals by which to control and direct one's life.

Anti-Urban Bias   The popular perception that cities are places of crime, immorality, loneliness, and impersonality. This bias is reflected in classical urban theory in the description of urban society as the cause of social disorganization, stress, alienation, and anomie.

Classical View of Urbanization   The view, associated with the work of many early sociological theorists, that urbanization results in the destruction of cohesive small communities and the creation of impersonal, socially disorganized, and alienating social relationships.

Cultural Heterogeneity   Lack of agreement and consistency in cultural beliefs, values, and attitudes.

Cultural Homogeneity   Agreement and consistency in cultural beliefs, values, and attitudes.

Division of Labor   The organization of work roles in society into specialized tasks.

Extended Kinship System   A system of family relationships in which close and frequent social relationships and ties based on mutual assistance and obligation are maintained with a large number of kin outside of the nuclear family.

Mechanical Solidarity   Social solidarity based on shared cultural beliefs, attitudes, and values.

Modified Extended Family   A kinship system in which major emphasis is placed on nuclear family relationships but significant ties are maintained with extended kin.

Nuclear Family   A kinship system in which the major emphasis is placed on relationships between the mother, father, and children.

Organic Solidarity   Social solidarity based on a system of exchange relationships between individuals in specialized roles in a complex division of labor.

Sacred Orientation   A cultural orientation in which the justification for an activity or belief is based on an appeal to religious beliefs.

Secular Rationality   A cultural orientation in which the ultimate justification for an activity or belief is an explanation based on logic and systematic observation of measurable phenomena.

Segmental Social Relationships   A network of social relationships in which relationships are specialized by function and the people one knows in different social situations do not know each other.

Social Disorganization   A societal condition in which norms are inconsistent, cultural values are in conflict, kinship and other relationships are weak and unstable, and individuals feel anomic.

Solidarity   The sense of shared identity, cooperation, and agreement which holds a society or community together.

Total Social Relationships   A network of social relationships in which the same people interact with one another in a number of different social situations while occupying a number of different roles.

Traditional Orientation A cultural orientation in which beliefs and activities are justified on the basis of past practices and beliefs.

SUGGESTED READING

Coontz, Stephanie. 1992. *The Way We Never Were: American Families and the Nostalgia Trap.* New York: Basic Books.

Fischer, Claude. 1976. *The Urban Experience.* New York: Harcourt, Brace, Jovanovich. A landmark work, emphasizing the positive effects of size, density, and heterogeneity.

Fried, Marc. 1969. "Grieving for a Lost Home." In *The Urban Condition,* edited by L. Duhl. New York: Simon and Schuster. A description and critique of the anti-urban bias.

Friedman, F. G. 1953. "The World of La Miseria." *Partisan Review* 20:218–31. A widely reprinted description of Italian peasant life which thoroughly challenges the romantic view of traditional rural village life.

Hutchison, Ray, ed. 1993. *Research in Urban Sociology: Urban Sociology in Transition.* Greenwich, CT: Jai Press.

Jacobs, Jane. 1961. *The Death and Life of Great American Cities.* New York: Vintage Books.

Powers, Ron. 1991. *Far from Home: Life and Loss in Two American Towns*. New York: Random House. This story of two communities—Cairo, Illinois, and Kent, Connecticut—explores the erosion of community ties in the United States.

Rubin, Lillian. 1994. *Families on the Fault Line*. New York: Harper-Collins. A description of the impact of social and economic changes on blue-collar families.

Schaeffer, Peter V., and Scott Loveridge, eds. 2000. *Small Town and Rural Economic Development: A Case Study Approach*. Westport, CT: Praeger.

Wirth, Louis. 1938. "Urbanism as a Way of Life." *American Journal of Sociology* 44:1–24. The most influential summary statement of the classical view of the nature of social life in urban society.

4

Problems of the Urban Disadvantaged

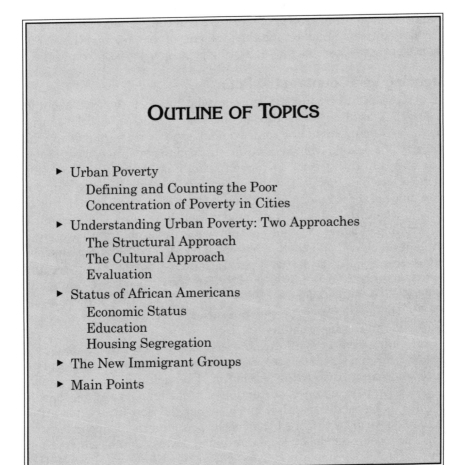

OUTLINE OF TOPICS

- Urban Poverty
  Defining and Counting the Poor
  Concentration of Poverty in Cities
- Understanding Urban Poverty: Two Approaches
  The Structural Approach
  The Cultural Approach
  Evaluation
- Status of African Americans
  Economic Status
  Education
  Housing Segregation
- The New Immigrant Groups
- Main Points

Unequal treatment and unequal living conditions are facts of life in all societies. Urban society is no exception. Inequality is a pervasive characteristic of urban social structure. In this chapter, we will examine those aspects and consequences of inequality which have been a particular concern of those who study urban problems. Our focus will be primarily on those people for whom inequality is a persistent, unpleasant reality: nonwhite racial groups and the poor.

URBAN POVERTY

Obviously, poverty is not just a problem of urban areas. Still, about 42 percent of the poor in the United States live in central cities, and their presence is associated with a number of uniquely urban problems. We will examine who the urban poor are, where they live, and what special problems urban poverty creates. We will then discuss attempts by social scientists to understand the problems of the poor and the significance of those attempts for suggesting policies to assist poor people.

Defining and Counting the Poor

It may seem surprising to someone who has not thought about it before, but deciding who is poor in an affluent, industrial society turns out to be a complicated and controversial issue. No one would deny the poverty of someone who lacks sufficient food to stay alive, wears rags, and sleeps in the street. The person is *absolutely* deprived. Even in a rich society like the United States, we see absolute poverty, hunger, and homelessness among a small proportion of our population. But in an industrialized, generally affluent society like ours, the concept of poverty extends beyond those people who cannot obtain a bare minimum level of food and shelter. We consider as *relatively* poor someone whose conditions of life are substantially worse than average and whose standard of living is lower than that considered minimally acceptable by most members of society. Thus, relative poverty is the lack of things that most people in a society take for granted as necessary and can routinely obtain.

Defining poverty in relative terms makes it more difficult to decide who is poor and who is not because we lack agreement on what constitutes an acceptable living standard. The definition of acceptable depends, in part, on one's perception of an attainable and reasonable level of living conditions. How much is enough? How little is too little? Where do we draw the line between the poor and the nonpoor?

The most commonly used definition of poverty is that employed by the federal government. The *official poverty line,* set by the U.S. Department of Health and Human Services, is calculated based on the cost of food. An estimate of what it costs to purchase a minimally adequate diet is made. That figure is then multiplied by three. (The questionable assumption is that all other necessities will require not more than twice what must be spent for food.) Thus, in 2000 the poverty line for an individual living in an urban area was $8,959, and for a family of four it was $17,761 (U.S. Census Bureau, 2001a). Anyone with less income than this is counted as officially poor by the government. Inflation will mean that the poverty line constantly rises, although it is not directly linked to the cost of living.

The official poverty line is only an approximate measure of poverty, and from time to time attempts are made to measure poverty differently. In the 1980s, for example, officials in the Reagan administration argued that if the value of government programs were counted, poor people's incomes would rise substantially. They introduced an alternative measure of income that included the cash value of government services such as Food Stamps and Medicaid. More than one-third of poor families automatically became nonpoor when the estimated costs of these services were added to their income. This change in accounting greatly reduced the size of the poverty population, a change they argued more truly reflected actual poverty rates (Weinberg, 1995).

Other experts argue that the number of people in poverty is understated, not overstated, due to recent social changes. As more women have entered the labor force, for example, working families have had to meet additional costs for child care. Some scholars argue that the number of poor families would increase if child-care costs were taken into account when measuring family income. Moreover, although housing prices have risen dramatically in some parts of the country in recent years, no adjustments have been made for different costs of living in different regions (Citro and Michaels, 1995).

Economists and even government agencies do not always agree on who is poor. This lack of agreement means that we should be cautious about statistics concerning poverty. The official poverty line (counting cash income only) represents just one attempt to estimate who is poor and who is not. It is probably a fairly conservative estimate. But since the federal government publishes most of its statistics based on the official definition of poverty, that is the measure most researchers use.

It is also important to note that poor people are not necessarily unemployed. About half of all poor families belong to the *working poor*. They live in households where at least one member works but their income is insufficient to raise them over the poverty level (Mishel, Bernstein, and Schmitt, 1999). Whether a working household is poor depends, to an extent, on the number of people in it. For example, in 2000, a person working full-time at the minimum wage earned $10,712 per year. This income, although low, was over the official poverty line for one person. If, however, the wage earner was supporting even one other person, that income put them into poverty.

A related issue is underemployment. Many people who are working can find only part-time jobs. Of course, some people prefer to work part-time and do so voluntarily. An increasing problem for working people in the United States, however, is involuntary part-time employment. A recent study showed that one quarter of all part-time jobs are filled by people who would have preferred full-time jobs but were unable to get them (Tilly, 1996).

Given these considerations, how many poor are there and where do they live? According to the U.S. Census Bureau (2001a), in 2000 some 31 million people were poor, about 11 percent of the population. Four-fifths of these poor people lived in metropolitan areas, and only one-fifth lived in rural areas. About 16 percent of central-city residents were living below the poverty line in 2000, compared with 8 percent in suburban areas and 13 percent in nonmetropolitan areas (U.S. Census Bureau, 2001a). As the proportion of the population living in the suburbs increases, the number of poor people living in the suburbs has increased too. Although the rates of poverty are lower in suburban areas than in cities, in absolute numbers, almost as many poor people now live in suburban communities than in central cities.

Concentration of Poverty in Cities

No matter where the poor live, they experience—and create—problems. Despite some stereotypes of the carefree poor, being poor is no fun. For instance, besides real material deprivation, the poor are more likely to be victims of crime, experience unemployment, die younger, and spend time in jail or a mental hospital.

However, the experiences and problems of the poor are not all the same. The problems of the poor in cities are different from those of the poor outside the cities, since poverty is more geographically concentrated in urban areas.

We must first remember that most people living in cities are not poor, and most people in cities, even most poor people, do not live in neighborhoods characterized by high concentrations of poor people. But the proportion of poor people living in such concentrated high-poverty areas is increasing. This is a disturbing trend because it further separates the poor from the rest of society. As a result, poor people living in high-poverty areas have fewer ties to nonpoor people and to mainstream social institutions than do poor people living outside of these areas. Such isolation has important implications for their opportunities to get out of poverty. A person's knowledge of and ties to the outside world are crucial for obtaining employment beyond the bare minimum. Yet these outside ties are difficult to establish for poverty-area residents because of the insular nature of poor neighborhoods. In addition, their neighborhoods typically contain few businesses that would provide good employment opportunities (Ellwood, 1988; Bourgeois, 1995).

As a result, individuals living in high-poverty areas often work in the *informal sector* of the economy, sometimes called the underground economy. These are hidden businesses that flourish in areas of concentrated poverty. Jobs in the underground economy include drug dealing, selling stolen goods, prostitution, and organized gambling, as well as working "off the books" at jobs that would be legal (e.g., construction, running errands, or driving unregistered taxis) if they were reported. People work at these jobs because they provide the best economic opportunities in an environment where legitimate work is either not available or not well paid. The fact that the work is illegal, however, means that participants in the informal sector run the risk of getting a criminal record, which makes it even harder for them to obtain regular employment (Sharff, 1987). Of course, not everyone in high-poverty neighborhoods works in the informal sector, but its growth is a sobering result of the concentration of poverty in certain city neighborhoods.

Another important characteristic of poor neighborhoods is that concentrations of poverty vary by racial group. Most poor whites live among people who are not poor. The fraction of poor whites living in high-poverty areas (those where more than 40 percent of all residents are poor) is quite small and is remaining constant, while the fraction of poor whites living in areas of moderate poverty (20 to 40 percent of residents are poor) has decreased slightly. Among African Americans, however, we see a steady increase in the concentration of poverty. Between 1970 and 1990 the proportion of poor African Americans living in areas of extreme poverty rose from 37 percent to 45 percent (Jargowsky, 1994).

The trend toward increasing concentrations of poverty is especially pronounced in large cities. The number of extreme poverty neighborhoods grew significantly between 1970 and 1990. During the 1970s the increase in extreme poverty census tracts was highest in the city of New York, followed by Chicago, Newark, Philadelphia, Cleveland, and Detroit. During the 1980s the cities most affected by the trend were first Detroit, then Chicago, Milwaukee, Houston, and New Orleans (Kasarda, 1993). (Although the data for 2000 are not yet available, sociologists expect that this trend continued during the 1990s.) In many concentrated poverty areas, racial segregation and economic deprivation have combined to form types of neighborhoods that some researchers call *hyperghettos*—areas with unfavorable conditions far more extreme than those in other African-American neighborhoods (Wacquant and Wilson, 1989).

Special Problems of the Urban Poor

Most of the special problems of the urban poor are related, in one way or another, to their concentration in large, homogeneous neighborhoods. That is why the increasing numbers of the poor in such neighborhoods is so disturbing.

Such geographical concentration has a number of implications. It means that the physical environment, not just one's own housing, is deteriorated and unhealthy. For instance, children can be attacked by rats or develop lead poisoning from old paint flaking off the walls. The squalor of slum neighborhoods is made worse by gutted, open, abandoned buildings, the danger of fire (accidental or not), and inadequate efforts at public sanitation. In poor neighborhoods, the general level of public services is low. Garbage collection, street repair, the level of police protection, the speed with which emergency services arrive, and conditions in the schools are all worse in the poorer sections of our cities.

Residents of poor neighborhoods are also likely to experience a number of other problems. Compared to other groups, they are much more likely to be victims of crimes (committed by the poor people around them). Their children are likely to go to neighborhood schools that are not only of lower quality but also contain mostly other poor children. These children are more likely to have learning problems, and the peer group pressures are likely to discourage academic achievement and encourage nonconforming behavior. Even relatively simple things can be a problem in a poor neighborhood. Lacking a car, the poor person is likely to have to shop at neighborhood stores which offer a limited range of merchandise at much higher prices than available elsewhere.

Special Problems Created by the Urban Poor

Large concentrations of poor people with poor people's problems in our central cities have created serious problems for those cities. Poor neighborhoods need more services from government. Social service costs are just part of the problem. Fire protection costs are higher. The need for police protection is greater. The need to deal with deteriorated or abandoned buildings imposes a costly burden on city government. Public transportation is more essential. Children of the poor need more educational services.

At the same time, poor people are not a good source from which to raise taxes. Slum dwellings do not generate much real estate property tax, and poor people do not have much income to tax. This is part of the reason central-city governments face growing financial problems (see chapter 7). It also helps explain why government services to the poor are of such low quality.

The growing concentration of the poor in central cities also plays a direct and indirect role in the movement of the white middle class and working class away from the central cities. Fear of the poor, mixed with racial fears, and the desire to avoid paying taxes to help the poor may have contributed to the movement to the suburbs, further complicating the central cities' attempts to raise tax revenues and contributing to the process of urban decay.

UNDERSTANDING URBAN POVERTY: TWO APPROACHES

The urban poor, given their large numbers and their manifest problems, have been a major focus of research among those concerned with urban social problems. Much of this research has attempted to determine the causes of the problems of the poor. The ultimate hope has been that this research would eventually result in a better understanding of the urban poor, which would provide a basis for effective public policies to assist them.

Two general approaches have emerged from research on the urban poor; one stresses the social and economic structure of the society, the other stresses the culture of poor people. Both approaches try to understand why we continue to have poverty in a rich society like the United States. This is a complex question having to do with a number of factors, some very remote from poor individuals themselves (e.g., trends in the national and international economies) and some much closer to home (e.g., whether they are married, how much education they have). The structural approach tends to emphasize the more remote factors, analyzing the way the economy and society create opportunities and distribute them, while the cultural approach tends to stress the closer factors, analyzing people's learned attitudes and behaviors and how these help them succeed or fail at work. The two approaches have different implications not only for understanding what causes poverty but also for attempting to create policies that will reduce the amount of poverty.

The Structural Approach

The structural approach says that poverty is the result of an unequal distribution of opportunity within our society (Braun, 1991). That is, the society is structured in such a way that there is only a certain, limited number of good jobs to go around. The proponents of this view portray the social structure of the United States as a sort of stubby pyramid, with a few highly desirable, well-rewarded positions at the top; a relatively large but still limited number of acceptable, comfortable positions in the middle; and an equally large number of inferior, undesirable positions at the bottom (including positions for the unemployed, as well as for those with bad jobs). They argue that the extent of poverty is to a large degree determined by how many good, middle, and bad positions exist.

One way to see the impact of economic structure on poverty is to observe the increases and decreases in the number of unemployed people as the national economy goes through periods of growth and recession. But proponents of the structural approach examine the quality as well as the number of jobs that exist. They point out that the types of jobs individuals hold, in addition to whether or not they have jobs, are relevant to their poverty or nonpoverty status. They argue that the increase in the number of working poor in recent years is an indication of a severe structural problem in our economy, caused by a transformation in the types of jobs that are available.

Structural theorists hold that the shift from a manufacturing-based economy to a service-based economy and the consequent deindustrialization we examined in chapter 2 are a major cause of changes in people's economic status. Danziger and Gottschalk (1995), for example, argue that it is becoming more and more difficult for people to find secure jobs with good wages, fringe benefits, and opportunities for promotion. The manufacturing jobs that used to provide those opportunities are either being replaced by machines or moved overseas. On the other hand, structural analysts argue, the service jobs that are increasing in number do not provide many opportunities for upward mobility. While a certain proportion of the growing service sector is made up of high-level jobs such as attorneys and computer analysts, a larger proportion is made up of low-level jobs such as janitors and fast-food cooks. Most importantly, the low-level jobs in the service sector do not have career paths leading to promotions. They tend to have very little mobility and act as a dead end, without opportunities for people to gain experience and move ahead. Thus, in the future, we can expect our society to become more divided into rich and poor, more polarized (Reich, 1991).

Urban poverty has become an increasing problem, according to this view, because of the movement of jobs and industry out of the cities. Whereas in the past cities offered job opportunities, today they are attracting fewer employers. Instead, suburban industrial and office parks now contain an increasing proportion of jobs, leaving large areas of the central cities devoid of any jobs. Inner-city residents without access to transportation may not be able to reach the jobs that do exist. Thus, the changing structure of the economy has affected the geographical distribution of jobs as well as the quantity and quality of jobs available (Kasarda, 1989).

While it may seem that the structural approach deals only with very large-scale, remote explanations for poverty, it also looks at how individuals get recruited into positions of poverty or affluence. In particular, structural theorists have pointed to certain institutions, especially schools, as having an enormous impact on people's economic status. They argue that schools act as gatekeepers, selecting the students who will succeed and fail economically, and contributing to their chances of success or failure at every stage. Although the students' success or failure is supposed to be based on their intrinsic merits (intelligence, ambition, hard work), structural theorists find that school personnel's expectations and attitudes toward a student are heavily influenced by his or her family background, income, sex, race, and ethnicity. Thus, a self-fulfilling prophecy often occurs, increasing the probability that a child from an affluent background will be thought of as bright while one from a disadvantaged background will be thought of as slow or unmotivated (Oakes, 1985).

The policy proposals that flow from the structural theory are directed toward increasing opportunities for employment. There are two variations, however—one politically more liberal and one politically more conservative. The conservative proposal is for government to cut taxes and regulation as an incentive to businesses to locate in high-poverty areas. An example of such a policy is the establishment of enterprise zone programs, in which states give corporations tax breaks in return for building plants in certain inner-city neighborhoods (see chapter 2). Liberals criticize the program as insufficient, maintaining that the small number of jobs created and the typically low pay offered will not go far toward solving problems of poverty (Wilder and Rubin, 1988).

The liberal proposal is that government should take the responsibility for increasing not just the number of jobs but also their pay and the degree of access to them. That is, government should directly address the issues of economic structure and job distribution. One application of this policy would be the creation of public sector jobs to supplement those in the private sector, especially in areas of high unemployment. Another is regulating the minimum wage, to ensure that employed people earn more than a poverty income and that wages rise with increases in the cost of living. Although Congress raised the minimum wage to $5.15 in 1997, its real value, adjusted for inflation, is less than the value of the minimum wage in 1956 (U.S. Department of Labor, 2001). A third policy would be to provide increased access to good jobs to those individuals who have been excluded. This might include access through training programs for those who need credentials, through transportation to job-rich areas for those who cannot reach them, and through government-funded day care facilities for those who are limited in finding work by family obligations. These increased services and opportunities for the poor could be funded by increased taxes on the well-to-do, thus helping to narrow the widening income gap. Conservative critics disagree with these approaches, arguing that increased taxes on businesses or on the affluent would hamper economic growth.

The Cultural Approach

The central claim of the cultural approach to poverty is that the poor have a special subculture (a set of values and beliefs different from those held by most people in society). In a sense, the poor are seen as operating in a separate social world with a different definition of reality, a different set of rules for behavior, different goals, and different definitions of success. This subculture is seen as being passed on from generation to generation through the socialization of children and as being deeply rooted in the personalities and way of life of the poor. As a result, the poor behave differently and, from the point of view of the rest of society, in an inappropriate and sometimes dysfunctional fashion.

Different theorists have emphasized different characteristics of this *culture of poverty*. However, the classic version derived from the work of Oscar Lewis (1966) emphasizes certain values and beliefs that are seen as shaping the behavior of the poor. The most important of these are fatalism (or a lack of aspirations) and present-time orientation.

By fatalism or lack of aspirations theorists mean to imply that the poor have given up hope for improvement in their lives. The poor do not believe that they can, by their own actions, control what happens to them. They no longer hope for conventional middle-class success. The poor, according to this view, no longer believe in the middle-class success ethic that discipline and hard work will lead to a better life. Hence, they see sustained efforts to improve their situation as pointless.

Because they have no long-term goals toward which they are willing to work, the poor, claim these theorists, are unwilling to discipline themselves or plan ahead. Rather, the poor display a present-time orientation. They live for today—with no concern for what tomorrow will bring. They do not organize their lives. They are unwilling to defer gratification (to sacrifice present pleasure to achieve some long-term goal). Rather, they live from moment to moment, seeking pleasure when and where they can.

The consequences of this view of the world, say culture of poverty theorists, are predictably bad. Given opportunities to improve their lives the poor will not take effective advantage of them. Given money, they will waste it on frivolous pleasures. They cannot maintain stable, intimate relationships with others, so family relationships will be unstable. Poor neighborhoods will be socially disorganized: social ties between people in the community will be weak, participation in voluntary organizations will be low, and a sense of community identity and obligations will be lacking.

In recent years, a variant of the cultural approach has focused on one group of the poor, the persistently poor. This subset of the poor consists of those not only in extreme poverty and living in concentrated poverty neighborhoods but also highly likely to be living in female-headed families, dependent on welfare as the main source of income, and having little history of or prospect for legitimate work. What distinguishes this so-called "urban underclass" from the rest of the urban poor, in the eyes of researchers, is the families' isolation from mainstream social life and the long duration of their poverty, often persisting from generation to generation (McLanahan, Garfinkel, and Watson, 1988).

Some observers view the subcultural attitudes of the persistently poor and their lack of participation in mainstream society as a kind of trap, not only preventing them from getting ahead but also condemning their children to the same fate: dropping out of school, getting arrested for selling drugs, having babies as teenagers. The home and neighborhood surroundings in which the children grow up, according to these writers, place too little importance on work, stable marriage, and education as means of upward mobility. (See, for example, Lemann, 1988.)

Where do these subcultural attitudes and behaviors supposedly come from? One explanation sees them as traditional adaptations to life in urban slums. In areas with few real opportunities for upward mobility, cultures develop around the needs of immediate daily survival. The point is not so much that poor people do not value working, saving money, marriage, and education but that they see these things (perhaps correctly) as not possible for them. They therefore define the seemingly inevitable alternatives (dropping out, unmarried pregnancy, petty crime) as acceptable (MacLeod, 1995).

A more controversial explanation blames social welfare policy for fostering these subcultural attitudes and behaviors. In this view, persistently poor people have become dependent on social welfare programs, especially the recently dismantled Aid to Families with Dependent Children (AFDC), which provided cash payments to low-income families with children. Proponents of this view argue that AFDC destroyed both the work ethic (by providing welfare payments as an alternative to wages) and the two-parent family (by providing single mothers with incomes) among the poor (Murray, 1984).

As with the structural approach, the policy proposals stemming from the cultural approach can be either liberal or conservative. In the 1960s, many policies of the national "War on Poverty" were derived from the liberal version of culture-of-poverty theory. The main thrust of the policies was to intervene in the poverty cycle by teaching poor people the attitudes and behaviors they needed to succeed in mainstream society. Many government-sponsored antipoverty programs, such as Head Start and the Job Corps, were aimed at exposing poor individuals to so-called "middle-class" beliefs, values, and experiences. (Other programs, such as the Model City Program, were oriented toward increasing the level of economic opportunity in poor communities and so were more structural policies.) Today, the federal government runs fewer of these programs, but the cultural approach has been adopted by self-help groups in a number of poor neighborhoods. Often associated with churches or religious sects, these groups offer strong support for mainstream attitudes by organizing teenagers against gangs, drug use, and premarital sex and emphasizing education, work, and marriage as achievable goals.

In the past decade, conservative policy focused on cutting back welfare programs, especially AFDC. Welfare opponents argue that the poor will not learn proper attitudes toward work as long as they have government programs on which to rely. By tightening welfare eligibility and cutting payments, government can ensure that anyone who reasonably could be expected to work will be working. An offshoot of this policy direction is *workfare*, which requires welfare recipients to work off their payments at less than the minimum wage, thus making welfare a less attractive alternative to work for all but the truly needy. There is also a liberal version of workfare; the difference is that the conservative proposals are more oriented toward discouraging people from applying for benefits while the liberal proposals are more oriented toward helping them to enter the paid labor force.

In 1996 Congress passed so-called "welfare reform" legislation—the Personal Responsibility and Work Opportunity Act—that made sweeping changes in welfare programs, particularly the AFDC program (see table 4.1). The legislation eliminated the federal government's responsibility to provide payments to eligible recipients (known as an entitlement) and gave that responsibility to those states that chose to accept it. It established limits of two years at a stretch and five years in a lifetime for any adult to receive welfare benefits. It added a work requirement of 20 hours per week for adults to receive food stamps. It also made immigrants ineligible for public assistance unless they become U.S. citizens (Greve, 1996).

Table 4.1
From AFDC to TANF

The main public assistance program in the United States, Aid to Families with Dependent Children (AFDC) was replaced in 1996 by a program called Temporary Assistance to Needy Families (TANF). The following is a summary of the provisions of the legislation, called the Personal Responsibility and Work Opportunity Act. This law:

- ends the federal guarantee of cash assistance to needy families
- gives states discretion over the amount of money they will spend on programs for the poor
- gives states discretion over the level of benefits they will pay
- establishes a lifetime limit for adults of 60 months of assistance
- mandates that states require adult recipients to work (education and job training programs do not count)
- makes noncitizens (including legal permanent residents) ineligible for TANF, Supplemental Security Income (which assists the elderly and disabled), food stamps, and Medicaid

SOURCES: Albelda, 1996; Greve, 1996; Reuss, 1996.

Evaluation

What evidence exists to support each of these approaches? Is one correct and the other incorrect? Or can some elements of each be combined to provide a more complete understanding of the causes of poverty?

There is a great deal of evidence to suggest that poverty is, at some fundamental level, caused by the structure of the economy. Take, for example, the increase in the number of poor people since 1979. This is not an isolated phenomenon but one facet of a more general trend toward greater inequality, or *polarization,* of incomes in the United States. At the same time that the poverty population is increasing, the numbers of the very rich are also increasing (but not as quickly), and the middle class is shrinking in size (Mishel et al., 1999).

These changes in income distribution are the result of several identifiable trends in the U.S. economy. First, working people's wages are not keeping up with increases in the cost of living. When adjusted for inflation, the wages of 80 percent of male workers and 50 percent of female workers fell between 1989 and 1995 (Mishel et al., 1996). The incomes of the well-to-do, however, have increased rapidly. Between 1988 and 1997 the average salary of Chief Executive Officers rose 31 percent, compared to a mere half of one percent for all workers (Mishel et al., 1999). The average CEO now makes 115 times what the average worker makes, up from 56 times the average worker's pay as recently as 1989. So polarization in wages has contributed to polarization in incomes.

Second, because of economic restructuring, many workers have been permanently laid off from their regular employment. They are *displaced workers* because the jobs they were trained to do have disappeared, and there is little hope that they will become reemployed in the same job. One study showed that of all the long-term employees displaced by plant closings and downsizings between 1991 and 1993, fewer than half were able to obtain full-time jobs at pay levels comparable to their former jobs (U.S. Bureau of Labor Statistics, 1996, table 7).

Third, in recent years, the U.S. economy has been producing many more bad jobs than good jobs. The 1980s and 1990s saw a shift from high-wage to low-wage sectors of the economy. The fastest growing job sectors in the 1990s were temporary services and retail—both low-wage industries. These two sectors produced 79 percent of all new jobs created between 1989 and 1997 (Mishel et al., 1999). Not surprisingly, the expansion of low-wage jobs means that many full-time workers do not make enough to support themselves. The incomes of many full-time workers even puts them below the poverty level. Since 1979, the proportion of full-time workers earning less than poverty wages has increased from 24 percent to 29 percent.

Fourth, there is a geographic mismatch between the types of jobs being produced and the skill level of the people who need jobs. According to several analysts (see Ihlanfeldt and Sjoquist, 1998, for an overview), the good jobs that are being created in cities are mainly in the information-processing industries of the service sector. These jobs have high educational requirements and do not provide opportunities, even at the entry level, for the masses of young, unemployed urban dwellers. The move of lower-skill manufacturing and service jobs to the suburbs has made it more difficult for city dwellers to gain entry-level employment. Because poor, unemployed inner-city residents have low rates of automobile ownership, and because public transit routes are designed to take people from residential neighborhoods to central business districts, many suburban job sites are barely accessible by public transportation.

Thus, the structural approach gives us many insights into the larger causes of poverty. It shows how the economy influences the amount, type, and location of poverty in our society. It helps us understand why we see certain contradictory trends in our cities: increases in homeless people and beggars on the streets at the same time that the market for expensive condominiums heats up and chic new clubs and restaurants open daily.

The structural approach does not, however, give us much information about how *individuals* become poor, stay poor, or become upwardly mobile. It tells us that certain categories of people (members of racial minorities, women and children, people without much education) are most likely to be poor. But it does not tell us why individuals from the same neighborhoods or even the same families can turn out very differently. From a structural point of view, a great deal of the difference in occupation or income between individuals with similar backgrounds (parents' income, educational level, etc.) is due simply to luck.

The cultural approach may help fill in the missing links between the remote causes of poverty and the ways in which specific individuals or groups become poor. How do people's attitudes and behaviors affect their chances of becoming or remaining poor? Are there systematic differences between the cultures of poor and nonpoor people, and, if so, how do these affect their chances for the future?

One question that has been raised is whether persistent poverty is the result of a culture of welfare dependency. To what extent do the poor constitute an underclass of people spending most of their lives on welfare, and not trying to get ahead? Some important data on these issues are provided by the Panel Study of Income Dynamics (PSID), which has studied five thousand families since 1968. One study based on PSID data asked how many of the poor are persistently poor (defined as poor for eight or more years out of a ten-year period). The researchers found that, although 40 percent of the people in the study were poor *at some time* during a twenty-year period, only 1.1 percent were persistently poor (Devine and Wright, 1993). An earlier study based on the PSID showed that, although about a quarter of the people in the study received some government welfare (AFDC, food stamps, or another form of public assistance) during a ten-year period, only 4.4 percent received welfare persistently and less than half of them (2 percent of the total group) derived more than half of their family income from welfare programs (Duncan, 1984). The authors of the study conclude that:

> . . . [T]he popular conception of "the poor" as a homogeneous, stable group is simply wrong. Although the series of snapshot pictures of poverty provided by the Census Bureau surveys shows fairly constant numbers and characteristics for poor families each year, actual turnover in the poverty population is very high. (Duncan, 1984:60)

Researchers also have studied the issue of individuals' attitudes and their impact on poverty. The cultural approach holds that when people learn attitudes such as fatalism and lack of future orientation within a subculture, those attitudes make them less likely even to try to get ahead. In effect, the culture discourages them from thinking they can succeed. The Panel Study of Income Dynamics examined this question of people's attitudes and their impact on poverty. Since the PSID is a longitudinal study, one that traces the same individuals over a long period of time, it lets researchers examine the relationship between people's attitudes at one time and their economic level at a later time. The PSID tested the subjects' achievement motivation, sense of control over their lives, and orientation toward the future. Surprisingly, their attitudes on these dimensions had no relation to their economic success or failure seven years later (Duncan, 1984). This study confirms other research done with smaller groups (MacLeod, 1995).

Should we conclude that the cultural approach to poverty is simply wrong? Not necessarily, but social scientists are beginning to realize that the relationship between social structure, attitudes, and behavior is very complex. Living in a poor neighborhood and growing up in a poor family can have an impact on whether people get ahead, but there is no automatic relationship between the two (Mayer and Jencks, 1989). In addition, individuals from the same neighborhood and even from the same family can grow up with different attitudes toward success and achievement. To complicate matters further, positive attitudes do not necessarily make a person likely to succeed, although consistently negative attitudes must certainly hurt the chances of success.

A more realistic view of the causes of poverty is one that combines three factors. The first is the structural or objective constraints people face (opportunities for good jobs, competition in the labor market, labeling by schools, and so on). The second is the way people interpret their situations through the eyes of the cultural groups of which they are a part, especially their families and friends. The third is the actions they choose based on both of those factors, and, finally, the consequences those actions have for their life chances. In no sense do these factors guarantee poverty, although they may make it more or less predictable in some cases. (See MacLeod 1995 for a more thorough discussion of the way these factors interact.)

The conclusion we reach is that a distinctive culture is characteristic of only a small proportion of the poor and that it is less a cause of poverty than one means by which poverty may be perpetuated among some poor people. This is hardly a new idea. The late Oscar Lewis, who originally formulated the culture-of-poverty concept, argued that only about one-fifth of the poor population displayed unique cultural traits (Anderson, 1974). That estimate fits very well with more recent assessments of the size of the persistently poor underclass.

What about the majority of the poor not in this small subgroup? Most of them are people who did not start out in poverty and frequently get out of poverty when employment opportunities and life circumstances permit. Other than that, about all they have in common is low income. Some are the temporarily unemployed who eventually find employment. Another group is former workers who are permanently unemployed, usually because of plant closings or permanent layoffs. Older workers frequently find it difficult to be rehired because of their age. Some of the permanently unemployed are part of the thousands of workers disabled on the job each year. Many single-parent families are poor because they are headed by women (often with young children) who have been divorced or deserted and have, as a consequence, slipped into poverty. Retirement on inadequate pensions or social security benefits often results in a working-class family slipping below the poverty line. A large proportion of the poor, especially women, are working but receiving wages too low to raise them above the poverty line.

The fact that most of the poor are people such as these (and their children) seems to explain why so many studies have failed to find a majority of the poor displaying culture-of-poverty traits. Most of the poor are not members of a multigenerational impoverished class with a history of welfare dependency and social pathology. Rather, they are working-class people who have had bad luck and/or are struggling to survive in marginal working-class jobs.

If this interpretation of the evidence is correct, it has important implications for public policy toward the majority of the poor. What poor people need is not just jobs (many already work), but good jobs, providing an income that will actually get them out of poverty. However, job opportunities have to be combined with creating conditions in which the poor can take advantage of those opportunities. This would entail such measures as effectively preventing racial, sexual, and age discrimination; providing education and training opportunities; providing child care for single-parent families; and retraining people with disabilities. Finally, there is the issue of those who are poor for reasons beyond their control but cannot be employed (e.g., the severely disabled and the elderly). Adequate levels of public assistance are obviously the only way in which their conditions of life could be improved.

There remains the problem of the persistently poor underclass. Fortunately, they represent a minority of those who are poor. However, in absolute numbers there are significant concentrations of these poor in certain neighborhoods of our central cities. What policy response is appropriate for this group depends on a number of considerations. First, to what extent is their behavior really the result of subcultural differences and how deeply embedded is that subculture? Second, to what extent is it possible to design workable programs that will actually have a significant impact on improving their (and, especially important, their children's) lives? These policies will probably have to go beyond providing job opportunities and include ways of convincing young people that they can actually take advantage of these opportunities. Unless they see school and work as viable routes to upward mobility, young people have no reason not to engage in behaviors like teen pregnancy, gang warfare, taking drugs, and dropping out of school.

An interesting experiment is now going on and may give us increased insight into an effective policy direction. Beginning with philanthropist Eugene Lang in 1981, a number of wealthy individuals have adopted classes of elementary school children from poor inner-city neighborhoods and promised to pay their college tuition on the condition that they stay in school, avoid drugs, and not become teenage parents. Several cohorts of young people have now been the beneficiaries of such private scholarship programs. Although the results are uneven, it appears that the students in these classes, exactly like their peers in every other way, are experiencing much higher rates of high school graduation and college entrance than their age-mates. Of the 61 sixth-graders to whom Lang offered scholarships in 1981, 90 percent completed high school and 60 percent went on to college or post-secondary training (www.ihad.org). In addition to individual benefactors, several organizations such as the Urban League have begun scholarship programs for young children. The successful programs seem to be those that begin in elementary school, have high expectations for the children's academic achievement and personal conduct, and provide mentoring, tutoring, and enrichment on a regular basis throughout the school years.

Observers may ask why we need to rely on private individuals and organizations to take innovative steps toward improving poor people's chances for the future. Unfortunately, as poverty has worsened since 1980, public policy has turned away from attempts to solve the problem. The trend away from public antipoverty policy is largely based on three faulty assumptions. First, some commentators argue that because unemployment rates are relatively low, anyone who wants a job should be able to find one. As we have seen, however, having a job is no guarantee against poverty, as the economy produces too many jobs at poverty wages and not enough jobs at livable wages. Second, some observers contend that government policy is ineffective in solving problems of poverty. Critics of government programs claim that the antipoverty programs of the 1960s were ineffective, but government policy actually has had a major impact on poverty. Since 1980, consistent increases in government Social Security payments have reduced the rate of poverty among senior citizens from 15 percent poor to 10 percent poor (a lower rate than the rest of the population), while cutbacks in child welfare programs helped to raise the rate of poverty among children to over 16 percent. Thus, due in part to the effectiveness of government programs to help the elderly, children have now replaced them as the poorest age group in the population (U.S. Census Bureau, 2001a). Third, many writers have accepted the notion that government programs actually cause poverty by encouraging dependency. But in truth, most aid recipients are short-term recipients and many use aid to supplement their low wages. By eliminating welfare programs, such families are often pushed into deeper poverty.

We are compelled to conclude that an effective government policy to address the problems of poverty is both possible and necessary. It cannot be a simple, one-factor type of policy because of the complexity of the problem. At a minimum, it must include:

(1) economic policy to create a sufficient level of jobs with good wages, adequate benefit levels, and opportunities for promotion;
(2) programs of training and education to enable people to gain employment at good jobs as well as the supports (social services, transportation, health care, child care) they need to enable them to undertake and complete the training; and
(3) an adequate social welfare system to provide for those who cannot work, those who are facing temporary drawbacks, and children whose families cannot provide for them.

STATUS OF AFRICAN AMERICANS

Cities are often associated with racial and ethnic minority groups, and quite rightly so. For more than a century, immigrants to the United States have settled in cities, and for more than a half century, rural-dwelling African Americans have migrated to cities in large numbers. Members of both groups typically value cities for their promise of economic opportunities and a better life for their families. Yet many members of minority groups, particularly people of color, have also encountered discrimination, marginalization, and grinding poverty in their urban settings. In the remainder of the chapter we will explore the conditions among the most significant racial and ethnic minorities now residing in cities: first we will look at the experience of African Americans and then turn to recent immigrants to the United States.

Economic Status

More than three decades have passed since the landmark civil rights legislation and Supreme Court decisions of the 1960s that barred racial discrimination in employment, education, voting, and the rental or sale of housing. At least in terms of the law, they removed many long-term barriers to the full participation of African Americans in the society and economy. The relative speed with which court challenges and legislation brought down the legally sanctioned color bar in much of the nation generated some optimism that African Americans would soon be able to compete equally with whites in the economy. As we will see, however, economic progress has been uneven for African Americans since the mid-1960s. By examining indicators such as income, wages, poverty rates, employment, and ownership of wealth, we can assess the current economic status of African Americans relative to whites.

In the area of family income, the pattern over time seems to be one of modest progress for African Americans compared with white families. In 1965, African Americans earned 55 percent of the income that white families earned, or $3,393 to the whites' $7,251. By 2000, after a series of ups and downs, African-American families were doing slightly better, earning 66 percent of the incomes of white families—$30,439 to $45,904 (U.S. Census Bureau, 2001d). Obviously there is still a long way to go, but by this measure, the gap between the two groups is narrowing.

Trends in family income levels, however, provide only a partial picture of the actual situation. Average family incomes are the statistical result of a number of different and sometimes contradictory influences, such as whether people are employed, how much their wages are, how many people in the household are working, whether there is income from anything other than wages (such as government payments, alimony, or interest), and a number of other factors. If we look at the earnings of employed workers, for example, we find that African-American male workers' wages have decreased relative to those of white males since 1979, while African-American women's earnings have remained stable compared to those of white women workers (Swinton, 1993).

A favorable sign is that, in recent years, education has had an increased payoff in earnings for African Americans. While African-

American workers are still, as a group, paid less than whites with similar educational levels, these wage differences have been decreasing, and the racial pay levels are closest among workers with graduate degrees (Thomas, 1993).

If we look at unemployment levels, however, we find that African Americans are more likely to be unemployed compared to whites than in the past. In addition, once laid off, African-American workers tend to be unemployed longer and have a harder time finding new jobs than white workers (U.S. Bureau of Labor Statistics, 2001). Unemployment has become especially severe among younger, urban African-American males, many of whom are not even counted as unemployed because they have stopped looking for work. Instead, they are counted as not in the labor force.

Perhaps the most sobering statistics about the economic differences between African Americans and whites are those relating to poverty. During the past three decades, the poverty rate among whites has fluctuated between 7 and 12 percent of the population, while the poverty rate for African Americans has fluctuated between 23 and 35 percent (U.S. Census Bureau, 2000b). Although currently it is at the low end of that range, almost half of all African-American children are now poor. Poverty has also deepened among African Americans due to ever-decreasing incomes among the very poor and an increasing tendency toward chronic poverty. In the 1990s the rate of chronic poverty (defined as being poor in every month in a two-year period) for African Americans was 15 percent, while for whites it was only 3 percent (Eller, 1996).

Not surprisingly, African Americans own less property than do whites. The most recent national survey of wealth ownership, conducted in 1995, showed that African-American households own only one-seventh as much wealth as do white households (U.S. Census Bureau, 2001c). They are substantially less likely than whites to own such common possessions as a house, a car, or even an interest-bearing savings account. The large differences in wealth between African Americans and whites is not due solely to the income differences between the races. When households of similar occupations and incomes are compared, the white households still have substantially larger wealth holdings than the African-American households. Surveys by Melvin Oliver and Thomas Shapiro (1995) show that three factors have disadvantaged African Americans compared to whites: whites are much more likely to inherit or be able to borrow from their parents; whites are much more likely to have access to loans and mortgages to allow them to buy homes; and the property that whites own has tended to appreciate in value far faster than property owned by African Americans.

When we ask how African Americans are doing relative to whites, we get different answers depending on which group of African Americans we are discussing. Many sociologists now think that economic polarization, the widening of the gap between the rich and the poor, is one of the most important trends affecting the African-American population. As we saw earlier, economic polarization has been occurring among the entire population of the United States, but some analysts argue that it has been taking place even more rapidly among African Americans than among the population as a whole.

One factor that seems to be related to economic polarization among African Americans is the changing family structure and the different impact that has had on white and African-American families. On the one hand, single-parent families are more likely to be poor than two-parent families, and poor African Americans are increasingly likely to be living in families headed by a single mother. Unfortunately, this fact has consequences for the future as well as the current living standard of poor families. Single-parent families are not only more likely to be poor than two-parent families, but they also tend to stay poor for longer periods of time (McLanahan et al., 1988). On the other hand, the trend toward two-earner couples has helped some African-American families make rapid economic gains. High-earning African-American families, although small in number, have been slowly closing the income gap with their white counterparts (Swinton, 1993).

It is also important to look at the overall economic context. Negative trends in the economy tend to hurt African Americans more than whites. During recessions, for example, African-American workers are more likely than white workers to be laid off because they are concentrated in the secondary labor market—the less-skilled, low-wage, non-unionized jobs most affected by workforce cuts (Thomas, Herring, and Horton, 1994). Another contextual factor is that African-American workers are heavily concentrated in northern central cities. As basic changes in the economy have moved manufacturing job opportunities to different regions, the industries most affected have been those employing the largest numbers of African-American workers (Wilson, 1987). Furthermore, the wages for the industries and the types of jobs held by African-American workers have tended not to keep up with inflation.

Racial discrimination also affects the economic position of many African Americans. Although for the past thirty or more years racist attitudes among whites (or at least the proportion of the population admitting to them) have been declining, many patterns of racial inequality persist. Because of past discrimination in hiring, for example, African Americans often have less job seniority than white workers. Because workers are usually laid off in order of seniority, the African Americans are more likely to be laid off when companies cut their workforces. Past discrimination also means that there are large numbers of older African-American workers who were locked into low-wage, low-skill jobs when they were younger. Denied access to education, training, and the chance to work at jobs that would improve their skills, their opportunities now are severely limited. Another problem is that residential segregation can limit economic opportunity, especially among the very poor. Those extra poor, socially fragmented inner-city neighborhoods that have been called hyperghettos are affected by economic problems more intensely than are other types of neighborhoods. When the economy is bad, they are hurt worse than other areas, yet when the economy recovers, they recover less than other areas (Wacquant and Wilson, 1989). Finally, African-American workers are still paid less than white workers with the same education, even though the pay difference is gradually decreasing (Thomas, 1993).

Many of the economic gains African Americans have made are at least partly the result of social policy. Antidiscrimination legislation helps African Americans, women, and other minority groups access many educational and employment opportunities formerly closed to them. Equal opportunity hiring and promotion programs, guidelines that spell out affirmative action procedures for companies seeking contracts with the federal government, and legislation mandating local governments to do a certain amount of business with minority-owned firms help African Americans compete in the business world. Despite these policies, the economic gains of African Americans have been uneven at best. As the move to dismantle affirmative action and other race-based programs proceeds, this modest progress could easily be reversed. In any event, it is likely that for the foreseeable future the United States will continue to see deep economic divisions between the races.

Education

Racial economic divisions have persisted despite major gains in the amount of education African-American children are receiving. The gains have been most spectacular in terms of the rates of high school graduation. In 1965, 56 percent of African Americans between the ages of 14 and 24 and 78 percent of whites of the same age group had completed high school. By 1999, the percentage among African Americans was 77 percent and among whites it was 84 percent (U.S. Census Bureau, 2001b). Clearly, the education gap between African Americans and whites at the high school level has been closing. The racial gap in achievement scores for students is also steadily narrowing (Mishel et al., 1996).

A larger proportion of African Americans are now pursuing higher education. In 1985, about 11 percent of African Americans over 25 and 20 percent of similarly aged whites were college graduates. By 1999, the figure for African Americans was 15 percent and for whites 26 percent (U.S. Census Bureau, 2001b).

The fact that African-American children now attend school for almost the same length of time as white children does not necessarily mean that the educations they receive are identical. African-American students still receive lower scores on standardized achievement tests than white students. In addition, an overwhelming difference between African-American and white students' educations stems from continued racial segregation in the schools. African Americans are still likely to be consigned to schools in the central-city school districts in which the students are predominantly members of racial minority groups.

That is a problem for several reasons. School integration has been a constitutionally mandated goal of government policy for a generation. Continued segregation represents evidence of a serious failure of public policy. Continued segregation in the schools is symbolically important too. Segregation in the schools is highly visible evidence of our society's failure to operate in a racially blind fashion.

Prior to the antisegregation legislation of the 1960s, school segregation came in two varieties: *de jure* (in law) segregation was based on laws that mandated separate schools for the races. De jure segregation existed mainly in the South. The other kind of segregation, called *de facto* (in fact), was the result of racial residential segregation and the practice of assigning students to the school closest to their home. De jure segregation has been easier to address through changes in school policy such as court-ordered mergers of segregated schools. De facto segregation has been more difficult to address. Although schools in some parts of the country are now fairly well racially integrated, the majority of African-American students attend schools that are highly racially segregated. The reason for this continued school segregation is that residential patterns in major metropolitan areas, home to most African-American students, continue to be highly segregated (Rivkin, 1994). Because low-income African Americans live in the areas with the fewest white students, they are more affected by de facto segregation than their middle-class peers (Orfield, 1994).

Consider the case of Hartford, Connecticut. Although the state of Connecticut has the highest per capita income in the nation, Hartford contains a large proportion of relatively low-income minority residents. The student population of the public schools is 94 percent African American or Latino, and three out of four students live in families whose incomes are below the poverty line. Several students joined together to sue the state, proposing that the school districts be enlarged to include both minority and white populations in roughly equal numbers. The students' attorney argued that they were being denied access to an equal education because of their race. In 1995, however, the State Superior Court denied their claim, stating in its decision that since the state did not create the segregation it did not have an obligation to help reduce it (Gleick, 1995).

In areas that have attempted to desegregate the schools, significant differences exist, related to the type of desegregation plan adopted. In southern cities such as Atlanta, Memphis, Dallas, and New Orleans, the progress toward desegregation has been dramatic. This is at least partly due to the aggressive stance of the courts in enforcing strong desegregation plans. Many northern cities, such as New York, Chicago, and Philadelphia, have had no court-ordered desegregation and have experienced either steadily high or increasing levels of school segregation. In those cities outside of the South where court-ordered programs have been implemented (such as Los Angeles, Milwaukee, and Indianapolis), school segregation has decreased (Farley, 1984).

Public sentiment on racial segregation and desegregation is mixed. Recent polls show that although nearly 90 percent of all Americans agree that school segregation should be illegal, fewer than 20 percent approve of integrated communities as a way of reducing school segregation (McAneny and Saad, 1994). Furthermore, there is some evidence that white residents of more affluent communities are less welcoming to minority students in their schools than are white residents in less affluent communities (Miller, 1990).

Some cities have drawn new school district boundaries to include additional white students in the school population. Louisville, for example, merged the city and suburban school districts into one metropolitan district in 1976. The expanded pool of white students makes it easier to achieve racial balance in the schools. At the same time, white families cannot move to the suburbs to find all-white schools, since the suburban schools are part of the same system as the city schools. As a result, Louisville has succeeded in reducing the separation of minority and white students (Rusk, 1993). Since school segregation today is mostly the result of minorities and whites living in different school *districts* (not, as previously, their living in different *neighborhoods* within the same school district), these merged-district desegregation programs are the most effective avenue for decreasing school segregation. Unfortunately, in some cities outside of the South where these plans have been proposed, they have been blocked by suburban communities whose residents want their schools to remain virtually all white.

Rather than redrawing district lines, some districts have attempted to desegregate by assigning students to schools based on a lottery or some factor other than the students home addresses. In the 1970s and 1980s many school districts adopted policies to create a consistent racial mix in each school, often by transporting students to different neighborhoods within the city. These mandatory reassignment or so-called "forced busing" programs were frequently unpopular with parents (especially but not exclusively white parents), who often resisted them by withdrawing their children from public schools or by moving to a different community (Rossell, 1995).

Since the early 1980s, urban school districts have increasingly adopted voluntary desegregation programs instead of mandatory programs. Voluntary programs encourage students to select their school based on its curriculum or reputation rather than simply its location. An increasingly widespread type of voluntary desegregation plan is a *magnet school* program, in which certain types of courses are offered at different schools. A city may, for example, concentrate the performing arts at one school, computing technology at another, and foreign languages at a third. Magnet schools can address segregation when programs that would be attractive to white students are placed in schools with large African-American populations and vice-versa. Voluntary desegregation programs are less effective at desegregating schools than are programs that redraw the boundaries of school districts or merge urban and suburban districts. Within individual school districts, however, voluntary desegregation programs are about as effective as mandatory school reassignment programs. This may be due to the fact that voluntary desegregation programs cause less white flight from the public schools than do mandatory desegregation programs (Rossell and Armor, 1996).

In city schools, problems of finances compound those of racial segregation. Poverty and underfinanced schools are most visible in those inner-city areas where per-pupil spending can be only a small fraction of the amount spent in adjacent suburban districts (Kozol, 1991). Students in these highly segregated, low-income schools suffer not just from isolation but from inadequate facilities and often from a lack of hope for success. Even in areas that have made substantial progress toward reducing school segregation, however, we still see a relationship between the racial composition of the student body and the quality of education the students receive. A study of Texas schools revealed that schools with higher proportions of minority students had less experienced, less qualified teachers and larger classes than schools with lower proportions of minority students (Kain and Singleton, 1996).

The question still remains, what difference does it make if students go to segregated schools? On the subject of achievement test scores, the evidence is mixed. Some studies have found that school segregation contributes to differences in academic achievement (Bankston and Caldas, 1997), but others have found that even in integrated schools, a substantial racial gap in test scores persists (Puma, 1997). When other factors besides test scores are considered, researchers find that attending integrated schools can provide positive long-term advantages for African-American students. Studies that have followed the life choices of students from kindergarten through adulthood have found that African-American students who attended integrated schools are, as a group, more likely to work in a high-prestige occupation, to succeed in integrated workplaces, and to adapt to heterogeneous living situations (Crain and Strauss, 1985; Dawkins and Braddock, 1994).

Social science research has gone beyond the question of segregation versus integration to examine the racial interactions that take place within the schools. Each school has a particular culture, and interaction between and within racial and ethnic groups takes place within the wider culture of the school. Even in schools that appear to be racially integrated, for example, African-American and white students may enroll (or be enrolled) in different classes and may be socially separated from students in the other group. In addition, classroom observation studies show that teachers often treat students differently (whether deliberately or not) based on their race and sex. Overall, African-American students have been found to receive more negative feedback from teachers than do white students (Irvine, 1985).

Some studies have reported a school culture that expects African-American students to be low achievers (Ogbu, 1991) and in which teachers do little to prevent low-income minority students from dropping out of school, as they might with white students (Fine, 1991). Anthropologist John Ogbu (1990) argues that African-American students often develop an attitude of little enthusiasm for school and low motivation for success as a reaction to their perceptions of the outside world. Because they feel that the deck is stacked against them for college, work, and success, Ogbu argues, they reject the idea that they should try to excel in school. Studies of African-American students who do well in school show the reverse of this process. Some high-achieving African-American students report that their success requires that they give up their identities as African Americans— members of a group—and adopt an attitude of individualism and "racelessness" (Fordham, 1988).

Other research stresses that predominantly African-American schools, even in inner-city neighborhoods, can create cultures of achievement and excellence in which students are prepared for success (Wilson-Sadberry, 1995). One of the problems facing such schools is the difficulty of recruiting young, bright, educated African-American teachers. Changes in the economy and in higher education in recent decades have provided African Americans with an expanded choice of careers, and teaching has become a less popular occupational choice for African-American college graduates (King, 1993).

Discouraged by the prospects for their children in urban public schools, middle-class and working-class African-American parents sometimes seek other educational alternatives. One popular choice is to enroll children in private schools, often Catholic schools in cities where they are available. Such parents frequently cite a lack of discipline and a perceived lack of commitment to a quality education as their reasons for rejecting the public schools (Jones-Wilson, Arnez, and Asbury, 1992). The reputation of urban private schools may exceed the reality, however. One large national study of African-American and Latino students in public and Catholic high schools showed that, when individual background factors (such as parents' income) were held constant, the students in the Catholic schools had achievement levels only slightly better than the students in the public schools (Keith and Page, 1985).

Another newer alternative to public schools is the independent African-American school. Some proponents argue that the creation of independent schools gives parents control over their children's education that is absent in public or other private schools (Bell, 1989). A number of these schools are experimenting with Afrocentric curricula, a philosophy based on the contributions of African civilizations to world civilization and the uniqueness of the African-American experience (Shujaa, 1992).

What can we expect for the future of education for African-American young people in urban areas? Over the past three decades, desegregation has proceeded unevenly, succeeding in some places but not in others. The areas of greatest progress are those in which the courts have been most aggressive at reversing deliberately segregated schools. In 1995, however, the Supreme Court ruled that some school districts will be allowed to terminate their desegregation plans. Thus, we are likely to see continued high levels of de facto school segregation in the large cities. But achieving integration is not the only way of improving education for African Americans, and the evidence is mixed on whether (and to what degree) going to school with whites improves the life chances of African-American students. The question left for us to weigh, then, is not whether school desegregation is possible, or whether it increases the achievement of African-American students, or whether it is the only avenue to increasing their quality of education. Even if we were to answer no to the above questions (which would by no means be justified by the evidence social scientists have gathered), we still need to weigh whether school desegregation may be an end in itself—a public commitment to decreasing racial isolation, indifference, and antagonism in our society.

We should not think of schools as the only factor affecting the intellectual and educational achievement of African-American children, moreover. Youngsters' economic levels, social supports, recreational opportunities, and work opportunities are also very important in shaping their development, from what they learn to how long they stay in school. Thus, real improvement in educational attainment for African-American young people is most likely to occur in the context of an overall improvement in opportunities within their communities (Haynes and Comer, 1990).

Housing Segregation

As should be obvious to even a casual observer, neighborhoods in the United States remain highly segregated by race. The extent of residential segregation has changed slightly over time, but the changes have been modest and the overall degree of segregation remains high.

Segregation of African Americans actually increased in cities in each of the decades between 1900 and 1960 (Taeuber and Taeuber, 1965). Since then, in each decade we have seen overall rates of segregation that either remained stable or declined modestly. In the thirty metropolitan areas with the largest African-American populations, the segregation index reported in the 1990 census was .665. This means that to even out the African-American and white population so that they would be in the same proportion in every neighborhood throughout the metropolitan area, 66.5 percent of the African Americans would have to move to another neighborhood. The figures for 1970 and 1980 were .753 and .683 respectively (Massey and Denton, 1993). Segregation levels are highest and the slowest to change in established, large metropolitan areas; they have decreased more rapidly in newer, growing cities of the South and Southwest (Squires, 1994; Farley and Frey, 1994).

Since 1970, we have seen an increase in the number of African Americans moving to suburban areas. Between 1970 and 1990 the proportion of African Americans living in the suburbs doubled, going from 16 percent to 32 percent, and it now stands at 35 percent (U.S. Census Bureau, 1996a, 2000e). The rate of suburbanization, however, is uneven. In the past decade, African Americans have been most likely to live in racially mixed suburban neighborhoods in a small number of relatively affluent communities, all constructed since 1980 (Marshall, 1994). Different regions of the country also have different rates of African-American suburbanization: in the South, 34 percent of African Americans live in the suburbs compared to 28 percent in the North and West (U.S. Census Bureau, 1996a).

Living in a suburban community does not always lead to racial integration for African-American residents. The available evidence indicates that suburbanization of African Americans often results in their resegregation within suburban towns. Since 1970, the traditional pattern of suburban settlement for African Americans has changed. Traditionally, they tended to be concentrated in semi-rural enclaves or in segregated communities in older industrial towns. The new pattern of settlement is more varied. Some African-American suburbanization consists of central city neighborhoods simply spilling over into the inner ring of older suburbs. In other cases, particular sections (often older, less desirable ones) of the suburbs are undergoing racial change and being converted into predominantly African-American communities, experiencing problems similar to those of inner-city ghetto areas (Keating, 1994). About the only exception to these patterns may be among the most affluent African Americans, who do seem to be achieving a more dispersed pattern of residence in predominantly white areas.

What accounts for this continued pattern of residential segregation by race? Many whites believe, erroneously, that a large majority of African Americans prefer to live in separate neighborhoods. Surveys of urban African Americans consistently indicate that an overwhelming majority would prefer to live in racially mixed neighborhoods (Bobo and Zubrinsky, 1996). In addition to desiring integration itself, many African Americans want to obtain housing and services better than those available in predominantly African-American areas. Regardless of income level, African Americans obtain housing which is of lower quality than that obtained by whites at similar income levels and pay as much or more for that housing (Yinger, 1995). It is no wonder, then, that African-American residents express higher levels of dissatisfaction with their neighborhoods than do whites in the same metropolitan areas (Darden, 1987).

If segregation cannot be explained by African Americans' preferences, neither can it be explained by economic factors. African Americans are not concentrated in the central cities simply because they cannot afford housing in the suburbs. In city after city, studies have shown that if families bought or rented their housing solely on the basis of their incomes, racial segregation would decline dramatically. In our large metropolitan areas, only a fraction of the middle-class African Americans who can afford to live in the suburbs actually live there, and only a tiny fraction of poor whites have poor blacks as neighbors (Massey and Denton, 1993). In fact, it is one of the sad ironies of urban housing markets that, for a given level of housing quality, African-American families usually pay higher prices than white families living in comparable housing.

What then accounts for the continuation of residential segregation? The overwhelming weight of sociological opinion is that widespread, systematic (though covert and subtle) racial discrimination in housing continues to occur in the United States. It may be illegal, but literally millions of whites are finding ways to get around the antidiscrimination laws. On the face of it, this may seem a curious conclusion given what is known about the change in white racial attitudes. In the last few decades, most surveys have indicated that acceptance of the basic principles of integration, equal opportunity, and racial justice has increased steadily. In surveys, a large majority of whites state support for the principle of equal housing opportunity for African Americans (Farley and Frey, 1994). But simply agreeing with the principle of integration is not enough to prevent discriminatory behavior in regard to housing.

Housing discrimination rests on a complex of beliefs, perceptions, and preferences (see figure 4.1). The white middle class has a strong preference for neighborhoods in which people like themselves predominate. The problem is that whites often regard African Americans as people very different from themselves. They stereotype African Americans as poor and as having different character traits and cultural traditions. Many whites believe that the entry of African Americans into a white neighborhood will bring higher crime rates and lower property values. Many whites also believe that the movement of a small number of African Americans into a neighborhood guarantees that the neighborhood will become predominantly African American very soon thereafter (Farley et al., 1994).

A good deal of evidence shows that these beliefs are unfounded, or at best half-truths. African-American residents moving into predominantly white neighborhoods are similar in most social characteristics (education, occupation, income, family type) to their white neighbors. In addition, several studies show that there is no predictable relationship between racial change and property values in neighborhoods. Sometimes property values decline, but they are just as likely to increase (Yinger, 1987). There is also no evidence that integrated neighborhoods will inevitably become all African American (Saltman, 1989). Sometimes these beliefs, however, can act as self-fulfilling prophecies, actually producing the feared outcome. If large numbers of people put their houses on the market at the same time, the prices are likely to decline; if whites flee from a neighborhood, it is likely to become increasingly populated by African Americans, and so on. Thus, an underlying white uneasiness about changing neighborhoods (even when not expressed openly as racial prejudice) can be a powerful force affecting where people of different races live.

The result, despite laws to the contrary, is that whites have contrived a number of ways of maintaining segregation through discriminatory practices. Documenting these practices is difficult because they are informal and secretive to avoid the possibility of legal prosecution. Yet, they quite clearly occur. Thus, in most large cities, a *dual housing market* exists: a situation in which African-American and white home seekers have very different choices for housing available to them. Let us examine three examples of mechanisms by which this situation perpetuates itself.

One widely reported practice is that of "steering" prospective customers by real estate agents. Real estate agents in some cities make it a practice to encourage African Americans to look at housing in neighborhoods with an established or growing minority population (Yinger, 1995). The techniques range from subtle (e.g., only mentioning houses in particular neighborhoods) to not so subtle (e.g., missing appointments with African-American customers or telling them that a particular house listed for sale has just been sold). Similarly, the agents assume whites will not be interested in housing in integrated neighborhoods and act accordingly. Although the practice of racial steering is illegal, real estate agents often act as the gatekeepers who channel people into the "proper" areas.

In many urban neighborhoods, especially tightly knit, white, working-class neighborhoods, the market for housing is handled informally. Homes for sale are not routinely listed with realtors, and rentals are normally not advertised in the newspaper or other public outlets. Instead, neighbors and family members circulate word of vacant apartments or of people who are looking to buy homes. In such neighborhoods, the informal social networks establish rules about who belongs and act as a screen to keep family and friends in the neighborhood while screening out outsiders (DeSena, 1994).

More blatant and uglier is the very real threat to African Americans of white violence if they do manage to surmount discriminatory barriers and move into a white neighborhood. Violent episodes such as vandalism and arson create real fear among African Americans and may make them feel as if they will be targets of hateful acts (Logan, 1988). Research in Detroit indicates that although African Americans overwhelmingly preferred to live in integrated neighborhoods, most were reluctant to be the first African-American family to integrate an all-white neighborhood (Farley et al., 1993).

Besides practices that serve to keep African Americans out of white neighborhoods, segregation continues because whites tend to leave central city neighborhoods into which African Americans have moved. There is some debate as to the reasons for this phenomenon.

Some observers emphasize that the resegregation of neighborhoods once African Americans move in is the result of white flight fueled by fear. They argue that the entrance of African-American residents, beyond a certain proportion, sets off fear of neighborhood deterioration among whites, who then decide to leave in large numbers. In some cases, this white flight is hastened by real estate speculators manipulating residents' fears to increase sales activity. This illegal practice consists of systematically canvassing neighborhoods in which a few African-American families live and informing the white residents that their neighborhood is "changing" and the property values are about to fall dramatically. The speculator offers to pay cash for their homes if they will sell immediately at a price under normal market values. In a panic, the whites sell out. The speculator then turns around and sells to African-American families at inflated prices, making a large profit.

Other observers de-emphasize the role of white flight in racially changing neighborhoods. They argue that resegregation is not so much a matter of racially motivated flight from a neighborhood as it is a failure of whites to move into a changing neighborhood. As housing units become vacant in the normal course of events (such as a family

Figure 4.1
Major Causes of Residential Segregation

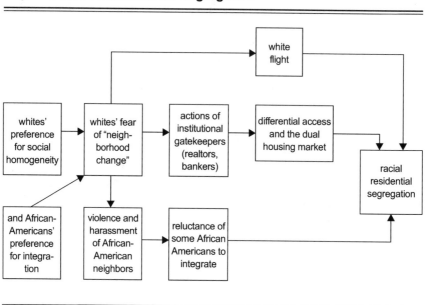

growing and moving) only African Americans move into the neighbor-hood. Farley and his associates (1978, 1993) traced changes in whites' attitudes about the conditions under which they would move out of or into a racially mixed neighborhood. They found that since the 1970s, the proportion of whites who said they would move out of a mixed neighborhood did not change but that the proportion who said they would be willing to move into one increased modestly.

To summarize: the single most important reason for the degree of segregation that exists in the urban housing market remains discrimina-tory practices and white behavior because a significant proportion of the white population rejects the prospect of having African-American neigh-bors (Bobo and Zubrinsky, 1996). If the trends of the 1990s continue, African Americans will make increased progress on two dimensions of housing: improving the quality of their housing relative to whites and modestly increasing overall integration, especially in newer suburbs. If present trends continue, however, our largest cities will remain highly segregated and may even become more segregated in the future.

THE NEW IMMIGRANT GROUPS

Immigration to the United States from abroad has been on the rise in recent decades. The number of immigrants legally accepted into the country each year is governed by law. In the past, large waves of immigrants arrived during the 1870s and 1880s and again from 1900 to 1920. Then Congress placed severe restrictions on immigration, and for about forty years, the number of newcomers slowed to a trickle. Since 1965, a series of laws have permitted increased numbers of immigrants to enter the country, with special categories for skilled workers, political refugees, and foreign citizens seeking to join family members already living in the United States.

By 1997, the United States was home to more than 25 million immigrants (U.S. Census Bureau, 1999a). Because of changes in U.S. immigration laws and economic or political conditions in other areas of the world, hundreds of thousands of immigrants have arrived since 1965, especially from Asia and Latin America. They have, to a great extent, settled in the largest metropolitan areas of the United States. The city with the highest proportion of recent immigrants is Los Angeles, which has been called "the new Ellis Island," but sizable numbers of newcomers have arrived in most large cities (Portes and Rumbaut, 1996).

The region of the world from which the United States receives the largest group of immigrants is Latin America, especially Mexico, Central America, the Dominican Republic, and Cuba. (Puerto Ricans are not immigrants since Puerto Rico is legally part of the United States.) They, along with smaller numbers from South America, the Caribbean, and Spain, are counted together in the census as Hispanic, although they more commonly refer to themselves as Latino. Together they constitute the fastest growing ethnic group in the population (U.S. Census Bureau, 2000c). As a group, the socioeconomic status of Latinos, based on such measures as income and rate of unemployment, is slightly higher than that of African Americans but still well below that of whites.

Latino immigrants' settlement patterns vary depending on their country of origin. While Cubans tend to be concentrated in suburban areas, Puerto Ricans are mainly central city dwellers and Mexicans are found predominantly in rural areas. The regions of residence also vary greatly, with Cubans located disproportionately in the South and Mexicans in the Southwest. Puerto Ricans are the most segregated from whites and have the lowest socioeconomic status of all of the Latino groups (Woolbright and Hartmann, 1987).

Immigration from Asia to the United States was a minor part of total immigration until about 1970. Until that time, 90 percent of all immigrants from Asia came from one of three countries: China, Japan, or the Philippines. But Asian immigration accelerated in the aftermath of the Vietnam War. Between 1980 and 1990, the Asian-American population doubled, and it is expected to double again by 2010 (Lee, 1998). Because of political changes in Asia, significant numbers of people, some of them refugees, chose to migrate to the United States from Vietnam, Laos, and Cambodia. In addition, economic changes in Asia drew many educated or wealthy immigrants from India, Korea, Taiwan, and Hong Kong to the United States. Thus, the Asian-American population is becoming not only larger but also more diverse. Only about half of Asian-Americans now have Chinese, Japanese, or Filipino origins.

Like the Latino groups, the Asian groups from different nations vary in their socioeconomic status, degree of segregation, and region of settlement. The Chinese are the most highly urbanized with a large proportion living in New York City, while more than half of Korean immigrants live in suburban areas. As a group, Asian immigrants have disproportionately settled in the western United States, but while 80 percent of the Japanese are located in that region, fewer than half of the Koreans and Vietnamese are living in the West (Woolbright and Hartmann, 1987).

Despite the increase in immigration and its impact on large cities, there is little evidence that the United States is becoming a true "melting pot." Studies of the destinations and residential patterns of immigrants show that immigrants live in highly clustered groups, most within only ten metropolitan areas of the United States. This clustering is particularly apparent in the Latino and Asian groups. One-fifth of all Latinos in the United States live in the Los Angeles metropolitan area, for example, while 58 percent of all Latinos live in the ten metro areas, including Miami, New York, and Chicago. More than two-fifths of all Asian Americans live in three metro areas: Los Angeles, New York, and San Francisco. Although several smaller metropolitan areas have also experienced an influx of immigrants (for example, Las Vegas, Houston, Seattle, and Washington, D.C.), there is little dispersal of the new immigrant groups into other areas of the country (Frey, 1998).

One interesting and perplexing phenomenon sociologists have explored is the apparently greater success some of the new immigrants have achieved in the United States compared to that of African Americans. Although there are significant internal variations, as a group both Latino and Asian immigrants have more rapidly dispersed into white areas and have achieved a higher standard of living relative to whites than African Americans (who have been here much longer) have been able to achieve. This is partly the result of lower (although still significant) levels of housing and job discrimination against Latinos and Asians. Several other factors, however, have been identified as contributing to their higher success rate.

For one thing, certain countries' immigrants have been drawn from the most educated, skilled, and wealthy segments of the native population. Most Cubans who left immediately after the revolution in 1959, and Vietnamese who left during the revolution in the early 1970s fall into this category. When they arrived, even without a knowledge of English, they had the education and financial resources to establish themselves in the middle class (although many could not obtain as high a level of occupation as they had had in their native country).

A second factor in their favor has been the tendency to form *ethnic enclaves,* ethnically homogeneous neighborhoods in which housing, businesses, and all economic activity can be dominated by a single ethnic group (Logan, Alba, and McNulty, 1996). Groups such as the Chinese and Koreans have been very successful at establishing businesses run by and for members of the ethnic group. This not only provides jobs to the group's members, it also circulates members' money within the ethnic community rather than paying it to outsiders. New immigrants have frequently used strong family and kinship networks for economic advantages such as borrowing money at low interest rates, hiring free (or low-paid) workers, getting free child care, and living in groups to save on rent (Kasarda, 1989). Finally, many recent immigrants come from ethnic groups in which attitudes of extreme frugality and even self-exploitation are common. Almost no sacrifice of self or family members is too great when the goal is entrepreneurial success (Zhou, 1992). This range of ethnic-based strategies has either not been available to most African Americans or has not been applied consistently enough to enable them to move ahead economically as rapidly as the new immigrants.

Immigrants have historically been a source of controversy among people who were born in the United States. During the nineteenth and early twentieth centuries, anti-immigrant movements were common, and anti-immigrant agitation prompted the laws that curtailed the flow of newcomers in the 1920s. Although many native-born citizens recognize the contributions that immigrants make to the culture and the economy of the nation, they can often be suspicious because the newcomers seem so different. Especially in times of economic stress, natives can perceive newcomers as competitors for jobs, housing, and public services. This general suspicion of difference can lead to full-fledged *xenophobia,* or fear of foreigners. In the past three decades, the differences between natives and newcomers have become more visible, in part because of the frequently darker skin color of the immigrants from Asia and Latin America, compared with the previous European immigrants.

The large increase in immigration since 1965 has, perhaps predictably, caused a backlash socially and politically in some regions of the country where large numbers of newcomers have settled. Opponents of immigration charge that immigrants abuse welfare programs, evade taxes, and refuse to learn English. In 1994, California voters approved a ballot measure called Proposition 187, which targets illegal immigrants. If enforced, it will make illegal immigrants ineligible for any public services, including schools, and will require public employees, including teachers, to turn in any illegal immigrants to the immigration authorities. In 1996, the welfare reform legislation passed by Congress made legal immigrants ineligible for benefits under most welfare programs. These measures are likely just the beginning of a more concerted effort to restrict immigration.

Is the view that immigrants are a drain on public and private resources justified? Social scientists who study the impact of immigration report that immigrants have a higher rate of employment and a lower use of public assistance than do nonimmigrant citizens. Immigrants who entered the United States between 1970 and 1992 paid some $25 to $30 billion more in taxes than they used in all public services, including public schools (Passel, 1994). Overall, the larger the immigrant group, the more jobs they create, largely through the types of entrepreneurial activities mentioned earlier. Furthermore, immigrants often take jobs that native-born workers avoid. Some economists argue that without immigration, certain sectors of the economy would suffer from severe labor shortages (Muller, 1993).

What should we expect for the future? Past waves of immigrants clustered initially in selected urban neighborhoods, then gradually dispersed in subsequent generations. The dense clustering of immigrant settlements we see in contemporary North American cities is likely to continue as long as the incoming stream of immigrants remains sizable. If the opponents of immigration succeed in drastically curtailing that stream as they did in the 1920s, it is likely that current immigrants will slowly disperse.

Regardless of the level of immigration, the general trend will probably be much as it has been with past immigrant groups: a tendency to adapt to life in the United States. Ungar (1995), for example, shows that the current wave of immigrants is very similar to the newcomers who arrived from 1880 to 1920. Both groups aspire to work, save, and succeed economically. With time, the culture of each immigrant community takes on more characteristics of the mainstream American culture.

MAIN POINTS

1. The official count of poverty probably understates the true number of poor people.
2. Poverty can result not only from the lack of work but also from employment at jobs that do not pay adequate wages.
3. Although most urban dwellers are not poor, there is an increasing tendency for poor people to be found living in neighborhoods where the majority of the population is poor. This is especially true for poor African Americans.
4. There are two sociological approaches to explaining poverty. The structural approach stresses the ways in which jobs and

income are channeled by social institutions. The cultural approach stresses the ways in which individuals learn behaviors that contribute to making or keeping them poor. Each of the approaches has different implications for reducing the amount of poverty.

5. Racial inequality continues to be a serious problem in U.S. cities. Although the educational achievement of African Americans is approaching that of whites, their income levels remain substantially lower than those of whites.

6. The African-American population, like the white population, is experiencing increased income polarization into wealthier and poorer segments.

7. Many public schools that were desegregated in the 1960s and 1970s have become resegregated. Smaller school districts and those systems that merge city and suburban schools have the best records regarding school desegregation.

8. Residential segregation by race is still very pronounced in U.S. cities. African Americans and whites do not have access to the same housing; rather, a dual housing market operates in most metropolitan areas.

9. Housing segregation cannot be explained mainly by racial differences in income nor by African Americans' preference for living with other African Americans. Any explanation must include racially motivated preferences and choices of whites.

10. Immigration into the United States, especially from Latin America and Asia, is having an important impact on our cities, since most new immigrants are settling in urban areas.

KEY TERMS

Culture of Poverty A theory that claims the behavior of the poor is the result of socialization to different values than those of middle-class people.

De facto Segregation Racial segregation that results from the decisions people make about where to live, where to send their children to school, and so on.

De jure Segregation Racial segregation that is created by law, such as separate schools, restrooms, and so on.

Dual Housing Market The situation in which whites and African Americans have substantially different housing choices available to them solely due to race.

Ethnic Enclaves Neighborhoods in which a single ethnic group controls most housing and businesses.

Hyperghettos   Minority neighborhoods whose high degree of racial segregation is accompanied by extreme poverty.

Informal Sector   Jobs that are either illegal or unreported to authorities, also called the "underground economy."

Magnet Schools   A type of voluntary desegregation program that encourages students to attend schools they might not otherwise attend based on their race or neighborhood.

Official Poverty Line   The most commonly used estimate of the amount of income necessary to escape poverty. It is generally considered a low estimate.

Polarization of Income   The increasing gap between the rich and the poor.

Structural Approach to Poverty   This theory holds that poverty is the result of the unequal distribution of resources and opportunities within the social structure.

Working Poor   That subgroup of the poor who work full-time but at wages too low to put them over the poverty line.

Xenophobia   Fear of foreigners.

SUGGESTED READING

Duneier, Mitchell. 1992. *Slim's Table.* Chicago: University of Chicago Press. An ethnographic study of working-class African Americans in the city.

Edin, Kathryn, and Laura Lein. 1997. *Making Ends Meet: How Single Mothers Survive Welfare and Low-Wage Work.* New York: Russell Sage Foundation. An inside look at how poor women combine work and welfare to meet the economic needs of their families.

MacLeod, Jay. 1995. *Ain't No Makin' It.* Boulder, CO: Westview Press. An ethnographic study of two groups of poor teenagers in an inner-city neighborhood.

Portes, Alejandro, and Ruben Rumbaut. 1996. *Immigrant America: A Portrait.* 2nd ed. Berkeley: University of California Press. An overview of the causes and consequences of immigration.

Squires, Gregory. 1994. *Capital and Communities in Black and White.* Albany: State University of New York Press. A study of the impact of economic changes on African-American and white communities in the United States.

5

Housing and Urban Decay

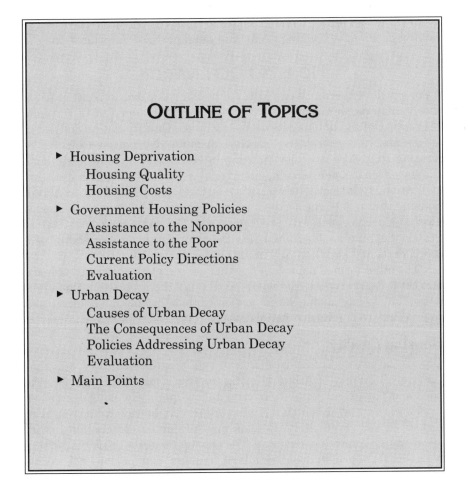

OUTLINE OF TOPICS

- Housing Deprivation
  - Housing Quality
  - Housing Costs
- Government Housing Policies
  - Assistance to the Nonpoor
  - Assistance to the Poor
  - Current Policy Directions
  - Evaluation
- Urban Decay
  - Causes of Urban Decay
  - The Consequences of Urban Decay
  - Policies Addressing Urban Decay
  - Evaluation
- Main Points

Housing represents one of the largest expenditures in the average family's budget. It is normally the largest purchase ordinary people make and constitutes their most important asset. It is also a basic material necessity. Weather-tight, physically safe, sanitary, and affordable housing is something everyone needs. At the same time, the housing people can afford in terms of its comfort, convenience, and aesthetic qualities is a major determinant of a family's standard of living and quality of life. Additionally, housing is an important social symbol that reflects social rank and prestige. As a consequence, the condition, cost, and availability of housing is both a critical concern to individuals and a major indication of material well-being in society. To be deprived of adequate housing is a major form of deprivation and disadvantage.

Our discussion here will be limited to two major problems that urban areas face in regard to housing. Our first concern will be the nature and extent of housing deprivation. We will then turn to the related problem of housing decay and neighborhood deterioration.

HOUSING DEPRIVATION

A person can experience two kinds of housing deprivation, either separately or in combination. First, a person can be deprived in terms of the quality of the housing he or she occupies. Quality can be defined in either absolute or relative terms. Absolute deprivation consists of housing that does not meet minimum standards in relation to such things as space per person, structural soundness, cleanliness, and sanitation. Relative deprivation consists of not being able to obtain housing that meets one's expectations in terms of lifestyle preferences, aesthetic preferences, and prestige needs. For example, in the United States the middle-class ideal has traditionally been ownership of a large, detached single-family home on a spacious lot.

The other form of deprivation is that caused by the high cost of housing. Such deprivation exists when people find themselves with no alternative but to pay such a large portion of their income for housing that their ability to purchase other necessary items is substantially impaired.

Housing Quality

One of the great accomplishments of the twentieth century was that the overall quality of urban housing improved markedly and the proportion of the urban population living in low-quality housing decreased.

Precisely how much things have improved, however, has not been measured very accurately. Census measurements of housing quality are unreliable and inconsistent. The census makes a basic distinction between standard and substandard housing, but defines the terms inconsistently. In different censuses, substandard has meant some combination of the following: absence of a complete kitchen, absence of a complete bathroom, absence of central heating, presence of peeling paint, presence of noticeable cracks, and crowded conditions (in excess of one person per room). As a result, census reports on housing may understate the amount of substandard housing and certainly make comparisons over time difficult. Since 1974, the federal government has conducted an annual or biennial *American Housing Survey* which contains more detailed and consistent data on housing conditions.

The available evidence points toward general improvement in housing quality over the long term. For example, in 1973, 6 percent of all families were living in crowded housing (defined as more than one person per room). Only 3 percent of these families lived in crowded housing by 1996 (U.S. Census Bureau, 1996c). Similarly, the quality of new homes (defined by size, number of bathrooms, attached garages, central air conditioning, and the like) has steadily increased from the 1940s onward. Also, the proportion of people living in homes they own has increased. In 1940, less than half of households (44 percent) owned their own homes, but by 1999, two-thirds (67 percent) of all households were homeowners (U.S. Department of Housing and Urban Development, 2000). Overall, urban areas have seen a major decline in grossly inadequate housing and significant increases in the quality of housing occupied.

This general increase in housing quality does not mean that the problem of inadequate housing has been solved. Progress toward eliminating substandard housing has slowed in recent years. In its 1999 *American Housing Survey,* the U.S. Census Bureau found that almost seven million families were living in inadequate housing. These households lived in homes or apartments with major structural problems, such as the lack of a complete kitchen, holes in the roof or foundation, or inadequate plumbing, heating, or electrical systems. A further problem with unsound housing in urban areas is that it tends to be highly concentrated geographically, with some low-income inner-city neighborhoods plagued by both abandoned housing and occupied but substandard housing. Housing quality also varies depending on the population group to which the household belongs. While homeowners enjoy better than average quality, renters suffer from worse than average housing quality. Those groups with the least adequate housing are low-income renters, African Americans, and Latinos (Gilderbloom and Applebaum, 1988).

Federal policies that have been developed to deal with inadequate housing have primarily addressed the problem by removing inadequate units from the housing stock. Beginning with programs in the 1930s to build public housing, legislation required the demolition of one substandard housing unit (single-family house or apartment) for every new subsidized housing unit built. Later in the 1950s and 1960s, slum clearance became a major urban policy goal, and cities used federal funds to demolish a good deal of deteriorated housing.

While this type of policy was effective in decreasing the number of substandard housing units, it was not necessarily effective in replacing them with low-cost, adequate housing. So some of the statistical improvement in the housing stock has been due to an overall reduction in the supply of low-cost housing.

Zoning and Housing Quality

One of the hidden factors complicating the issue of housing quality in urban areas is the role of suburban zoning ordinances in distributing different types of housing. In most metropolitan areas, at least some suburban communities practice *exclusionary zoning*. By requiring builders to use a sizable housing lot (often a half acre), large square footage plans for new homes, and sometimes even particular building materials, existing residents ensure that only the well-to-do can afford to move in. Some areas institute outright bans on certain types of housing: mobile homes, attached single-family dwellings (e.g., townhouses), or apartment houses. The result is that these towns literally become exclusive—that is, they exclude those families whose incomes do not allow them to live in their upscale type of housing. As a result, in most metropolitan areas, low-cost housing is highly concentrated in the central cities. This concentration limits the kinds of neighborhoods from which low-income households may select their housing and narrows the choice of neighborhood amenities such as schools, shopping, and recreational facilities that are attached to the housing decision.

As a response to the lack of available housing, several states have attempted to limit exclusionary zoning and to encourage or require communities to allow low-cost housing to be built within their boundaries. In New Jersey, for example, a state supreme court decision (called Mount Laurel II after the community that was charged with practicing exclusionary zoning) required that all towns develop plans to construct low-cost housing. Each suburb must take its "fair share" of units based on the size of the town and the amount of buildable land available. The mechanism used in New Jersey, as well as in California and other areas, to achieve the integration of low-cost units into suburban areas is called, appropriately enough, *inclusionary zoning*. By this mechanism, new housing developments must include a certain proportion of low-cost units in order to be approved for construction. If developers want to build, for example, fifty houses, about ten of them (usually 20 percent of the total) must be priced for low- and moderate-income families. Inclusionary zoning has had modest successes in New Jersey and has provided a model for several other states (Mallach, 1988).

The significance of this legal change is that it increases housing choices for many families and allows access to the suburbs for many who were formerly priced out of those areas. Eliminating exclusionary zoning is hardly a panacea for housing quality problems, however. Not

everyone wants to or can move to the suburbs, and even if more households do move out of the central cities, attention must be given to
increasing the quality of deteriorated housing for those who remain.

Housing Costs

Past gains in housing quality were the result of two long-term trends.
The first trend was toward steady increases in average real purchasing power in the general population. One of the major things people
did with this rising purchasing power was to upgrade the quality of
their housing. The second trend, reinforcing the first, was that the cost
of new housing increased at a slower rate than average income from
1945 until 1965 (Stone, 1986).

Since 1965, however, these trends have reversed. Real purchasing
power has not increased, and the cost of housing has risen more rapidly than income. The result has been a growing problem of cost deprivation in housing, in which more and more people either cannot afford
the kind of housing to which they have become accustomed or must
devote a large share of their income to housing. Thus, analysts have
now come to the conclusion that the main housing problem in the
United States today is not the overall supply of housing but the dwindling supply of affordable housing. In short, we have developed a
housing affordability crisis.

Affordability Crisis

Housing prices have increased rapidly in recent years. In 1970, the
median rent in the United States was $108. By 1999, it had risen to
$614 (U.S. Census Bureau, 2000f). Homeowners also saw housing costs
soar: the median sales price of new homes increased from $23,400 in
1970 to $138,000 in 1999 (Hughes, 1996; U.S. Census Bureau, 2000f).
But these average increases in housing prices mask the differences
among regional housing markets. Although housing prices in the middle of the country rose only modestly, those on the coasts soared during
the 1980s and 1990s. In 1994, the price of the average existing (not
new) house was $110,000 nationwide, but it was $146,700 in the West,
and $256,000 in the San Francisco metropolitan area (Hughes, 1996).
By the summer of 2000, the price of a single-family home had risen to
$370,000 in the Bay Area, preserving San Francisco's lead as the most
expensive metropolitan area for housing (Schevitz, 2000).

The increase in housing prices is so profound that it has changed
our very definition of reasonable housing costs. Until the mid-1970s,
economists and realtors used a guideline for rent or housing payments
of 25 percent of a household's income. Housing prices have risen so
much faster than incomes that the 25 percent rule has now been
raised to 30 percent. Even if we use this higher figure to define "reasonable" housing payments, however, we find that about a third of all

households are paying an excessive amount for their housing. Whether homeowners or renters, many of these people pay so much for housing that they are, in the terms of one economist, *shelter poor*. That is, although they are technically not poor, once they have paid their rent or made their mortgage payment, the remainder of their income is insufficient to meet their other needs (Stone, 1986).

Several factors caused the increase in housing prices beginning in the late 1970s. Land prices soared, especially in the West. Costs of material, labor, and financing (mortgage rates) also rose. The tremendous demand for housing created upward pressures on the price as the large baby-boom generation looked for housing. The rental housing market was caught in a particularly vicious circle. High financing and construction costs, changes in the tax law, and a lack of people able to pay the high rents necessary to make a profit from new units all made new construction less profitable. So fewer units were built. The resulting shortage of rental units drove rents up further. At the same time, people unable to purchase single-family houses turned to the option of purchasing condominium apartments (partly to escape rising rents). They made condo conversion profitable: landlords could make more money by selling their units to their tenants as condominiums than they could by renting them. This further tightened the supply of rental units and drove up the price. In some cities, the economic booms of the late 1980s and 1990s attracted new, highly paid workers who were willing to pay higher prices for housing, thus further driving up the costs in the market.

The overall impact of these changes in the housing market has been to produce an increase in the supply of higher priced housing and a decrease in the supply of lower priced housing. Thus, although housing units are being produced, they are not concentrated in the price range where most buyers or renters can afford them. Nationally, only 40 percent of all households can afford to buy an average priced home in their area, and only 10 percent of renter households can afford to buy an average priced home in their area (Dreier, 1997).

The housing affordability crisis has affected the middle class, but it has hurt low-income families the most. While the supply of low-cost units has been decreasing, the number of low-income families has been increasing. The result of these two trends is a growing gap between what low-income people can afford to pay for housing and what they must actually pay to keep a roof over their heads. This gap between incomes and housing costs affects not only people who aspire to buy a house but also people who simply cannot afford their rent. In 1997, according to the Department of Housing and Urban Development (2000), some 5.4 million poor families either paid more than half of their income for rent or lived in severely inadequate housing. This number represents an all-time high in HUD's "worst housing needs" category, and the number has been growing rapidly.

Some groups have fared better and others worse as housing prices have soared. Households headed by women supporting one or more dependents have had particularly rough going. Women heads of households are more likely to be renters and are more likely to be poor than male household heads or single adults. While many two-parent families have been able to keep up with housing prices by becoming two-earner households, single-parent families obviously do not have that option. Besides high housing costs, women often face discrimination which further limits their housing choices. Although technically illegal, it is common for landlords to reject women applicants, especially those with children (Pearce, 1990).

What does the future hold for housing costs and availability? Despite generally high housing costs, the economic prosperity and low interest rates of the 1990s helped many households buy their own homes. By 1999, rates of homeownership in both cities and suburbs had reached record highs (U.S. Department of HUD, 2000). But this achievement was accompanied by growing rates of shelter poverty and homelessness. The reason for the seeming contradiction is that very little housing is being produced for low-income households. Unless we see a reversal of the pattern of declining incomes compared to increasing housing costs, we will continue to experience the housing affordability crisis that has been growing for the past thirty-five years.

The Homeless

The most dramatic consequence of the housing affordability crisis has been the appearance of an increasingly large group of people without permanent homes. Although homelessness is a problem in rural and suburban areas, it is—like so many social problems—more concentrated and more visible in cities.

The most visible groups of the homeless, such as beggars and people with obvious psychiatric problems, have given many people a false impression of the nature and extent of homelessness. The homeless are a highly diverse group with many different specific paths by which they became homeless. What they all share, as Elliot Liebow (1993) has so eloquently pointed out, is low incomes. Some, approximately half, have a psychiatric problem or a drug or alcohol dependency that prevents them from functioning normally or working on a consistent basis. Others are perfectly normal, middle- or working-class people who have lost their housing due to a traumatic event: a house fire, a severe illness, a divorce, or loss of a job. A large and growing proportion (estimated at 35 to 40 percent) are mothers and children who either have been denied (or cut from) public assistance or whose incomes are too low to pay the high rents in urban areas. A rapidly growing group of homeless people are senior citizens who either do not have families to care for them or who cannot live with their children.

Homelessness is a relatively new problem, a new manifestation of poverty in our society. Although there have always been poor people, people who needed psychiatric help, and single mothers, these groups did not suffer from homelessness in large numbers until the mid-1970s. Economic trends during the past thirty years, and particularly the virtual disappearance of the cheapest types of housing, have precipitated the large-scale homelessness we see today. The rising housing prices that have affected all segments of the population have literally driven out many low-income households, as landlords have been able to charge higher rents. Some alternative types of housing, like the old single-room-occupancy hotels (SROs) that formerly housed many single, elderly people, have been demolished or converted to luxury apartments as some downtown neighborhoods have become gentrified. An additional factor leading to increased homelessness has been the deinstitutionalization of large numbers of psychiatric patients without adequate supervision to ensure their reintegration into community life. Thus, a number of independent factors—higher housing costs, stagnating incomes, increasingly stringent welfare programs, housing demolition, and psychiatric policy—converged in an unfortunate manner in the 1980s and 1990s to produce increasing homelessness (Timmer, Eitzen, and Tulley, 1994).

Policy responses to homelessness have been, by all accounts, inadequate. The federal government supplies some funding to cities through the McKinney program. These funds, first allocated in 1987 as an emergency food and shelter program, were expanded in the 1990s as a response to requests from local governments (Hays, 1995). Federal policy, however, has not been able to coordinate programs for the homeless, and local governments have approached the problem in wildly different ways. Some cities have passed ordinances to get rid of their homeless by preventing them from sleeping in public, begging, and scavenging in dumpsters, or even by giving them one-way bus tickets out of town. Others have provided temporary shelters but have kept the facilities stark and primitive so that they do not attract additional homeless from other areas. A few cities have established comprehensive policies ranging from alcohol and drug counseling to job placement to housing subsidies. Others have attempted to forestall people from becoming homeless by intervening to prevent them from being evicted from their housing when they are in financial difficulty.

Solving the problem of homelessness is a complicated business. No one solution or program will address homelessness adequately because homelessness has many different causes. First, at the minimum, we need policies to increase the availability of low-cost housing in cities. It is unreasonable to expect low-income people to be able to pay the standard two-months' rent as a down payment before moving into a private apartment, yet the supply of public housing has also decreased in recent years, as we will see shortly. An adequate supply of affordable housing provides a foundation for preventing homelessness.

A second policy component to solving the problem of homelessness is maintaining jobs and income for poor households. Too many people become homeless simply because they have no financial cushion to carry them through a spell of illness, the loss of a job, a fire, or other misfortune. A significant number of homeless people work but still cannot amass the savings needed to get into decent housing. As we saw in chapter 4, the stagnation of wages and the decrease in stable, well-paid blue-collar jobs have caused income polarization and pushed additional people into poverty, as have the policies of cutting welfare benefits and removing people from the welfare rolls. Because low incomes put people at risk for homelessness, if the incomes of the people at the bottom are raised—even slightly—the ranks of the potentially homeless will be thinned.

The third policy direction for dealing with homelessness is to provide adequate services to individuals with personal or household problems such as substance abuse, psychiatric disorders, and domestic violence. Simply providing housing for people is not sufficient if they lack the life skills to be able to live independently. They may need counseling, job training, medical attention, child care, and other support services. In previous generations, our society dealt with problem individuals by institutionalizing them for long periods of time. Few present-day experts advocate a return to long-term institutionalization as an effective response to the problems of troubled individuals. Instead, many advocate community-based treatment with adequate professional care that allows individuals both to receive the treatment they need and to live in as normal a setting as possible (Dear and Wolch, 1987).

Currently, the burden of providing for the needs of homeless people falls mainly on local governments and on nonprofit organizations such as churches. These groups do their best to provide temporary shelter, food, and perhaps clothing to homeless individuals. Unless our society adopts a more comprehensive approach to homelessness, however, we will continue to treat symptoms without addressing the causes of the problem: poverty, available housing, and social service needs.

GOVERNMENT HOUSING POLICIES

Over the last sixty years, the federal government has attempted to reduce housing deprivation through a number of different programs. One set of programs was designed to help more affluent working- and middle-class families purchase single-family houses. Another set of programs attempted to reduce the absolute housing deprivation of the poor (and, thereby, eliminate slum housing).

Assistance to the Nonpoor

Since the 1930s, the federal government has provided major assistance to those seeking to buy housing. Most of these subsidies have gone to relatively affluent home buyers.

The single most expensive housing program is the *homeowner's tax deduction,* an income-tax deduction allowed for the cost of interest on a mortgage, combined with deductions for state and local property taxes. Currently, the cost to the federal government in lost taxes is about $60 billion per year. (That compares to $10 billion spent on housing subsidies for the poor.) The more affluent a person is, the larger the total amount of the subsidy. Of households earning $100,000 or more, 80 percent receive a deduction, which averages $4,500, but of households earning between $30,000 and $50,000, only 25 percent receive the deduction, and the average amount is less than $1,000 (Dreier and Atlas, 1994). This is due partly to the fact that the more affluent tend to buy more expensive houses and thus pay more (deductible) mortgage interest than the less affluent. A second reason is that since the incomes of the affluent are taxed at a somewhat higher rate than those of the less affluent, the deductions represent a greater tax savings to people at higher income levels. The homeowners' tax deduction is much larger than other federal housing subsidies.

In addition to this subsidy, the other major subsidies to home buyers have been the *FHA* and *VA mortgage programs.* These programs primarily subsidized suburban housing construction and played a major role in suburbanization after 1945 (see chapter 1). Because the government insured the loans, private lending institutions were willing to provide relatively low-interest, low down payment mortgages to home buyers. Changes in the FHA program in the 1970s meant that some less affluent families in central cities began to participate in the program, but the bulk of the loans have continued to go to the nonpoor. Through FHA and other programs, the federal government also plays a major role in making sure that adequate funds for mortgages are available in the banking system.

Federal assistance to the nonpoor has been successful in promoting housing ownership. It played a central role in the post-1945 housing boom that created the suburbs and made possible an increase in home ownership. It generated a tremendous amount of housing. While its direct beneficiaries were the more affluent, its supporters argued that the middle class and poor would also benefit from these programs. As each well-to-do family moved into new housing, its former residence would become available to another (presumably less affluent) family, which would in turn vacate its former residence, and so on. Thus, a vacancy chain would be created by which housing of each higher income group would *filter* down to each lower income group. Critics such as Dreier and Atlas (1994) point out that these programs are an expensive and inefficient way of producing housing, as well as a boon to those who need help least. They argue that limiting the deduction (say, to $300,000 per family) could save billions of dollars in federal expenditures.

Assistance to the Poor

The set of programs designed for the poor has always had much more limited success. These programs have taken two major forms: the construction of *public housing* and the provision of housing subsidies to the poor. In recent years, housing programs for the poor have largely been coordinated through the Department of Housing and Urban Development (HUD).

From the 1930s through the 1960s the primary focus of federal programs to help the poor obtain decent housing was the construction of low-income public housing projects. Initially, this was a small program of low-rise projects built during the 1930s. They housed relatively few poor people, but met with modest success. Most of the people they housed were temporarily poor working-class people left unemployed in the Depression. In general, this early public housing was well maintained and did not have major problems of vandalism and crime.

This limited success was followed by the decision to construct large-scale public housing projects. Officials hoped to provide a significant amount of decent housing for the poor at a reasonable cost to the taxpayers. It soon became apparent, however, that these two goals were in conflict with each other.

The main problem was that Congress never provided sufficient funds to ensure the success of the program. This failure had many repercussions. While public housing construction was funded by the federal government, the operation of the buildings was left mainly to the cities and towns in which they were located. That meant that, like private landlords, the local housing authorities in charge of public housing projects had to take in enough in rents to cover their expenses such as utilities, maintenance, and administration. At the same time, however, changes in federal regulations (and in the private housing market) transformed the clientele living in public housing from the Depression-era temporary poor to the poorest of the poor. While operating expenses for public housing rose throughout the 1960s and 1970s, rents were nearly frozen due to the extremely low incomes of the residents and legal limitations on the percent of their income they were allowed to pay for rent. As federal operating subsidies fell farther and farther behind what was needed, many local housing authorities could not meet the necessary expenses for maintenance and security. These problem projects, usually located in very poor parts of larger cities, became not only eyesores but also dangerous to their inhabitants. (See Bratt, 1986, for a history of the public housing program.)

Funding problems were compounded by serious design failures. To keep costs down, public housing built during the 1960s tended to be clusters of high-density apartment blocks, separated by large open spaces. Designers gave little effective attention to creating structures that provided safe public space, adequate meeting and shopping areas, access to transportation and places of employment, and means for parents to keep an eye on their children. Political pressure also guaranteed that public housing reinforced racial segregation by being located in low-income, African-American neighborhoods. The most notorious example of the failure of this type of cheap, large-scale warehousing of the poor in public housing was St. Louis's Pruitt-Igoe project, which became so deteriorated and dangerous that it was demolished less than twenty years after it had been built (vonHoffman, 1996).

Another important problem of the large-scale public housing projects is that they have often been regarded as visible symbols of poverty for many of those who live in them. A certain address can immediately mark and stigmatize children in school, job-seeking adults, and social service clients as different and undesirable. These negative attitudes so common in the United States are largely absent in Europe, where public housing is more widespread, serves a broader cross-section of the population, and is better integrated into the community (Popenoe, 1985).

In fact, in the United States as well, many public housing projects are highly successful. The most popular and successful are those reserved for senior citizens, but some people do not know that these projects are part of the public housing program. Other successful types of projects are the small (under 100 units) developments that have comprised most of the public housing construction since 1980 and the *scattered site* developments in which individual units of public housing are located among the private housing units in residential neighborhoods. Many of the large superblock projects have recently been replaced or downsized to provide better living environments for the tenants. To a large extent, the bad reputation of public housing is undeserved. As one report stated, "Nobody likes public housing except the people who live there and those who want to get in" (Bratt, 1986:343).

In the 1970s, the federal government began to move away from building publicly owned and operated housing. Instead, it developed a number of programs encouraging private landlords to make additional apartments available for low-income households. One aspect of this strategy was a mortgage construction subsidy program through which housing developers received low-interest mortgages subsidized by HUD. In return, the developers agreed to rent to low-income households for a certain period of time (usually about 20 years). While these construction programs augmented the stock of low-cost housing, the units were only temporary additions to the low-cost inventory. As the time limits expired, and as market conditions changed, many landlords chose to convert their apartments from subsidized to market-rate units, raising rents to whatever the market would bear.

Another way in which the federal government reoriented its housing subsidy strategy was by providing rent subsidies to tenants seeking housing in the private market, so-called *rental assistance programs.* Under the Section 8 rental assistance program, landlords charge the prevailing market rate for apartments, while the low-income tenants pay a proportion of their income for rent (usually 30 percent), and the federal government makes up the difference. Direct rent subsidies are supposed to provide more flexibility for tenants and a cheaper, less bureaucratic alternative to public housing. Since both tenants and landlords have to apply to be accepted to Section 8, however, the program has its own bureaucratic problems. Moreover, since fair market rents have increased dramatically, the price of the subsidy has skyrocketed. Critics argue that in some areas, rent subsidies have actually contributed to pushing up rents since they have allowed landlords to charge low-income people higher rents than they would otherwise have been able to pay. In other areas, government-approved prevailing rent levels have not kept up with actual rents in recent years, discouraging landlords from entering the program.

The newest and currently fastest growing rental assistance program is rent vouchers. The program operates by providing a coupon or voucher to approved low-income households and allowing them to spend it on any rental unit they can find. Although voucher systems are less bureaucratic than Section 8 rental assistance, they tend to raise rents even more than Section 8 (Widrow, 1987). Probably the most significant problem with all forms of rental assistance, however, is that the amount of money the government allocates to them is so small that only one-tenth of the low-income renters who need assistance receive it (Dreier and Atlas, 1992).

Current Policy Directions

Since the 1970s, the federal government has instituted three profound changes in the direction of national housing policy: reducing government involvement and relying more on the private market to provide housing; relinquishing federal control of housing programs to states and cities; and emphasizing residential mobility as a way of solving housing problems.

The first policy change is reducing government intervention in the housing market. Probably the most significant aspect of this change was the decision to cut back the public housing program by not producing any new units and by selling existing units either to tenants or to private landlords. This took the federal government out of the business of producing housing. A related aspect of this change was raising the rents in subsidized units (public housing and Section 8). Initially, rents went up from 25 percent to 30 percent of tenants' incomes. Currently, with the voucher system, rents are not based on the renter's income but on the market value of the housing. In addition, Congress has repeatedly cut funding for housing assistance programs to low-income families. The overall impact of these changes has been greatly to reduce the role of the federal government in providing low-cost housing.

The second major policy change adopted by the federal government is relinquishing federal control of programs through the creation of *block grants*. Block grants are pools (or blocks) of money that states and cities receive for broadly defined purposes, for example education or community development. The *Community Development Block Grant program* has taken the place of individual funding for several specific housing programs. Thus, rather than the government setting up programs and providing the cities with money to implement them, the federal government provides money for community development but lets the local governments decide how to spend it. The advantage of block-grant funding is it gives the localities the flexibility to address problems in their own ways. The disadvantage is there is no guarantee that the local community will spend all or even most of the money to aid low-income residents or to provide housing.

Recently we have witnessed the third profound change in housing policy, namely an emphasis on residential mobility as a solution to housing problems. Critics of public housing have long argued that it concentrates too many of the poor within small geographic areas, thus creating significant "negative neighborhood effects" for the residents. They particularly point to problems of crime and poor schools (Newman and Schnare, 1993). To counteract the concentration of poverty, HUD developed a strategy of deconcentrating assisted housing. By placing low-income families outside of concentrated poverty neighborhoods, proponents argued, they could access better educational and employment opportunities. Hence the strategy's name: Moving to Opportunity (MTO). MTO is controversial because it is often used as a mechanism for racial desegregation as well as improving housing opportunity. Encouraging low-income public housing tenants to move to nonpoor neighborhoods often means encouraging African Americans to move from inner-city projects to racially mixed urban or suburban neighborhoods. Although this type of move can result in successful adaptations to the new neighborhood and neighbors, skeptics ask how many low-income African-American residents can be absorbed by middle-income, predominantly white neighborhoods before a backlash sets in (Rosenbaum, 1995).

The Housing Act of 1990 added two new initiatives that support and enhance the three main directions cited above. The first initiative is the HOPE program, which stands for Housing Opportunities for People Everywhere. This legislation supports homeownership for the poor in three ways: by allowing public housing tenants to purchase their apartments, by encouraging tenants in subsidized private housing (e.g., Section 8) to purchase their apartments, and by encouraging nonprofit housing providers to build housing to sell to low-income families. The second initiative is the Family Self Sufficiency program. This legislation aims to "wean" households from reliance on public housing (and other forms of public assistance) by providing social services to address the household's economic and social needs. Both of these programs take the point of view that what low-income households need is social mobility, not government assistance. The assumption behind them is that, ". . . the barriers to a decent, middle-class existence are primarily individual in nature, rather than built into the opportunity structure of the economy" (Hays, 1995: 259).

Over the past thirty years, the federal government has retreated from its earlier goal of providing low-cost housing to compete with the private market. As a result, nonprofit groups have increasingly taken on the role of housing developer. Local governments, community organizations, churches, and labor unions have formed or supported nonprofit corporations to produce subsidized housing, called nonprofit or *social housing*. While state and local governments may provide matching funds, other sources such as charitable foundations and individual contributions (of money, materials, and labor) form the basis of the funding. Some of these nonprofit corporations construct rental housing or rehabilitate older apartment houses for rental. Others produce single-family homes and sell them at low prices to low-income households. One of the most prominent national groups, Habitat for Humanity, relies largely on donated materials, volunteer labor, and the "sweat equity" of low-income people who work building houses to gain credit toward a home of their own. Although such volunteer-based programs do good work, their limited scope means that they can serve only a small fraction of the families in serious need of better housing.

Supporters of the nonprofit housing sector use the example of Canada—which has channeled government housing funds through nonprofit organizations for the past thirty years—as a model for the United States to follow. While Canada still has some housing problems, it has been able to produce more than 300,000 well-designed subsidized units that integrate lower- and middle-class residents, carry little social stigma, and cannot by law be sold to private owners or converted to condominiums. Canadian social housing complexes are also cheaper to operate than private apartment complexes because their tenants often manage them cooperatively and thus benefit from using their resources efficiently (Dreier and Hulchanski, 1993).

Evaluation

Government housing programs have without a doubt helped increase the amount of housing produced in the United States. In general, our housing standards are quite good and have improved steadily in recent decades. The chief problem with housing assistance, however, is that as a society we give the largest portion of our housing subsidy to the households who need it the least. Upper- and middle-income people benefit from having a homeowners' tax deduction, but they probably do not need this incentive to persuade them to buy homes. The federal tax deduction does help them buy more expensive homes, however, with other taxpayers making up for the taxes the affluent homeowners do not pay. If Congress eliminated or reduced this subsidy, it would have little impact on the housing quality of most citizens but would save billions of dollars.

The vastly smaller amount of funds that we allocate to the poor is more visible and more politically controversial. Take public housing, for example. Originally constructed to provide temporary housing for the unemployed, in many cities it was gradually transformed into permanent warehouses for the persistently poor. Because of public housing's bad reputation, the federal government is providing money for the demolition of selected public housing projects. Some residents, however, express skepticism that their homes, if demolished, will be replaced (Ritter, 1996). As public housing disappears, what else will take its place? Programs such as Moving to Opportunity, which disperse public housing residents to middle-income neighborhoods by giving them housing vouchers, have initially shown signs of success. As the number of participants in the program has grown, however, city residents often find that too few apartments in nonpoor neighborhoods are available to absorb the number of tenants needing housing (Popkin et al., 2000). In addition, the Section 8 and housing voucher programs are chronically underfunded, resulting in extremely lengthy waiting lists for assistance. The recent emphasis on encouraging homeownership for the poor sounds good but does not work for everyone. Many poor families simply have incomes too low to support the financial requirements of homeownership and would risk losing their homes if financial disaster in the form of an illness or layoff occurred.

Federal housing programs have encountered many problems, chiefly the lack of adequate funding and the opposition of the real estate industry. Despite these drawbacks, one fact is clear. If the government does nothing to provide more and better housing for low-income people, the supply of affordable housing will continue to shrink. The economics of the situation are clear: private developers and landlords prefer to invest in high-cost, high-profit housing units. Government programs literally help put a roof over the heads of many low-income people. It is disturbing to speculate on the consequences of a continuation of our current direction: generous subsidies for the well-to-do and free-market "solutions" for the poor. These can only deepen the inequalities in social class, push more people into bad housing or into the streets, and widen the growing gap between the housing "haves" and "have-nots."

URBAN DECAY

Urban residential decay is the process by which the physical condition of housing in a whole neighborhood or major section of a community deteriorates. Fundamentally, it is a reflection of two basic facts. First, urban areas are home to large numbers of poor people who cannot afford to spend very much for housing. Second, in a profit-oriented society such as ours, housing is produced (built, mortgaged, rented) only if it will make a profit for someone.

Even as the overall quality of housing in metropolitan areas has risen, the central cities (home for the poor and centers of low-rent housing) have experienced declines in the quality of their housing stock. They have been decaying. In a few of the worst hit cities, that decay has spread to a majority of the neighborhoods. All central cities, however, have experienced some decay in the last few decades. A number of factors have contributed to or accelerated that process.

Causes of Urban Decay

The age of the housing stock in the central cities makes central-city neighborhoods vulnerable to decay. Simple age, however, does not guarantee decay, as old housing is often structurally sound and repairable. Because most of the housing in our northern central cities was built prior to 1930, at the very least, it requires higher maintenance and heating costs than newer homes. Older structures also lack the amenities that became popular after 1945, such as large yards, garages, and multiple bathrooms. The older housing also is often multiple-family rental housing which has fallen out of favor in recent decades.

After World War II, the vast majority of the new housing being constructed was in the suburbs. The suburban exodus from the cities, which had begun in the 1920s, accelerated. Older urban housing gradually lost its appeal as middle-class housing, and less affluent families began to move in. Landlords could not charge as much rent to cover operating expenses, maintenance, and financing costs. Less affluent homeowners could afford to do less maintenance. Initial deterioration began.

The rate of deterioration, however, was much accelerated after 1945 by the in-migration of the rural poor. At the same time that the middle-class housing market was weakening in the cities, there was a tremendous demand for low-rent housing. The old slum neighborhoods could not accommodate the new wave of the poor. Thus, the stage was set for rapid conversion of neighborhoods for use by low-income families.

The process of urban decay is not a simple combination of an aging housing stock, market forces, and demographic trends. Several government policies have had the unintended effect of encouraging slum creation. As we saw in chapter 1, government housing and tax policies subsidized the middle-class movement to the suburbs, leaving a shortage of middle-class whites to buy housing in the central cities. Not only did the FHA mortgages encourage this suburban movement, until the mid-1960s it was virtually impossible to get an FHA mortgage for an existing property. This meant that the federal government's housing resources were highly concentrated in the suburbs, drawing not just people but also investment money out of the central cities. Federal highway construction and urban renewal destroyed substantial quantities of low-income housing, forcing the poor to move to new neighborhoods or into public housing. Because of the government's failure to provide sufficient low-cost housing, many of these displaced residents ended up in overcrowded or otherwise inadequate quarters.

Banks and other major lending institutions have also contributed to the decline of inner-city neighborhoods. Since the 1940s, banks have frequently *redlined* or disinvested in many central-city neighborhoods. This means that they seldom grant conventional mortgages to people seeking to purchase homes and rental properties in older neighborhoods. Redlining especially affects neighborhoods with a large proportion of nonwhite residents. In redlined neighborhoods, rather than borrowing from banks, people must borrow from lenders who require extraordinarily high interest, large down payments, and large monthly payments over a short period of time. In redlined areas, the reason that banks and other conventional lenders turn down loan applicants is not because of the borrowers' own credit-worthiness but because of the location of the property they wish to buy. The result is that average families and small investors virtually cannot purchase housing in many central-city neighborhoods.

Researchers are debating exactly how widespread the practice of disinvestment is. There is little doubt, however, that many inner-city neighborhoods simply are not granted mortgage loans by conventional lenders (Wyly and Holloway, 1999; Yinger, 1995). Such disinvestment is a prime cause of urban decay because lenders can cause a neighborhood to decline simply by predicting that it will decline and withdrawing vital resources from it. While government agencies such as the FHA theoretically should step in to provide financing in these neighborhoods, until recently they did not. The FHA's criteria for mortgage lending were for many years based on the same assumptions as those of the private banks. This further depressed the market for urban housing and also favored the involvement of real estate speculators (who had access to financing) in older central-city neighborhoods.

In a dramatic reversal, the FHA began to lend more or less indiscriminately in central cities during the early 1970s, with equally poor results. Unscrupulous developers made cosmetic repairs to many deteriorated homes, bribed FHA inspectors to approve the faulty construction, and sold the units with a government-guaranteed mortgage to unsuspecting low-income first-time home buyers. In a short time, when the structural flaws in the homes became apparent and the homeowners could not afford to repair the substantial problems, they simply abandoned the properties. The FHA, which had guaranteed the mortgages, was left owning these useless houses (Squires, 1994).

Destroying a neighborhood can be profitable to real estate speculators, at the expense of the existing residents of the neighborhood. One common strategy has been for high-income investors to use the purchase of old apartment buildings as a tax shelter. Investors buy old buildings cheaply on high interest, short-term mortgages. To cover the cost of the large mortgage payments they do almost no maintenance and subdivide the apartments to create more rental units, "milking" the buildings by running them down. Hence, the buildings generate enough money to pay the mortgages and, perhaps, even generate income for the owners. However, the real payoff for the owner has come from the Internal Revenue Service. For tax purposes, buildings are assumed to decline in value over time, an accounting device known as depreciation. The amount the buildings depreciate each year is counted as a business expense since the owners are, on paper, losing the value of their investments. Thus, even though the owners do not lose any cash income, they can subtract substantial paper losses from their taxable incomes. When the buildings are fully depreciated, they can still be sold for enough to cover the initial down payments. Thus, the investors do not lose any actual money but save substantial amounts of income tax. The buildings, neglected and overused, rapidly deteriorate. (Changes in the tax laws over the past twenty-five years have alternately made this type of tax write-off easier and more difficult for investors to claim.) Banks have also found these speculative practices profitable because of the high interest rate they charge speculators to take out mortgages on properties that they would not have lent on otherwise—that is, areas that were redlined for purposes of individual homeownership (Feagin, 1988a).

A final cause of urban decay, not found in all areas but very dramatic and devastating where it does occur, is the deliberate destruction of property through arson. When landlords are unable to make money on their buildings through the normal rental process, they may resort to burning them for the insurance money. Arson-for-profit frequently occurs in neighborhoods with high degrees of absentee ownership, abandoned buildings, housing code violations, and overdue property taxes, where owners are taking the final step with their slum properties. Other areas that may experience arson-for-profit are those undergoing gentrification. Here a fire serves the useful purposes of evacuating current (usually low-income) tenants and providing an insurance payment which can help finance renovation of the building for a more upscale clientele at higher rents. Arson is a serious problem in many large cities, displacing tens of thousands of residents and taking more than a thousand lives each year (Working Group on Housing, 1989).

The Consequences of Urban Decay

Quite obviously, urban decay results in the deterioration of large portions of the residential areas in the cities. It means that the poor continue to live in bad housing. However, that is not the whole story. Ultimately, urban decay results in the destruction of large numbers of housing units. The end process of urban decay in a neighborhood is usually abandonment.

Abandonment has reached epidemic proportions in our central cities. As a neighborhood runs down further and further, a number of things occur. The buildings deteriorate until they are barely habitable. Those who have any economic resources move to slightly less decayed neighborhoods in search of better housing. To attract any tenants at all, landlords have to decrease their rents. In turn, this leads the landlords to further decrease the level of maintenance and services. Unworkable plumbing, broken windows, collapsing stairs, unrepaired furnaces, lack of heating fuel, and broken wiring become more and more common in the buildings. Building owners drop any pretense of trying to pay their taxes to the city, and the city's service levels are often cut in response. The residents of the neighborhoods become almost exclusively the poorest of the poor. Vandalism, crime, juvenile gangs, and unsanitary conditions in the buildings and the streets make the neighborhood a nightmare in which to live. The stage is then set for abandonment.

When this stage of decay is reached, it is no longer possible to make a profit out of a slum rental property. Rents are too low and vacancy rates are too high, so that the costs of keeping the building open exceed what the owner can make from the rent. The building has been milked dry. At this point, many owners default on the mortgage and walk away from the building; they may even disappear through a scheme such as owning the building through a "dummy" corporation, which simply goes out of business with no assets left to seize. The city takes over ownership of the property because of the many years of back taxes owed on the building, boards it up, and schedules it for demolition at city expense. The buildings remain as burned-out or vandalized shells until the city can afford to bulldoze them. The city ends up the owner of acres of vacant rubble in a depopulated neighborhood.

This reduction in the number of housing units through abandonment has had two important results. It has contributed to the shortage of housing (especially rental housing) in our urban areas at a time of inadequate construction of new housing units and rapidly rising housing costs. (Many abandoned housing units were salvageable prior to reaching the final stages of decay.) At the same time, it has withdrawn from the tax rolls of our central cities significant numbers of formerly tax-producing properties. Thus, abandonment has contributed to tax-base erosion, which is part of the reason central-city governments face a continuing, serious financial crisis (see chapter 7).

Policies Addressing Urban Decay

The federal government began to address the problems of housing deterioration in the 1930s when Congress passed its initial public housing legislation. The emphasis of federal policy for the first thirty or more years was on eliminating deteriorated housing by demolishing it. This so-called "bulldozer approach" reached its peak in the urban renewal program administered by the federal government between 1949 and 1974.

Under the *urban renewal* program, cities were given federal money to identify slums, raze existing buildings, and prepare the land to be sold to private developers. Many older, northern cities such as Chicago, Boston, New Haven, Newark, Philadelphia, St. Louis, New York, Washington, Pittsburgh, and Detroit bought and demolished great tracts of property in the late 1950s and throughout the 1960s. Officials hoped that by cleaning out slum properties they would prevent blight from affecting sound neighborhoods and would attract developers to build new, more modern housing in the central cities. Despite legal restrictions, however, urban renewal land proved to be more valuable to developers as sites for nonhousing related uses and more valuable to city officials as space for central business district growth. Thus, much of the low-income housing torn down was not replaced with new housing. Rather, the cleared land was used for convention centers, university expansions, parking lots for the downtown business buildings and—ironically—luxury housing (Kleniewski, 1984). Frequently, the neighborhoods destroyed were not even the worst slums, but fairly stable working-class ethnic neighborhoods. The net result was that the modernization of downtown areas was obtained through the forced displacement of low-income people, reduction in the supply of low-income housing, and destruction of potentially salvageable neighborhoods. Despite some belated efforts to provide relocation assistance after early gross abuses, this program also often created real hardships for the people living in the neighborhoods slated to be demolished: difficulty finding affordable replacement housing, disruption of social ties, moving costs, and psychological stress.

In the mid-1970s, the urban renewal program was discontinued and another federal program, *historic preservation,* was begun as a way to address urban decay. Realizing that the urban renewal approach had destroyed many usable buildings, Congress enacted a provision of the tax code allowing investors to get federal income tax deductions for renovating historically certified buildings (Logan and Molotch, 1987). The goal of this policy was to save many older buildings which, under urban renewal, would have been demolished and to convert them to modern uses—for example, converting warehouses to offices and making manufacturing lofts into apartments. The Historic Preservation Act was successful in saving many buildings and providing subsidies for their renovation. The program, however, has done little to stem overall urban decay, nor has it helped provide housing for low-income people. Since it is designed to benefit investors, it does not provide assistance to homeowners and, indeed, much of the benefit has gone to developers of commercial properties rather than residential properties.

Two more far-reaching pieces of legislation adopted in the 1970s are the *Home Mortgage Disclosure Act* (HMDA) of 1975 and the *Community Reinvestment Act* (CRA) of 1977. Both laws make it more difficult for banks to discriminate against individuals or neighborhoods when they give mortgages. The HMDA requires that lenders disclose publicly the characteristics and addresses of applicants for home mortgage loans, both successful and unsuccessful. The CRA requires that federally chartered banks and other lenders provide services, including loans, within the areas in which they are located. These laws are the result of lobbying by community groups to address banks' disinvestment practices in their neighborhoods. Since their passage, they have been resisted and criticized by the banking and thrift (savings and loan) industries, which have lobbied Congress to have the laws rescinded. According to community groups, the laws have not always been enforced, allowing lending discrimination to continue (Bradford and Cincotta, 1992). Currently, however, both laws are being enforced, and they have resulted in an increase in the number of loans being granted in cities in recent years (Bogdon and Tong, 1999). The reason these laws are so powerful is that the banks must produce evidence of their lending records as a condition of having their federal charters renewed. If the bank regulators continue to take these requirements seriously, we may see some stemming of property decline, or even a modest revitalization in cities from the increased investment.

Under the Clinton administration, HUD attempted to coordinate the many urban programs into a unified effort. The 1995 urban policy statement entitled "Empowerment" contained a six-point program: improving employment opportunities, attracting capital investment to cities, expanding the stock of affordable housing, reducing crime, increasing residential mobility for urban residents, and targeting economically distressed areas for special federal assistance. This approach had two advantages over previous policies: it recognized that a number of urban problems were interrelated, and it encouraged local communities to build on their individual strengths. Despite its innovation and creativity, however, HUD had to face an uphill battle for funding its programs and was nearly eliminated altogether by Congress in 1996. Overall, the federal budget for urban programs has been dramatically cut since the early 1980s.

Evaluation

What is the record of government's attempts to eliminate slums and urban decay? Most government programs aimed at reducing urban decay have, according to critics, simply moved it around. They remove bad housing from one area but often force the residents of those areas to crowd into other neighborhoods, creating new slums. Programs that have brought young, white, middle-class households into the city have also displaced many low-income households of various races and ethnicities from their traditional neighborhoods by driving up rents and property taxes. While local officials may be happy to see the property values (and thus tax revenues) increase in gentrifying areas, they inevitably have to face property decline somewhere else as low-income people move on. For this reason, it is important to recognize that the problem of urban decay cannot be solved without addressing the problems of poverty and racial discrimination.

Urban decay is more than a problem of blight or property deterioration. It is rooted in two facts about our cities: first, that there are significant numbers of people who do not have enough income to pay for adequate housing, and second, that the people who own and manage property do so mainly to make a profit. (See David Harvey, 1973, for more on this subject.) Government policy seriously aimed at solving the problem of urban deterioration must be oriented toward obtaining a more equal distribution of income and better access to decent housing for everyone. Otherwise, cities will continue to look like mosaics, with some good areas and some bad areas intermixed, and with new investments in one area implying withdrawal of resources from another area.

MAIN POINTS

1. Housing quality has improved, on the average, in the past fifty years. Improvements have been accomplished mainly by removing substandard units from the housing stock.
2. Gains in housing quality must be weighed against increasing housing costs, however. Since 1970, housing costs have risen

more rapidly than people's incomes, creating an affordability crisis for low- and even middle-income households.

3. Rising costs have contributed to the increase in homelessness in urban areas.

4. The largest federal housing assistance program, the homeowner's tax deduction, is designed to benefit the nonpoor. Affluent homeowners benefit most and lower-income homeowners benefit least from this program.

5. Housing programs for the poor, mainly public housing and rent subsidies, have been chronically underfunded by the federal government and have achieved only limited successes.

6. Since the 1970s, federal housing policy has relied more on the private market to provide housing rather than having government help provide housing.

7. Nonprofit corporations have become important housing providers, especially for poor people, since neither the private market nor the government is currently providing adequate low-cost housing.

8. Urban decay has been a significant problem for cities since the 1940s, when suburban growth began to outstrip city growth. Deliberate property destruction for profit often speeds up the process of decay.

9. Community groups have succeeded in obtaining laws requiring banks to lend in urban areas that have experienced disinvestment.

10. Federal policies addressing urban decay have often focused on property rather than people. The most recent policy direction is to address a community's economic needs rather than simply its decayed property.

KEY TERMS

Abandonment The final stage of residential decay in which building owners abandon their buildings and residents flee, leaving the neighborhood a depopulated wasteland.

Community Development Block Grant Program The main program the federal government uses to fund cities' and states' housing and urban development efforts.

Community Reinvestment Act A federal law requiring banks to grant loans in their service areas.

Exclusionary Zoning The practice of allowing only certain (usually expensive) housing to be built within a community.

FHA and VA Mortgage Programs Special federal programs sponsored by the Federal Housing Administration and the Veterans' Administration to make it easier for potential homeowners to borrow money for a home.

Filtering   The approach to housing that relies on the notion that by subsidizing housing for the nonpoor, the poor would eventually benefit.

Historic Preservation   A government program that gives tax incentives to developers to rehabilitate older properties.

Home Mortgage Disclosure Act   A federal law requiring banks to report on the geographic scope of their loan activity.

Homeowner's Tax Deduction   The deduction for mortgage interest and property tax payments given to homeowners on their federal income tax.

Housing Affordability Crisis   The situation in many communities in which a significant number of households cannot afford adequate shelter within their incomes.

HUD   The U. S. Department of Housing and Urban Development.

Inclusionary Zoning   The practice of requiring a certain amount of low-cost housing to be built in growing communities.

Public Housing   A government program to construct and operate rental housing.

Redlining   The practice of refusing to provide conventional mortgage financing for the purchase of housing in particular neighborhoods; also known as disinvestment.

Rental Assistance Programs   Programs such as Section 8 and vouchers in which the federal government pays a portion of low-income households' rent.

Scattered Site   Locating individual units of public housing among the private housing units in residential neighborhoods.

Shelter Poverty   A form of housing deprivation in which people pay such a large portion of their incomes for housing that they cannot afford other necessary items.

Social Housing   Housing produced by nonprofit organizations and not intended to be privately owned.

Urban Renewal   The major federal slum clearance program.

SUGGESTED READING

Hays, R. Allen. 1995. *The Federal Government and Urban Housing.* Albany: State University of New York Press.

Snow, David, and Leon Anderson. 1993. *Down on Their Luck: A Study of Homeless Street People.* Berkeley: University of California Press.

Squires, Gregory, ed. 1992. *From Redlining to Reinvestment: Community Responses to Urban Disinvestment.* Philadelphia: Temple University Press.

Shelterforce, a monthly magazine of housing. Published by National Housing Institute, 439 Main St., Orange, NJ 07050.

6

Transportation

A number of years ago, a Gallup poll of city dwellers asked the question, "What do you regard as your community's worst problem?" People ranked transportation-related problems as worse than education, poor housing, and high taxes (Washington Post, 1975). Even now most people, it seems, are dissatisfied with urban transportation. For the majority of the urban population, the underlying problem is a car culture, which resists and overwhelms all alternatives. Most commuters do not want to adhere to fixed routes and schedules, whether they be buses, car pools, or van pools (Kamin and Ibata, 1990d).

What we will discover in this chapter is that transportation is, indeed, an urban problem. However, the nature of the problem is much different from what most people think. The fact is that, compared to other times and other places, the American urban transportation system is a very fast, flexible, and convenient system (except for some groups). The real problem is not how well the system moves people (which it does very well), but the huge and increasing costs and problems the system creates in exchange for the flexibility and convenience it provides.

THE CONTEMPORARY URBAN TRANSPORTATION SYSTEM: THE AUTOMOBILE

In the typical large American city of eighty years ago, a very different pattern of urban transportation existed than exists today. Automobiles were still relatively rare. Walking and riding slow-moving electric trolleys were the primary means of transportation for the average citizen. (A few cities had faster subways and elevated trains.) Most transit lines radiated out from the central business district, and, as a result, getting places other than downtown on public transportation was a slow and complicated process. Main streets and downtown areas were at least as congested as they are today. Traffic moved slowly as clumsy, underpowered trucks, horse-drawn wagons, cars, trolleys, and pedestrians tried to get around each other. The automobile was being hailed as a solution to a very serious hazard to health and pedestrians: horse manure on the streets. As we have already seen, these transportation difficulties resulted in cities that were compact and densely settled as a way to minimize distances between work, home, stores, and places of recreation. Since that time, urban transportation has undergone fundamental change.

The story of urban transportation in the 1900s is basically the story of the rise of the automobile to almost total dominance as a means of moving people. As recently as 1940, public transit was still responsible for about 30 percent of all passenger miles in urban areas. (A passenger mile is defined as one person traveling one mile and is a measure of transportation use.) The use of public transit for the journey to work, according to the U.S. Census, declined from 12.6 percent in 1960 to 4.6 percent in 1989. By 1999, however, the use of public transportation for the trip to work had increased slightly, to 4.9 percent (U.S. Department of Transportation, 1994a; U.S. Census Bureau, 2000f). In fact, mass-transit ridership grew faster than highway use for three consecutive years (1998–2000), according to the American Public Transportation Association and the Federal Highway Administration (Layton, 2001). However, no one expects mass transit to displace the primacy of the automobile any time soon, since more than 85 percent of workers in 1999 commuted via automobile (U.S. Census Bureau, 2000f).

There were several reasons for this almost total takeover of urban transportation by cars in the post-1945 period. Probably the most important reason was car ownership finally became affordable for the majority of people. In 1950, 41 percent of all families did not own a car. By 1970, only 17 percent did not own one (Kemp and Cheslow, 1976). Motor vehicle registrations have increased steadily since 1970, reaching more than 211 million vehicles in 1998. In particular, truck registrations—which after 1985 included minivans and sports utility vehicles—increased 58.2 percent between 1988 and 1998 (see figure 6.1).

Figure 6.1
Motor Vehicle Registrations

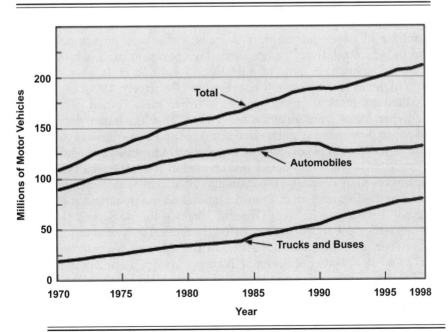

SOURCE: *Our Nation's Highways: Selected Facts and Figures*, 1998.

As we have seen, this nearly universal car ownership played a major role in suburbanization. In turn, suburbanization encouraged increased car use. The majority of the urban population now lives in low-density suburbs. In addition, about two-thirds of new jobs created in the United States from 1960 to 1980 were located there. Consequently, by 1975 a majority of all urban workers lived in the suburbs, but only about a third of them commuted into the central cities (U.S. Census Bureau, 1979). For reasons discussed later in this chapter, traditional mass transit just did not fit in with changing commuting patterns.

Government also played a role by encouraging car use and discouraging mass transit. The role of the Interstate Highway System was especially important in the development of the contemporary urban transportation system. The decision to route these highways directly through most urban areas and to add various beltways (circling routes) and short connectors in urban areas turned the program into a thinly disguised subsidization of urban expressway construction. With the Highway Trust Fund picking up 90 percent of the cost of construction, the temptation to build expressways to provide urban transportation was almost irresistible for state and local governments. It was simply the cheapest way, from the point of view of these governments, to deal with urban transportation needs.

While government lavished money on expressways, public transportation was allowed to languish. No federal aid to urban mass transit was available at all until 1961. Initially, the funds provided were very modest and limited to the construction of new facilities and the purchase of new equipment. That meant the local government still had to bear a relatively heavy burden of operating costs, which made mass transportation more of a drain on local and state governments than highway construction (Congressional Quarterly, 1978).

Real attempts at giving support to urban mass transit began with the Urban Mass Transportation Act of 1964. This legislation, designed to aid urban development, authorized grants of up to two-thirds of construction, as well as reconstruction and acquisition of facilities and equipment. A single mass-transit authority was created in 1968, the result of a reorganization plan dividing responsibility for urban mass transportation between the Department of Transportation and the Department of Housing and Urban Development (Weiner, 1988:45–46, 54; *Beyond Gridlock,* 1988:54–59, 62–63). During the 1970s the federal government increased its support of public transportation. In the thirteen years between the 1977 and 1990 National Personal Transit Surveys, a number of subway and metro systems were either opened or expanded in Washington, Baltimore, Atlanta, and Miami, and older subway systems in New York, Boston, Chicago, and Philadelphia were extended. Newer systems have been more characteristic of commuter rail than of traditional subway systems, with much wider spacing between stops, higher speeds, and—above all—more of a focus on serving the commuting needs of high-income suburbanites (Pucher and Williams, 1992).

However, this increased federal effort never came close to matching that devoted to highways (see figure 6.2). Moreover, federal expenditures for infrastructure, including mass transit, went down by almost 20 percent in actual dollars between fiscal 1980 and fiscal 1991. Between 1960 and 1987, the federal share of spending for all infrastructure dropped from 31 percent to 23 percent of total expenditure. During the same time period, state expenditures declined from 29 to 24 percent, while local governments increased their outlay from 41 to 53 percent (Broder, 1990a). Of the $17.5 billion in public funding for transit in 1997, the federal government contributed 27 percent. This represented a slight increase from recent years, though it remains well below the peak of 43 percent reached in the early 1980s (U.S. Department of Transportation, 1999).

Government policy can also be seen as having indirectly contributed to the growing reliance on the automobile. As we have already seen (chapter 1), government played a major role in subsidizing the construction of suburban housing and the relocation of employment to the suburbs.

Perhaps less important, but still significant, is the evidence that powerful private interests benefited from and successfully worked for the destruction of mass transit in some cities. The most famous example was the role of General Motors, Firestone Tire, and Standard Oil of California in eliminating electric streetcar systems for several cities. These companies contributed money to "holding companies" that bought the privately owned transit companies in cities such as Los Angeles and converted them to diesel buses (which GM made). As one critic has written:

> Diesel buses have 28 percent shorter economic lives, 40 percent higher operating costs, and 9 percent lower productivity than electric buses. . . . In short, by increasing costs, reducing revenues, and contributing to the collapse of hundreds of transit systems, GM's dieselization program may have had the long-term effect of selling GM cars. (Snell, quoted by Brown, 1979:14)

More generally, the so-called "highway lobby" has been credited with a major role in encouraging highway construction and blocking funds for mass transit. This group consists of the large highway construction contractors, automobile makers, oil companies, trucking companies, and automobile supply companies who have a major stake in continued highway construction and car use. It is generally recognized as one of the better organized and funded lobbying groups in Washington (Brown, 1979:14). A current example of the highway lobby's efforts is the eight-mile stretch of tunnels being built through downtown Boston—the most expensive stretch of road in the whole country. This

Figure 6.2
Highway Expenditures by All Units of Government

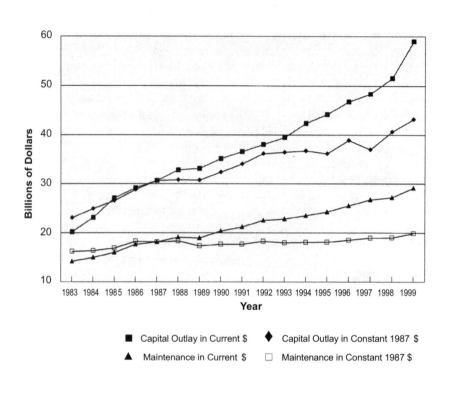

SOURCE: Federal Highway Administration, Office of Highway Policy Information, "Highway Statistics 1999."

stretch will replace an obsolete, traffic-clogged elevated highway. The ultimate question is: will this effort end Boston's gridlock? The priority of the automobile in transportation is plainly evident (Rimer, 1996).

In recent years, however, commuter rail has been significantly improved. Many American cities—because of the nature of their street systems and parking facilities—find it increasingly difficult to accommodate the growing number of cars. Commuter rail service has become an increasingly attractive alternative. Ridership on existing systems has grown significantly in the last ten years, for example, in Washington, D.C., Los Angeles, San Jose, Dallas-Ft. Worth, and Miami (Layton, 2001).

One final note about automobile dominance is in order, however. The national patterns we have been examining tend to hide the fact that, in some cities, mass transit is still a significant form of transportation. A few of our older, larger cities have "inherited" quite extensive mass-transit systems that still move large numbers of people. Most notable are the cities of New York, Boston, Philadelphia, and Chicago. These systems were built prior to 1920 and have remained in use for a number of special reasons. Two of the cities are major centers of corporate headquarters which require movement of large numbers of office workers to downtown locations. All of them experienced most of their growth prior to the appearance of the automobile. As a result, their basic physical structure is such that automobile use is usually inconvenient. In addition, these cities were willing to subsidize the continued losses of their transit systems to keep them going (Kemp and Cheslow, 1976:297).

OTHER CHARACTERISTICS OF URBAN TRANSPORTATION

The combination of suburbanization and heavy automobile use has, in turn, had a number of other consequences for the nature of contemporary urban transportation.

Multiple Destinations

As we have seen, suburbanization has meant that the location of work, retail shopping areas, recreation facilities, and the like have been dispersed to a large number of widely separated locations. Radial movement to centrally located downtowns and concentrated industrial districts is a much smaller proportion of the total movement of people in urban areas than previously. The typical urban commuter, in fact, drives from a suburban residence to a suburban work location (see figure 6.3). In many urban areas, there is even a "reverse rush hour" in which central city residents commute to dispersed suburban locations.

Increased Travel Distances

The spread-out, low-density, and decentralized nature of suburban areas also means that the distance traveled (especially to work) has tended to increase in most urban areas. Despite this fact, however, travel times have not increased as much. Automobiles provide faster door-to-door service because the traveler does not have to walk to a transit stop and wait for a bus or a train. Generally, automobiles also average higher travel speeds. Hence, the switch to the automobile allowed people to travel further distances without major increases in the time devoted to travel.

More drivers today use cars that are more fuel-efficient. However, improvements in car efficiency are negated by both the increasing number of drivers and the greater distances driven. In 1970, Americans drove 5,722 miles per capita, but by 1995 the figure had risen to 9,867

Figure 6.3
Urban Movement Patterns in 1920 and 1990

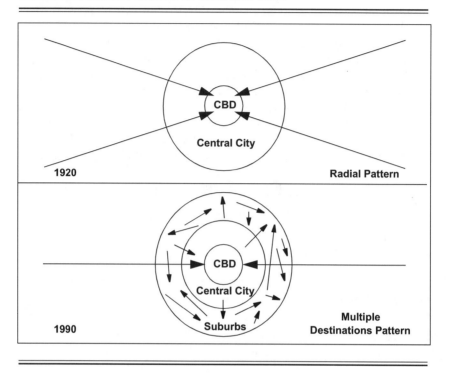

miles (Kendall and Washburn, 1996). How is this to be explained? First, the United States has more households today, and more drivers per household, including women workers. Second, we have had a pattern of governmental policy choices reinforcing inappropriate land use, which contributes to urban sprawl. More people have to drive to work, school, day care, and shopping. It isn't simply that people like their cars, but rather that they have few alternatives to driving.

Approaching Gridlock?

Despite the past success of the urban highway system in moving people, more recently, in a number of urban areas, the highway system has not expanded rapidly enough to keep up with the growth of traffic.

Travel congestion on the urban interstate system has steadily increased over the years. In 1990, 48 percent of the peak-hour travel on this system occurred under conditions of congestion, while 56 percent occurred under such conditions in 1998. The peak, moreover, is now much longer than one hour, both in the morning and afternoon *(Our Nation's Highways,* 1995, 1998). The result is increasing *gridlock:* during peak commuting hours the number of cars attempting to use the highway system exceeds the capacity of the system. Cars are increasing in number twice as fast as people. Despite the expenditure of huge amounts of money on highway construction and maintenance, funding levels have not kept pace with increasing car use. The rapid increase in inter-suburban commuting is a major source of the problem. Suburbs have few main arteries, and thus a rapid and efficient flow of traffic is inhibited (*Our Nation's Highways*, 1998).

The annual cost of traffic delays is nearly $501 billion, or about $640 per driver. The standard remedy for dealing with congestion is expanding capacity—that is, building more roads. Transportation researchers, however, have identified several paradoxes with this remedy and conclude that expanding the road system is ineffective or counterproductive. First, even if new highway construction and building mass transit were cheaper, it would still be very difficult for transportation departments to build their way out of the problem. Congestion itself causes much rush-hour traveling to be canceled, diverted, or rescheduled. Measures for relieving congestion are thus partly undone by latent demand, since rush hours begin earlier, end later, and affect other routes. Another reason highway expansion alone does not work is that congestion is inappropriately priced. Since drivers do not pay for the time loss that they impose on others, they make socially inefficient choices concerning how much to travel, when and where, and what route to take. The combination of latent demand and mispriced congestion is such that an expansion of capacity either brings about no change in congestion, or even makes it worse (Arnott and Small, 1994).

EVALUATING THE URBAN TRANSPORTATION SYSTEM

How should these changes in urban transportation be judged? That depends on what standards one uses to judge them. In some respects the urban transportation system works very well. In other respects our automobile-based transportation system verges on a national disaster.

The Benefits of Automobile-Based Transportation

For the vast majority who now own automobiles, the automobile serves them well as a method of transportation. It provides them with a degree of mobility that is a highly valued form of personal freedom in our society. As the trends just discussed indicate, with minimal effort, we can move directly and quickly from home to another location whenever we want to. The automobile is comfortable and private. We do not have to wait for others or depend on others. We can live where we want to, not just where a mass-transit line happens to run. In short, the automobile offers flexibility, independence, reasonable speed, comfort, and convenience. From the point of view of the individual user, the automobile quite simply provides a level of transportation service that is superior to all other modes of transportation.

The Costs of Automobile-Based Transportation

The basic dilemma of automobile transportation is that it delivers its superior level of service at such a high (and increasing) cost. In the past, given the extraordinary wealth of American society, that high cost seemed to many an acceptable burden to bear in return for the satisfaction of individual preferences. The problem we face now is that the costs may be finally exceeding our ability to pay.

Transportation by car is indeed a relatively expensive operation, involving not only purchase costs and repairs, but also routine maintenance, insurance, and ultimately, replacement. Although U.S. drivers enjoy more reasonable gasoline prices than those in many other countries, there is no guarantee that gasoline price rises will remain moderate. This became apparent in 1990 when the Iraqi invasion of Kuwait caused gasoline prices in the United States to soar.

The cost of owning and operating a vehicle in 1998 ranged from 31.3 cents per mile for subcompacts to 50.8 cents per mile for a full-size utility vehicle (*Our Nation's Highways,* 1998). In other words, the average vehicle (at a cost of 44 cents per mile and an average annual mileage of 13,000) costs about $5700 per year, compared to $50 per month ($600 annually) to use the PACE bus system on a monthly pass basis (PACE, 2001).

In addition, we should not look at the cost of an automobile-based transportation system only from the point of view of the individual. Because the automobile is the most expensive mode of land transportation, our reliance on it means that as a society we spend more of our national income on transportation than other, less auto-dependent societies.

The expense of the automobile to society as a whole is probably best illustrated by the demands it places on our scarce and expensive energy supplies. Indeed, this is probably the single most serious problem with continuing our present approach to urban transportation. Oil imports contributed to our massive trade deficit in the 1980s and 1990s. Increasing dependence on foreign oil has left the United States more vulnerable economically to disruptions in foreign production. A real roadblock to reducing energy costs has been the tendency for Ford and General Motors to concentrate on big cars, in order to increase profits. Moreover, low fuel prices have resulted in both consumer and producer losing interest in fuel economy. At the same time, taxing policies, while restricting consumption somewhat, have not been geared toward discouraging the purchase of less-efficient cars (Renner, 1989:103–6).

Automobiles also continue to be a major source of urban air pollution, despite the addition of pollution control devices. Motor vehicle

emissions contribute to four of the six criteria pollutants as determined by the Environmental Protection Agency. Most notable among
these are lead and carbon monoxide. The major control strategy to
reduce lead emissions has been to phase out leaded gasoline, which
has produced significant reductions (though health officials now feel
lead has detrimental effects on human health at much lower levels
than formerly believed). Catalytic converters, installed in all nondiesel
American cars since 1975, have proven to be an efficient and effective
means of reducing carbon monoxide and other harmful emissions,
although this effectiveness is impaired by poor auto maintenance and
illegal tampering with pollution control devices (Nadakavukaren,
2000). These gains also have been diminished by the immense growth
in traffic volume.

In 1990, Congress passed several amendments to the Clean Air
Act designed to beef up pollution control efforts. The amendments
established specific annual emission reduction goals to ensure steady
progress, with penalties (such as cutting off federal highway construction funds) for nonattainment areas. Because a number of metropolitan areas in the United States still do not meet these goals, several
states have adopted inspection and maintenance programs. Such programs require all autos registered within a given area to have their
tailpipe emissions tested on a regular basis. The amendments also call
for the use of reformulated gasoline and less-polluting alternative
fuels such as ethanol and methanol (Nadakavukaren, 2000).

The automobile also has contributed to urban decay. It played a
very significant role in suburbanization, thereby accelerating the
decline of downtown retail business and central-city residential neighborhoods. The interstate expressway system, begun in the late 1950s,
accented this trend, enabling easy access both to adjacent suburbs but
also to newly built suburban industrial plants, offices, and shopping
centers. The suburbanization process was (and is) very closely linked
to the building and proliferation of roads, and the geometric increase
in the number of automobiles (Palen, 1987:118, 182–87).

It also should be kept in mind that not everyone enjoyed the convenience and mobility that conversion to an automobile-based transportation system provided for the majority of urban residents. One of the worst
transit problems in the United States is the tremendous inequality in
mobility among different socioeconomic groups. The poor, the elderly, and
the handicapped make less than half as many trips per capita as the rest
of the population. Due to financial constraints, these groups have less
access to automobiles. Since most recreational, shopping, and employment sites are almost totally inaccessible without cars, disadvantaged
groups are thus further discriminated against by a transit system that
drastically limits the mobility of anyone without a car. The distribution of
transit subsidies, moreover, is not equitable, since the largest subsidies

go to rail services used by affluent riders, and the smallest to inner-city bus services used mainly by the poor (Pucher and Lefevre, 1996).

What this means is that one of the real problems for many of the urban poor, elderly, and handicapped is that they face major obstacles to mobility. Given the limited nature of mass-transit systems in all but a few cities, they may have to undertake long walks to reach transit lines; endure tedious rides in slow-moving, infrequently scheduled buses and long waits to make transfers; and pay increasingly expensive fares. Often, this dependence on public transit means that these people simply cannot get to many places (especially in the suburbs) or travel at certain hours of the day. This is an especially severe problem for the working poor. As we have seen, employment opportunities have become increasingly limited in central cities. The suburbs are where a large portion of the jobs, especially the good jobs, are located. Lacking cars, many of the poor have simply been unable to go where the jobs are.

TRANSPORTATION ALTERNATIVES

As a result of these problems, there has been a growing emphasis on making urban transportation more efficient and effective for all groups in the population. The difficulty is that of finding a system that will actually meet contemporary transportation needs. How can we find a system that will provide something which approximates the kind of superior mobility to which we have become accustomed and also move large numbers of people efficiently?

Traditional Mass Transit

Most of the public discussion of how to improve urban transportation has centered around creating new public mass-transit systems. Generally such systems are conceived as being cleaner and faster versions of the kind of mass-transit systems already operating in some of our central cities. The choice usually discussed is seen as being between publicly supported and subsidized rail systems (e.g., subways or surface rail rapid transit) or "line bus" systems (large buses following a fixed route). The popular view seems to be that if you provide people with good, cheap, fast subways or buses, they will leave their cars at home. A survey taken by a metropolitan bus system found, in contrast, that nine out of ten people surveyed felt that mass transit was less convenient than driving. Over half surveyed felt that bus trips were too long. Low bus ridership seems to be due to low population density in suburban areas (Kamin and Ibata, 1990d).

The solution of urban transportation problems will not be simple. The idea that building traditional mass-transit systems will provide a relatively quick, efficient, and effective way to move a major portion of the urban population neglects a number of problems of traditional mass transit.

Traditional mass-transit systems have generally been designed on the assumption that people will walk to the transit line. In addition, to make transit attractive to people, service on a given route must be frequent: people will not wait long periods of time or change their work habits just to use mass transit. As a result, each mass-transit route must attract a large number of people to justify the number of trains or buses to be run. There is no efficiency in running a train or large bus almost empty. The problem is most severe in the case of rail transit. The huge cost of building the rail system means that a very large number of people have to use it to justify the cost of construction. One estimate is that each rail line must carry 25,000 people a day.

As we have seen, the suburbanization process resulted in urban areas of low population density. Single-family houses on large lots mean that a relatively small number of people are spread over a relatively large area. Under these conditions, the problem low density creates for mass transit should be obvious. Not enough people live within easy walking distance of the mass-transit route to provide enough passengers to justify the cost of frequent service (in terms of fuel, equipment, or labor costs). The only place this is not a problem is in the large, old central cities with high densities and inadequate highway systems. It is no accident that it is there that traditional mass-transit systems have fared best in competition with the automobile. The problem of low density is worst in those areas that now contain the majority of our urban population: suburbs and the newer metropolitan areas of the South and West.

Traditional mass transit also is designed to serve a centrally located downtown or other location that attracts a very large number of people. People are picked up along the route and deposited in one central location. Yet, current urban transportation patterns based on car use have evolved toward people going to a very large number of dispersed locations. Only a minority of workers and shoppers now head for the central business district.

Moreover, there is no simple way to restructure traditional mass transit to serve dispersed locations. Again, we run into the requirement that each route in the system must carry large numbers of people to be efficient. Not enough travelers are going to the same locations to meet this requirement.

Surface rail and subway systems present another problem: they are monumentally expensive to construct. For surface rail systems, land must be acquired at a very high cost. Subway tunnels are very expensive to dig. In addition, rail, control systems, maintenance yards, and rail cars are all very expensive. Again, what this means is that a large number of people must use the system to make it economically viable.

There are other financial barriers to be overcome. To attract users, fares have to be kept low. Partly, this is because people do not calculate the true cost of operation when they compare using their cars to mass transit. They usually think only in terms of the gas and other basic operating costs of their cars. Also, they consider the obviously greater convenience of traveling by car. Hence, only very low fares are likely to attract riders to transit systems. Generally speaking, the fares have to be set so low that they do not generate enough income to cover the cost of constructing the system. In fact, most systems require subsidies to cover operating costs. The result is that actual users of the system do not pay for it.

This need to subsidize the huge cost of a rail system makes for several problems. For reasons already discussed, only a small minority of urban residents are likely to use and directly benefit from the system. Thus, the net gain to the whole community really is relatively small. On the other hand, new subway systems in a number of cities, for instance San Francisco and Toronto, have resulted in a very considerable expansion of business and economic development ("Big City Metro," 1990).

It should also be kept in mind that constructing a rail system, like constructing an expressway, can be very disruptive to the areas through which it passes. It is true that real estate values go up along such a line (especially near the stations) because of the increased attractiveness of the land for commercial development. However, that is not much consolation to the neighborhood residents. Moreover, the period of construction can destroy small merchants, and surface rail systems bring with them noise and visual blight which can make an area very unattractive for residential use.

There is simply no escaping the fact that the automobile is the most attractive and convenient method of urban transportation from the point of view of the user. Despite the stereotype of the frustrated commuter trapped in a traffic jam, most people actively prefer to travel by automobile. Despite the high cost of automobile use, many people are likely to be able to afford to commute via automobiles for a long time to come.

In contrast, traditional mass transit is relatively inconvenient to use. The choice of destinations is limited. It is crowded during rush hours. People worry about riding transit at night because of the fear of crime. Commuters have to walk to the transit line and wait for at least a short period of time. Lumbering buses trapped in traffic are much slower than traveling by automobile. Many of these inconveniences are minor. Some of them can be partially corrected by proper transit design and operation procedures. But the basic fact remains that people who use traditional mass transit tend to be those people who have no other choice. Those who have a choice, opt for the automobile. People have grown up in a setting where cars are the only way to get from one place to another. It is harder, therefore, to convince people to use public transportation. A survey in the Chicago suburbs revealed that 90 percent of suburbanites feel mass transit is not as convenient as the automobile. This study also showed that two-thirds resented fixed schedules (Kamin and Ibata, 1990d).

Hence, the traditional approaches to mass transit are not likely to attract a large number of riders who voluntarily choose to leave their cars at home. Major new approaches to making transit attractive and convenient will be required.

Finally, recent legislation on behalf of the handicapped raises the issue of providing them with equal access to the mass-transit system. Equal access assumes that the quality of service will not change when access is made possible. Such availability will increase transit costs in a number of ways. Equipment expenses, as well as access at stops, for both suburban trains and subway cars as well as buses, may well sky-rocket. Ridership of those not needing such assistance may decline considerably, due to the longer time schedules necessitated by greater loading time required for handicapped riders. This decline might be especially apparent during rush hours. Fares may very likely increase, to compensate for decreasing ridership (Houston, 1989; Walberer, 1989; Washburn, 1989; *Wall Street Journal,* 1989).

The end result is that there are growing doubts about the useful-ness of rail transit systems as the primary transit system for most urban areas. Certainly, these systems will have to be limited to those few cases where the rail system can move very large numbers of peo-ple and provide major advantages to justify the high initial cost. More-over, the cost must be compared to other alternative systems of transportation, such as bus systems, which may provide more flexibil-ity at a lower initial cost. City governments do not have an infinite amount of money to spend on public transportation. Even if a tradi-tional rail system will ultimately pay for itself (over a twenty- or thirty-year period), the question remains whether another approach would cost less to begin with, move as many people, and, hence, pay for itself sooner. As we will see later in this chapter, there is a good possibility that such alternative approaches exist.

Do all these problems mean that traditional mass transit has no role to play in urban transportation? Not necessarily. Such transporta-tion probably will play a limited role in urban areas. There are things that traditional mass transit does very well. It does move large num-bers of people efficiently to a downtown location. With increasing num-bers of middle-class workers who work in these downtown areas choosing to live in central-city residential neighborhoods, traditional mass transit could enjoy a modest revival of popularity. In the lower density, more dispersed sections of newer urban areas, however, tradi-tional systems will probably play a much smaller role (Shannon, 1980). In the foreseeable future, therefore, such systems will not move a majority of urban travelers. Rather, traditional mass transit must be seen as just one part of a larger transportation improvement strategy.

The Mixed-Systems Approach

If the public is to have real alternatives, transit networks, appropriately including various types of transit, must be designed in the context of urban planning. For example, this can be done by synchronizing schedules of different modes of transportation, and by structuring convenient transfers from one type of system to another. A multiple approach, using several different forms of mass transit in conjunction with each other, can make mass transit much more attractive and efficient. This in fact has been done in a number of places (Renner, 1988:47, 49–51; Barry, 1989; Koepp, 1988; Work, 1987). Such a comprehensive approach would enable the user to have the best of many worlds: the combining of cars and other forms of transit according to one's personal, daily needs. To reduce auto congestion, transit alternatives should be focused on the needs of the various transit populations. Projects for discouraging auto use should be worked out with the participation of those affected. This indeed must be done if such plans are to really be effective (Kapinos, 1989; Prewda, 1989; Renner, 1989:111; Work, 1987). A number of proposals have been put forward to combine more efficient automobile use with more innovative forms of public transit and some use of traditional mass transit. This is what might be called the *mixed-systems approach.* Some of the elements of such an approach include: (1) redesigning the automobile, (2) changing car-use patterns, (3) altering mass transit, and (4) transforming consumer preference.

Redesigning the Automobile

Suburban sprawl requires the automobile as a primary mode of transportation. There is a huge fixed investment in the existing "built environment" of our suburbs, and that environment has been designed for auto use. Hence, the problems of energy use and pollution will have to be addressed, in part, by the introduction of much more efficient cars. There was a considerable emphasis on small, fuel-efficient cars after the Iranian oil crisis of 1979 (Lave, 1979). As the price of gasoline leveled off during the 1980s and 1990s there was an accompanying desire for larger and more prestigious vehicles. While small, fuel-efficient automobiles are definitely a large percent of production, an increasing number of new models are larger and less fuel efficient. The notion of the car as a status symbol returned, especially for the younger, wealthier buyer. American buyers are more likely to prefer showier cars (Renner, 1988:33; Greenwald, 1990). Minivans and sports-utility vehicles have also become very popular with American consumers. However, the potential savings derived from converting the national car fleet to more fuel-efficient vehicles is immense. Such cars could meet most individual needs in urban areas as well as bigger cars do now. Additional benefits of the conversion would include being able to accommodate more vehicles in existing parking facilities and, to a lesser extent, on the highways.

Changing technology, such as the increased use of electrically powered vehicles, may provide a more efficient and environmentally sound mode of transportation than gasoline-powered vehicles. Once again, however, there are no simple solutions. The state of California, which had adopted a requirement that 2 percent of all cars sold within the state by 1997 be electrically powered, rescinded this requirement. Opponents of the requirement argued that electric vehicles were simply too expensive and too limited in range to be practical (Passell, 1995). Automakers voiced approval of the rescindment. Air quality advocates and members of the emerging electric car industry called the changed law a sellout to the automobile and oil industries (*Chicago Tribune,* 12/27/1995). Others argued that the changes will give automakers a few additional years to develop and test electric vehicles, leading to better performance and pricing that better competes with conventional vehicles (Moore, 1996).

Changing Car-Use Patterns

What can be done to cope with gridlock? Highway construction will not solve the problem of traffic congestion because the required increases in spending are too massive. Cities must adopt a multifaceted approach involving construction of appropriate freeways, mass transit, and regulated land use. Organizations studying America's transportation needs and noting the different segments of the transportation market may be able to suggest alternatives that people find cheaper and more convenient than driving alone. For example, transportation planners in many areas now concentrate on developing strategies encouraging people to use mass transit and ride sharing rather than driving alone (Edmondson, 1994).

Because most metropolitan-area dwellers drive to work alone, just increasing the average number of people per car to two would reduce the total number of cars during rush hour in most urban areas by about 40 percent. The result would be a reduction in energy use, pollution, congestion, and the need for more highways. The benefits to individuals would also be substantial. The cost per trip would be reduced by almost half. The need for a second automobile would be reduced, while the flexibility and convenience of door-to-door service provided by the car would be retained. During the 1980s and 1990s, public agencies spent billions of dollars to promote car pools, buses, and other transit alternatives. Relatively few Americans, however, are willing to use alternatives to the one-person car, and in fact, the percentage of Americans using this form of transportation to go to work rose from 64 percent in 1980 to 78 percent in 1999 (U.S. Census Bureau, 2000f).

A number of programs to promote car pooling have been developed. Companies in Southern California have provided incentives for employees to join pools. A 1987 study found that when several companies paid employee expenses for parking and car pool expenses, worker participation increased to more than 50 percent. The success of such an approach in this region may be due to tough legislation designed to reduce the number of employees driving to work without passengers, the alternative being the payment of stiff fines (Kamin and Ibata, 1990a). More than 2,000 van pools have been formed in the northern Virginia suburbs of Washington, D.C. However, results are not uniformly hopeful. Some large businesses in the Chicago suburbs have organized TMAs (transit management associations) to promote van and car pooling by enlisting the participation of local businesses and companies. To date, only about 1 percent of the employees have participated. In contrast is the response of a branch of Sears and Roebuck, whose car and van pool effort netted 40 percent of workers (Kamin and Ibata, 1990d).

Altering Mass Transit
The traditional form of mass transit may not attract many passengers, but it is possible that the system could be changed so that a gradually increasing share of urban travelers might be attracted to a modified system—especially in the case of those traveling to central locations. Most proposals of this sort involve the use of various forms of buses, rather than rail systems. Buses have the advantage of being able to travel flexible routes and requiring smaller initial investment than rail systems.

One of the chief disadvantages of traditional bus service is that it is so slow. One possible solution is the creation of special bus lanes on urban expressways to allow for express bus service. A number of cities have already created such lanes. In one variation of this approach, the bus makes a passenger pick-up "loop" in a suburban area and then runs at high speeds downtown. The "park-ride" approach involves passengers driving to the central pick-up areas, parking their cars, and finishing the trip by bus. This approach also works to feed passengers from suburban areas onto commuter rail lines or subway systems at the edge of the city. The park-ride concept has the dual advantage of allowing frequent, high-speed service and overcoming the problem of low population densities in the suburbs. It is also a very efficient way to use the existing freeway system. An excellent example of such an approach is that of metropolitan Toronto. Synchronizing of schedules enables convenient transfer between different routes as well as different modes of transit. Such multi-destinational systems work well in a number of North American cities (*Transit in Toronto*, 1987; Renner, 1988:49–51).

The so-called "minibus" (large passenger van) system has also been suggested as a possibility—usually for smaller urban areas.

These vans can pick people up from their homes, either by being radio dispatched in response to a telephone call or by a prearranged schedule, and then deliver the passengers to some common location (an office complex, a subway station, or a large factory). The small size of the van minimizes the time spent collecting people and could allow the creation of a system that serves many dispersed locations. In effect, the system would function something like a car pool, except that people would not provide their own vehicles and there would be more people per vehicle. Where such a system feeds into an existing traditional mass-transit line, it could provide enough passengers to justify the operation of high-speed rapid transit and overcome the problem of low density in suburban areas. Finally, another suggested role for the minibus system is that of providing flexible, door-to-door bus service to the handicapped and elderly. This would save the expense of modifying the whole transit system to allow for special access facilities and could provide, if properly developed, higher quality service (U.S. Department of Transportation, 1994a).

One approach used in some smaller cities across the United States to help persons who are handicapped and/or needy to obtain transportation is the car subsidy. Those eligible register with the city and are issued a card and a number. Riders are limited to a certain number of trips per month. Those using this system pay the company either a lower or subsidized fare. The balance is paid to the company by the city every month. The city, in turn, receives state and federal subsidies. This approach has the advantage of using existing equipment and personnel while at the same time providing affordable service to the user (Bolton, 1989).

When properly planned, transportation programs can increase inner-city residents' access to job opportunities. Chicago's Suburban Job-Link Corporation's "Job Express" program is an example of an innovative effort to bring the chronically unemployed from their neighborhoods on Chicago's West Side to the industrial parks beyond O'Hare Airport. Job Express combines van-pooling and ride-sharing activities with employment counseling, job-skill training, and instruction in personal grooming and interactive skills. The Greater O'Hare Association of Industry and Commerce helps its member companies by participating in this project to obtain badly needed labor for entry-level positions *(Chicago Tribune,* 7/9/1995). Job Express's task is far from easy. The organization's efforts to set up car pools for Chicago's West Siders are difficult because drivers are often afraid to pool with strangers and members of other ethnic groups. But with all its difficulties, the program, generating 250 positions, returns more than three million dollars annually to the West Side.

Other mass-transit solutions involve using resources already available. For example, it might be possible to use interstate corridors as sites for metropolitan trains connecting suburbs. Abandoned and underused rail freight lines could also be put to use. These approaches could provide a more rapid means of getting people from one suburb to another in an era in which an increasing number of jobs (and traffic problems) are in the suburban area *(Chicago Tribune, 2/27/1989)*.

Not all mass transit should be downtown-centered. The PACE system (Chicago suburban bus service) is an example of this philosophy. This agency has built a transportation center in Schaumburg, a suburban office center northwest of Chicago. This facility is designed to combine a number of transit types: a bus depot, taxi and limousine stands, a large garage for cars, and car rental agencies. Buses terminating at this center operate as links for nearby suburbs to office buildings and an adjacent mall. Direct bus service is available both to Chicago and O'Hare Airport, as well as to convention centers and hotels *(Chicago Tribune, 3/22/1989)*. PACE also has started an express service linking southern and western suburbs—a first step in linking suburbs distant from one another. Those needing work and living in the south suburbs can thereby get to the many jobs available in the west suburbs. PACE promotes cooperation and communication between employment services and employers in both sets of suburbs *(Chicago Tribune, 8/14/1989;* Kendall and Washburn, 1996:3; City of Schaumburg, 2001).

A vital factor in commuter rail extension is the enthusiastic response of the local community; an example of such is when local leaders and business owners agreed to build stations and parking lots along the new 53-mile Wisconsin Central line, running from downtown Chicago to Antioch, Wisconsin. This collaboration helped make it possible to get generous state and federal funding. Existing freight tracks were brought into use for suburban commuters. Such a cooperative community spirit could very well assist similar efforts in other parts of the country *(Chicago Tribune, 7/16/1994)*.

How will such ongoing expansion occur? These commuter lines are extended in order to follow population growth. As with the addition and expansion of freeways, so it is with metropolitan rail lines. Both transit alternatives are desired by an increasing number of middle- and upper-class citizens who continue to work in Chicago's central business district. These people are very likely to vote, not only for those seeking national office, but also for their state representatives and senators. Moreover, the suburbs, with their growing populations, have an increasingly larger percent of representatives and senators in the legislature. Legislators from this growing edge of the metropolitan area— the more outlying suburbs and the exurbs—vote the wishes of their constituents, and these include funding for expansion of both highways and also rail lines in this region. This situation is true not only for metropolitan Chicago, but throughout the United States *(Chicago Tribune, 7/16/ 1994, 6/5/1995;* Lowe, 1994; Pucher and Williams, 1992; Stein, 1994).

Another rail alternative is light rail, a smoother, quieter version of the old-time trolley. It costs considerably less (about 20 percent) to build than traditional mass-transit systems and does not require an exclusive, separate right-of-way: it can run down the middle or side of a road, or in auto-free malls, utility corridors, or even back alleys. This flexibility reduces construction costs by avoiding the need for expensive, time-consuming underground tunnels and elevated tracks. Light rail construction can cost as little as ten to fifteen million dollars per kilometer, on average one-fifth to one-third as much as a surface metro and one-tenth the cost of an underground subway (Lowe, 1993).

Ensuring that investments in rail lines provide an adequate economic return can be accomplished only by including environmental and social criteria in the accounting process. Mass transit's worth to society extends far beyond the income generated by fares. Having commuter rail and intercity railways as alternatives to driving represents immeasurable gains: avoiding the high costs of pollution, traffic congestion, oil dependency, and road accidents. Moreover, economists agree that infrastructural improvements are a sound benefit to the national economy. A ten-year $100 billion increase in public transportation spending was estimated to boost worker output by $521 billion, versus a $237 billion increase in output resulting from the same level of spending on highways. In addition, public transit investments were shown to return net benefits almost three times as rapidly as highway investment (Lowe, 1993).

Transforming Consumer Preference

Rapid increases in the cost of car use could provide a major incentive for people to use alternative transportation systems. However, most discussions of urban transportation have concluded that changes in the mass-transit system to make it more attractive will have to be linked to changes that make car use less attractive and convenient.

The basic goal of such a policy would be to reduce single-occupancy car use in favor of either public transportation or car pooling. Obviously, care would have to be exercised to assure that such policies would not simply discourage car use to one particular location. Restricting car use in downtown areas, for example, might simply encourage relocation of stores and places of employment to suburban locations.

A number of policies are possible. Special lanes can be designated in freeways for vehicles with several passengers. Fees for low-occupancy or single-rider vehicles can be levied. Access fees can be charged for use of congested roads (Renner, 1988:49).

Outlook for the Mixed-Systems Approach

Clearly, approaches such as these would take time to implement, encounter some public resistance, and involve substantial, regionally based planning. Overall, however, the mixed-systems approach should have several advantages. It would retain much (but not all) of the flex-ibility and convenience of the present system. It can be adapted to our low-density, suburban pattern of land use. Hence, it would not require rapid, massive changes in residence, work, and travel patterns. That means it could begin to be implemented now, and we could begin to reap the benefits of increased efficiency sooner. Also, many of the changes do not require massive capital investments by government. At the same time, it is an approach that can be introduced gradually, and costs can be spread out over a number of years. Finally, it is a flexible enough approach that it can be tailored to the specific needs of each urban area. However, such a strategy does require some signifi-cant federal and state expenditures and, just as importantly, coordi-nated government planning and intervention. Whether such a government effort is likely to be forthcoming in the near future seems dubious, given current efforts to reduce government expenditures and to rely increasingly on private economic initiatives to provide services.

The city of Toronto offers us one model of an integrated transit system. Many of Toronto's subway stations provide commuter parking as well as fast transfer to surface routes (both bus and light rail). Dial-a-bus systems provide service to commuter trains. Parking is available for either the entire day, or for short-term use. Since 1963, a policy of expanding and updating transit systems to effectively serve established and growing sections of metropolitan Toronto has been fol-lowed. This plan has made it possible for 95 percent of this area's resi-dents to be within half a mile of some transit route (*Transit in Toronto*, 1987).

One of a region's basic economic assets is its transit system. A recent study of transit in Chicago provides some ideas for other cities as well. The report suggests that the region first must challenge tradi-tional assumptions concerning land use, the use of public funds, and transit districts. Residences and job sites could be clustered around transit stations and retail-service centers; and transit agencies in the metropolitan area could be consolidated. Second, transit could be made more attractive by improving existing transit services, decreas-ing travel time, making facilities and vehicles clean and safe, and developing regional travel centers in outlying areas. Flexible services such as jitneys and subscription van pools could connect dispersed populations having diverse destinations ("A Vision," 1994).

A few encouraging signs point to a hopeful outlook for mass tran-sit. Overholser (2000) noted a significant change in both attitudes and behaviors toward mass transit. She cites a recent report from the American Public Transportation Association noting a rapid increase in the use of mass transit, both in the long and short run. Ridership increased to 9 billion trips on mass transit in 1999, compared with 6.5 billion in 1972, while ridership went up 4.5 percent in 1999 compared to 1998. A Princeton Survey Research Association poll found that 26 percent of urban and suburban dwellers saw urban sprawl as their communities' worst problem. That transit ridership increased before gas prices did suggested that it reflected a basic change in behavior. Kathleen Sullivan (2000) noted that in Washington State, a 1999 Hart Research Poll found that suburban voters favored transit over road building by more than three to one.

Another study (Keyser, 1999) found that use of the St. Louis Metro light rail system benefited rural areas by increasing public awareness of public transportation, changing views of public transit, improving the economy of outlying areas, stimulating economic development and tourism, as well as providing effective alternatives to automobile travel. A similar development has taken place in Portland, Oregon, whose western corridor experienced land value increases even before new light rail infrastructure was in place (Knaap, Hopkins, and Ding, 1999).

Sullivan (2000) notes that a voluntary Commute Trip Reduction Program—a state incentive program designed to encourage riders to leave their cars at home and commute by bus, train, and van or car pool—has been not only popular but successful. The $3.8 million investment takes 18,500 cars off the roads of Washington State every day. Thus, the business community and its employees are able to get to work faster and are more productive.

EVALUATION

To a large extent, modern urban areas are a creation of the automobile. This is even more true of our newer urban areas in the Sunbelt and Mountain states. Patterns of land use, the single-family suburban house, shopping malls, and a lifestyle based on easy mobility all have resulted from nearly universal car ownership. But many urban problems and much of our wasteful energy practices are also attributable to the automobile. Central-city decay, pollution, the decline of public transit, rising transportation costs, visual blight, neighborhood destruction, and much suffering and death from auto accidents are part of the legacy of our decades-long love affair with the automobile. It now appears that this love affair has finally become too costly to continue.

The next few decades will be a period of transition for urban and metropolitan transportation. New approaches are being tried. Numerous studies show that adding and widening roads do not reduce traffic. Rather, they increase gridlock. Solutions that move people and products, not just vehicles, are in the interests of everyone. The general public needs an effective and efficient mix of solutions, a variety of viable, affordable transportation choices.

MAIN POINTS

1. Contemporary urban areas rely almost exclusively on the automobile for transportation—despite some recent revival of public transportation in some cities.
2. Automobile dependence came about as a result of increasing car ownership, suburbanization, government subsidies of highway construction, government neglect of public transit, and the influence of special interests.
3. The combination of heavy car use and suburbanization has meant that people travel more often, for more reasons, to more dispersed locations, longer distances away, and at higher speeds. However, rapidly rising traffic volume has produced gridlock in some urban areas.
4. The automobile has meant a high degree of mobility and convenience for most urban residents.
5. The flexibility provided by the automobile has been bought at a high cost in terms of economic waste, energy inefficiency, pollution, urban decay, and the creation of a group of "transportation disadvantaged."
6. Traditional mass transit has a number of problems which limit its usefulness in contemporary urban areas. These problems include those associated with low population densities, multiple destinations, high construction costs, consumer resistance, and dubious benefits to the transportation disadvantaged.
7. An alternative approach to urban transportation needs is the "mixed-systems" approach. Such an approach would include redesigning the automobile, changing car-use patterns, creating innovative approaches to mass transit, and changing consumer transportation preferences.

KEY TERMS

Gridlock   The severe traffic congestion and extremely slow travel speeds caused by traffic volume greater than the capacity of the highway system.

Mixed-Systems Approach   The strategy of designing an urban transportation system which employs a number of different modes of transportation to meet the needs of different areas and groups of travelers.

Multiple Destinations   The pattern of contemporary urban travel in which urban travelers are moving to a large number of widely dispersed destinations.

Traditional Mass Transit   A system of transportation which relies primarily on the use of high-speed rail cars and fixed-route line buses.

Transportation Disadvantaged   Those persons having less mobility because they are not able physically or financially to drive cars.

SUGGESTED READING

Goddard, Stephen B. 1994. *Getting There: The Epic Struggle Between Road and Rail in the American Century.* New York: HarperCollins, Basic Books. This book gives an appropriate account of the ongoing conflict between two important transportation elements.

Kapinos, Thomas. April 1989. "Attitudes Toward Mass Transit." *Mass Transit:* MIT 10-15. An outline of public views toward mass transit and its implications for mass-transit planning.

Kemp, Michael, and Melvyn D. Cheslow. 1976. "Transportation." In *The Urban Predicament,* edited by W. Gorham and N. Glazer. Washington, DC: Urban Institute. A reasoned overview of urban transportation problems that considers alternative policy approaches.

Knaap, Gerrit J., Lewis D. Hopkins, and Chengri Ding. 1999. *Do Plans Matter? Effects of Light Rail Plans on Land Values in Station Areas.* Cambridge, MA: Lincoln Institute of Land Policy.

Pucher, John, and Christian Lefevre. 1996. *The Urban Transport Crisis in Europe and North America.* London: Macmillan Ltd. This book gives up-to-date, detailed information about the nature and problems of transportation in these two continents.

Reconnecting Rural America: Report on Rural Intercity Passenger Transportation. 1989. Washington, DC: U.S. Department of Agriculture, Office of Transportation. Traces recent attempts to restructure a national bus system, with attention to both rural and small-town systems, and their relation to intercity systems.

Renner, Michael. 1988. *Rethinking the Role of the Automobile.* Worldwatch Paper 84. Washington, DC: Worldwatch Institute. Exploring the evolving role of cars in developing and developed nations, with a focus on environmental effects.

7

Urban Political Systems

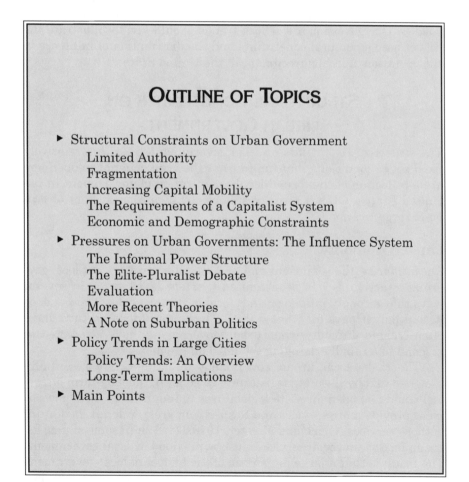

OUTLINE OF TOPICS

Urban residents rely heavily on the services provided by local government. The overall quality of life, as well as the health, safety, and economic opportunities of most urban residents depend partly on how efficiently and effectively local government delivers a wide range of services. The next chapter will examine how well local urban governments are doing in providing specific services. However, before we can consider those services we need to understand something about the general nature of urban government. In particular, we need to examine how responsive local government is to the demands placed on it by its citizens. That depends on the structural constraints that limit what local governments can do and how they go about doing it, and the distribution of political influence in the community, which determines to whom government is most likely to respond. Our discussion will conclude with an examination of recent trends in the policies pursued by city governments. Those trends should vividly illustrate the role of both structural constraints and the distribution of influence in the operation of local government in the United States.

STRUCTURAL CONSTRAINTS ON URBAN GOVERNMENT

The *structural constraints* on local governments refer to a relatively fixed set of conditions that limits what they can attempt to do. Some are a reflection of the formal legal organization of government in the United States. Others are a result of our capitalist system of economic organization.

Limited Authority

The *authority* (the legal right and responsibility) to carry out local government activities has been limited by state legislatures in several ways that strongly influence what local government does, how it does it, and how it pays for what it does. These limitations, in turn, have often created difficulty when urban governments have attempted to respond to a rapidly changing set of urban problems.

The tasks local urban government undertakes are essentially assigned to it by the state legislature. In general, the long-term historical trend has been for state legislatures to require that local government provide more services and to specify in greater detail the nature of those services (Gluck and Meister, 1979:211–12). In some states, for example, certain social services must be provided by local government. The result is that a large proportion of the budget of local government usually goes to provide services that are required by state law. For example, local governments devote about half of their total expenditures to education, the nature of whose provision is closely regulated at the state level (Wolman and Goldsmith, 1992:108). Conversely, local government is not allowed to perform other activities that the states have reserved for themselves. Setting pollution standards, for example, may be a state responsibility.

State legislatures also generally determine the basic form local government can take: for example, how much authority the mayor can have, the make-up and form of election of the city council, and the extent to which the school board is independent from the city council. In addition, states have increasingly specified in great detail how local government agencies are to operate. For example, many states specify the number of days schools are to be open, qualifications for police officers, civil-service procedures for government employees, and the nature of zoning procedures.

Finally, the type of taxes a local government can impose are usually strictly limited by state government. In practice, what this has meant is that local government relies very heavily on the real-estate property tax for its tax revenues. As of 1990, about 75 percent of local government revenues came from property taxes (about half in the case of larger municipal governments). Fees and charges for services (e.g., water, trash collection) were the second largest revenue source (Wolman and Goldsmith, 1992:111–13). Other major sources of tax revenue are generally reserved by the state. As we will see later in this chapter, this reliance on the real-estate property tax has been one source of the financial difficulties of many cities.

These limitations on local government arose for a variety of reasons, some of them very good ones. Some restrictions date to the nineteenth and early twentieth centuries, when state legislatures were controlled by representatives from rural areas. These rural representatives were fearful (partly because of the large number of foreign immigrants in the cities) of the growing size and economic power of the cities. Accordingly, they sought to impose limitations on the political power of the cities and maintain rural dominance over state government. Other restrictions grew out of a concern that local governments were not performing needed services in an adequate, equitable, or efficient way. States intervened to correct the situation by forcing local governments to undertake certain activities and mandating the level of service to be provided. In other cases, city governments were dominated by powerful and corrupt political machines, and state governments stepped in to control local corruption (Gluck and Meister, 1979:71–6).

However good the intentions of such limitations, they have often created problems for local government. The actual freedom of action of local government officials is quite limited. They have a limited ability to raise revenues and much of that revenue is committed to required programs. The ability to develop new programs, change priorities among existing programs, and respond to citizen demands and complaints is therefore not great. Local government is thus relatively inflexible in terms of the activities and programs it can undertake. That means that it also tends to be relatively unresponsive to changing citizen needs and expectations.

Not surprisingly, as new urban problems confronted urban governments in the post-1945 period, they often appeared paralyzed. They lacked both the resources and the authority to do very much to deal with the developing problems, even in those rare cases where there were both popular support and the political leadership to back new initiatives (Gluck and Meister, 1979:12–15).

New programs, and the funding for them, had to come from state and (increasingly) federal government. During the 1950s and 1960s both federal and state urban policy primarily took the form of programs either directly administered or tightly regulated by state and federal agencies. For instance, most of the urban renewal projects begun in the 1950s were dependent almost exclusively on federal funds, and each project required detailed approval at the federal level. These sorts of efforts reached their peak in the 1960s under the auspices of the Johnson administration's "Great Society" program. This only served to diminish further the independence and significance of local government. And, for better or for worse, it meant that urban policy and programs were determined mostly at the state and federal level, rather than locally. To a very large extent, what constituted urban policy in the United States had become essentially a federal responsibility. In addition, the growth of federal welfare programs created another set of de facto urban programs in the large central cities with major concentrations of the poor.

In the 1970s the federal government attempted to provide money to urban governments with fewer restrictions on how it was spent. For example, the revenue-sharing program essentially transferred federal money directly to cities for use in their general budgets with few stipulations on how it was to be spent. This may have increased local policy autonomy somewhat in the short term. However, it also made local budgets increasingly hostage to decisions made in Washington.

This dependency on state and federal government became so pervasive that Warren (1956) argued that local government agencies had essentially become tied to agencies at higher levels of government. These "vertical ties," he argued, had become more important than decision making at the local level in determining what local government did. Similarly, both Alford and Friedland (1975) and Gottdiener (1987) characterized local government as being in an essentially dependent relationship with the higher levels of government. This dependence has increasingly rendered local politics and decision making less and less relevant to understanding what local government does.

One of the major policy initiatives of the Reagan administration was the set of proposals labeled the "new federalism." These proposals explicitly sought to address the growing federal role in state and local government. They involved consolidating funding for a myriad of federal programs for states and localities into large block grants (e.g., all programs relating to transportation). States or localities were to be free to allocate money for specific programs within "blocks" as they saw fit. Overall funding was simultaneously to be substantially reduced. The policy was billed as a way of increasing state and local autonomy in relation to the federal government. It was never fully implemented because it was viewed by opponents (in Congress and state and local officials) as a disguised way of destroying many of the social programs created in the 1960s and 1970s. The fear was that drastic funding cuts could not or would not be made up at the local level. In addition, there was concern that programs targeted towards the poor and minorities would suffer the most because of their lack of political power at the state and local level. As we will see, the major funding cuts that did occur and the partial implementation of block grants that Congress approved appear to have had that result. It can be argued, moreover, that any increased autonomy (mostly obtained at the state level) was counterbalanced (especially at the local level) by the constraints imposed by reduced federal funding (Fainstein and Fainstein, 1989). Cuts in federal aid to the cities (and states) continued in the 1990s, although the rate of decline slowed. By the middle of the 1990s the total reduction in key federal urban programs since the early 1980s ranged between 30 and 100 percent. Hence, the role of federal assistance is now much smaller than it was a generation ago (Penner, 1998; Eisinger, 1998.)

At the same time, what has come to be called *devolution* continued at the federal level. The federal government has surrendered direct administrative authority to the states in a number of program areas. The most dramatic recent example was the 1996 welfare reform. The federal government now provides a fixed block grant to states to operate the new TANF welfare system within a loose set of federal guidelines. There is some indication that states have also been moving toward limited devolution to localities in some program areas. De facto devolution as been occurring because states have been reducing some kinds of aid to localities, leaving local government with more responsibility to determine funding levels. More explicit, formal devolution has occurred in a few states where legislatures have actually shifted the administration of some programs, including TANF, to the local level. However, the extent of this devolution is still very limited and whether devolution from states to localities will become more widespread remains to be seen (Watson and Gold, 1999).

Another trend in the relationship between state and local government also deserves mention. Some observers believe that the political power of central cities in state government has declined substantially. Margaret Weir summarizes this argument:

> The decline of urban population [in central cities], the rise of the suburbs, and the increasing power and fragmentation of state legislatures have all disrupted an older pattern of policy-making based on logrolling across regions. In addition the growing disconnection between state and local politics has encouraged state politicians to enact policies with little regard to their effect on localities. (1996:35)

Finally, it should be pointed out again that many federal decisions on general national policy can also be regarded as a form of "urban" policy making that fundamentally shapes the problems and opportunities faced by local government. For example, we have seen how federally supported mortgage loan guarantee programs (FHA and VA) helped determine both the form and extent of post-1945 suburbanization. The role of the federal government in shaping the economic changes of the 1970s and 1980s (discussed in chapter 2) provides another example of "indirect" urban policy making.

Wolman and Goldsmith conclude that the ability of local governments to *autonomously* affect the overall well-being of their citizens, while real, is quite limited:

> Our conclusion is that local governments . . . possess autonomy in limited, but not unimportant spheres. We end, however, by noting that this autonomy represents merely a potential which local governments may choose to exercise or not as they wish. Whether they do is a question of local government initiative and responsibility. (1992:47)

Fragmentation

American metropolitan areas are governed not by one local government but by many. The list of local government units is almost endless: city governments, suburban governments, county governments, sanitation districts, pollution control authorities, and so on. The typical large metropolitan area is governed by several hundred, usually autonomous, government units whose jurisdictions frequently overlap. The United States has a staggering total of more than 80,000 local government entities (Wolman and Goldsmith, 1992:65).

This fragmentation of local government authority has occurred for a number of reasons. Rapid urban growth meant that urban populations quickly spread out beyond central city boundaries. In the nineteenth and early twentieth centuries, cities responded by annexing these new urban areas. Cities grew very rapidly both in terms of their geographical area and population. However, except in some areas of the South and Southwest, annexation was soon stopped—usually by state legislatures (see chapter 1). Urban reformers in the early 1900s added to fragmentation by advocating the creation of numerous independent boards and agencies to encourage citizen control and weaken the power of the corruption-ridden city political machines. Also, as problems such as transportation and sanitation became regional, independent agencies (e.g., the New York Port Authority) were created to provide special services to those areas. Finally, state and federal programs to provide services to local areas added yet another set of government agencies, independent of local control and, often, of each other (Gluck and Meister, 1979:155–56; Greer, 1962; Wood, 1964).

Traditionally, most urban sociologists have been highly critical of this urban government fragmentation (Keating, 1995). For one thing, they argued that one result is poor coordinating and planning between the various government agencies attempting to deal with problems that affect a whole metropolitan area. Each governmental unit jealously protects its jurisdiction and attempts to work out solutions to problems, often with only minimal concern either for what other agencies are attempting to do or for the needs of the area as a whole (Keating, 1995:119–20; Lineberry, 1970).

Critics of fragmentation have also claimed that it leads to inefficient delivery of services and perhaps unnecessary duplication of services. For instance, both city and county government may operate police forces and build jails to serve much of the same area. Many small departments (e.g., police, fire, water) may not be as efficient as one large centralized department (Orfield, 1997; Keating, 1995:119; Wood, 1964).

Another frequently cited result of fragmentation is that the quality and level of services will vary substantially within a metropolitan area. For example, the financial difficulties of the central cities, in part a result of the loss of more affluent taxpayers to the suburbs, have resulted in a disastrous deterioration in their public schools. Within the suburbs themselves, some localities with less affluent residents may find themselves unable to provide even such basic services as sidewalks, sewers, or a professional fire department. Meanwhile, nearby suburbs with affluent residents can enjoy elaborate public services. These service differences point out again that the suburbs are not homogeneous, middle-class "bedroom" communities, but include some communities of predominantly working-class and poor residents. As a result, suburban governments have varying abilities to raise revenues and provide services (Logan and Schneider, 1981; Wood, 1964). Mark Gottdiener (1987:198) contends that this inequality in the ability to provide services also becomes self-perpetuating. Poorer communities are unable to attract more affluent residents and desirable businesses because of their inferior service provision. The resulting weak tax base makes it impossible to improve services. At the same time, wealthier communities are able to use their zoning powers to keep the less affluent out. This exclusionary zoning thus represents a method by which the more affluent attempt to insulate themselves from the problems (and taxes) of both the central city and their less affluent suburban neighbors (Orfield, 1997; Wolman and Goldsmith, 1992:75).

Fragmentation also puts pressure on urban governments to avoid policies and tax levels that would encourage the more affluent residents and business owners to move to other communities (Wolman and Goldsmith, 1992:74). For example, as we saw in chapter 4, this is the dilemma that "within-district" racial integration of central-city schools has created in many of our major metropolitan areas. Middle-class and business tax flight has also played a role in U.S. suburbanization for the last half century.

In addition, Newton (1976, 1978) argues that there is a direct relationship between fragmentation and the very low level of citizen participation in urban politics. Fragmentation means that each small political unit is unable to address the major problems of the metropolitan area. Hence, local politics only addresses the more minor problems within each small jurisdiction. These issues do not evoke much interest on the part of citizens. A case study of suburban politics by Gottdiener (1977) supported Newton's claims.

Small governments are also inherently less powerful in their dealings with higher levels of government. They have limited resources and small staffs. Moreover, they represent only a small fraction of the population of their urban area.

These criticisms of fragmentation have generally been cited by urban reformers as the impetus for creating metropolitan-wide governmental units for at least some local government service functions (Rusk, 1993). However, a number of researchers have called the critique of fragmentation into question (e.g., Ostrom, 1983; Bish and Ostrom, 1973; Popenoe, 1985; Parks and Oakerson, 1989; Stein, 1989; Keating, 1995; Wattenberg, 1999; Gordon and Richardson, 2000). They note that there is little evidence that centralized, metropolitan service departments are actually more efficient. Indeed, small service units may often be more efficient. Moreover, "public choice" theorists argue that small government units may be more responsive and accessible to citizens and provide people with a form of local autonomy which they prefer. The large number of local governments can be thought of as a "market" in which citizens choose the type of government and mix of services that best conform to their preferences and needs. As a consequence, the overall distribution of services in a metropolitan area may better reflect citizen preferences because of fragmentation. In addition, these theorists have argued fragmentation means that capital is most successfully raised by those governments that are more fiscally responsible and efficient. Hence, fragmentation assures more efficient allocation of capital investment.

The controversy over the merits and limitations of metropolitan government is likely to remain unresolved at the academic level:

> The technical arguments about consolidation versus fragmentation have proved inconclusive. This is partly for lack of data, partly because of difficulties in measurement but mainly because the items which are to be measured are themselves politically contested or normative . . . For example, we have seen that consolidation may provide the resource base for more redistribution and the sense of community which could sustain such a policy. On the other hand, it might bring into the city suburban and conservative votes disinclined to vote for politicians favoring redistribution. . . . Generally speaking, people with a beneficent view of government will support consolidation. . . . People who regard government as a necessary evil . . . will tend to favor small-scale, fragmented government. (Keating, 1995:131–32)

There have been a few successful government consolidation efforts (e.g., Indianapolis, Nashville, Columbus). At least some observers would rate these efforts as effective experiments in governmental reorganization (e.g., Rusk, 1993). However, the practical reality is that political opposition to government consolidation is widespread. Local officials whose power or positions might be threatened often oppose consolidation. Public opposition to consolidation appears to be strong. That opposition has a number of sources. For example, suburban residents may be concerned that their taxes will be raised to support central-city services or that busing to achieve racial integration would be mandated in a consolidated school system. Both suburban and central-city residents may fear the loss of political autonomy (Baldassare, 1989,1994).

Other proposals for dealing with urban problems on a metropolitan-wide basis have argued for more limited forms of government cooperation and coordination. Such proposals are believed to be more likely to muster political support because they are less threatening to suburban interests. For example, Myron Orfield points to the success of such regional cooperation in the Minneapolis area (Orfield, 1997, 1998). Christopher Leo and his associates believe there is a real possibility that a system of "regional growth management" could curb the worst problems associated with urban sprawl and attract major political support (1998).

Increasing Capital Mobility

As was pointed out in chapter 2, the United States economy has come to be increasingly dominated by large corporations serving a national and/or international market, often from a large number of geographically dispersed facilities. Modern communication and transportation systems allow administrative control to be exercised far from centers of administration. Fewer and fewer corporations are tied to a single metropolitan market. There is less reason to locate in one particular urban area because of geographic factors, quality of labor supply, physical infrastructure, or transportation facilities. For an increasing number of corporations, this *capital mobility* means there are numerous urban areas which are more or less interchangeable in terms of their desirability as places to locate corporate facilities. At the same time, pressures created by increased international competition have made the search for more cost-effective locations a major corporate priority (Sassen, 1994, 1996). For example, the last two decades have witnessed a major further dispersal of the auto industry away from its traditional location in or near Detroit (Kantor, 1987:506–7).

As a consequence, urban areas find themselves in an increasingly fierce competition for corporate investment. Indeed, the fragmentation of metropolitan government means that even within a given urban area, local governments compete with each other. This puts large corporations in a very favorable bargaining position. They can demand subsidies, tax relief, favorable regulatory policies (e.g., zoning laws), and other special treatment as the price for deciding to locate in a particular urban area (Kantor, 1987:507; Gottdiener, 1987:199; Fainstein, 1996; Sassen, 1994, 1996; Jaffe and Blackmon, 1998). For example, in 1989, Chicago and the state of Illinois (representing the Chicago area) found themselves in an intense bargaining war with other metropolitan areas to obtain a commitment from Sears Corporation to locate a major portion of its central headquarters operations (previously all centered in Chicago) in their areas. (Suburban Chicago "won," after agreeing to provide major subsidies to Sears.)

Such competition is a major constraint on the actions of local government. Loss of corporate investment to more aggressive competing localities is increasingly possible. As a consequence, local leaders have come to see protection and expansion of the local economic (and tax) base as a central priority of government, even if it means paying less attention to other pressing needs or citizen demands. Corporate preferences and concerns tend to take precedence. Various schemes to attract corporate investment consume a major portion of governmental effort and resources (Kantor, 1987:510–11; Molotch, 1988:32–35; Logan and Molotch, 1987: 57–62; Fainstein, 1996; Sassen, 1994, 1996).

The Requirements of a Capitalist System

A number of "neo-Marxist" sociologists have suggested that the most fundamental constraint on urban government (as well as on all other levels of government) in the United States derives from the nature of capitalism itself. In this view, a capitalist system has certain fundamental requirements if it is to continue to operate. The activities of local governments are seen as necessary to meet some of those requirements. Hence, there are some things which urban government simply *must* do.

The most common form this argument has taken is associated with the so-called structuralist neo-Marxist theory of how the political system operates (see O'Connor, 1973; Habermas, 1975). These theorists contend that modern capitalism has become increasingly dependent on government action. In this view, corporate profitability has come to depend upon obtaining government subsidies (e.g., labor force training at public expense, government supplied infrastructure, and special tax breaks). This is the so-called "capital accumulation" function of government. Consequently, not only are local governments motivated to attract capital investment by assisting corporations, the survival of the capitalist system depends on it. In addition, government is called upon to alleviate some of the consequences of corporate activity (e.g., pollution, periodic unemployment, and inadequate housing for the poor). In part these activities are imperative to assure the survival of the labor force needed by capitalist enterprises (again, assisting "capital accumulation"). No less important, they also reduce public discontent caused by the negative consequences of corporate action. Controlling discontent is the so-called "legitimation" function of government. Thus, action to assist in capital accumulation and legitimation on the part of government at all levels is one of the "imperatives" of capitalism.

A different view of what government, of necessity, must do to preserve capitalism is offered by Gottdiener (1987). He contends that there are two levels or tiers of government operation. The first tier is constrained by the requirements of capitalism. This tier enforces the system of private property and wage labor that is the fundamental defining characteristic (and requirement) of a capitalist economy. It does so through its "social control" activities (i.e., the police and legal system). For example, local government cannot allow strikers to seize or destroy corporate property during a labor dispute. Gottdiener does not deny that the activities specified by the structuralists may be undertaken by urban governments. However, he does not see them as a fundamental requirement for the survival of capitalism. Rather, they are activities undertaken in the second tier of government operation, which affects the distribution of wealth rather than the more fundamental system of private property. Gottdiener contends that what determines the policies of government at this second level depends on the struggle for influence over government by various groups in the community, not just corporate needs.

Economic and Demographic Constraints: Local Resources and Needs

We have already examined the key trends in economic development and population movement in U.S. urban areas. From the viewpoint of local officials, the results of these trends place both policy demands upon them and determine the local resources available to support public policy.

The most obvious and basic of these economic and demographic constraints in the United States is that class, racial, and ethnic groupings tend to concentrate in certain jurisdictions. Central cities tend to have a high concentration of the disadvantaged in terms of class, race, and ethnicity. As we discussed in chapter 4, this population places heavy demands on cities for certain kinds of crime control, special educational services for less affluent children, low-cost housing, and the like. At the same time, there has been a substantial erosion of the central-city economic base due to the loss of traditional manufacturing jobs, the movement of some office operations to the suburbs, the relative decline of central shopping districts, and the like. City officials find themselves confronted with demands for services and programs to serve a needy population and a declining tax base to support those programs. At the same time, they are aware that major efforts to attract new economic activities are required in an environment in which private investment has become highly selective and mobile. Given their limited revenue sources, city leaders find themselves constantly torn between service delivery and economic development activities.

Demographic and economic constraints for suburban governments are different and more highly variable, depending upon the particular mix of economic activities and the demographic characteristics of the different suburbs. High-status residential suburbs, for example, enjoy an enviable tax base because of their high property values. Yet their governments face a host of constraints. Their mostly fiscally conservative residents have become increasingly resistant to tax increases, but demand some very high quality services—especially in regard to schools. Commercial development would increase the business tax base, but runs into resistance from residents who wish to maintain the exclusionary zoning for residential use to maintain their property values and quality of life. Hence, even in a high-status suburb, government resources are limited, while the demand for services continues to grow. At the other end of the suburban spectrum, older blue-collar suburbs may be encountering residential decay; a changing mix of residents by class, race, and/or ethnicity; and changing service demands caused by that changing population composition.

Further examples need not concern us here. It should be clear that urban local governments do not confront all the same problems with the same resources. There is a tendency in the literature on urban politics to focus on larger central cities. The discussion here is based on that literature and cannot attempt the complex analysis needed to redress this unbalanced emphasis. Hopefully, this discussion has at least made the variability of the constraints facing urban governments in the same metropolitan area an explicit issue.

PRESSURES ON URBAN GOVERNMENTS: THE INFLUENCE SYSTEM

The policies pursued by urban governments are not determined completely by the structural constraints they face. Those constraints simply represent the general environment in which decisions are made. Within the limits imposed by that environment, urban governments enjoy considerable potential latitude in adopting specific policies.

In principle, the formal procedures of electing public officials by universal suffrage is supposed to assure that public decision making reflects the distribution of preferences among citizens. However, few scholars of electoral systems believe that elections actually achieve that result. They fail to do so for a number of reasons. For example, in local elections, only a small (unrepresentative) minority (less than 20 percent) normally bother to vote. Voters tend to be poorly informed, and their sources of information are limited. Elections provide limited candidate choice and rarely provide citizens with clear issue choices. Once elected, officials need not be bound by their campaign promises. Many policy decisions are really made outside of public view and/or by appointed civil servants (Marger, 1987:227–54). In short, elections are, at best, "crude blunt instruments" of popular control.

The Informal Power Structure

More crucial to policy outcome than the formal system of elections is what might be called the "informal structure of power." The *informal structure* consists of a system of political "influence" relationships. *Influence* is a kind of political power that exists outside of the official framework of authority created by laws or government charters. It consists of the ability to affect the decisions of government without going through the procedures (e.g., voting) called for by the system of laws. For example, if a wealthy individual can obtain a tax reduction by making a large campaign contribution to a politician, we say that the person has political influence.

In general, social scientists have viewed influence in group terms. Various groups are seen as having common interests and certain resources which allow them to exercise influence to achieve goals that serve their interests. A number of such groups can be identified in any urban political system.

Business Leaders

There can be no doubt that local business leaders exercise considerable influence on local government. (Just how much we will discuss in a moment.) They have the ability to make substantial campaign contributions, and they have both the information and the political skills necessary to become involved in local politics. In addition, the local media (press, radio, television) will tend to reflect the interests of business either because they are owned by local business interests and/or because they do not wish to offend local advertisers. Business leaders also have considerable prestige in most communities, so they are able to affect public opinion. Business leaders are frequently asked to serve on government commissions and advisory groups because of their leadership skills and prestige. Finally, they are often in a position to directly affect the economic health (and tax base) of a community since they are major employers. In some cases, this includes the ability to move their businesses out of the community if local government policy on such issues as zoning and taxation is not to their liking. We have already seen that this is not an idle threat, as the older central cities in the North have discovered.

Formally Organized Interest Groups

Every urban area has a large number of organized groups that attempt to influence local government. These include such groups as labor unions, professional associations, charitable organizations, civic improvement associations, neighborhood improvement associations, and the PTA. Frequently they have, or are in the position to collect, money from their members to make campaign contributions. They can get their members to vote for candidates endorsed by the leadership. They also can be a source of campaign workers (a very important role that many labor unions play), and their leaders can often attract media attention and influence public opinion. Many of these organizations (e.g., charitable groups) also provide a political platform for business leaders, who often are the leaders of these voluntary organizations.

Government Officials

In the last two decades scholars have paid increasing attention to government officials as a group with political interests and the resources to pursue them. At the very least, they have an interest in increasing their own power and privileges. The primary means of doing so is to expand the scope, power, and resources of government itself. Besides their formal authority, such officials also possess specialized knowledge about what government is doing and how government operates. They can use this information to their own advantage. Elected office also is a "bully pulpit" (in T. R. Roosevelt's famous phrase) from which to influence public opinion. Moreover, they have easy access to other influential people in the community.

Local Government Employees

Especially in larger cities in the North, government employees have emerged as a major political force. As the (somewhat ironic) result of efforts to prevent corruption and favoritism, many local government employees have civil service protection and cannot be threatened by loss of their jobs or promotions by elected officials. Moreover, elected officials depend on the permanent bureaucracy for the specialized knowledge and skill needed for planning and implementing policy. City employees also provide very visible and critical services that can be disrupted to put pressure on elected officials and the public. Thus, for example, the police can develop "blue flu" (call in sick in large numbers) or write large numbers of parking tickets to press their demands. Of course, in some cities, government employees also exercise influence as formally organized interest groups through their labor unions. Consequently, public employees are in a position to block policies of which they disapprove and make demands for the recognition of their economic interests. For instance, when the first black mayor of Gary, Indiana, was elected, he had considerable difficulty changing government operations because of the opposition of the city bureaucracy and, very importantly, the police.

Unorganized Voting Blocs

Most urban areas have at least some divisions in the electorate based on such things as ethnicity or religion. Often these voters are represented by informal groups. Even when they are not, they may tend to vote together as a bloc based on a sense of shared identity, interests, and tradition. Hence, elected officials may feel obliged to make special efforts to please these groups in hopes of obtaining their support. The result is that their concerns may carry more weight than other, less homogeneous groups which are less likely to vote together. For example, in most cities, middle-class voters have an influence on local government much greater than their sheer numbers in the electorate might suggest. This is because middle-class voters are much more likely to be informed and concerned about local political affairs and are much more likely to vote. In contrast, lower-class voters are much more likely to be politically apathetic and, hence, their concerns and problems can be more safely ignored by local government. (However, some observers feel that the large numbers of welfare recipients in the central cities may have become a significant voting bloc, despite low voting turnout, simply because of their large numbers and their dependence on government.)

New Urban Social Movements

Beginning in the 1970s an increasing number of urban sociologists began to point to a new form of politically mobilized group that either actually or potentially could have a major impact on local government: "new urban social movements." Fainstein and Hirst, in a recent review of the literature, suggest that such groups are unlike traditional work-based labor unions and other essentially class-based movements in that they

> . . . typically challenge government's role in producing or reinforcing an uneven distribution of power and resources. . . . [T]heir objectives transcend specific policy concessions . . . [and aim at] changing urban meaning . . . by break[ing] down the material and social hierarchies structuring urban life and produc[ing] in their

stead a city organized around use values, autonomous local cultures, and decentralized participatory democracy. . . . (1995:183)

In other words, these groups are oriented toward racial-ethnic, cultural, and quality-of-life issues. Examples of such groups in the United States in the last few decades would include racially/ethnically based community groups, neighborhood groups seeking to protect some aspect of local community life, ecology groups seeking to limit some aspect of local regional development, religiously based groups seeking public recognition of their rights and values, gay rights organizations, feminist groups seeking to empower their members, homeowners or renters groups, and xenophobic anti-immigrant groups seeking to defend some aspect of the dominant culture (Fainstein and Hirst, 1995:184–96).

The Elite-Pluralist Debate

How much influence do these various groups have? In the last several decades, social scientists have made a major effort to determine the relative weight of the various groups in the political influence system at the local level. In the 1950s and 1960s this research took the form of "community power studies." Two contradictory views developed: the pluralist and the elite views.

Pluralists argued that influence is fairly widely distributed between various segments of the community (Dahl, 1961; Polsby, 1963; Judge, 1995). These segments were viewed as being represented by some more or less organized groups (which pluralists called *interest groups*) that actively work to influence local government in favor of the people they represent. Interest groups were seen as fairly representative of the range of political concerns in the community: most people have their interests protected by at least one, and usually more, organized interest groups.

Pluralists argued that the political leadership of a community is usually not unified on most issues. Different leaders are important for influencing different government policies. Community leaders represent different groups, and these groups have clearly different goals and concerns. For instance, Robert Dahl, in his classic study of the city of New Haven, identified three critical local issues (school decisions, urban renewal, and political nominations) and found different sets of leaders attempting to influence government on the different issues.

Moreover, each interest group has some effective means for exercising influence in areas that are of concern to it. Hence, the pluralists contended that no one group or its leaders is powerful enough (or even interested enough) to dominate local government on every issue. Local policy, as a consequence, was seen as a compromise between a limited set of interest groups. Faced with conflicting demands of the different interest groups, government officials and politicians try to find a compromise that is acceptable to all the involved groups. Thus, according to the pluralists, the role of political leaders is that of "honest brokers" (negotiators) who put together coalitions (alliances of interest groups) backing a compromise policy. Government officials themselves were seen as relatively neutral participants who simply seek to keep the various interests satisfied. No one group gets everything it wants, but almost everybody has some indirect influence on government policy. It is not a perfect system, said the pluralists, but one that is reasonably responsive to citizen desires.

For pluralists, the big danger from this sort of system is not that it is undemocratic, but that it may lead to paralysis and stalemate. The various groups' positions may be far apart, and they may so effectively block each others' influence that no policy compromise can be achieved. Hence, no government action at all can take place. This sort of problem is most likely to arise in the case of major issues that affect many groups and where the issues involved are extremely controversial. Under these conditions the politics of compromise may become the politics of inaction and drift. Thus, the dilemma of the influence system is that the very process that makes the political system democratic may also render government incapable of acting on the most important issues it faces.

Elite theorists of community power (e.g., Hunter, 1952) did not necessarily deny that such interest groups exist and function the way the pluralists said they do. The key difference in the elite view is the notion that one group has overwhelming political influence, and the other groups are of only secondary importance. This dominant group, the power *elite,* is usually identified as consisting of major business leaders in the community: for example, bankers, newspaper owners, real estate developers, owners of large retail enterprises, and executives of large local corporations.

The basis of this elite's power, said elite theorists, is shared interests, coordination of political activities, and the possession of resources that can be used for maintaining political dominance.

According to elite theory, members of the elite have a sense of shared interests based on their economic and social positions. Simply put, they want a "good business climate" in the community. The goals are to minimize local government interference in their business operations (including keeping taxes low) and to obtain services which benefit local business activity (e.g., "reasonable" zoning policies).

Given their shared interests, the elite can be expected to work together to achieve them. Through informal meetings, regular social contact in clubs and organizations, and even secret political strategy meetings, they develop common positions on issues. Often, they attempt to stay out of the political limelight and work through other people who function as their representatives. Thus, leaders of charita-

ble organizations, local politicians, and the like really are only representatives of powerful community leaders who prefer to work behind
the scenes.

Elite efforts are more consistently successful than the efforts of
other groups, argued the elite theorists, because the political resources
they control are much greater than those of other groups. They have
more money to contribute. Media control is in their hands. The economic fate of the community can be fundamentally affected by their
business decisions. In a real "showdown" they have more ability to
protect their vital interests than do other groups.

The consequences of elite influence is clear, said elite theorists.
Local government policies tend to reflect elite interests and concerns.
For instance, money may be appropriated for urban renewal, but the
money will go for improvements for the downtown business district
while the housing needs of the poor will be ignored or given only minimal attention. Parking lots and convention centers will be built,
expressways will cut through working-class neighborhoods, and business interests will be the prime beneficiaries.

The problem created by elite control is therefore seen as the subver-
sion of democratic control. Behind the noise of election campaigns, con-
flicts in city council, and the demands of the contending interest groups,
a small group of business leaders actually chart the political course of
the community. Government is viewed as a creature of the business
elite, rather than a reflection of general community interests and
desires. (See Harding, 1995, for a recent summary of the elite tradition.)

Evaluation

Which view is right? There is no simple answer to that question. As
Walton (1966) pointed out, the two approaches use different methods
to reach their opposing conclusions. Elite theorists use the "reputa-
tional" approach to identify the elite, and pluralists use a "decision-
making" approach to determine which groups participate in making
policy. Thus, the conclusions of the two theoretical approaches appear
to be a consequence of the methods of research they employ. As long as
there is no clearcut way to decide which method is better, there is no
way to decide which theory fits the evidence best.

Some researchers have attempted to get around this stalemate by
concluding that the whole theoretical debate between the pluralists and
the elite theorists is essentially ideological and really misses the point.
Rather than insisting that urban government is always either pluralist
or elite in structure, these researchers suggest that the extent to which
a community is pluralist or elite in structure is a matter of degree, and
communities vary quite a bit in the nature of their influence structures.
Hence, some communities may have relatively strong political elites,
others may be primarily pluralist, and still others may fall somewhere

in between. Thus, the degree to which local political influence is centralized in the hands of an elite is highly variable. Urban governments can be ranked on a continuum (a graduated scale) from high to low in terms of how centralized political influence has become. The task of research on urban influence then becomes to identify characteristics of cities associated with high or low centralization and how the degree of centralization affects policy decision making (Clark, 1968).

More recently, a number of theorists have attempted to combine and/or modify the pluralist and elite perspectives in various ways to develop a general theory of influence at the local level. All these new theoretical approaches recognize a role for conflict and contention between competing interest groups at the local level. All of them also identify a special role played by a particular elite group. However, how they treat the role of nonelite interest groups and their depiction of the nature and behavior of elite groups varies considerably. To illustrate these various new approaches we will briefly examine four recent theories: (1) state managerialism, (2) regime theory, (3) the city as growth machine, and (4) the two-tiered state.

More Recent Theories

Pluralist theory views local government officials as relatively neutral brokers between interest groups. Traditional elite theory treats those officials as essentially passive agents of business interests. The emergence of what is called the "neo-Weberian" approach calls both of those views into question. This theory is usually called *state managerialism* (Gottdiener, 1987:66).

Theorists employing this approach (e.g., Pahl, 1977; Lipsky, 1976; Block, 1980) argue that government officials (state managers) represent an independent "interest group" that seeks to influence public policy to benefit itself. Most of these theorists argue that what state managers want is to increase their own power and the resources under their control by expanding the role of government. They are free to pursue their own goals because authority over the government administrative apparatus provides them with resources that allow them to free themselves from outside control. For instance, they have access to specialized knowledge on government operations which no one else possesses. Civil service bureaucrats are protected from easy dismissal, and they are given considerable latitude on how they perform their tasks (Gottdiener, 1987:66). The result, argue these theorists, is that the characteristics of local government organization and the preferences of state managers play a powerful independent role in shaping the nature of urban government policy. For example, Pahl (1977) argues that those groups that are best able to deal with complex bureaucratic rules and procedures will get the most resources from local government simply because officials find it less difficult to deal with those groups.

State managerialists differ, however, in how they view the relationship of state managers to other groups. Some implicitly seem to assume that there is an essentially pluralist system in which state managers enjoy an especially strategic position to determine the nature of policy (e.g., Lipsky, 1976). Others (e.g., Block, 1980) argue that business interests are the chief group putting pressures upon and constraining the behavior of state managers. State managers dare not pursue policies which so threaten business interests that they become unwilling to invest in the economy. At the same time, other citizen groups cannot be completely ignored. State managers need at least the grudging support of average citizens, if for no other reason than to avoid mass political discontent and disorder. Hence, state managers will sometimes—especially in times of crisis and impending mass discontent—adopt policies favorable to average citizens, even if it runs contrary to the immediate interests of business.

Closely related to managerialism is *regime theory*. Gerry Stoker (1995:54–71) provides an overview of this new view. It emerged as a major approach to urban politics in the mid-1980s and explicitly rejects both the pluralist and elitist traditions. The best-known regime theorist is Clarence Stone, whose writings reflect his work on politics in Atlanta (1989, 1993, 1995). Regime theorists adopt an essentially neo-Weberian view of local government officials as relatively autonomous, while accepting as a given the constraints imposed by a capitalist system of political-economy and acknowledging the privileged position of business. At the same time, like pluralists, they acknowledge at least the potential for urban government paralysis created by a political system fragmented into a large number of competing interest groups. Indeed, the central question for regime theorists is: how do urban government officials manage to govern at all given the powerful competing demands placed on them and the very real constraints on their freedom of action?

The answer to this problem of governance is the creation of the "regime." Stone defines a regime as an ". . . informal yet relatively stable group with access to institutional resources that enable it to have a sustained role in making governing decisions" (Stone, 1989:4). Such a group usually consists of a network of cooperating organizations (including government) that recognizes the essential role each plays in making and implementing public policy. This network differs from a pluralist interest group coalition in that it is not based on single-issue, short-term bargaining by otherwise unobligated groups. Rather, it is a more stable system of ongoing relationships linked by a sense of solidarity, loyalty, and mutual support that the participants view as necessary for governance in their mutual interest.

Regime theorists do not assume that public policy is a simple aggregation of the interests of the participants in the local urban political regime. Instead, public policy emerges out of the attempt to find a shared sense of purpose and direction. That shared sense of purpose is strongly shaped by what the participants consider feasible for government to do. In turn, the emphasis on feasibility turns the regime toward the concerns of resource-rich groups. That approach almost assures a concern with major business interests, but almost always has to be linked to the interests of other politically mobilized groups in the local community. As a consequence, public policy tends to reflect three factors: (1) the makeup of the governing regime, (2) how the relationships between the major members of the regime develop, and (3) the kinds of resources each member of the regime brings to governance (Stoker, 1995:61).

Stone (1993) argues that four general types of urban regimes have characterized urban politics in the recent past. Stoker summarizes this typology as follows (emphasis added):

> *Maintenance regimes* seek not major change but rather to preserve what is. Their core governing task of routine service delivery requires relatively straightforward relationships between government officials and nongovernmental actors. A *developmental regime* in contrast needs more resources and is attempting a more complex governing task. Such regimes are concerned to take positive action to promote growth or counter decline. *Middle-class progressive regimes* in contrast seek environmental protection and control over growth and/or social gains from growth. Such regimes engage in a complex form of regulation as their core governing task. Finally, Stone identifies *lower-class opportunity expansion regimes* which in order to achieve their ends require substantial mass mobilization. Such regimes face resource and coordination prerequisites that are often absent in American cities. (1995:61)

Regime theory has enjoyed considerable support among students of local politics in the last decade. Numerous studies have used this framework to analyze specific urban governments (Kantor, Savitch, and Haddock, 1997; DiGaetano, 1997; DiGaetano and Lawless, 1999; Lauria, 1997). Probably the most commonly cited problem these studies have revealed is that ". . . regime theory neglects to specify the ways in which external or nonlocal forces shape the processes of urban governance" (DiGaetano, 1997:865; see also Sites, 1997). As has already been stressed in this chapter, external constraints on urban government play a powerful role in what these governments do.

A much different view is provided by Molotch (1988) and Logan (Logan and Molotch, 1987), who argue that urban governments function as *growth machines*. While it has significant similarities to the traditional elite view, this view represents a major modification of that earlier approach. It also incorporates many of the basic insights of another major recent approach to urban politics called the "political economy" perspective. These theorists also acknowledge at least some role for the citizen interest groups of pluralist theory.

The growth machine consists of those interest groups that have the most to gain from rapid economic growth in a given local political jurisdiction: real estate developers, local business leaders, providers of professional services, financial institutions, and newspapers. All such groups stand to obtain major direct financial benefits from local growth. Even local universities, cultural centers, and social service agencies are likely to view growth as a source of increased students, clients, and patrons. On the other hand, there are many groups that are not the direct beneficiaries of development and do not participate in the growth machine. Large corporations not headquartered in the area and/or having operations in many locations have little stake in the success or growth of one area: they can locate anywhere. In addition, Logan and Molotch argue that rapid local growth is probably not in the interest of most average citizens. Growth increases such things as housing costs, congestion, pollution, crime, and taxes. While all groups suffer from these problems of growth, only those in the growth machine reap major benefits. For example, poor people may not benefit from increased job opportunities because many of the new jobs go to better qualified migrants. An increasing tax burden may fall mostly on homeowners.

Why does the growth machine have its way, even if the benefits of growth are spread among the interest groups so unevenly? Logan and Molotch answer with an essentially elite-theory answer. The growth machine, through such things as campaign contributions and control of the media, has a major say in the selection of the political leadership.

However, Logan and Molotch do not consider their theory as simply an extension or refinement of elite theory. Rather, they present it as a synthesis of previous theorizing. They acknowledge that factors emphasized in other theories, including pluralism, limit the power of the growth machine. These factors are outside constraints on the growth machine. The most important of those constraints is that identified by "political-economy" theorists: the danger that corporate capital will either fail to invest or remove its capital investment to more attractive localities. We have already discussed the implications of this constraint. Logan and Molotch regard other constraints as much less important in affecting the actions of the growth machine. They accept the notion that the competence, unity, and preferences of state managers may have some minor influence on the success of the growth machine coalition. The least effective constraint, they argue, is the impact of the efforts of average citizen groups: established interest groups, voting blocs, and political movements. Their successes in opposing the growth machine are likely to be limited in scope (achieving minor concessions) and short-lived (once the group disbands).

John Logan and associates, in a recent review of twenty years of empirical research on growth machine theory, argue that the main claims of the theory have been supported. Growth is the central issue of most local politics, and pro-growth interests are usually the most successful influence groups at the local level (Logan, Whaley, and Crowder, 1997).

Finally, Gottdiener (1987) has proposed a theory which he regards as a balanced synthesis of recent theorizing about the local state, which he calls the theory of the *two-tiered state*. As we have already discussed, the first tier refers to those state activities directly constrained by the requirements of a capitalist system. The second tier refers to state activities that affect the distribution of wealth in society (e.g., tax policies, the provision of services to different groups, and government subsidies). Contrary to most neo-Marxist theorists, Gottdiener does not regard the second tier as being directly constrained by the requirements of the capitalist system. Rather, policy outcomes in the second tier are the result of the conflict among three general groups: state managers, business interests, and citizen groups. To further complicate the struggle between these groups, each of them is frequently divided into factions pursuing their own interests. For example, public employees may seek to increase their wages and job security, creating problems for elected officials. Thus, Gottdiener proposes a model of conflict which has some similarities to the pluralist view. However, agreeing with the managerialists, he treats state managers as having their own set of interests, rather than treating them as neutral coalition builders (the pluralist view).

Thus, Gottdiener argues that elite theory and more recent neo-Marxist theory oversimplify how influence is exercised. He also recognizes the contribution of pluralist and managerial theorists. However, he argues that the result of politics at the local level is quite similar to that suggested by the elite theorists and neo-Marxists:

> Local government in the United States is nourished currently by political crumbs falling from the table of higher state levels. Its functions are defined by the interplay between systemic needs of the larger social structure and the actions of powerful interests that bind decision-making to specific social outcomes. Democratic participation in this process has very little to do with the way this system functions. (Gottdiener, 1987:269)

A Note on Suburban Politics

With the exception of research on political fragmentation, most research on urban politics has had a strong bias toward larger urban political systems, usually the central cities. In principle at least, the theoretical models just discussed should be applicable to the smaller governmental units in metropolitan areas. We should expect most of the same kinds of limits on direct citizen rule and the kinds of interest groups found in the cities. On the other hand, suburbs differ from cities and one another in terms of such characteristics as population size, class composition, economic base, and the nature of the business community. Consequently, certain types of suburbs in particular metropolitan areas might, to use Stone's terminology, be characterized by different sorts of "regimes." For example, high-status suburbs often use exclusionary zoning and growth restrictions to maintain their character as primarily upper-middle or upper-class residential enclaves (Logan and Molotch, 1987:135; Logan et al., 1997: 612–14). Along with fragmentation, what this potential diversity means is that any urban area is probably characterized by substantial diversity and complexity in the actual operation of the totality of the governments that seek to govern it. Any attempt to discern a single, focused system of political influence for an entire metropolitan area is probably doomed to failure. Instead, the best way to think of government at the level of a whole metropolitan area is that of a complex array of interests, some region-wide, some local, all trying to influence a "crazy quilt" of governments and agencies.

POLICY TRENDS IN LARGE CITIES

Ultimately, politics "matter" because they create public policy. As we have seen, at least since the 1960s, the old central cities of the North have been confronted with a growing array of problems that are commonly viewed as making up the contemporary urban crisis. While no two cities have responded to this crisis in an identical way, it is possible to identify certain general tendencies that are common to most of them. We have already looked at some of them in previous chapters. Looked at from the perspective of almost a half century, it is possible to discern a basic trend in the policy orientation of big city government. We now turn to a brief overview of that trend.

Policy Trends: An Overview

Recall that by the 1960s the governments of big cities were facing a number of alarming trends: industrial stagnation or decline; loss of downtown retail dominance; rapid suburbanization of younger, more affluent households; growth of low-income populations, in part because of rapid African-American migration from the South; stagnation or decline in population and tax base; growing social problems associated with a growing poverty population; increasing racial tension around such issues as school integration, crime, and police brutality; and an aging, deteriorating housing stock and public infrastructure. The continued vitality of downtowns (especially in corporate headquarters cities such as New York and Chicago) remained one of the few bright spots for the big cities.

Local revenues were simply inadequate to fund programs designed to deal with social and economic change on this scale. As their populations declined, these cities had fewer people to tax. The population that remained was poorer and less able to pay taxes. Property taxes on real estate yielded less income as property values declined (or increased slowly) in poorer neighborhoods. There were more poor neighborhoods as the middle class left and the poor arrived. A decline in industrial and retail trade further reduced taxable property. As tax rates were increased to compensate for this decline in the *tax base* (value of the property available to tax), opposition to further increases grew. Higher rates threatened to encourage more affluent homeowners and businesses to move to the suburbs or other areas. Finally, the limited authority of urban city governments to impose new kinds of taxes, and the unwillingness of state legislatures to grant them new taxing authority, made it difficult to tap new tax sources (Petersen, 1976; Bahl and Schroeder, 1978).

For a while, city governments got around these revenue limitations by obtaining more and more federal aid. Federal aid for the "urban redevelopment" of downtowns, construction of public housing (and later, other forms of housing subsidies for the poor), various types of antipoverty programs, "revenue-sharing" grants for neighborhood revitalization and economic development projects, mass-transit subsidies, job-training programs (e.g., the CETA program of the early 1970s), and the like steadily increased during the 1960s and early 1970s. Based primarily on federal largesse, central cities appeared to be mounting aggressive efforts to revitalize their downtowns, deal with social problems and poverty, and encourage business investment. However, the result was that city governments became increasingly dependent on federal aid for a large share of their operating budgets. In most large cities by the mid-1970s federal aid equaled about half of all the money raised from local sources (Bahl and Schroeder, 1978; Reischauer, 1978).

The period of growing federal subsidy and additional funding for new programs effectively came to end in the mid-1970s. With some fluctuations, after that, federal aggregate spending for cities entered a period of gradual decline in "real dollar" terms (after adjustment for inflation). Moreover, there were major shifts in where the money went. Fewer dollars were funneled through programs run by the cities (e.g., job training, mass transit, and local public housing authorities) and more went directly to individuals (e.g., housing rent subsidies). The result was a large (on average, over 50 percent) decline in federal funds as a percentage of local government budgets (Eisinger, 1998; Park, 1994; Parker, 1995; Morgan and Hirlinger, 1993; Fainstein and Fainstein, 1989; Peterson, 1985).

The direct budgetary result for big cities in the North was almost perpetual fiscal stress for all of them and intermittent budgetary crises for many of them. All these cities found that past budgetary increases were not sustainable and that major budgetary reductions in some program areas were necessary to balance expenditures with available revenues. Each year city officials have had to make hard decisions about what services to maintain or cut, and/or what taxes to increase, to balance their budgets. This constant strain to balance very tight budgets is known as *fiscal stress*. In some cities, unanticipated revenue shortfalls, increased costs, and/or reductions in federal or state aid levels (not to mention just poor planning) quickly led to budgetary crises. Officials found themselves confronting a rapidly widening gap between revenues and expenditures that threatened the ability of these cities to pay their obligations. Faced with potential bankruptcy, drastic budgetary reductions and tax adjustments were necessary to resolve these crises (Pammer, 1990; Morgan and Hirlinger, 1993).

The response to fiscal stress and/or fiscal crisis resulted in more than budgetary reductions. It resulted in a major shift in big city policy concerns. Programs oriented toward the poor were particularly likely to be trimmed. Cities that operated social programs with federal funds and then lost that funding in the 1980s were not likely to maintain the programs with their own funds. Cities were more reluctant to cut "basic services" (e.g., police and fire protection), but many eventually did so. Expenditures on physical facilities were selectively reduced. Those programs viewed as contributing to business investment were maintained or, if possible, even increased. Others (e.g., neighborhood parks, school buildings) were allowed to deteriorate. Some services were privatized. In some cases that meant the city simply stopped providing the service and allowed private businesses to deliver it for a fee. In other cases, cities contracted the service out to private business at a set price. Some cities even tried to give away some services (e.g., city-owned hospitals or colleges) to other levels of government, such as counties or states (Eisinger, 1998).

On the revenue side, cities made limited attempts to increase tax levels. Concern over the effect of increased taxation on business investment both limited the amount of the increase and tilted it toward taxes on citizens (e.g., sales taxes). A very common form of "revenue enhancement" was to institute users' fees for city services. It should be noted that in most cases, such fees impose the greatest burden on the poor, since they have the least ability to pay them (Eisinger, 1998).

Despite often quite draconian service reductions, most cities did not actually reduce their budgets very much. That is because they increased their efforts to encourage business investment. For example, major projects were undertaken to refurbish downtown business districts to make them more attractive for corporate offices. Cities provided direct subsidies or tax relief to developers of downtown office centers and corporations willing to build factories. Government "development bonds" were issued to provide low-interest loans for the same purposes. Those cities in the most financial trouble and/or with the highest unemployment rates were the ones that spent the most to encourage investment. Ironically, most research suggests that such programs may have limited impact on the actual investment decisions of corporations. What is offered is usually only of marginal economic significance to the corporations. Moreover, in a situation in which almost all localities now offer incentives, it is hard for any one locality to offer a significantly better deal. Other scholars have argued that what benefits accrue from economic development are primarily concentrated in the hands of local developers and their allies, rather than being spread to the whole community (Eisinger, 1998, 2000; Kaplan, 1995; Thomas and Savitch, 1991; Morgan and Hirlinger, 1993; Rubin and Rubin, 1987; Ganz, 1985; Kantor, 1987; Logan and Molotch, 1987; Kirby, 1985). Peter Eisinger sums up these changes:

> The new mayors speak the language of modern public management and run their administrations accordingly. They believe in reinvention, innovation, privatization, competition, strategic planning, and productivity improvements. They favor economic development and low taxes, partnership with the business sector, and good housekeeping. (1998:320)

Long-Term Implications

Budget reductions have had a crippling effect on city services. As we will see in succeeding chapters, balanced budgets in the old central cities have been obtained at the price of crumbling streets, understaffed police departments, closed library branches, and further deterioration in already crisis-ridden school systems. In the newer, growing urban areas, avoiding financial crises and maintaining lower tax rates have meant continued low levels of service and an inability to respond to the problems of growth.

The cumulative effects of years of neglect are now becoming apparent. Central cities are failing to meet the challenge of educating a labor force with adequate skills to meet the needs of a changing economy. Crumbling public facilities threaten the ability of business to either expand or improve efficiency. Ancient bridges, poorly maintained highways and public transit systems, inadequate fire protection, an overwhelmed criminal justice system, and overburdened water and sewer systems all make for a poor business climate. Nor should we ignore the human costs of service reductions. For the least advantaged, basic needs are even more poorly provided than before. Cuts in city-provided medical facilities make access to low-cost medical care more difficult in many cities. Poor quality schools make it harder to escape poverty. Reduced fire and police protection threaten the poor the most because they are at the most risk of criminal victimization and fire. User fees exclude the poor from services and facilities previously accessible to them. For all of us, less reliable public services and deteriorated facilities adversely affect our quality of life.

MAIN POINTS

1. Urban government is limited in what it can do by four structural constraints: limited authority, fragmentation, high capital mobility, and the general requirements of a capitalist system. In addition, urban governments face economic and demographic constraints. The most obvious of these is that class, racial, and ethnic groupings tend to concentrate in certain jurisdictions.

2. Taken together, these constraints limit how effective urban governments can be in dealing with the problems of urban areas and being responsive to citizen demands.

3. Besides the effect of structural constraints, urban government actions are strongly shaped by pressures exerted by a number of groups with political influence: business leaders, organized interest groups, government officials themselves, public employees, and unorganized voting blocs.

4. Traditionally, there have been two theories of how much influence various groups have over local government: elite theory and pluralist theory.

5. Pluralists believe that influence is relatively widely distributed between the various groups, and, as a result, local decisions are relatively democratic in nature. The problem is that this may result in paralysis when the various groups refuse to compromise.

6. Elite theorists believe that business leaders have the ability to dominate local government, and the problem of local government is that it is undemocratic and not responsive to the needs of all groups in the community.

7. More recent theorizing about political influence at the local level has attempted to combine the two older theories.

8. State managerialist theorists emphasize the strong, independent role of government officials—pursuing their own interests—in shaping public policy. Some of these theorists argue that this "political elite" operates within the context of an essentially pluralist system of competing interest groups. Others argue that the most important group with whom state managers must contend are business interests.

9. Regime theorists acknowledge the structural limitations of a capitalist system of political economy but emphasize the creation of a relatively enduring network of groups with political resources as the basis of a governing coalition. Several different regime types characterize recent urban political systems.

10. Logan and Molotch argue that there is a coalition of interests—which they call the "urban growth machine"—that consists of

those who benefit the most from rapid economic growth and have a disproportionate influence on urban government. However, they acknowledge the role of other groups or factors in limiting the power of that coalition.

11. Gottdiener argues for a "two-tiered state" theory. The first tier is constrained by the nature of capitalism itself to enforce the system of private property through the use of police powers and the courts. The second tier engages in activities that affect the distribution of wealth in society. Policies undertaken by this tier are determined by a complex struggle between government officials, capitalists, and workers. In this struggle, a number of factors operate to give capitalists the greatest advantage.

12. During the 1970s most of the large cities of the North experienced growing fiscal stress because of rising expenditures, an inability to raise local revenues, and a growing reliance on external aid.

13. The response to the fiscal crisis was major cuts in public service expenditures (especially for the poor) and increased user fees and nonbusiness taxes. Growing emphasis was placed on policies to promote business investment.

KEY TERMS

Authority The power conferred on a person or agency of government by laws, constitutions, charters, and other recognized legal means.

Capital Mobility The ability of large corporations to shift their investments and business operations to different locations with relative ease.

Devolution The transfer of responsibility for a government program from a higher level of government to a lower one.

Elite As used by elite theorists of community power, the elite consists of that group of business leaders and the wealthy who dominate the informal structure of political influence in a community.

Fiscal Stress The growing difficulty of city governments to keep their budgets in balance because of such factors as rising service costs, stagnant tax bases, and declining federal aid.

Fragmentation The division of government authority in urban areas between a large number of local governments and agencies.

Influence A kind of informal political power that exists outside of the official framework of authority created by laws.

Informal Structure A system of political influence relationships.

Interest Group A group of people (more or less formally organized) with a shared political goal that attempts to influence government policy.

Pluralist   As argued by pluralist theorists of community power, the view that political influence is fairly widely distributed between various segments of the community.

Structural Constraints   The relatively fixed set of conditions within which governments operate that limits what they can do.

Tax Base   The total assessed value of the property of a community on which taxes are levied.

SUGGESTED READING

Judge, David, Gerry Stoker, and Harold Wolman, eds. 1995. *Theories of Urban Politics.* Thousand Oaks, CA: Sage. A set of articles summarizing the major theoretical developments in the study of urban politics from the pluralist-elite debate to the present.

Logan, John, and Harvey Molotch. 1987. *Urban Fortunes: The Political-Economy of Place.* Berkeley: University of California. Probably the best-known of recent attempts to reexamine the issue of community power.

Orfield, Myron. 1997. *Metropolitics: A Regional Agenda for Community and Stability,* rev. ed. Washington, DC: Brookings Institution. A clear argument about why government fragmentation makes solving metropolitan-wide problems difficult and a blueprint for how to begin to change things.

Urban Affairs Review, 30(5), May 1995. A special issue of the journal devoted to essays by leading urban scholars on the past and future of urban policy.

Urban Government
The Delivery of Services

Concentration of large numbers of people under conditions of relatively high density is only possible and reasonably tolerable if at least some minimum level of government services is provided. Preindustrial cities were places in which the ability and concern of government to deliver safe water, remove wastes, maintain public order, and assist the helpless were limited. Consequently, they were places of disease, disorder, squalor, and frequent misfortune for a majority of their residents. Indeed, conditions were generally so bad that the death rate exceeded the birth rate, and population was only maintained by the continued addition of new residents from the countryside (Sjoberg, 1960). Conditions in contemporary urban areas are so much more tolerable and safe in large part because of a massive effort on the part of government to maintain a high level of basic services.

The range of services provided urban residents by government is immense. It would be impractical even to list them all here. However, it is possible to distinguish between two general categories: (1) physical services and (2) social welfare services. *Physical services* consist of those activities that provide residents with a habitable environment and meet certain basic physical needs best provided collectively. They include waste disposal, water supply, and disease control. *Social welfare services* refer to a wide range of efforts to assist people in their day-to-day social activities and to make collective social life possible. They include such activities as assistance to the needy and helpless, maintenance of public order and safety, and education. Our concern in this chapter is to examine a few of the more critical of these physical and social services with an eye to evaluating their quality and some of the problems government faces in delivering them.

PHYSICAL SERVICES

Most physical services have as their common goal the maintenance of an acceptable level of public health and safety. Here we will focus on four areas which are particularly fundamental to achieving this goal and which, in the past, most North Americans have taken for granted: air quality, water supply, waste disposal, and infrastructure maintenance. As we will see, we cannot take these services for granted any longer.

Air Quality

Until fairly recently, government played a relatively minor role in trying to control urban air quality. That was not because air pollution was not a severe problem. Coal burning (and before that, wood burning) created very foul and unhealthy air over our cities in the past. However, public resignation and a limited ability to do much about the problem meant that control measures were crude and indifferently enforced, when anything was done at all. It was only in the 1960s that increased public awareness of the problem and increasing research evidence on the effects of air pollution created political pressure for a nationwide effort to curb air pollution.

The Clean Air Act Amendments of 1970 provided the first comprehensive program for attacking air pollution on a national level. Among other things, this legislation set National Ambient Air Quality Standards for six of the most common and widespread air pollutants, known as criteria pollutants (Nadakavukaren, 2000). Since 1970, aggregate emissions of the six criteria pollutants have been cut 29 percent. (During this same period, energy consumption, vehicle miles traveled, and the U.S. gross domestic product increased significantly.) Despite this progress, the EPA estimates that 121 million people still live in areas with pollution levels above the national air quality standards (U.S. EPA, 2001a).

Exposure to air pollution is associated with numerous deleterious health effects, including respiratory problems, hospitalization for heart and lung diseases, and even premature death. Children, the elderly, and asthmatics are particularly vulnerable. Particulate matter, for example, irritates the respiratory tract when inhaled. Epidemiological studies conducted in six U.S. cities from 1975 to 1988 have demonstrated a link between high levels of fine particulate air pollution (2.5 micrometers or less) and death due to lung cancer, respiratory disease, and heart ailments (Nadakavukaren, 2000). Sulfur dioxide and nitrogen oxides, the primary components of acid rain (acid deposition), are respiratory system irritants and can increase susceptibility to such ailments as pneumonia. Moreover, acid deposition can cause several dangerous metals, including aluminum, mercury, and lead, to become more soluble and thus able to leach into the surrounding environment, potentially contaminating household and municipal water systems. Vehicle exhaust contains carbon monoxide and also contributes to the formation of ground-level ozone, which can inflame airways and trigger wheezing, coughing, and pain when breathing. It also can aggravate asthma and increase a person's vulnerability to respiratory illnesses like pneumonia and bronchitis (Nadakavukaren, 2000; U.S. EPA, 2001b).

Air pollution results in great harm not only to health but also to nature. The acidification of lakes and streams can destroy aquatic ecosystems. Air pollution also damages forests, reduces crop yields and increases plant vulnerability to disease and pests, and impairs visibility in our national parks (Nadakavukaren, 2000). Moreover, many historical monuments (including the Statue of Liberty and Washington Monument) are being slowly degraded by airborne pollutants.

After the early gains in air quality of the 1970s, the 1980s were marked by inaction and a failure to implement certain regulations deemed unfavorable to industry. This situation was improved significantly with passage of the Clean Air Act Amendments of 1990, which strengthened air quality legislation and addressed problem areas (e.g., acid rain) that had not been part of the 1970 legislation (Nadaka-vukaren, 2000). Though the bill by no means represented the desires of the strict environmentalists, neither did it represent a complete surrender to pollution control opponents. Hence, the question is no longer one of values or public concern; the environmentalists seem to have won the battle for public opinion. The challenges now are those of getting governmental action in the current political environment and adopting policies based on solid scientific evidence (Broder, 1990b; Easterbrook, 1990).

An example of current air pollution control policy is the EPA's Acid Rain Program, begun in 1995. This initiative employs both traditional and innovative approaches to reduce sulfur dioxide and nitrogen oxide emissions. The program's restrictions on fossil-fuel fired power plants have resulted in substantial reductions of sulfur dioxide. Ultimately, in 2010, the program will result in a 10-million-ton reduction from 1980 emission levels. The results for nitrogen oxides are mixed. While the average emission rates of power plants participating in the Acid Rain Program have decreased 42 percent since 1996, total emissions of nitrogen oxides have not decreased significantly because electricity generation and vehicle use (and therefore fuel combustion) have increased (U.S. EPA, 2001c).

Generally speaking, U.S. air quality has improved significantly over the last three decades. However, serious problems remain. Vehicle emissions are one such problem. Vehicle emissions contribute indirectly to ozone, which has shown the least progress of the six criteria pollutants. In fact, in some areas of the United States ozone levels have worsened in the past ten years (U.S. EPA, 2001a). Levels of criteria pollutants in a number of urban areas still remain high enough to endanger the health of residents. These "nonattainment" areas violate the standard for one or more criteria pollutants, usually ozone or carbon monoxide, both related to vehicle emissions. Critics charge that auto manufacturers have been reluctant to meet standards set by the federal government. Consumer preferences for sports utility vehicles, minivans, and other less fuel efficient vehicles haven't helped. Others question whether the Environmental Protection Agency has adequately enforced the Clean Air Act provision which bans the use of federal funds for new highway and industrial construction in areas not complying with that act's mandates.

Plans developed for the Los Angeles area provide some idea of the kinds of policies that appear likely to be adopted in the near future. A twenty-year air quality plan was developed by California's South Coast Air Quality Management District (AQMD). The plan includes a heavy emphasis on car pooling. Methanol-fueled buses have already been adopted, while the use of rechargeable batteries is a growing possibility for cars and mass-transit vehicles. There also are plans for a subway (Weisman, 1989).

Future policy initiatives are likely to be in the direction of cleaner fuels, cleaner technology, and energy efficiency. For example, readily available measures could reduce electricity demand by 15 percent in the Midwest, the region producing one-third of sulfur dioxide emissions. The ACEEE (American Council for an Energy-Efficient Economy) has concluded that savings of from $4 billion to $8 billion would result if emission control and conservation were national policy. Increased recycling would not only save scarce landfill space, it also would eliminate some pollution by reducing the emissions from production facilities—such as those producing aluminum and paper (French, 1990:111–12). Alternate fuels (e.g., methanol) may reduce ozone but produce much more formaldehyde than does gasoline. A more viable approach would be to produce automobiles both low in emissions and high in fuel economy. In summary, waste minimization and energy conservation are more hopeful and realistic strategies than is air pollution control alone. The U.S. Office of Technology Assessment (OTA) concludes that United States industry has the potential to lower waste and pollutant production by 50 percent in the near future (French, 1990:113–14).

The Urban CO_2 Project is one of several projects sponsored by the International Council for Local Environmental Initiatives, an affiliate of the U.N. Environmental Project created in 1990. The project involves fourteen cities working together to develop carbon dioxide emission inventory targets for carbon dioxide emission reduction. United States cities included in the project are Miami, Denver, Minneapolis-St. Paul, Portland, and San Jose. The targets for reduction include such strategies as switching fuels, using renewable energy, and facilitating bicycle use. The cost of achieving a carbon dioxide emission limitation will be lowered as policies are put into place to maximize energy efficiency. For example, normal rates of equipment and power plant turnover will provide opportunities to achieve significant gains in energy efficiency. Moreover, there are significant cost advantages and energy savings in designing new buildings to minimize energy use. Land-use planning focused on more compact, pedestrian-oriented cities would significantly reduce growth in transportation demand. All of these strategies are part of the Urban CO_2 project.

Water Supply

Clean, abundant, and cheap water has been something most urban residents in the United States have come to expect. And, indeed, the total national supply of water is not in doubt. The problem lies in getting enough water of adequate quality to where it is needed at a reasonable cost. Despite past successes in doing so, current trends suggest that many urban areas face a real possibility of a serious water supply crisis in the near future.

The problem is most severe in the West and Southwest. On the average, this is an area of light rainfall. Massive efforts have been required to create the current water-supply system. Most traditional sources of water have been tapped and are being used at near or even beyond their long-term capacity. The most important single source is the Colorado River. A complex system of reservoirs and diversion canals have now fully exploited this source. Other smaller rivers are also heavily utilized. Pumping of groundwater out of wells is depleting this source faster than it is being replaced by nature.

Yet, demand for water is still increasing. Agriculture based on irrigation (the largest single user, and waster, of water) is a major regional industry and a significant contributor to the national food supply. Rapid industrialization, urbanization, and population growth have also resulted in rapid increases in water use. Future growth will impose yet additional water demand. Thus, the West and Southwest are faced with the prospect of water demand outstripping existing supply systems in the near future (Nadakavukaren, 2000; Postel, 1992).

Building dams and reservoirs has been the traditional response to growing water demand in the West. Reservoir capacity in the United States grew steadily, an average of 80 percent increase per decade, between the 1920s and the 1960s. The list of appropriate dam sites, however, has decreased, while at the same time their cost has risen sharply (Postel, 1985).

Hence, better management and more efficient use of existing supplies of water appear to be necessary. Today, in many metropolitan areas, the strategy for ensuring adequate water resources has shifted from increasing *supply* to managing *demand,* or conservation. Water can be conserved in several ways. For example, present irrigation practices in the West are not sustainable—agricultural water users will have to become more efficient. Means to this end include raising water prices for irrigated water to a realistic level. Water is currently so cheap that few farmers in the West attempt to improve their efficiency. They probably would do so, however, if prices were raised. Recycling irrigated water and using more efficient watering equipment (e.g., drip irrigation systems), will also aid the water management effort. In Texas these practices resulted in a decrease in water use of 28 percent between 1974 and 1987. In West Texas, water savings from the use of irrigation control devices such as drip systems and underground pipelines saved nearly 200 million cubic meters of water as of 1995 (Postel, 1996:57). Adoption of such measures by farmers frees water for use by urban communities. While there is a trend in this direction, a conflict over resources between agricultural interests and urban areas is increasing in intensity, particularly in California (Postel, 1996; Reisner, 1989).

In addition, a number of approaches that attempt to decrease water demands by industry and households have been enacted. Within the past ten to fifteen years, increasingly strict federal mandates requiring the treatment of industrial wastewater prior to discharge have given industry a strong incentive to recycle and reuse process waters. Such efforts have resulted in sharp declines in water withdrawals in many industries. In some areas, water flowing in and out of power plants is being used by adjacent greenhouses and fish farms (Deutsch, 1999). Recycling metals such as aluminum from scrap (rather than using ore) reduces the amount of water discharged by over 95 percent. Household fixtures, a traditional culprit in water waste, have been improved so that new toilets and shower heads can reduce consumption by at least 50 percent. New models of dishwashers and washing machines offer a savings of at least 30 percent. Communities in Arizona and Southern California have initiated measures to discourage water wastage associated with landscaping practices. Such measures include promoting desert landscaping and enacting legislation that restricts the amount of yard space property owners can devote to grass. Storing surplus runoff underground also offers a number of advantages. Competition for valuable land is decreased, and the great loss of water through evaporation that occurs with surface storage is prevented. Congress provided funds for this type of approach in seventeen western states in 1984. These efforts offer modest hope that conservation and better management can avoid disruptive water shortages (Postel, 1985; Nadakavukaren, 2000).

The eastern United States faces much different problems. On the whole, the total amount of water available from surface runoff is more than adequate. The problem is getting clean water to heavily populated areas. Part of the problem is that water sources near heavily urbanized areas tend to be polluted. As a result, urban water systems face the choice of cleaning up the local supply or moving clean water long distances. Both approaches are expensive. Past neglect has meant that rivers in urban areas received sewage that was only minimally treated. Nor would conventional treatment methods completely solve the problem. Industrial pollution dumps dangerous chemicals that are difficult or impossible to remove into water supplies. Hence, expensive controls at the plant site are required. Some urban areas face the additional problem of not being located near water sources adequate for their needs.

Water development has been dominated by a simple formula: estimate the demand for water, and then obtain the needed supply. This approach may work in the short term in a world of resource abundance, but certainly is a problem in the long run. A more adequate plan should include a set of practical, measurable steps of good water management. Unless water is reserved for the larger environment, cities, agriculture, and industry will overuse and misuse it. What, however, constitutes appropriate conservation or use—for instance, for rivers? Such measurability is very complex. Nevertheless, setting even tentative goals for the amount of water to be left in rivers could help maintain sufficient quantities, as science in the meantime moves toward a more adequate model for measuring and monitoring water supply. In regions where rivers are already over-drained (e.g., much of the western U.S.), meeting such minimum requirements requires diverting water from farm and city and keeping it in the environment (Postel, 1996:54).

Some progress has already been made to this end. In 1994, California and federal officials signed an agreement to limit the amount of fresh water that can be diverted from the San Francisco Bay area. Farmers and city dwellers will face shortages in the short term, but California's citizens in the long run should benefit, as economic activity comes into a more balanced relationship with the water supply. This agreement has a broad base of support, including farmers, environmentalists, and urban residents, as well as state and federal officials (Postel, 1996:54–55).

Another strategy to conserve water resources is that undertaken by private organizations and government agencies, which have purchased water rights and then dedicated them to restoring the aquatic environment. The Nature Conservancy of Arlington, Virginia recently performed such an action in the Chesapeake Bay area.

Solid Waste Disposal

Urban areas face the immense task of removing huge amounts of residential trash and garbage as well as construction and industrial wastes. In 1999, U.S. residents, businesses, and institutions generated more than 230 million tons of municipal solid waste (U.S. EPA, 2001d). In the past, costs were kept low by careless dumping or burning. Open dumps created disease and pest hazards, allowed wastes to leak into the environment, and were public nuisances. Uncontrolled burning was a major source of air pollution. Hence, urban governments moved to create sanitary landfills where waste could be carefully buried.

About 61 percent of solid wastes generated in the United States are disposed of in sanitary landfills. However, dwindling capacity at existing landfills, the difficulty and expense of siting new landfills, and increasing public disfavor have forced many communities to explore alternative disposal methods (Nadakavukaren, 2000). New York, Chicago, and Los Angeles were already having difficulty finding places to dump their solid wastes in the 1970s (Bukro, 1975); the solid waste dilemma now confronts every urban area. In addition, there have been a number of accidents involving private dumps in which dangerously toxic chemicals were carelessly buried and resulted in environmental damage and illness.

In addition, recent findings suggest that refuse does not simply rot away, but rather lasts a long time. Landfill conditions tend to preserve rather than dispose of garbage (Bukro, 1989) and may result in the accumulation of dangerous amounts of methane gas. There also has been growing concern recently at both the state and federal levels about the threat of groundwater pollution by municipal landfill leachates. (Half the population depends on groundwater for its water supply.)

About 340 of the federal "Superfund" sites slated for multimillion dollar cleanup programs are former municipal landfills. New federal landfill requirements that became effective in 1993 now mandate groundwater monitoring wells and methane detection systems—measures that will help prevent past pollution disasters from being repeated. However, the increased cost of implementing such measures has resulted in a sharp drop in the number of operating landfills in the United States (from approximately 8,000 in 1988 to about 2,314 in 1999), although overall landfill *capacity* has not declined as sharply. In fact, only a handful of states that provided data on remaining landfill space reported having less than ten years of capacity. For the foreseeable future, it appears solid waste will be transported longer distances to fewer, large regional facilities that are better designed and operated than those of the past (Glenn, 1999; Nadakavukaren, 2000).

Despite improvements in landfill operations, state and local officials need to develop new, more sustainable waste management strategies for the decades ahead. However, there is considerable disagreement as to how the solid-waste crisis should be handled. For example, the incineration of trash to produce electricity or simply to reduce waste volume gained popularity in the 1980s, particularly in the Northeast where landfill space was scarce and landfilling fees were skyrocketing. However, the problem of disposing of the incinerator ash—which frequently contained dangerous levels of heavy metals—and the high cost of construction and operation of incinerators curbed their use. By the end of the 1990s, only 7.5 percent of municipal solid waste in the U.S. was disposed of by incineration (Nadakavukaren, 2000).

As a consequence, source reduction efforts and a heavy reliance on recycling to reduce waste volume are more viable alternatives over the long term. Both consumers and manufacturers play vital roles in a strategy to reduce waste generation at the source. Such a strategy includes producing products without excessive packaging, avoiding single-serve and disposable packaging, substituting reusable products for disposable ones (e.g., cloth napkins, china dishes, cloth diapers), and so on. Copy machines that print on both sides of a sheet of paper and a greater use of e-mail can vastly reduce waste in the workplace.

There is great potential for recycled products, although it will take time to develop markets for them. As the demand for these products increases, recycling will become more efficient and economical. One problem with recycling is that it sometimes meets resistance—some people do not want to take the time and trouble to sort their trash. However, recycling has made impressive gains since the late 1980s. In a 1999 report, *BioCycle* magazine reported the highest recycling levels ever—31.5 percent of all solid waste, nearly four times the level recycled in 1990 (*BioCycle*, 1999).

To encourage recycling, state and local governments have enacted policies and set recycling goals. One of the most successful approaches has been the curbside collection program in residential areas. By 1999, curbside collection was provided by more than 9,000 municipalities, serving more than 140 million people. In some jurisdictions, laws mandate that certain products contain a minimum percentage of recycled material. Government purchasing policies that require government agencies, state universities, and public schools to purchase supplies that are recyclable or that contain recycled material are another tool through which recycling is encouraged by boosting the market demand for recyclables (Nadakavukaren, 2000).

About 38 percent of municipal solid waste is paper and paper products, which have a recycling rate of about 42 percent. Plastics make up 10.5 percent of the waste stream, and have a recycling rate of 40 percent for soft-drink containers, with varying rates for other types of plastic containers (U.S. EPA, 2001d). According to the American Plastics Council (2001), plastic bottle recycling increased six-fold between 1990–1998.

Old automobile tires have been a major solid-waste disposal problem for some time. Now, however, recycled tires are being used in a great variety of products, including shoe soles, mats for erosion control, or temporary roads. Crumbled rubber is made into hockey pucks and running tracks. Rubber mixed with asphalt is useful for paving. Another important use of discarded tires is that of energy production. With a BTU content greater than coal, tires release a great amount of energy when burned. In Modesto, California, for example, a high-temperature incinerator burns tires at a rate of 700 per hour to generate power for a local utility. Cement kilns are other potential consumers of used tires. Although pollution-control equipment is necessary, the high temperatures in the kilns result in near-total combustion, leaving little in the way of by-products (Nadakavukaren, 1995). In 1985, the EPA estimated that less that 6 percent of all scrap tires were recycled, but by 1990 the figure had risen to 10.7 percent. By 1994 one-third of all tires were being recycled (McConnaughey, 1994).

Deutsch (1999) describes the pioneering efforts of Triad Energy Resources, a company that is developing eco-industrial parks that turn industrial by-products into raw materials for other uses. The company's founder came up with the idea after touring a plant that burned old tires and noting that it paid haulers to cart away gypsum— a by-product of the process that happens to be used in plaster, toothpaste, and other products. Other companies are now following suit and are either buying their neighbors' wastes or selling their own.

While many advocates of recycling feel that it lowers waste disposal expense, most evidence leads to the conclusion that high rates of recycling are more expensive than alternate forms of solid waste treatment. The basic comparison between recycling and incineration comes down to the fact that recycling is labor-intensive; thus it is more expensive.

Moreover, a strong alliance has surfaced consisting of reproducers of waste (the packaging lobby and the plastics industry, for example), and the disposers of waste (the private-sector waste management companies). This pro-incineration bloc challenges the efforts of environmentalists and governments to control waste growth via recycling and waste reduction. The view that there is an inevitable movement toward a recycling society is in conflict with the market-centered nature of the economy, dominated by the private producers and disposers of waste material. To compound the problem, many urban areas face a political conflict between environmental demands for comprehensive recycling strategies and efforts by urban administrators to balance their budgets. In some cases, this has resulted in a shift away from comprehensive recycling toward the increasing use of incineration (Gandy, 1994: 2–3, 114–16).

Infrastructure Decay

The condition of the basic physical service systems and facilities *(infrastructure)* in most urban areas has been steadily deteriorating. For example, the bridges, subways, highways, water, and sewer systems of New York City are currently in terrible shape. The cost to repair New York's infrastructure will approach if not exceed $50 billion. This city's situation is paralleled by that of large cities across the nation (CBS, 1989; Szabo, 1989). Infrastructure decay means that urban areas now face the need to undertake expensive repairs to make up for past neglect. If they fail to do so, not only will urban residents face growing inconvenience from service breakdowns, but industries and businesses which rely on the physical services system will face growing operating costs.

Why did infrastructure decay occur? Quality infrastructure has been taken for granted by the public. It was assumed to work properly until a breakdown occurred. Hence, there was little political pressure to maintain infrastructure. This tendency toward complacency and neglect was powerfully reinforced by the mounting financial problems of urban governments in the last twenty-five years. In growing urban areas there has been, at the same time, increasing use of and even greater stress on these facilities (Giglio, 1988).

Building deterioration is a long-term problem given recognition only recently. An increasing number of buildings in city centers have experienced masonry deterioration, resulting in broken materials falling to the sidewalks below, sometimes resulting in serious injury or even death of pedestrians. In New York City, the basic cause is that of an inadequate inspection system. Simply put, requirements for repairs are not enforced (Kennedy and Sullivan, 1998). Chicago's inspection ordinance of 1978 was a landmark action, followed by similar laws in cities across the nation. Yet Chicago continues to have serious problems of high-rise structural deterioration as the result of an aging infrastructure and a lapse of nearly twenty years in effective inspection due to an inadequate number of qualified inspectors and a lack of funding. Buildings in cities (like Chicago) that have consistent freeze-thaw cycles and heavy precipitation are the most vulnerable (Mendell, 2000). In the spring of 2001, after another incident involving a deteriorated building facade, the Chicago City Council passed an ordinance making the inspection process of older buildings more stringent (Washburn, 2001).

Decay of the transportation infrastructure is particularly widespread. Over one-third of all major U.S. highways (nearly 250,000 miles of roads, bridges, and overpasses) are in poor or mediocre condition, according to a report released by the AAA-Chicago Motor Club. As of 1994, one-third of the nation's nearly 600,000 bridges were either structurally deficient or functionally obsolete. Of this number, 14 percent were not safe for the volume and type of traffic using them. The remaining 19 percent could be used if traffic speeds over them were strictly adhered to (Our Nation's Highways, 1995:21). The backlog of existing road and bridge repairs needed on major U.S. routes is estimated at $315 billion, which the Federal Highway Administration says will require an annual capital investment of more than $70 billion over the next five years. That figure is $37 billion more than presently is spent annually by federal, state, and local governments (Jiminez, 1996). How could this immense expense be covered? Some suggestions include putting to use the $25 billion in gasoline and airline ticket taxes currently in trust funds, and ending the use of gasoline taxes for nontransportation purposes.

Besides increasing government expenditures on infrastructure, some observers suggest increased involvement of the private sector. For example, this approach has been proposed regarding toll roads. The U.S. Chamber of Commerce has recommended the enactment of user fees in the financing of construction, maintenance, and rehabilitation of these roads (Szabo, 1989).

Evaluation

Providing clean water, removing solid wastes, assuring breathable air, and maintaining service systems and facilities are all activities that the public has a reasonable right to expect of government. However, governments are increasingly hard pressed to deliver such services. The problem is not primarily technical: technologies exist or are being developed which enable governments to pursue these activities. Rather, the problem is one of cost and the public's willingness to pay. To continue to enjoy the current high level of physical services and to clean up past environmental abuses is likely to require increasing expenditures by government and industry. That means diversion of capital badly needed for the industrial modernization required for continued economic growth. It means higher taxes, increased user charges for public services, and higher prices for consumer goods. In an already slowly growing economy, with rising costs for other government services, at least some economic sacrifice will be required.

The question is: who is going to sacrifice how much? Effectively dealing with the problems of physical services ultimately implies some "trade-off" between private consumption and collectively provided services. Allocating the burden of who will pay or be worse off will be no easy matter. However, failure to act will also impose major sacrifices in terms of filthy, unhealthy air; an inadequate water supply; and the dangerous accumulation of improperly disposed solid waste. In that event, everyone will suffer, though the less affluent will suffer more because they lack the ability to buy alternative services or run away from the problem.

Some have proposed *privatization*, the transfer of public services into the hands of profit-oriented contractors. Phoenix has been touted as a model for such privatization. This city's administration has attempted to divide garbage collection into public and private sectors to decrease costs. John Donahue (1989) provides considerable insight into the appropriateness and validity of privatization. Efficiency is the rationale usually given for such transfer. Yet, there are no data clearly demonstrating that private water or utilities are less expensive, and there is only limited evidence suggesting that private airline and rail systems are more cost effective. There is, however, significant research showing that private trash disposal is less expensive. Overall, the available research suggests that there is no guarantee that it is cheaper to contract out city services to the private sector. Donahue concludes that privatization has the most potential use for those service activities whose performance can be easily specified and monitored, such as garbage collection.

Realistically, no major expenditure initiatives seem likely in the near future. The reality is a declining federal budget in the area of domestic "discretionary" expenditures, increasing pressures on state and local governments as the federal government transfers more responsibility to them, and strong resistance to tax increases at all levels of government. These changes seem likely to be major constraints on urban service delivery.

At the same time, at the federal level, the current battle is over whether to *weaken* the federal regulatory role in favor of states and localities. Competition for corporate investment and the strength of business interests in most state legislatures seem likely to create a process in which states and localities compete to offer corporations a more "sympathetic" regulatory environment.

Under these circumstances, local governments appear likely to simply "muddle through." Reallocation of existing resources to meet emergency service needs, public-private partnerships, new recycling technologies, more flexible and cost effective regulations, and other *ad hoc* policy initiatives offer some hope of avoiding major deterioration in physical services, and there may even be some scattered areas of improvement.

SOCIAL WELFARE SERVICES

During the twentieth century government played an increasing role in providing assistance to people in need. Prior to 1930, the provision of these services was almost exclusively a state and local affair, and the range and extent of the services were quite limited. Private philanthropy augmented these efforts. The massive problems of the Depression in the 1930s overwhelmed these limited state and local efforts. In response to the problem, the federal government's "New Deal" intervened with a wide range of emergency assistance programs. In the process, the whole notion of government responsibility for helping citizens meet their social needs gradually changed. Increasingly, the government assumed the responsibility of assuring a minimum level of material well-being, helping people deal with their personal problems, and providing opportunities for economic and social advancement. The idea of the "welfare state" was born. Out of the welter of emergency programs designed to deal with the problems of the Depression emerged a permanent system of social welfare programs. This complex system of federal, state, and local programs (all of which were increasingly federally funded and mandated) attempted to assist the poor, the disabled and handicapped, the socially disadvantaged, the uneducated, and the emotionally disturbed (Wilensky and Lebeau, 1965).

Quite obviously, the provision of social welfare is not an exclusively urban problem or function. However, urban social welfare represents one of the major service efforts of government at all levels, and a significant minority of urban residents rely on those services. Central cities, as we saw in chapter 4, bear an especially heavy burden because of the concentration of poor people with problems within their boundaries and the limited resources available locally for assisting them.

General Problems of the System

Given the complexity and range of social welfare services that exist, a review of individual programs is not possible here. However, despite their complexity and number, these programs constitute a system—albeit a ramshackle one—with certain general characteristics and problems. Obviously, not all programs share these characteristics and problems to an equal degree. But enough commonality exists to make some limited generalizations about the system as a whole.

Unclear Goals

Social welfare remains a controversial program, and there is still no real public consensus on what the system should be trying to do. In addition, many existing programs evolved out of *temporary* New Deal programs. They are now being asked to do things they were not originally designed to do, such as providing long-term support and assistance. There is little notion of what the system as a whole is supposed to be accomplishing. Rather, individual programs have been added piecemeal to deal with specific problems either as they arose or as political pressure to do something mounted. Often, programs developed for one purpose end up being used for something else. For example, during the 1970s, the CETA program was officially designed to provide employment and training for the unemployed. It was instead used to subsidize the payrolls of financially distressed cities.

This lack of a clear set of central goals means that priorities are not clear. What things need doing first, which programs deserve the most support, and what efforts are most important are hard to determine. Effective, rational allocation of resources is therefore difficult.

Weakness at the Local Level

Relatively little control or authority over the social welfare system resides in local government. Partly this reflects a lack of initiative or concern at the local level. This has been especially true in the Sunbelt, but has also been true of other areas. When local governments do have some freedom over the use of federal money they tend to spend it on the nonpoor. For instance, one study of the Community Development Block Grants program found that only 5 percent of the funds (intended to prevent neighborhood deterioration) went to low-income neighborhoods in 1976—with 26 percent going to moderate-income neighborhoods, 30 percent to middle-income neighborhoods, and 39 percent to high-income neighborhoods (Heumann, 1979:242). Some of this inertia and reluctance to provide help to the really disadvantaged also reflects the reality of the distribution of political influence at the local level. Those who need the help most have the least political power. However, weakness at the local level is also a reflection of the general lack of resources and authority at that level. Local governments have very limited authority to control the kinds of programs they undertake and to fund locally controlled services.

Thus, social welfare is primarily funded and controlled at the state and federal level. Combined with local inertia, this virtually guarantees a system that is not very sensitive to local needs. Decisions are made by distant bureaucrats who are unaware of local conditions, protected from public scrutiny, and insulated from the demands of both frontline case workers and their clients by multiple layers of bureaucracy.

In the 1980s the Reagan administration attempted to reduce the degree of detailed control that federal agencies have over some programs by granting states greater flexibility in meeting federal standards and reducing the proportion of the social welfare budget provided through categorical grants. However, this flexibility was accompanied by reduced federal funding. The federal budget from 1982 through 1984 included cuts of 10 percent each year for social programs. Food stamps, child nutrition, AFDC, and unemployment compensation, to name a few, were cut drastically. The basic strategy used was to increase eligibility requirements in order to decrease the number of those who could apply. This approach cut about a half million people off AFDC, and in the process also caused them to lose Medicare benefits. At least one million people were no longer able to receive Food Stamps (Johnson, 1987:167–68).

In 1996, Congress passed welfare reform legislation that further eroded the federal government's responsibility to provide social assistance to the poor. The AFDC program, the main public assistance program in the United States, was replaced by a temporary assistance program that eliminated the federal government's guarantee of payments to eligible recipients and gave the responsibility to those states that chose to accept it. The legislation also included work requirements and lifetime limits on the receipt of benefits.

Rising Costs

As the range and size of service programs have increased, the total cost of the social welfare system has grown immensely. For example, though federal and state government allocations were almost nothing in 1900, by 1929 they had risen to about $4 billion. This figure grew to $24 billion by 1950, accelerating to $770 billion by 1986. Cash allocations to poor people went from $2.5 billion in 1950 to $104 billion by 1986 (Bixby, 1988). The sum total of welfare expenses in America, both public and private, amounted to 13.5 percent of the Gross National Product in 1968, rising to 33 percent by 1993 (Kerns and Glanz, 1988; Kerns, 1997). Recent federal administrations, reacting to public resentment against welfare, were able to slow the increase of many welfare programs, and to decrease others. This is, though, a temporary trend. Growth probably will go on, albeit at a less rapid rate than during the 1960s and 1970s. There has been no reversal of social trends resulting in the need for welfare. Increases in existing problems will continue (e.g., children born out of wedlock, illiteracy, drug abuse, and school dropouts). Unemployment and underemployment will continue to be high. In addition, such concerns as AIDS and spousal abuse will probably require welfare funding (Popple and Leighninger, 1990:54).

The American public appears to favor a social policy that combines welfare and work (Califano, 1993; Gueron, 1993), and the 1996 welfare reform act calls for measures in this direction. This legislation required states to present plans to replace AFDC by July 1997. Each state received a lump sum to manage its own welfare and work programs. Major provisions of the new legislation include the following: the head of every family on welfare must work within two years or lose benefits; lifetime benefits will be limited to five years; states can provide payments to unmarried teenage parents only if a mother under age 18 stays in school and lives with an adult; future legal immigrants will be ineligible for most federal benefits during their first five years in the U.S.; states must provide Medicaid for anyone who qualifies under current law; and food stamps will be limited for adults not raising children *(New York Times,* 1996).

Disparities in Service Levels

The quality, range, and extent of social welfare services continue to vary widely on a regional basis. Where a person lives profoundly affects the amount of assistance she or he can expect in time of need. The major variation is between the old industrial states of the North Central and Northeast regions and the South. Traditionally, the South has had extremely low levels of social welfare services. These low levels appear to be attributable to a number of factors. In part, in the past, they reflected the relative poverty of the South, which severely limited government taxing power. However, these low levels also reflected a greater degree of upper class domination of the political system at state and local levels. The "political culture" (generally accepted political beliefs and values) also was one which tended to downplay the role and responsibilities of government (Lupsha and Siembieda, 1977).

Evaluation

It is relatively easy to enumerate the manifest problems of the social welfare system and criticize various specific aspects of its functioning. However, it is not so easy to evaluate the significance of these specific problems in trying to judge the system as a whole. One's overall evaluation of the system depends on the political perspective from which one views its specific problems. Hence, there are several ways to look at the system.

From a conventional liberal political perspective, it can be argued that for all its problems and failures the social welfare system functions as a real "safety net" of basic services that assure significant protection against personal disasters. It has brought about an unprecedented degree of basic security in the sense that the general population is assured that its most basic needs will be met and the neediest and weakest in society will not be totally neglected. Liberals press for measures to help single parents as well as married couples in which both spouses work. This reflects the liberal view that the traditional family (breadwinner-homemaker) is no better than other family forms. Liberals also advocate providing child-care assistance to employed parents (Cherlin, 1999).

Conservatives, on the other hand, argue that the whole notion of a welfare state is based on faulty premises, and the consequences of the system may be socially dangerous. For one thing, they say, it is simply wrong to assume that government can or should intervene in a major way in the lives of individuals. Government is not wise enough, and large governmental bureaucracies are not manageable enough to achieve the intended results. The waste, disorganization, and growing body of wrong-headed bureaucratic regulations are the predictable results of the mistaken idea that government can successfully engage in effective social engineering. The unfortunate consequence is that we are paying dearly for the effort. In this view, the social welfare program has resulted in the weakening of individual initiative and moral responsibility, the restriction of individual rights, and the partial destruction of traditional family and community structures. The immense cost of the system has, at the same time, diverted resources from private consumption and investment, reducing the efficiency of the economy and long-term economic growth (Murray, 1984).

Leftist observers couch their evaluation of the social welfare system in a more general criticism of the social and economic system. They see the social welfare system as an attempt to deal with and contain the symptoms of more fundamental social failures which reflect economic and political inequalities in society. They argue that the social welfare system cannot possibly be expected to deal with the problems of individuals effectively because those problems are rooted in the basic organization of society itself. Hence the various programs, quite predictably, fail. However, from the point of view of the powerful in society, the system really is a success. Elite power and privileges are not fundamentally threatened by the system. In addition, the social welfare system provides just enough assistance to the underprivileged to prevent widespread political discontent and channels the aspirations and frustrations of the underprivileged in individualistic, nonpolitical directions. The system also deflects efforts for social reform away from fundamental social changes that would endanger elite interests. In this sense, the social welfare system is really quite effective, not at helping people, but as a system of political and social control (Piven and Cloward, 1971).

Near-Term Prospects

Although the size of government did not decline during the Reagan-Bush years, its focus did. Rights and freedoms of business were expanded, while government support of individuals, especially the disadvantaged, was cut back. Conservative efforts at the presidential and/or congressional level during the 1980–1996 period to free business from "threats" to profitability led to decreased environmental regulation, reduced work safety enforcement, declining "real" (after inflation) minimum wage and welfare benefit levels, and significant cutbacks in other social spending—except for Social Security and Medicare (Rubin, 1996:116–17).

The 1980s and 1990s thus can be characterized as a period in which the general willingness to blame the poor and otherwise needy for their own problems came to be reflected in public policy. Health care reform is but one example of the general unwillingness to use government policy to meet social welfare needs. Despite widespread concerns about cost and availability of health care services, it was very difficult for President Clinton to formulate or sell a universal program to Congress (even under Democratic Party control). At the same time, steady declines in support levels and tightening eligibility requirements in poverty programs in the 1980s and 1990s culminated in "welfare reform" in 1996. This reform (with some qualifications) essentially represented a triumph of the conservative view of the welfare system, both in Congress and the White House. The assumption of the new legislation was that there are enough entry-level jobs that will lead to eventual employment above the poverty-line income level if access to and length of time spent on AFDC is limited. Block grants to states (at a fixed level) to run their own welfare programs are believed to provide funds to those who know best what the poor need in their areas (Rank, 1994:160–61).

Early state experiments in welfare reform have provided a preview of how the new system will work. Advocates of the new state system in Michigan claim it will save substantial sums and help keep families together. In Michigan, nearly 30 percent of welfare clients earn a paycheck (more than three times the national average). Welfare caseloads in 1995 were the lowest in over twenty years, and state officials claim the Department of Social Services spent $100 million less for welfare. But many economists and sociologists who have studied the features of the new system are not so sure. Many of the jobs available pay so little that a family cannot rise above the poverty line and get off state aid. Thus, the Michigan system may just lock the working poor into a position where they require state aid, with limited if any savings (Kilborn, 1995).

The "Wisconsin Works" program was intended to shrink the welfare system by keeping people off the system in the first place. In order to receive benefits, people who apply for assistance are required to work in the private sector if work is available, in the public sector if jobs are not available, or in job-training programs if the worker needs such help. Wisconsin also subsidizes child care, but only in conjunction with work. Public sector pay is kept low to encourage recipients to seek jobs in the private sector (Raspberry, 1996:26). Officials acknowledge that initial costs of this program will be higher than the old AFDC program but believe it will save money in the long run. Others contend that, under the new program, some families will lose assistance and have to pay for child care and health care out of very limited incomes. A key question remains: will there be enough jobs in the private sector? Critics contend that welfare recipients will get stuck in low-paying jobs with no chance of advancement (Johnson, 1996; Kuczka, 1996).

The General Accounting Office (GAO) study of welfare programs in seventeen states found that the number of families who found work after leaving public aid is much larger than previously reported—between 63 percent and 87 percent, depending on the state. But many families are having a tougher time than when on welfare. A study by the Center for Budget and Policy Priorities found that 10 percent of families with the lowest incomes actually lost an average of $860 in annual income between 1995 and 1997, when welfare reform went into full effect. The GAO study tended to support this research. Nevertheless, in Wisconsin and South Carolina, former recipients felt their lives were better than when on welfare, even though they were more likely to have trouble making ends meet ("Welfare Reform's Good Report Card," 1999).

Whether the new welfare system "works" will depend in large part on how well state governments respond to the challenge. Past failure of many state welfare programs, in both the distant and recent past, are certainly cause for some skepticism about the current reforms.

EDUCATION

Operating the public school system has traditionally been one of the most important roles of urban governments. Education budgets constitute a major portion of the total local government budget, and education has been the focus of much public concern and interest. Most families are directly affected by educational policies and programs, either as users of the system or as taxpayers. In addition, the public expects much of the educational system. The schools are expected to transmit the dominant values of society and teach social skills. Simultaneously, they are called on to make sure that the whole population acquires the basic knowledge, discipline, and literacy skills necessary for participation in the labor force and to prepare a minority of the population for more advanced training. People in this society have also put enormous faith in the ability of the school system to equalize occupational opportunities and provide a channel for upward mobility for talented children of the disadvantaged (Dentler, 1977:311–19).

Not surprisingly, these expectations have proven difficult to meet. The public school system has never really done the things expected of it very well. Probably no more than 40 to 60 percent of the students in the public school system have ever emerged psychologically more adjusted, acculturated, and competent in basic literacy and job skills as a result of their experiences in school (Dentler, 1977:314). And this modest rate of success has been even more modest for the children of the lower classes. Consequently, the ability of the public school system to provide a real channel for mobility and a means of equalizing opportunity has always been much less than the general public has believed (Jencks et al., 1972).

The reasons for these more general difficulties of the public school system are beyond the practical scope of the present discussion. We will focus instead on those problems that have further increased the already enormous difficulties faced by urban public school systems. These problems threaten to make an already problem-ridden and chaotic system even more problem-ridden and chaotic.

Educational Finances

The most visible and fundamental problem facing urban school districts is finances. Total national spending on public schools has increased enormously in the last few decades in response to rising costs. Earlier, part of this increase was due to increasing enrollments as a result of the baby boom. However, stabilizing or falling enrollments in the 1970s and 1980s provided little relief from this cost spiral. In 1988–89 expenses for elementary and high schools were about $200 billion. This represented an increase of 21 percent compared to 1978–79. The rapid increases started in 1983, when the emphasis on school reform began (*Condition of Teaching*, 1988:51).

In 1999–2000, an average of $7,086 per pupil was spent on elementary and high school education in the United States. The amount varied considerably by state. Significant differences also occurred between school districts in the same state or city (National Center for Education Statistics, 2001).

Sixty years ago education was primarily funded at the local level. Since that time, the states and federal government have become progressively more involved. In 1998 the states provided 48 percent of school revenues, with 45 percent coming from local governments (National Center for Education Statistics, 2001). While federal expenditures are only a small part of the total federal budget, they play an important role in elementary and secondary education. They cover research, programs for special education (such as for disabled and disadvantaged students), and such programs as fighting school dropout rates.

Most of a school district's budget goes for salaries and benefits for teachers and administrators. The growth in per pupil expenditure during the last few decades is largely due to a decrease in the student-staff ratio. However, teacher salaries as a portion of total school expenses stayed about the same as they were in 1980–81 (National Center for Education Statistics, 1989, table 56). Higher costs are due also to the initiation of programs for those having particular needs, such as those with disabilities. Some such programs are required by state and federal governments. Costs for services required for the disabled are much greater—over twice as much per child in 1985–86 (National Center for Education Statistics, 1989:56, 113). In addition, the last few decades saw a major increase in the types of programs most school districts attempted to offer. Part of this was an attempt to upgrade the quality of programs. In central-city school districts, another major factor was the rapid increase in the proportion of children from disadvantaged families who needed special educational programs. State governments (and, to a lesser extent, the federal government) also mandated program changes and special services that increased costs. Central-city districts were additionally burdened by the costs of increasingly elaborate efforts to achieve racial integration in the 1970s. Moreover, additional security needs and the costs of repairing the damage from vandalism increased significantly (Coleman and Kelly, 1976; Griffith et al., 1989).

The problem with these cost increases was they occurred in the context of the growing financial crisis faced by urban governments. As we have seen (chapter 7), urban governments simply lacked the ability to raise sufficient revenues from local tax sources. The problem in education was compounded in many areas by the fact that school districts obtain their tax revenues from separate tax levies (mostly on real estate). Increases in these separate school taxes often require direct voter approval, but voters have been increasingly reluctant to approve increased school taxes (Coleman and Kelly, 1976; Parkinson, 1979; Griffith et al., 1989). In addition, the states did not increase their total aid levels enough to relieve the local funding crisis. Political opposition to increased state spending in general and spending for education in particular slowed the rate of increase in state aid for education. The already financially desperate central-city districts felt the squeeze the most, but even suburban districts found the slowdown in state aid increases put more and more pressure on their budgets as suburban voters also began to resist tax increases (Parkinson, 1979:168–73; Griffith et al., 1989:27–30).

Consolidation has been one attempt to cope with school expenses. School districts in the United States declined in number from about

100,000 in 1945 to only around 16,000 in 1987 (Griffith et al., 1989:27). To meet the decline in federal monies allocated for schools, states have used sales taxes (producing about one-third of state funding) as well as income taxes (which bring in one-fourth). State lotteries are growing as another source of revenue. The portion of school funding from local property taxes has slowly declined (Ballantine, 1989:241; Ornstein and Levine, 1985).

Central-city districts have had greater economic difficulties than suburban school districts. The formulas used to provide state aid to local districts have failed to compensate for the larger tax base of suburban districts and have resulted in continued disparities in expenditures per pupil between central cities and suburbs (Griffith et al., 1989:28–29). While attempts to shift school funding bases have often been rejected, some court decisions have given new hope to those pressing for equity. In a 9-0 decision, the Texas Supreme Court said that the considerable gap between richest and poorest school districts violated the state constitution's requirement for an adequate education. The court in its decision mandated a change in the system. This decision is one of nearly a dozen overturning state school funding mechanisms on the grounds they violate state constitutions.

Recent developments suggest an ongoing effort to remedy inequities in school funding. As of 1993, lawsuits had been filed in forty-one states challenging the traditional property-tax-based system. A number have come to the attention of state supreme courts, and some reforms are being implemented. Greater judicial action at the state level is a crucial factor in reducing dependence on the property tax. Since the U.S. Supreme Court in 1973 washed its hands of the issue, the state courts are the best place to argue the question of educational equity. In the several dozen cases filed since the mid-1980s, those challenging funding plans have relied on state constitutional guarantees of support for the education of all children. These cases focus on the inability of property taxes, even when bolstered by state aid, to raise poorer districts to the level of wealthier ones. The solution appears simple: move from the property tax to sales and income taxes as the sources of school funding. Politically, however, such a solution is not all that simple. In many state legislatures the percent of suburban representation is so high that the shift from property to income and sales taxes can easily be blocked. Local control and reliance on local property taxes are inseparable issues for many legislators and their constituents. While most states are involved in the issue of school funding change, a few are spared this issue of equity. Hawaii has one statewide school district, while Florida's county-based system tends to equalize funding (Henderson, 1993). Some states—Kentucky, Tennessee, and West Virginia—have raised more taxes at the state level, and then directed the funds to the poorer districts (Verhovek, 1993).

Another dimension of the equity issue is that of deteriorating school buildings. This issue has been emphasized in dozens of court cases that are crucial means for poor, minority children to obtain a more adequate education in safe and secure physical plants (Jackson, 1993). At the federal level, the Clinton administration announced an initiative to help finance repairs of the nation's deteriorating public schools, which are increasingly run down, overcrowded, and ill-equipped, according to the General Accounting Office. The President's $5 billion plan would generate $20 billion in construction. States would be allowed to decide how to spend the money, with the help of a federal subsidy if needed. Interest charges to states would be reduced up to 50 percent, with neediest school districts receiving the most assistance (James, 1996).

Given their financial difficulties, school districts have had very little choice but to implement cutbacks. Where possible, they reduced the size of pay increases. This was not always possible, however, because of the resistance of increasingly militant teacher unions. Some layoffs (especially in the North) were possible simply because of declining enrollments, and some school closings were possible for the same reason. Special programs were reduced or eliminated. However, in the extremely distressed central cities in the North, these relatively modest cutbacks were not enough. Major teacher layoffs, drastic curriculum reductions, limited replacement of textbooks, tight controls on supplies, reduced maintenance, and the elimination of all but the most critical capital improvements were employed to hold down budget increases or actually reduce budgets. Even that was not enough for many big city districts. Many faced outright bankruptcy and closed temporarily because they could not meet their payrolls and pay their suppliers. Others barely managed to keep operating.

The short-term prospects appear to hold continued financial difficulty. Cost pressures are not likely to abate even with declining enrollments. Maintenance cannot be put off indefinitely and books do not last forever. Pressures to maintain or increase teachers' salaries will not disappear. Yet, political opposition to increased taxes means that revenues are not likely to increase very rapidly. More and more districts will have difficulty operating at all. Most districts will experience financial difficulties to some degree.

Performance Levels

Much has been written about declining performance levels in public schools. The popular impression is that the schools are doing a much worse job teaching basic academic skills than before. The weight of the evidence appears to be in favor of the interpretation that some declines have occurred. However, it is not quite the kind of decline perceived by the public. Scores for the most basic kinds of skills acquired in the lower grades (through fourth grade) have actually risen. Basic reading, writing, and arithmetic do not seem to be the heart of the problem. Rather, it is the more sophisticated skills and knowledge taught in the upper grades which appear to have declined. These declines are probably significant and merit concern. (However, even these declines have to be put into historical context. Because skill levels rose until the late 1960s, the statistically average high-school graduate probably knows more than his or her counterpart in 1920.)

Explaining these declines is even more difficult than documenting them. According to Christopher Jencks, most theories that were advanced to explain performance decline in the 1970s do not hold up to close examination. Jencks argues that there is strong circumstantial evidence that these theories are wrong, and certainly no hard evidence exists to support them. Hence, the performance decline may not be the result of such things as changes in the kinds of students taking standardized tests, baby-boom enrollment growth, television, parental permissiveness, declining school expenditures, desegregation, curriculum changes, "grade inflation," or "watered-down" textbooks (Jencks, 1978).

In the 1980s the most influential report on performance levels was *A Nation at Risk* (Bell, 1983). This report stressed that the relative decline in quality of American schools had contributed to the economic decline of the United States during the last two decades. Moreover, the report expressed concern over the decline of an informed citizenry, due to less adequate education and training. Comparisons of student achievement tests showed U.S. students were considerably behind their counterparts in other industrialized nations. In addition, they were often badly in need of remedial work in math, spelling, reading, and writing. This resulted in great financial costs both to industry and to institutions of higher education. Significant declines in achievement scores also were noted for those entering college and those graduating.

A Nation at Risk caused much evaluation of the U.S. school system and prompted reform efforts. The solutions advocated included an ongoing commitment to educating minorities and the less fortunate, while simultaneously increasing for high school students the number of required years of math, science, and foreign language. Teachers were to receive higher quality training, and pay scales were to be increased. A higher level of funding for educational needs was strongly urged (*Congressional Record*, 1983).

What is the impact of school reform? Some benefits—for example, the cooperative learning approach—have been documented. In this approach, above-average students tutor those who are not doing as well. It has been shown to be particularly beneficial to disadvantaged students. Overall, uncooperative attitudes and stress among students are reduced, academic performance is improved, students feel better generally about school, racial and ethnic tension declines, while self-esteem increases (Shepard, 1996:408; Gelles and Levine, 1995:434).

James Comer, director of Yale University's Child Study Center, agrees with other social scientists that the way to make education work for disadvantaged children is to make the school the center of the community, a home away from home. In fifty such schools across the nation, the tactics seem to work. In New Haven, Connecticut, where this idea was first attempted, the school dropout rate decreased by 26 percent, while the number of students moving on to higher education grew from 45 to 73 percent during the 1980s (Gelles and Levine, 1995:434–35).

Still, the nation's schools are not training students to qualify for more demanding jobs. Lack of appropriate education is one of the basic causes of the employment difficulties for youth and the problems business has finding qualified workers (Hatfield, 1989). School dropouts are three times as likely to be unemployed as are high school graduates. A number of attempts are being made to cope with this situation. In Chicago, for example, corporations and higher education institutions are attempting to structure programs that train applicants both in basic skills and also in computer-related techniques (Goozner, 1988).

The Loss of Legitimacy

Jencks (1978) feels that at least part of the problem in education stems from a change in the social atmosphere of the schools. This, in turn, is seen as the result of a change in the nature of the "social contract" between the schools, students, and the community.

To the extent that schools succeeded in the past, they did so because a form of "social contract" (mutual agreement and understanding) existed between parents, students, teachers, and administrators. All parties recognized the school as an extension and embodiment of community values and standards. (In fact, these were the values and standards of the community's dominant social and economic group.) It was assumed that the educational professionals who operated the system accepted and enforced these standards and that the procedures and requirements of the schools were those appropriate to achieving the agreed-upon goals. Parents were expected to reinforce and support the demands and requirements of the school.

In return for compliance with the community-sanctioned norms of the schools, students could expect to receive annual promotion in grade level and to be "fairly" evaluated and sorted into appropriate career or job channels. In short, the demands and the authority of the school were viewed as legitimate—that is, considered morally right and consistent with the values of the community (Dentler, 1977). The fact that the underlying assumptions of this social contract were dubious did not matter as long as it did not occur to many people to question them.

In the 1960s and 1970s, however, increasing numbers of people did begin to question the nature of the contract. Educators became less certain of the appropriateness of what they were teaching and how they were teaching it. Racial and ethnic minorities became more sensitive to the cultural biases built into the system. The cultural and class differences in central-city schools between predominantly white, middle-class staffs and predominantly poor, African-American student bodies called into question the existence of value convergence between school and community. In poor neighborhoods, schools became viewed as alien outposts of an impersonal and uncaring governmental bureaucracy. Even in middle-class districts, the introduction of new teaching methods, courses, and texts was increasingly seen as evidence of a school system run by arrogant professionals with different values than those of the parents and community. For example, the endless debate about sex education and school prayer has pitted the courts and school professionals against parents. Students who were more cynical about the institutions of society and the utility of education were less likely to internalize the norms and goals of the school. The traditional social contract in the schools was, as a consequence, severely weakened, and the legitimacy of school authority badly undermined.

One result was that the ability of the schools to impose traditional academic standards on their bored and cynical charges was substantially reduced. Most teachers interviewed in a Carnegie Foundation study felt that disruptive behavior, absenteeism, student apathy, and lack of parental support were problems. Nearly 70 percent also noted theft and vandalism; nearly half, student violence; about one-third, racial discord; and more than one-fourth, violent behavior against teachers. More than 20 percent mentioned that over one-fourth of their students were poor. Nearly all reported that child abuse and child neglect were problems (*Condition of Teaching*, 1988:26). As a consequence, uncertain themselves of what they should be doing and faced with resistance from their students, the school staffs reached an uneasy accommodation with their students: they would not ask too much of the students if the students would not disrupt things too much (Jencks, 1978:39–40).

High School Dropouts

Among the issues dominating the 1980s was the high school dropout rate, about 25 percent of total enrollment in some systems (Ogintz, 1989a). Fortunately, rates for dropping out have declined over the last two decades. Between 1979–1989, the dropout rate fell from 14.6 percent to 12.6 percent. The 1999 dropout rate was 11.2 percent (National Center for Education Statistics, 2001). This decrease has been particularly noteworthy for African Americans. African-American dropouts aged 14-24 who either didn't attend or had not yet finished high school dropped from 22 percent in 1970 to about 12 percent in 1988. Rates for whites dropped only 1 percent in the same period, from 11 percent to 10 percent. Hispanic rates continued to be high: 25 percent in 1998 (U.S. Census Bureau, 2001b). Dropout rates continue to be significant for inner-city youths from low-income, single-parent families (Griffith et al., 1989:22, 23). Nonetheless, for pupils with low test scores (in the bottom quartile), whites are more apt to drop out than African Americans and Hispanics. Many dropouts come back to school, either to complete their course work or to obtain an equivalence certificate (Griffith et al., 1989:24).

A number of experiments have been tried to reduce the dropout rate. Colleges and universities have adopted approaches designed to motivate inner-city children for higher education. Assistance is given in order to help those interested become eligible. New York State passed legislation substantially increasing funding for both dropout prevention and college aid (Ogintz, 1989b; Hundley, 1988). Alternative schools are an attempt at a within-system answer to dropping out. Chicago city colleges began this program to help dropouts complete high school. Alternative schools offer smaller classrooms, personal instruction, and readjustment assistance. Dropouts are referred to this program by high school counselors, social work agencies, and the juvenile court. This approach offers a second chance to students who leave school because of family problems, gangs, and boredom (Robinson, 1987).

Chicago public school truancy rates have fallen since the beginning of Mayor Daley's reform in 1995. A considerable number of high schools, however, have shown either no improvement or a worsening of their situation. One explanation is that classroom instruction revolves around annual standardized tests. Students who don't do well become disconnected and stop coming to school. Others are absent because they work full time at night to support their families, have sick children, or are overwhelmed by their studies. Extensive efforts are being made to increase required attendance, including use of home visitation, technology training, and alternative schools, as well as night high school. The night high school program gives those students who are failing a course, have been thrown out of regular classrooms, or who need to work during the day a chance to catch up. Student retention at some schools is better than that for daytime students (Quintanilla, 2000a, 2000b).

The Community-Control Movement

The problems of urban school districts have given rise to numerous efforts to reform them. In the recent past, probably the best known of these reform proposals was the *community-control* movement. During the 1970s, a few large-city school districts (most notably, New York City) actually experimented with this kind of reform. The details of their programs varied, but they shared a common general strategy: that of giving people in each area of the city a direct voice in the operation of the particular schools serving their community. Power would shift from the distant and impersonal central school bureaucracy into the hands of the people directly affected and knowledgeable about conditions in their local schools. It was hoped that this decentralization of power would make each school more accountable and responsive to the needs of the community it served. This in turn would increase involvement of local parents with the schools and create support for improved educational programs. A further intent was to make sure that each school tailored its programs to the needs and cultural backgrounds of its students.

More generally, community control was viewed as an important democratic reform with implications for creating a more responsive system of urban government, increasing the legitimacy of governmental institutions, and training people in democratic participation (Orleans and Orleans, 1976).

A review of the various attempts at community control in a number of different cities suggests that, despite their early bright promise, such programs have not lived up to the expectations of their supporters. The programs often emerged out of genuine grassroots movements and initially enjoyed widespread community support and involvement. However, the impact of community-control boards was quickly blunted and contained by a number of factors. Funding for their operations often came from external sources, usually the federal government. This meant that local boards were hemmed in by outside controls and requirements which limited their freedom of action. It also meant that local boards became involved in federally mandated activities that required paid staffs of professionals. The boards tended to be deflected from their original missions by these service activities and increasingly controlled by "professional activists" more interested in providing services (and assuring their own organizational survival). Grassroots involvement withered away. At the same time, community-control programs ran into massive resistance from existing educational interest groups who felt their power and economic interests were being threatened. Central district boards were reluctant to surrender their decision-making authority. State educational agencies and the central district bureaucracy resisted community control for the same reason. Teachers' unions felt that the privileges and protections provided under their contracts might be lost. These various interest groups were usually successful in undercutting community control through political pressure and bureaucratic delaying tactics. The result was that real, democratic community control with effective decision-making power either was never achieved or did not last (Gittel, 1980).

Some observers feel that decentralization of schools will not in itself solve the problems of educational systems. The context of poverty, crime, and family disorganization will not simply disappear. Nor will any amount of participation by citizens and teachers help if they are not prepared or capable. The decentralization approach can, however, lead to opening up the system to new ideas and to accountability (Bakalis, 1987).

Lewis and Nakagawa (1995) found that in five major American cities, including Chicago, decentralization had little effect on administrative bureaucracy in urban educational systems. While decentralization was intended to upgrade local schools by involving parents in local-school administration, little change actually occurred in school reorganization to make them more effective in the learning process. In addition, the desires of local school boards to obtain more changes were not fulfilled. Thus, while decentralization has wide appeal, it just has not been effective. Such an approach gives the illusion of change while threatening neither the racial makeup of the schools nor the financial arrangements of society. Government is seen as the problem, therefore spending more money cannot be the answer. Changes in the way local schools are run—i.e., new forms of local participation and shifts in formal authority—mean little if real leadership and sufficient additional revenue are not present for dealing effectively with poverty and racism. They conclude that decentralization is a poor substitute for more far-reaching reforms that fund public schools more equitably and really improve the true quality of education (Lewis and Nakagawa, 1995:35–36, 167–73).

Recent Trends

Presently, there is a widespread belief that public schools are grossly wasting their funds without improving student performance. With growing public pressure for fiscal restraint and a slowdown in funding, some states—and districts and communities within states—will face continued budgetary problems. Instructional quality will probably suffer, especially where enrollments are on the rise. Many school districts have deferred essential maintenance on their buildings. Moreover, moving into the computer age is very expensive for schools. Because of both fiscal constraints and lack of public confidence that expenditures for education are effective, the main goal in education is to gain control of spending (Mandel et al., 1995).

How might specific proposals affect public education? More accountability will be required, using business models. Another business-oriented approach getting considerable support is competition, which is felt to compel schools to break down rigid regulations and work rules, and instead, to innovate. A study by Hoxby (1995) suggests that availability of more school alternatives can lead to lower spending levels and higher achievement.

One approach advocated in recent years is the voucher system, used in Milwaukee, where low-income parents can get money to send their children to private schools. Proposals to implement vouchers often, however, stir up great political opposition (Mandel et al., 1995). Free-market conservatives have made optimistic promises and claims regarding school vouchers: public schools would benefit from healthier competition; their classes would get smaller; needy students would get more attention; everyone would learn more; there would be no need for bureaucratic or state regulation. There have been numerous success stories of voucher students in Milwaukee who have developed into above-average pupils after failing in public schools; however, of nearly 1500 students attending voucher schools in Milwaukee, about 200 dropped out. Two of the seventeen participating schools have gone out of business, and two more are on the critical list, due to serious financial difficulties. Milwaukee voucher schools have yet to meet the promises of advocates, who claimed that private-public competition would markedly improve student achievement test scores. Recently, even student voucher advocates have called for more state oversight. What are the likely implications? The more public money is used for private schools, the more state regulations and bureaucracy may follow. So far, vouchers have usually been earmarked only for those schools the middle class has abandoned. Vouchers could be less a panacea than a last resort. Critics also argue that vouchers skim off the best of the least fortunate students, and those with the most conscientious parents, abandoning the rest. The basic implication of voucher education is that it tends to widen the gap between the talented and the average student, between middle-class and lower-class pupils (Page, 1996).

Another controversial policy proposal that has been implemented in some districts is that of privatization. The experience of Educational Alternative Schools (EAS), a Minneapolis-based firm, illustrates why this approach has attracted controversy. Initially, test scores indicated that EAS students were improving their performance; 1994 figures showed, however, that students in the privately run schools, such as the one in Baltimore, did a little worse on the standardized tests than their peers in the city's other schools (Henderson, 1993). When EAS signed a contract in 1994 to manage all the public schools in Hartford, Connecticut, it was closely watched by many in the business and education communities as it sought to improve performance in a school system with a large minority population and many other difficulties typical of urban systems. By hiring EAS, Hartford attempted to reverse declining test scores, reduce dropout rates, and repair a badly decaying infrastructure. Efficient management was to provide the Hartford school board with extra income for making various improvements. In January 1996, however, EAS abruptly terminated its contract. Privatization has been terminated not only in Hartford, but somewhat earlier in Baltimore and also in Florida's Dade County (Kirby, 1996). Such results suggest the difficulties in running a school system like a business. It can be argued that there still may be limited benefits to privatization, for example, in the maintenance of school property and equipment. Privatization, however, may not be a general answer to the problems of public education (Kirby, 1996). Perhaps the most important implication of the largely unsuccessful privatization approach is that the ingredients for a successful for-profit school are not that different from those required for a top public school: adequate funding, site-based management, dedicated teachers, and a vision shared by the whole community (Nifong, 1996).

Independently owned charter schools are one of the fastest-growing innovations in public education. In recent years, twenty states have passed charter school laws, resulting in 230 units. Advocates claim charter schools serve, are financed by, and are accountable to the public. They can improve upon the procedures and accountability of school bureaucracies, as well as provide new incentives for teaching staff. Opponents argue that such schools drain away the best students, leaving disadvantaged children unserved, reducing citizen involvement in and support of the public schools, and further decreasing funding for physical plant, programs, staff, and maintenance (*Chicago Tribune,* 3/15/1996). Charter schools, however, enroll larger percentages of minority students than nearby public schools in many communities, and many serve special needs. Advocates claim that traditional public schools have improved as a result of the emergence of charter schools (Walters, 1996).

Evaluation

The crisis in education is not new. Critics of the public schools have never lacked for evidence of various failures and problems in the system. That is because the schools have never fully lived up to their promises and the high expectations of the public. The past century is littered with the wreckage of various reforms, each of which promised some sort of "quick fix" for the long-term problems of the schools.

It should now be clear that the problems are more complex than the educational reformers have assumed. For one thing, we are asking more of the system than it can probably ever deliver. For instance, to ask educational programs to correct the deep-seated consequences of unequal opportunity and the inequalities of wealth and power in society is really to ask the impossible. Even if we knew how to design such programs, they would encounter the powerful opposition of the already privileged and those educational interest groups who benefit from the status quo. It can be argued that in many ways the schools function the way they do because it is beneficial to many powerful interests in society. For example, are the schools intended to teach democratic values or are they really designed to teach obedience and discipline to the future labor force? We should also remember that many of the schools' problems exist in the context of more general problems in the society: crime, drug abuse, poverty, racism, the declining legitimacy of major institutions, and economic and demographic trends.

None of this is meant to imply that we should be either complacent or despairing about the schools. Education has severe problems which simply must be confronted by public policy. Besides its more fundamental problems, we have just seen that a number of more recent trends threaten the ability of the system to continue to function at all. Past mistakes are not grounds for inaction, but only suggest the magnitude of the problems that will have to be faced.

CRIMINAL JUSTICE

From the point of view of the general public, one of the most important urban problems is crime (especially that associated with drugs). Primarily, this is a reflection of the widespread fear of being victimized by street crime, having one's home burglarized, or being caught in the violence generated by illegal drugs. These fears are reinforced by the tendency of the news media to give dramatic coverage to such crimes. These fears have some basis in fact. The kinds of crime most feared by the public do seem to have increased in the last few decades. We will also see, however, that public fears and perceptions of the crime problem are oversimplified. Such crimes as street crime, murder, and burglary are only one aspect of the urban crime problem. Other forms of crime, about which the public has tended to be much less concerned, are at least as serious in terms of the cost to society. In addition, we will see that an effective response to crime is much more difficult than most people think.

We also need to put the current problem of crime in better perspective. There seems to be a widespread belief that serious crime problems are a very recent development and that crime represents evidence of some sort of contemporary breakdown in society. In fact, U.S. cities have always confronted serious amounts of crime and violence, and the current level of public concern is not the first time the nation has been threatened by a breakdown in public order. At the turn of the twentieth century in New York City, some slum areas were so dangerous that police would only enter them armed and in pairs. Labor violence flared repeatedly in urban areas between the 1870s and 1930s. During the railway strike of 1877, many hundreds of people were killed across the country, and about two miles of railroad cars and buildings were burned in Pittsburgh as the result of violent clashes between strikers, railroad police, and the militia (President's Commission on Law Enforcement, 1967).

Officially Reported Crime

Traditionally, the focus of most government efforts to measure crime (as well as control it) has centered on a particular set of offenses that correspond to public perceptions of and concern about criminal activity. This represents a very biased and incomplete view of the total extent and nature of such activity. However, the crimes included in the "official crime rate" are serious ones which involve real public suffering, and therefore merit our careful consideration.

The Official Reporting System

The most important and best-known government effort to measure the extent of crime has been the *Uniform Crime Report* (UCR). For half a century, this report has been issued annually by the Federal Bureau of Investigation. It contains the official crime rates, which are calculated on the basis of reports sent to the FBI by local police departments (see table 8.1). The UCR does, however, have a number of problems and limitations. It is based on only a few kinds of crimes (rape, robbery, murder, aggravated assault, burglary, larceny-theft, and auto theft, for example). In addition, people don't always report these crimes. The UCR thus both understates the amount of crime, and gives a distorted image of the crime problem.

Trends in Official Crime Rates

Generally speaking, crime rates for both violent and property crime in the United States rose between 1960–1991. While the violent crime rate was about 150 per 100,000 people in 1960, by 1991 it had risen to 758. Similarly, property crime rates during this time period increased from about 1,800 per 100,000 to more than 5,000 (Federal Bureau of Investigation, 1995 in Macionis, 1997:222). Since 1991, the rates for both violent and property crimes have gone down.

Victimization Studies

A number of criminologists hold that a more realistic and extensive picture of crime is provided by victimization surveys (Barlow, 1990: 134–35; Spates and Macionis, 1987:384). In 1986, for instance, the *Uniform Crime Reports* indicated 91,460 forcible rapes, as compared to 129,940 such crimes noted by *victimization surveys*. In this same year such surveys recorded nearly twice as many aggravated assaults (1,542,870) as the UCR (834,320). Much less contrast was found for auto theft—about 1.2 million for the UCR, compared to about 1.4 million for victimization surveys. Victimization studies are certainly not without flaws. Their findings are based on recall and memory, which may be somewhat selective. Fear of being found out to have told about a crime may cause the respondent to lie or distort replies to questions (Barlow, 1990:135–38).

Table 8.1
The Official Rate of Crime

Year	Total Crime Rate*	Violent Crime Rate*	Property Crime Rate*
1981	5858	594	5264
1982	5604	571	5033
1983	5175	538	4673
1984	5031	539	4492
1985	5207	557	4651
1986	5480	618	4863
1987	5550	610	4940
1988	5664	637	5027
1989	5471	663	5078
1990	5820	732	5089
1991	5898	758	5140
1992	5660	758	4903
1993	5484	747	4738
1994	5374	714	4658
1995	5276	685	4591
1996	5087	637	4450
1997	4930	611	4319
1998	4616	566	4049
1999	4267	523	3744
2000	4124	506	3618
Percentage Change			
1991–2000	−30.1%	−33.2%	−29.6%

*Number of reported crimes per 100,000 inhabitants

SOURCE: U.S. Federal Bureau of Investigation, *Crime in the United States* (various years).

Variations by Size of Community

Popular conceptions of the crime problem tend to associate living in large central cities with a high risk of being victimized by crime. Crime is viewed as one of the major disadvantages of city life compared to smaller, safer communities. There is considerable truth to this view. It does nonetheless oversimplify a complex situation.

There is a general relationship between city size and the official crime rate. In the recent past, the overall crime rate has tended to be higher in larger communities than in smaller ones (see table 8.2). Both property crimes and violent crimes are, on the average, highest in metropolitan areas, and consistently decline with city size (Spates and Macionis, 1987:384).

Table 8.2
Rate of Crime by Size of Place in 1998

Size of Place	Total Crime Rate*	Violent Crime Rate*	Property Crime Rate*
250,000+	7058	1218	5840
100,000–249,000	6407	758	5649
50,000–99,999	5302	590	4712
25,000–49,999	4701	454	4247
10,000–24,999	4286	373	3913
under 10,000	4646	397	4249
Metro Areas	5000	630	4300
Rural Areas	1900	230	1800

*Number of reported crimes per 100,000 inhabitants

SOURCE: U.S. Federal Bureau of Investigation, *Crime in the United States* (various years).

These findings in regard to crime and city size must be qualified. A great number of crimes are not known, not reported to police, and carelessly recorded. Official data thus has very real limitations. National surveys show slightly over one-third of all serious crimes go unreported (Spates and Macionis, 1987:384). Hence, comparisons between cities based on official statistics must be approached cautiously.

There is no clear explanation for the relation of crime extent and city size. We do know, however, that urban crime is concentrated in a few areas of cities. These districts are characterized by ongoing poverty, unemployment, inadequate housing, teen pregnancy, and drug use (Flanagan, 1990:268). Most homicide victims and offenders are African American, relatively poor, males, and between 20 and 30 years of age. Most victims and offenders in rape cases are from relatively low socioeconomic areas in the largest cities. In the case of robbery, African Americans are victimized at three times the frequency of whites, though offenders tend to be African American (Barlow, 1990:155–56, 194, 221). Generally speaking, a disproportionate percent of urban poor show up in national crime data, both as accused and victims.

James Q. Wilson has argued that crime committed by those living in poor neighborhoods has increased because of the breakdown of inner control and the adoption of crime as a way of life (Wilson, 1983). Many have taken issue with Wilson. It has been suggested by his opponents that the level of wages available to poor, inner-city youth offer little incentive to work, since illegal activities offer much more in the way of financial rewards (McGahey, 1986:249). Others argue that inner-city residents are much more apt to see unemployment as permanent, making them more open to crime as an alternative way of life

(Duster, 1987:306–9). Rates for violent crime by youth thus reflect their limited choices in legitimate job markets. To survive in many neighborhoods, a person may have to become part of a gang. Gangs give personal protection as well as access into criminal income. Finally, procedures of arrest, sentencing, and pretrial and court arrangements show prejudice against African Americans and Hispanics. Police and the court system, particularly during the last decades, deal with the breaking of the law, not the context of the offender (Flanagan, 1990:272–75).

Recent Changes in Crime Rates

In the middle and late 1990s crime rates were down across the United States, some dramatically. How can this trend best be explained? Those in the criminal justice system point to new policing methods. According to a New York police commissioner, the falling crime rate is due in large part to the decentralization of policing, from headquarters to local precincts. Older police officers have been retired. Computerized crime statistics are compiled daily and used to spot areas where crime is on the rise. Police are then swiftly deployed to deal with these crime sites. Generally speaking, New York has replaced a reactive response with a proactive, preventative philosophy (*Economist,* 1996).

In New York, New Orleans, and other American cities, the downward trend in crime rates may be due to a combination of tougher and softer tactics. More aggressive action toward suspects is occurring at the same time police have become more involved in community policing, including more interaction with schoolchildren. Norval Morris, professor of law and criminology at the University of Chicago, suggests, however, that testing the actual effects of different efforts to deter crime is very rarely done (Lacayo, 1996:48–53). Other experts feel that the declining crime rate is only temporary and will reverse itself as the teen population grows (Lacayo, 1996; *Christian Science Monitor,* 1996; *Economist,* 1996).

At the same time, concern over police brutality has grown. Allegations by Amnesty International in 1996 against the New York Police Department claimed that the department has continued to use excessive force, in spite of recent reforms, especially against African Americans, Hispanics, and Asian Americans. Yet prosecutions and convictions of police remain relatively rare.

New York is not alone in confronting complaints of selective arrests and racially motivated abuse by police. Racial motivations surfaced as a major concern in the Los Angeles area after such incidents as the Rodney King beating and the testimony of detective Mark Fuhrman during the O. J. Simpson criminal trial.

During the past decade, the U.S. Civil Rights Commission, an independent panel appointed by the president, has investigated racially motivated abuse. However, most police agencies are reluctant to turn over internal data dealing with race and policing (Thomas, 1995). The Commission recommends the FBI begin gathering data nationwide on police abuse and discipline to help local police departments and citizens measure the extent of the problem. Meanwhile, many police departments have adopted their own measures to address this problem, including independent review boards, expanded sensitivity training of officers, and early warning systems to identify officers with emotional and psychological problems.

White-Collar Crime

The public perception of crime as a problem of the urban poor is based on the failure to recognize the significance and prevalence of an entire class of criminal activity that is not primarily a lower-class phenomenon: white-collar crime. This somewhat heterogeneous group of crimes has been variously defined. However, Herbert Edelhertz, former head of the Fraud Section in the Criminal Division of the U.S. Department of Justice, has suggested one definition: ". . . an illegal act or series of illegal acts committed by nonphysical means and by concealment or guile to obtain property, to avoid the payment or loss of money or property, or to obtain business or personal advantage" (cited in Demaris, 1974:15). Edwin Sutherland, who originally focused sociological attention on the problem, suggested a simpler, but narrower, definition that emphasized the class background of the offender. He defined white-collar crime as an act "committed by a person of respectability and high social status in the course of his occupation" (Sutherland, 1949:9).

Sutherland was among the first to document the frequency and variety of illegal business practices. Based on research extending up to 1944 on the seventy largest nonfinancial corporations, he found that the corporations had a total of 980 legal decisions rendered against them by a variety of enforcement agencies (about half by courts and the rest by other agencies). The violations involved such things as price-fixing among competitors, false advertising, unfair labor practices, trademark and patent violations, financial fraud, and violations of wartime regulations. Almost all the corporations had more than one violation. Sutherland likened the behavior of many of the corporations to that of habitual criminals (Sutherland, 1949:9).

The problem of white-collar crime is not just a matter of corporate misbehavior. There is a whole range of "respectable crimes" committed by individuals for individual gain. While some of these crimes are included in the official statistics (e.g., arson), it is generally believed that the official statistics grossly underestimate the extent of these crimes (Barlow, 1990: 284). Moreover, these crimes are not used in calculating the official crime rate. The majority of white-collar crimes involve some sort of fraud or nonviolent deception. They range from illegal tax evasion to embezzlement to phony insurance claims and charges for unnecessary medical procedures. There are no reliable statistics on the total cost of this kind of crime, but it is estimated to be very high indeed. Arson for profit (by building owners) reached epidemic proportions in urban areas and played a major role in increasing fire insurance premiums during the 1970s (Steglich and Snooks, 1980:438).

Some more recent forms of white-collar crime include insider trading, the corruption at HUD (Department of Housing and Urban Development) during the 1980s, the savings and loan scandal, and computer crime. Insider trading can be defined as the obtaining of inside information in advance of stock transactions. It is in effect the same as fixing a horse race or athletic game (Francis, 1988). The Mafia has had a key part in the manipulation of low-price as well as conventional stocks, involving extensive use of insider trading practices (Stern and Poole, 1989).

The HUD scandal involved allowing agency officials to use housing programs to provide loans for upper- and middle-class housing as well as for business developments. Members of Congress got grants and loans for themselves as well as for their constituents (Waldman, 1989; Cohn, 1989). The effects of those actions were both to deny housing loan assistance to the poor, as well as to disrupt real-estate markets and thereby collapse prices.

The savings and loan (S&L) scandals of the late 1980s and early 1990s are another example of white-collar crime. Three factors in particular contributed to the corrupting of S&Ls: the increase in deposit insurance to $100,000; power given (in 1982) to S&Ls enabling them to move from home mortgage loans to virtually any kind of higher risk venture; and the weak legal constraints at both federal and state levels. The resulting financial collapse of hundreds of S&Ls required a federal expenditure of hundreds of billions of dollars. This S&L "bailout" primarily benefits the Sunbelt (the region where most S&Ls failed). The rest of the country, however, pays for the bailout at a cost of about $2,000 per person. Tightened mortgage markets resulting from the S&L collapse have further eroded home ownership among the less affluent (Adams, 1989; Pilzer, 1989).

Finally, computer crime, the stealing of information from computers or damaging a computer, continues to be a major form of white-collar crime. This type of crime can take several forms: the changing of data to be entered or that's already in the computer, instructing the computer to perform unauthorized tasks, removing financial assets, modifying computer contents, and taking information from the computer, among other things. Losses from such crimes may run as high as $40 billion (Reid, 1988; Stoll, 1989).

Despite the fragmentary evidence, it is possible to make a few limited generalizations about the role of white-collar crime. First, it seems clear that white-collar crime is at least as serious a problem as the crimes used to calculate official crime rates. The total damage caused by white-collar crime certainly exceeds that caused by more conventional crimes. And it is certainly as common as other forms of criminal activity. The fact that white-collar crimes are committed by leading corporations and seemingly respectable people also contributes in a major, if unmeasurable way, to the diffusion of "criminal" attitudes and expectations in the population (Barlow, 1990:290).

Second, despite its seriousness, white-collar crime has failed to provoke the public concern and official control responses which other kinds of crimes have provoked. The general public does not conceive of the "urban crime problem" as a problem of rapacious corporations and greedy, dishonest, middle-class citizens. Reflecting these attitudes, the criminal justice system has made less of a sustained effort to detect and punish white-collar crime. As a consequence, most of the available evidence suggests that white-collar crime is fairly safe to commit. The risks of detection are probably fairly low, and the punishments for those crimes that are detected are often mild (Barlow, 1990:323–25).

Third, as its name implies, white-collar crime is committed primarily by middle- and upper-class people. This fact probably does much to explain both public and official apathy. Somehow, the criminal acts of a well-educated, articulate, white business person seem less serious than the crimes of a poor person. White-collar crime seems more an extension of "normal" (i.e., middle-class) behavior and is less likely to involve direct interpersonal, physical violence (though it may still kill people, as in the case of dumping dangerous chemicals). And, it should be remembered, white-collar crime is committed by people who have more political power and are better able to defend themselves in court than lower-class people.

Organized Crime

A major portion of the criminal activity in the United States consists of *organized crime*. This kind of criminal activity consists of more or less formally organized groups that operate "business" organizations which either provide illegal "services" or use illegal methods to provide legitimate services. Despite the sporadic investigations by law enforcement agencies and investigatory commissions, our knowledge of organized crime is very incomplete, and there remains considerable uncertainty about its precise nature, extent, and structure. There can be no doubt, however, that organized crime represents a serious problem, and most observers feel that the problem is most serious in major metropolitan areas.

Organized crime appears to dominate a number of areas of illegal activity. Very important is its role in the control of illegal gambling activities. "Loan sharks" (people who make loans to financially desperate people at extraordinarily high interest rates) also appear to be based in criminal organizations. Organized crime is also believed to be deeply involved in the production and distribution of pornography, the sale of stolen goods, prostitution, and narcotics. The sale of narcotics is especially important because a large number of street crimes are committed by narcotics addicts to support their habits. In addition, individuals connected with organized crime have used bribery, threats, and violence to infiltrate a number of labor unions where they attempt both to extort money from employers and to cheat the members by signing (for a price) weak contracts with employers. These criminals are also believed to have taken over a number of legitimate businesses that serve as covers for their illegal activities. Once involved in legitimate businesses, members of organized crime apparently use extortion and strong-arm tactics to eliminate their competitors. In many cities organized crime appears to have gained control of such activities as the vending-machine and jukebox industries, and to have major investments in bars, hotels, trucking companies, food companies, linen-supply houses, commercial garbage collection, and some factories (Cressey, 1969:xi). Organized crime also has been linked with stock-fraud schemes and real estate speculation in the Sunbelt (Stern and Poole, 1989).

Of growing importance in the recent past has been the appearance of large-scale drug smuggling and drug gangs. The President's Organized Crime Commission concluded that drug trafficking was the most serious activity of organized crime. Billions of dollars are made in these transactions, which are often interregional and worldwide in scope. Countless individuals, their families, communities, and not the least, governments, are severely hurt through the sale and use of drugs (Reid, 1988:345–47). Commerce in illegal drugs is the world's most rapidly growing business. The United States is the world's biggest market. Producers range from Thailand and Lebanon to Mexico and Colombia, to name a few. Though immense quantities of drugs have been seized by U.S. authorities, the supply is so great that the flow into this country is virtually unaffected. Entire nations have been disrupted through bribery and intimidation by drug bosses. Colombia is perhaps the most flagrant example. A coalition of criminal families there has transformed the cocaine trade into an international industry. This worldwide surge of illegal drugs makes traditional law enforcement virtually impossible. Latin American-U.S. relations have been severely tested by the tendency of the United States to use military action to suppress the drug trade (Kraar, 1988).

Ethnic gangs are also an important element in the changing face of organized crime in the United States. The newer ethnic groups, especially those from Central America, Asia, and the Caribbean, started by living off those of their own nationality. Once they became stronger financially, they expanded into the larger society. Crime syndicates from Hong Kong moved to the United States in anticipation of more stringent control when Hong Kong reverted to China in 1997. Taiwanese and Jamaican gangs are also present in the United States (*U.S. News and World Report,* 1988).

Inner-city gangs now have the chance to grow in power due to sales of "crack" cocaine and to the breakdown of the old organized crime groups. Contemporary gangs are much more violent than Mafia groups. Gang disputes and wars are no longer over neighborhood control, but rather over control of drug sales. Most such gang members are in their teens or early and mid-20s.

The total economic impact of organized crime is not known, and estimates vary widely. One early estimate stated that the total activity of organized crime amounted to more than twice the losses resulting from street crime (President's Commission, 1967). The problem of organized crime goes beyond the simple fact that it represents a violation of laws, leads to violence against citizens, and costs society tremendous sums of money. Organized crime subverts the basic institutions of society. Otherwise honest businesses are forced to make illegal arrangements to survive. Workers are forced to accept working arrangements that violate their supposedly legally guaranteed rights to be represented by organizations of their own choosing. Perhaps most importantly, organized crime corrupts government at a number of levels. Organized crime survives in part by the routine and widespread bribery and corruption of the police and the courts. Every few years, evidence of the bribery of elected officials and the role of organized crime in financing political campaigns comes to light and gets a lot of media attention. Quite literally, government has been heavily infiltrated by organized crime (Barlow, 1990:353–54).

This brings us to the most disturbing aspect of organized crime—it has proven to be almost impervious to efforts by law enforcement agencies to control or stop its activities. Indeed, organized crime has even defied efforts to discover the full nature and extent of its organization and operation. There is considerable debate, for example, about the extent to which various organized crime syndicates coordinate their activities and participate in regional or national organizations. Numerous reasons have been given for this failure of law enforcement to effectively control organized crime. Certainly, corruption of the police and public officials has played a role. In addition, organized crime has been very effective in intimidating potential witnesses and maintaining discipline among its members. Moreover, the operations of organized crime are both complex and sophisticated. Proving court cases against alleged leaders has proven very difficult and generally has exceeded the resources and ability of local law enforcement agencies. Finally, because organized crime provides services that a substantial number of people want or believe they need (gambling, prostitution, and illegal drugs), there is a germ of truth to the frequent justification used by these criminals for their activities: they really can exist only because there is a market for their services (Barlow, 1990:359).

Responding to Crime: The Dilemma

Crime is clearly a serious problem, and the public expectation that government should do something about it is understandable. The question is: what should be done? The fact is that public policy makers are faced with a number of problems dealing with crime which severely limit the available policy options.

A Limited Understanding of the Causes of Crime

There are a number of general theories about the nature and causes of crime. Each of these theories has its intellectual supporters, sources of empirical support, and some utility in explaining crime. However, these theories are frequently contradictory, many are fairly crude and incomplete, and none can claim overwhelming evidence which supports its claims. Hirschi suggests that two traits define crime. First, crimes tend to be committed by the young; crime rates are high among those in the late teens and on into the early twenties, but fall quickly afterward. Second, offenders tend to see life in terms of the short run, and are low in self-esteem (Macionis, 1997:231).

The Difficulty in Eliminating the Causes of Crime

Despite our limited understanding of the causes of crime, past efforts at attempting to understand and/or control crime have made one thing fairly clear: seeking to deal with crime by eliminating its causes is extraordinarily difficult. While sociologists may differ in regard to their specific theories of crime, there does seem to be some agreement on the general nature of those causes. Apparently, those causes are deeply embedded in the basic culture and social structure of United States society. Hence, "simple" solutions (no matter how desirable on other grounds or how hard to achieve) are not likely to substantially reduce the causes of crime.

The Harris thesis, for example, suggests that there is a connection between unemployment, AFDC, traditional male (macho) behavior, and the cultural acceptance of crime. Implied here is the larger context of a positive correlation between increasing inequality and crime. How can these relationships be explained? The rate of violent crime in the United States is disproportionately high because this country has a permanent, distinct underclass. The impoverished ghetto conditions where millions of African Americans and Hispanics live fosters both motive and opportunity for violent criminal behavior. The crucial explanation is not one of race or ethnicity, but rather long-term poverty and unemployment, with extremely high rates for African-American youth. African Americans are unemployed because available work does not provide enough money to exist. The employment situation of African-American and Hispanic males is compounded by their high dropout rate. Any policy seriously attempting to decrease ghetto unemployment will have to provide appropriate training and equal opportunities for the African Americans and Hispanics who live there (Harris, 1981).

It seems likely, then, that reducing the motivation or the pressure to commit crime would involve very fundamental changes in the nature of American society. For example, some suggested changes include major reductions in the degree of income inequality and wealth, changes in the opportunities available for mobility, changes in the economic environment in which corporations operate, changes in the control of corporate behavior, and changes in cultural values (Flanagan, 1990:272–74). These would be very major changes indeed. In the near future, they also are probably very unlikely. At the very least, this means that short-term policy options will be limited to efforts to control criminal activity and minimize the damage done by crime rather than eliminating the causes of criminal behavior.

The Dilemmas of Crime Control

As in the study of the causes of crime, efforts to determine what forms of crime control will work have met with limited success and remain a source of considerable controversy among scholars, government officials, and the public. Public perception of a "crisis" of crime and drug abuse has led to the imposition of harsher sentences and more limitations on parole. The result has been a massive upsurge in the prison population in the United States. The inmate population has more than tripled since 1980, with more than 1.5 million people imprisoned by the mid-1990s—at a cost of $26 billion. Much of the upsurge can be explained by increased imprisonment of drug offenders. In 1983 about 8 percent of state prisoners were drug offenders, but by 1992 the figure had grown to 30 percent. (About 70 percent of federal prisoners were also drug offenders). The bulk of the rest of the increase was for property crimes, since violent offenders were and are a small minority of those who are brought to trial and sentenced. Critics have also pointed out that African-American drug offenders have been particularly targeted because of the especially harsh sentences that the law requires for crack-cocaine-related offenses. Nearly 88 percent of the inmates serving time for such offenses are African Americans.

Whether or not increased imprisonment has been a successful strategy is a matter of some debate. Declines in the rate of violent crime in the 1990s may have been impacted in part by improved policing efforts and the threat of longer imprisonment. On the other hand, much of the decline is easily explained by the decline in the number of young males in the population (a very temporary trend) and, more speculatively, changes in gang subcultures and/or more orderly and less violent marketing agreements among rival drug distribution organizations. Most sociological experts on crime are willing to concede, at most, a very modest role for increased imprisonment on general urban crime rates.

What is clear is that having the highest rate of imprisonment in the world and a prison population approaching two million raises serious questions. For one thing, it is immensely costly—prison construction and operation in many states equals or exceeds the budget for higher education. Conditions of appalling overcrowding, enforced idleness, violence between inmates, inadequate health care, and brutality on the part of guards have been reported all over the United States and have resulted in federal court intervention (to prevent "cruel and unusual punishment" as specified in the U.S. Constitution). Most of those now in prison will be released. Brutalization and socialization into criminal subcultures is the routine result of imprisonment. Social stigma and difficulties finding employment plague ex-convicts and make their social adjustment difficult. Not surprisingly, over half of those imprisoned will be re-arrested for new crimes or parole violations and returned to prison. The prospect of having so many angry, difficult to employ ex-convicts returning to our urban streets and neighborhoods should be a matter of real concern (Myers, 1995).

MAIN POINTS

1. Urban social life remains reasonably safe and tolerable only because government delivers a wide range of physical and social services.
2. Air pollution creates serious health problems and physical damage. The efforts of the last several decades to control air pollution have met with only limited success; serious problems remain.
3. The western half of the United States faces a growing shortage of water which could hamper continued urban growth. The basic problems in the rest of the country are the pollution of potential water supplies, and the need to move clean water to areas of population concentration.
4. Safe, environmentally acceptable disposal of solid waste is likely to involve increasing costs, the development of new procedures, and the clean-up of dangerous old waste dumps.
5. The primary problem urban government faces in dealing with these physical services and problems are high costs in a time when economic resources are limited.

6. The last half century has seen the creation of a substantial social welfare system in the United States. This system faces the problems of unclear goals; weakness at the local level; bureaucratic inertia; poor coordination, program design, and evaluation; rising costs; and disparities in service levels.

7. The public school system has always had difficulty in meeting the demands of the public. There are serious problems of declining performance levels, financial difficulties, and increasing demands for services. A number of reform efforts have been undertaken, with mixed results.

8. The official crime rate is based on police reports of crimes against property and crimes against the person.

9. The official statistics underreport the true rate of most crimes; these can be corrected somewhat by use of data from victimization studies.

10. White-collar crime, committed by both corporations and individuals, is at least as common as traditional crime (and exacts an equal if not greater cost to both individuals and society). This type of crime has received more attention lately due to widespread scandals.

11. Organized crime is that perpetuated by organizations that provide illicit services and are involved in subverting legitimate businesses and unions. It is especially pernicious because of the ability of such a system to conceal operations and to corrupt public officials.

12. The recent spending on state and local criminal corrections may be a response more to public opinion than to actual indications of its effectiveness in reducing crime.

KEY TERMS

Community Control   In reference to school systems, the attempt to decentralize control of large school systems into the hands of local groups representing the community being served by a particular school or schools.

Organized Crime   Crimes committed by criminal organizations, usually involving either the provision of illegal services or the use of illegal means to provide legitimate services.

Physical Services   Those services which provide for the physical needs of the population and are intended to maintain the general level of physical health and safety of the community.

Privatization   The transfer of public services into the hands of private contractors.

Social Welfare Services   Services designed to help members of the community meet their social needs in areas such as education, protection against crime, economic well-being, and assistance in time of illness or need.

Uniform Crime Reports   The annual report issued by the Federal Bureau of Investigation that contains the official crime rates.

Urban Infrastructures   The physical systems delivering urban services, such as water, sewer, and transit systems, as well as streets and sidewalks.

Victimization Surveys   The effort made to obtain a more realistic set of data on actual rates of crimes by use of a large representative sample, in which people are asked if they have been victims of a crime.

White-Collar Crime   Crimes by individuals or corporations involving illegal acts committed by nonphysical means and by concealment and guile to obtain property, avoid payment or loss of property, or to obtain business or professional advantage.

SUGGESTED READING

Bell, Terrel. 1983. *A Nation at Risk*. National Commission on Excellence in Education, April 1983 report. Washington, DC: U.S. Government Printing Office. This report caused a terrific reaction and impetus for educational reform in the United States. It contains a set of proposals for improving the quality of education by raising standards for teachers, students, and curricula.

The Common Good: Social Welfare and the American Future. 1989. New York: Ford Foundation. A readable report providing a basic analysis of the nature of and problems of the welfare system, with proposals for reform. It seeks to present the welfare problem and proposed solutions in the larger context of national, society-wide problems and proposals for change.

Griffith, Jeanne, Mary Frase, and John Ralph. 1989. "American Education: The Challenge of Change." *Population Bulletin* 44. An interesting and comprehensive outline of recent developments in United States education, set in historical context with relevant tables.

Siegel, Larry. 2000. *Criminology*. Belmont, CA: Wadsworth. A comprehensive discussion of crime that relates variables and types of crime causation to characteristics of urban areas.

9

Urban Problems in
Other Societies

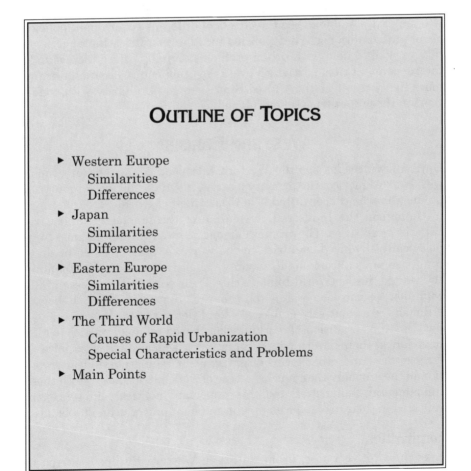

OUTLINE OF TOPICS

So far, the focus of this book has been exclusively upon urban conditions in the United States. However, before we attempt an overall evaluation of conditions in this country, we need to briefly examine urban conditions in other societies. In a single, brief chapter it is not possible to provide a comprehensive treatment of those conditions. The discussion, of necessity, will have to be quite general, and many of the generalizations made will not fit all countries equally well.

Such a comparative overview will serve several important purposes. First, it will allow us to consider the extent to which urban trends in the United States are unique or are the result of more general tendencies common to other societies. Second, comparison of our problems to those in other countries will provide a basis for evaluating their relative seriousness. Granted that we have serious problems, are we better or worse off than other countries? Third, such a comparison will make it possible to see the effects of different government policies on urban conditions. What policies in other countries have (or have not) worked to deal with urban problems? Finally, in an increasingly interdependent world, in which events in other countries are more and more likely to affect the United States, some familiarity with conditions in those countries seems advisable.

WESTERN EUROPE

Until a few decades ago the Western European countries were, along with North America, the primary location in which advanced industrial production was concentrated. They participated (with some difference in timing) in the Industrial Revolution of the nineteenth and early twentieth centuries. They remain among the wealthiest and most technologically advanced countries in the world. Average income in these countries ranges from slightly more to slightly less than that found in the United States (World Bank, 2000). Their economies are essentially capitalist (private ownership and reliance on markets), and their governments are relatively stable, electoral democracies. However, most have a strong tradition of working-class based political parties, which have forced their governments into a much wider range of social welfare services and other forms of government regulation and intervention in the economy than has been true of the United States. Both these fundamental similarities and this important political difference are reflected in their urban development and handling of urban problems.

Similarities

Like the United States, urbanization in Western Europe occurred in response to industrialization, and the overwhelming majority of the population now resides in urban areas. In the nineteenth and early twentieth centuries, European cities were even more compact and densely settled than their U.S. counterparts of the period. However, during the latter half of the twentieth century they also have experienced rapid suburbanization of population and industry. The result has been the kind of sprawling metropolitan areas surrounding the older industrial cities quite similar in their general patterns of land use to those in the United States.

Western European urban ecological structure primarily reflects the operation of market forces. The result has been relatively homogeneous areas in which particular economic activities occur (e.g., industrial districts) and the different social classes reside. Central downtowns remain the location of corporate headquarters, large financial institutions, and the like, and white-collar workers commute to them from the suburbs. Central cities have experienced industrial decline, both as a result of suburbanization and the contraction of older industries (e.g., steel and textiles) in response to foreign competition. The older industries and cities that specialized in traditional manufacturing have experienced drastic economic decline. Service-based economic activity has provided most of the urban employment growth. Older working-class areas in the central cities have increasingly become the residences of the poor, including immigrants either from the Third World (e.g., Turkey, Algeria) or poorer regions in Europe (e.g., Greece, Eastern Europe). A few large cities have retained their role as corporate and financial headquarters and have benefited from the internationalization of the command and control activities of large multinational corporations and the creation of an integrated world financial system (e.g., London, Paris, Frankfort, Geneva). Especially in these cities, gentrification of some central-city neighborhoods has also occurred; in fact, the term was first used to refer to developments in London in the 1960s and early 1970s (Hall, 1988; Light, 1983:222–31; Gottdiener and Hutchison, 2000:262–71; Cheshire, 1993).

Suburban areas include districts with more modern industrial activity (including high-tech corridors of electronics-related production) and working-class housing, as well as affluent, middle-class residential communities. In the last three decades, automobile ownership has become very widespread, and the proportion of commuting trips by mass transit has declined. Like cities in the United States, European cities have had to struggle to accommodate the resulting traffic congestion (Hall, 1988; Gottdiener and Hutchison, 2000:262–71).

Thus, much of what has been discussed in regard to urban trends in the United States is at least partially applicable to Western Europe. The same social, economic, and political factors that have shaped and reshaped our urban areas have also influenced Western Europe's urbanization. Like the United States, Western Europe is now undergoing major economic restructuring in response to global economic change. Many of the problems they have had to face are quite similar to those in this country. In addition, continued movement toward economic unification (the "European Union") means that Western Europe is emerging as a single market, with a single currency and coordinated economic policy, comparable in size and wealth to the United States. At the same time, economic unification means that both specific industries and whole metropolitan areas will have to adjust to their changing roles in the new economic system (Flanagan, 1999:373).

Differences

Despite their overall similarity to urban areas in the United States, those in Western Europe also display some significant differences. To the foreign visitor the most obvious one is that many (though not all) of the industrial cities of Europe were built around a historic core consisting of a preindustrial city. In the case of a few of these cities (e.g., London, Paris, Vienna), this historic core is quite large. During the nineteenth century the central parts of these areas were often substantially modernized, especially for government buildings and the construction of cultural centers. Since that time, at least in part because these areas are important tourist attractions, considerable efforts have been made to assure their preservation. Central business districts were consequently deflected slightly to the edge of the historic centers (often near central railroad stations). However, despite the preservation of some historic areas, the centers of Western European cities function similarly to those in the United States. In the recent past, residential neighborhoods near the historic centers (those that escaped commercial development) have become prime locations for gentrification (Light, 1983).

Western European governments have made more aggressive attempts to control and plan urban development than in the United States. Besides preserving their historic centers, after 1945 they also attempted to restrict and/or control the process of suburbanization. A number of the largest cities (e.g., London) established *green belts*. Usually located at the outer edge of the area of early suburban development, these green belts were rings of land several miles wide surrounding the central urban area in which most development was prohibited.

These governments also tried to reduce suburban sprawl outside the green belts by creating relatively high-density suburban towns (often located on mass-transit lines) in which most housing was multifamily. In the hope of reducing central-city congestion, they also encouraged industry and retail centers to locate in these suburban satellites. In some countries (e.g., Great Britain, Sweden) these communities were completely government planned and primarily government constructed *new towns*. In Great Britain the hope was that these new towns would become relatively self-sufficient industrial and retail centers that would divert development from London. In Sweden the new towns were intended essentially as residential centers with good transportation links for commuting to the central city. In other cases (e.g., France, West Germany) greater reliance was placed on employing land-use regulation to direct private development, although several massive suburban centers were constructed in the 1970s by the French government. In Holland, severe restrictions on the conversion of rural land to urban purposes has forced the more intense use (e.g., high-rise apartment buildings) of existing urban land (Palen, 1987:290–98; 305–9; Hall, 1977; Flanagan, 1999:365–74; Mackensen, 1993; Downs, 1998).

Historically, most Western European growth has been highly concentrated in a relatively few, very large urban centers (e.g., greater London, around Paris). In the 1960s and 1970s most Western European governments also tried to control the growth of large urban sprawls by encouraging economic development away from their largest urban centers. They did so primarily by providing subsidies to corporations to locate their facilities in smaller, more slowly developing urban centers and by providing other forms of assistance to local governments in those centers (Palen, 1987:294; Flanagan, 1999:365–71; Mackensen, 1993; Downs, 1998).

These interventions in the process of urban development achieved mixed results. At best, attempts to redirect the geographical location of urban development may have somewhat slowed the development of the largest urban centers, such as London and Paris. Several new towns were constructed around London and Stockholm, and they were reasonably successful in providing adequate housing and services (though sometimes criticized for their drabness and architectural monotony). However, the attempts to control suburbanization in London and Paris were overwhelmed by the sheer magnitude of the process. Private suburbanization of residence, industry, and retail centers occurred more rapidly than expected in those countries and created the familiar pattern of suburban sprawl and automobile congestion that their governments sought to avoid. Government ownership of much of the land around Stockholm made possible a higher degree of control over the suburbanization process in Sweden. The Dutch (faced by a very large population relative to the very small size of their country) have avoided the worst aspects of suburban sprawl by mandating high-density urban land use (Jones, 1988; Palen, 1987; Light, 1983; Flanagan, 1999:365–71; Mackensen, 1993; Downs, 1998).

Confronted with declining traditional industries and the European equivalent of the "rustbelt cities," the initial response was to try to subsidize or protect declining industries from foreign competition. The British, under Conservative governments, were the first to abandon this strategy and ultimately leave industry to compete in the changing global marketplace. The result was virtual collapse of a number of industries and entire industrial areas, especially outside of London. Other Western European governments proceeded more slowly and also provided more assistance to new industries. However, with the steady movement of the Common Market trading area toward a fully integrated European Union, protection of national industries has gradually been abandoned in favor of a more competitive market, and older industries have continued to decline. "Runaway plants" first sought to relocate in lower-wage areas of the expanding Common Market, such as Spain and Greece (Gottdiener and Hutchison, 2000: 365–71). With the collapse of the Soviet Bloc in Eastern Europe, Western European corporations now have a whole region in which to build low-wage factories on highly favorable terms (much as U.S. corporations do in Mexico).

Housing is another area in which most Western European governments have played a much greater direct role than in the United States. Many Western European countries faced a severe housing shortage after World War II as a result of wartime devastation. In all of them, slow housing construction during the 1920s and 1930s and rapid economic growth and modest population growth after 1945 further contributed to the need to provide additional housing units and replace worn-out, outmoded ones. In the face of this crisis, Western European governments embarked on a large-scale program to construct apartment buildings (or semi-detached row houses in Great Britain) and demolish the most deteriorated, older housing units. These new housing units were government-owned, and rents were heavily subsidized. More recently, greater emphasis has been placed on renovating older units (by government or through subsidies to individuals or nonprofit housing cooperatives), subsidizing private new construction, and providing housing subsidies to families. Sweden provides housing allowances to encourage larger families, Germany pays housing allowances to families based on income, and France provides general subsidies to families based on the number of children. Germany and the Netherlands give loans to nonprofit housing cooperatives. Great Britain provides rent rebates based on family income. Many provide mortgage subsidies of various kinds, even to middle-class households, to purchase privately constructed housing.

Overall, the direction of policy in the last twenty-five years has been toward less government construction of large-scale housing projects and more reliance on the private housing market. Beginning in the 1980s, the government in Great Britain drastically reduced its commitment to public housing construction. Most of the rest of Western Europe has seen a reduction in public housing and more subsidy for private home ownership. Public housing has gradually been moving toward a system designed primarily for very low income households (more like the United States). While internal population growth has been slow, heavy immigration during the 1980s and 1990s, both from Third World countries and Eastern Europe, has put pressure on the public sector of the housing market in most of these countries and created an increasing shortage of low-cost housing relative to the need. However, government regulation and subsidization remain much greater than in the United States (Palen, 1987; Marcuse, 1982; Light, 1983; Maclennan, 1993; Mackensen, 1999).

In part as a result of this government involvement, housing patterns and conditions are significantly different in Western Europe than in the United States. Overall, Western Europeans are very well housed in comparison to residents of most other countries, but their housing is less luxurious than that of the U.S. middle classes. Government subsidies have kept the average cost of housing within the reach of most citizens. On the other hand, the actual cost of housing (per unit of space) born by the combination of households and government is much higher than in the United States. This is in part due to more limited availability of land (and restrictions on its use for housing) and relatively limited housing supply. European governments also do not subsidize home ownership through general mortgage interest tax deductions and government guaranteed mortgages, as is done in the United States (Nivola, 1998; Mackensen, 1999).

These cost pressures mean that housing units are much smaller than in the United States and occupy much more limited land area. This creates higher average urban population densities in Western Europe (even in the suburbs) than in the United States. Except in Great Britain, even much of the middle class is likely to live in multifamily apartment units. In Great Britain the middle-class ideal is the semi-detached rowhouse with a tiny front yard and enclosed back garden. Government involvement in large-scale housing construction in the postwar period also means that a much larger percentage of the population lives in government-provided housing. For example, around one-third of the housing stock in Great Britain and Germany is government owned. Although the pattern is changing, public housing in Western Europe is not just for the poor, but for much of the working class (Palen, 1987; Light, 1983; Marcuse, 1982; Hall, 1977; Maclennan, 1993; Nivola, 1998).

Western European countries have managed to steadily increase their housing supply, and the quality of housing has generally improved. However, housing remains a problem. Construction has never quite kept up with the demand for new units, the need to replace old units, and the desires of an increasingly affluent population for improved housing amenities. The high rates of immigration in the 1980s and 1990s put further pressure on the public sector of the housing market. Long waiting lists characterize public housing. High costs for private housing confront middle-class households and limit the size, degree of privacy, and amenities available in the housing that they occupy. Substandard, slum housing exists to varying degrees in these countries and is occupied by the poor. Homelessness is a visible problem in France and Great Britain. Doubling up by poor families and postponement of marriage because of the lack of housing is widely reported (though hardly common in most countries). The percentage of income devoted to housing has been rising (Mackensen, 1999; Downs, 1999:50–51; Maclennan, 1993; Palen, 1987; Light, 1983; Marcuse, 1982; Hall, 1977).

Transportation patterns also differ from those in the United States. While car use has skyrocketed in the last forty years, mass transit (especially for commuting) remains much more important in Western Europe. On the other hand, suburban use of automobiles is much more similar to that of the United States. What explains this difference? Car ownership (and two-car families) are still less common in Western Europe than in the United States, but that difference is not enough to account for the difference in transit use. One factor is simple traffic congestion. In older parts of the cities the streets are very narrow and both driving and parking are thereby made more difficult. In addition, as part of government policy, there has been a reluctance to expand the automobile infrastructure rapidly in order to discourage commuting by car. Both highways and parking facilities intentionally have been kept inadequate. At the same time, more emphasis has been put on building and maintaining mass-transit systems. The rationale behind this policy is that it is cheaper for government, reduces the use of mostly imported petroleum, and discourages suburban sprawl. Heavy taxation of gasoline (again to reduce imports) also increases the cost of commuting by car (gasoline prices are more than triple those in the United States). Of course, the result is intense urban traffic congestion (Nivola, 1998; Jones, 1988:105; Palen, 1987:292; Light, 1983).

An increasing concern in Western Europe has been the effect of rising pollution levels. In general, Western Europe was slower to react to pollution than the United States. In addition, higher population density means higher densities of air and water pollution sources. The result has been very severe air, water, and soil pollution. For example, about one-third of the forests in Germany are dead or dying from the effects of air pollution. Despite some belated controls, the Rhine River basin is severely contaminated. Major damage to the lakes of Sweden has been reported as the result of acid rain (Brown and Flavin, 1988:6). Increasing pollution controls in the 1990s stabilized levels of some pollutants, but a high level of environmental damage continues (European Environmental Protection Agency, 1997).

Finally, at a more general level, there is a greater commitment in Western Europe (though France clearly lags in this regard and Great Britain has been changing) to provide certain services and pursue certain policies which reduce the kinds of inequality and poverty that were discussed in chapter 4. Especially after 1945, Western European countries created relatively elaborate "welfare states." Such benefits as (basically) free medical care, subsidized housing, free university education (to those who qualified), extensive unemployment payments, income support for the poor, a wide range of social services, and generous pensions represented an ambitious attempt to guarantee a relatively high minimum level of living for the whole population and eliminate extreme poverty. Compared to the United States, this system of welfare benefits and services to the whole population was much more extensive. Moreover, it did reduce some of the extreme disparities in living conditions that otherwise would have existed and that continue to characterize U.S. urban areas. However, the increasing cost of the welfare state (in part due to rising levels of chronic unemployment and an increasing elderly population), middle-class resistance to high tax levels, and concern with international economic competition have led most Western European governments to attempt to reduce some of the benefits and social services previously provided. Social spending has been most drastically reduced in Great Britain, where there was a concerted effort to dismantle much of the welfare state. In that country economic inequality has increased and poverty (and attendant problems such as crime) have become more severe. However, all Western European countries have made some move to curtail their social spending (Gottdiener and Hutchison, 2000: 270–71; Downs, 1998:49–50).

JAPAN

Japan rose rapidly to the first rank of the advanced capitalist countries after 1945. Currently it has per capita income and urbanization levels typical of the richest and most technologically advanced capitalist countries. Besides being among the largest and most economically important countries, Japan is of interest here because it achieved high levels of urbanization and industrialization later, but much faster, and under different circumstances than countries in North America or Western Europe. Unlike most of those countries, small, mountainous Japan had very limited agricultural land, virtually no natural resources, and a high population density relative to its arable land. Hence, its strategy was one that emphasized rapid technological development and productive efficiency to make its manufactured goods competitive in the world market. Government (continuously controlled by the same conservative, business-oriented political party until the 1990s) and the large, export-oriented corporations worked together closely to achieve economic development objectives. Policies not directly related to this goal were given low priority and allocated only limited resources:

> . . . the Liberal Democratic Party (LDP), [was] an "unabashed spokesman" for big business; in the interest of free enterprise, the LDP . . . resisted government intervention to protect the urban environment and . . . received in return generous subventions from big corporations. (Light, 1983:166)

In the late 1980s this export-driven economic growth began to falter. Japanese goods began to face more competition on the world market. Other industrialized countries had responded to the Japanese challenge with more competitive practices in their own industries and the threat of punitive trade sanctions to force open the heavily protected Japanese domestic market. Japanese industries also faced growing competition from low-cost, low-wage competitors in the rapidly developing Third World countries, especially in Asia. In response, many Japanese companies established "off-shore" productive facilities, either to avoid trade barriers in the North American and Western European markets or to take advantage of low wages in Third World countries (So and Chiu, 1995:179–85). After a deep recession and unprecedented unemployment, Japanese economic growth recovered slowly. Public economic concerns, combined with a series of scandals that reached all the way to the top of the Liberal Democratic Party, finally ended that party's long monopoly on power and control of the national government. After a brief period of rule by an opposition coalition and attempts at some constitutional reform in the mid-1990s, the badly fragmented conservative party resumed shaky rule as a coalition government. For the first time, serious debate occurred over some of the long-term policies that had supported Japan's export-oriented growth strategy (and some of the accumulating domestic problems it had caused). While most of its export industries continued to be successful in the 1990s, the overall domestic economy stagnated. Japan ended the 1990s with its highest unemployment rate in postwar history (around 4 percent). The Japanese political leadership seemed unable to embark on the basic economic reforms necessary to shake off the country's persistent economic stagnation (Pempel, 1999; Feldman, 1998; Japan Institute of Policy Research, 2000).

Our discussion of Japanese urban conditions will focus on the greater Tokyo metropolitan area. Japanese urbanization has tended to concentrate in a few very large urban areas, and Tokyo is the largest one. The Tokyo conurbation (including the cities of Yokohama, Kawasaki, and Chiba) alone accounts for almost 32 million people and one-fourth of the country's population (Waley, 2000:132). The problems of the other large metropolitan areas are less severe but the basic patterns of development are quite similar to Tokyo.

Similarities

The general ecological structure of the Tokyo region is similar to large metropolitan areas in the United States. The central area of the city of

Tokyo has progressively been given over to corporate headquarters, financial institutions, and business services, with mass retailing still important but losing out to satellite subcenters. In the 1980s Tokyo emerged as one of the centers of international finance and headquarters of multinational corporations, ranking it as one of the few global centers of the world economy (Sassen, 1994:161). Central Tokyo now specializes in administration and services, and most of the white-collar labor force commutes from the suburbs. Subcenters have emerged at points where suburban rail lines meet a loop railroad and commuters transfer from rail lines to other forms of mass transit for the trip downtown. They are primarily retail centers, but have developed as secondary office centers. (These subcenters are roughly similar to those that have been established at the intersections of urban expressways in places like Los Angeles.) Overall, the central "wards" of the city of Tokyo have been losing population and industry. Industry has been suburbanizing to the northeast (smaller manufacturing plants), south (large manufacturing), and to the southwest (small high-technology installations). The wards immediately east of the downtown are home to the older industrial districts (built on swampland next to the bay). They contain many small industrial enterprises and many of the older, declining industries (Waley, 2000: 129–36).

Working-class housing has expanded outward in the same sectors. The western and northwestern sectors of the suburbs are the primary location for higher status residential housing, although they contain some major industrial subcenters. Overall, in the last few decades most of Tokyo's (very substantial) economic development and population growth have occurred in the steadily expanding suburban ring (Nakamura and White, 1988). Thus, Tokyo land-use patterns are quite similar to those in the United States and reflect the predominance of market-based mechanisms and corporate interests in land allocation. Government intervention has been attempted, and relatively elaborate general plans have been drawn up, but with limited real impact. For example, in the 1950s a plan very similar to that for London was proposed. A large green belt was established at what was then the fringe of Tokyo, and new towns were planned beyond it. However, intense pressures for suburban development resulted in abandoning the green belt to residential development. The attempt to create new towns also had very limited impact on the pattern of suburbanization. Some existing towns were designated as new towns, and their development encouraged. One very large new town (Tama) was built by government, and an "academic garden city," containing a national university and some research institutes, was established. However, these towns were quickly swallowed up in the tide of unplanned suburbanization. Tama became essentially a residential suburb with the majority of its workers commuting to central Tokyo.

Similarly, programs have been announced repeatedly to encourage economic development of smaller urban areas in regions away from Tokyo, but their impact has been extremely limited (Light, 1983:165; Nakamura and White, 1988:143–44; Waley, 2000: 129–36).

Differences

While the pattern of urban land use is similar to the United States, the intensity of its use in Japan is different. Only about 15 percent of Japan's land area is level and arable (in a country with the land area of California). Urban areas must compete with agriculture for this limited land to accommodate an urban population of more than 80 million. In addition, government policy has had the effect of making the land available for urban uses even more scarce and expensive. A number of laws make it difficult to convert agricultural land adjacent to urban areas to nonagricultural purposes. For example, farmers are protected from paying taxes that would reflect the (very high) market value of their land and are paid large subsidies for their products. This makes it possible for them to farm profitably near urban areas and to hold on to their land until the price for it becomes very high. The official justification for this policy is the desire to maintain self-sufficiency in rice production and near sufficiency in other products. It also results in extremely high food prices for urban consumers. The policy also probably reflects the disproportionate political importance of the "farm bloc" because of its role in giving the Liberal Democrats the margin necessary to win each national election until recently (Fallows, 1986, 1989). Pressures from trading partners (e.g., the U.S.) to reduce agricultural protectionism and the growing discontent of urban residents over high food and land prices may ultimately lead to gradual modification of these policies. However, other, often well-intended, zoning and land development restrictions have further increased the cost developers need to charge to make a profit. In addition, prohibitive taxes on land sales (designed to discourage short-term land speculation) have encouraged landowners to hold on to undeveloped land. Landowners wait for the price to rise on their land until the transaction tax is offset by the higher price (Nakamura and White, 1988:146–47).

Concern over earthquakes (a real and serious threat, as the recent devastating earthquake in Kyoto demonstrated) and the effect of high-rise buildings on their neighbors (e.g., blocking out sunlight) also led to restrictions on the height of buildings. While some of these restrictions were eased for office buildings in the 1970s (because more earthquake-resistant building techniques were developed), most areas of Tokyo still restrict height. Average building heights remain little over two stories. Hence, the number of workers or residents that can be accommodated on a given parcel of land cannot be increased by building higher buildings (Nakamura and White, 1988:145).

The limited supply of urban land, restrictions on building height, and the tremendous demand for land as Tokyo grew had a predictable result. The price of urban land grew astronomically. If 1955 is taken as the base year in which the index price of residential land in Tokyo was 100, by 1983 the index price stood at 3,100. Primarily as a result of these high land prices, in 1983 the price of a condominium-type residence in central Tokyo was about twice as high per square meter of space as a comparable unit in London and slightly less than three times as high for such a unit in New York (Nakamura and White, 1988:140). The rate of price increases accelerated in the 1980s and led to a speculative boom in urban land prices (Fallows, 1989). As usually happens, the speculative boom proved unsustainable and was followed by a rapid deflation in urban land values back to the still high, but less absurd, levels of the mid-1980s (Waley, 2000:136).

The effect of these prices on housing conditions in Tokyo has been profound. The high price of land severely limits both the size and quality of the housing Tokyo residents can afford. In the city of Tokyo itself, lot size for a house is 100 square meters or less, and (as of 1980) average living space per person was about 10 square meters. While the percentage of housing units with full bathrooms has increased markedly, about 35 percent of Tokyo units still lacked them in 1980. As recently as 1980 almost one-third of Tokyo's housing units were still judged poorly constructed and highly flammable. More generally, the high cost of land leaves little money to invest in the house or apartment building itself, and consequently, even new housing tends to be flimsy and poorly constructed (Fallows, 1986). The high cost and crowded conditions of housing closer to central Tokyo has also forced increasing percentages of middle-class workers to seek cheaper housing further and further away from their places of work. By commuting sixty to ninety minutes (one way) workers can find housing built on land that costs "only" half as much as in the city of Tokyo. These still-astronomical (by U.S. standards) land costs mean that even distant suburban housing is likely to be on lots of little more than 100 square meters, and houses are likely to be built right up to the property line, with little or no open space between structures. A house similar to the typical new suburban house in the United States (but on a smaller lot) is financially out of reach for all but the rich in Tokyo. While about 40 percent of households in Tokyo own their residences, that percentage has not increased very much in the last thirty years, despite the fact that income levels have risen markedly. However, general measures of housing quality (e.g., indoor plumbing, amount of space) indicate slow but steady improvement over conditions in the past (Waley, 2000:148; Sterngold, 1994; Nakamura and White, 1988:140–41).

Most housing in Japan is provided privately. Public housing is quite limited and not necessarily even targeted toward the poor. One government agency does construct apartments (very small and often without such amenities as private bathrooms) for low-income households. Despite their unattractiveness, they are cheap to rent and demand for them greatly exceeds supply. Other agencies have constructed larger, better quality apartments in such areas as the new town of Tama. However, these agencies are required to break even financially and must charge rents that only more affluent households can afford (Hall, 1977:226; Palen, 1987:375).

The search for affordable housing has been an important impetus in Tokyo suburbanization. In turn, that suburbanization has meant steadily increasing time spent commuting and massive increased demands placed on the transportation system. Half of all commuters to central Tokyo in 1983 spent one hour (one way) to get to work, and one-fifth spent more than an hour and a half (Nakamura and White, 1988:141). As of 1984, the average total commuting distance for Tokyo workers was 50 kilometers (Yeung, 1988:161). While some workers commute by car, the grossly inadequate expressway system, narrow city streets, and the lack of parking make car use by most commuters out of the question. Only 12 percent of the land area of central Tokyo is devoted to streets, compared to 23 percent in London and 35 percent in New York (Hall, 1977:231). Nonetheless, car ownership and use in Tokyo has been steadily increasing. Traffic congestion has reached monumental proportions, and movement by street or highway is extremely slow, despite constant efforts to expand the expressway system. Most commuters rely on the mass-transit system. The suburbs are served by commuter railroads that terminate at several stations on a rail loop around the western edge of central Tokyo. Commuters then transfer to the city mass-transit system. At one time this system primarily consisted of streetcars and buses, but due to traffic congestion they were mostly replaced by a fast, efficient subway system in the 1960s and 1970s. More subways are under construction. The entire mass-transit system is well-engineered, fast, and provides easy access to all of central Tokyo. However, the number of commuters has consistently increased faster than the system has expanded. The result is a massively overcrowded system. The system has never carried less than 200 percent of its planned capacity (Nakamura and White, 1988:132–34; Sterngold, 1994).

Construction of basic physical infrastructure in Tokyo has been slow, and that city's basic systems are still not adequate. In the 1980s about one-fourth of the dwellings in Tokyo still lacked sewer connections, and the percentage of dwellings without sewer connections was even higher in many suburban areas. Complete provision of an adequate municipal water supply also has yet to be achieved. Public open space such as parks and recreational facilities are almost totally lacking (Hall, 1977:228; Nakamura and White, 1988:140).

Air, water, chemical, and noise pollution in the Tokyo area are arguably the worst of any urban area in an advanced capitalist country. Deaths directly attributable to pollution have been documented, and an estimated 76,000 to 200,000 people have been crippled as a result of exposure to pollutants in their communities or at work. Air pollution is the cause of a high level of respiratory disease. Sewage treatment is primitive, at best, and industrial pollution of rivers, bays, and groundwater is severe. Until the late 1960s pollution was treated by government as simply the unavoidable consequence of economic growth, and virtually nothing was done about it. Public protest since then has led to some efforts to control pollution, and the levels of some air pollutants have fallen. However, the control effort has been only partially successful, and the problem remains serious (Yeung, 1988:165; Light, 1983:165).

Most social services and welfare programs in Japan remain undeveloped relative to the United States and Western Europe. However, to some extent, this reflects the fact that economic inequality is substantially less than in any other industrial country. The very impoverished and socially marginalized population is relatively small. One feature strikingly absent from the urban landscape are large concentrations of the urban poor, though pockets of poverty do exist (Waley, 2000:149–50, 155). The government-funded retirement system is very limited, and most Japanese attempt to save a major portion of their incomes to provide for retirement. On the other hand, because of its importance for labor productivity, Japan places great emphasis on the educational system, and its elementary and secondary school systems obtain high performance levels from students (Fallows, 1989).

A relatively unique feature of Japanese urban life is the role of neighborhood associations. These associations are highly organized and cooperate with municipal government to provide services. For example, they take responsibility for keeping the streets clean in their neighborhoods. They also report fires and criminal activity to the authorities. Their activities may help account for the low crime rate and the relative safety of the streets in Japanese cities (Nakamura and White, 1988:139–40).

Finally, Tokyo faces the severe threat of a devastating earthquake. The last (very disastrous) quake was in 1923, and one of equivalent magnitude is overdue. The recent devastation in Kyoto was a warning of how much damage Tokyo might face. The modern high-rise buildings in downtown Tokyo theoretically are designed to withstand an earthquake, and emergency plans are in place. Nonetheless, other characteristics of Tokyo point to potential disaster: a high proportion of flammable wooden buildings, industrial and working-class residential zones constructed on unstable landfill, elevated expressways, huge numbers of commuters in subways during the rush hour, potentially explosive petrochemical complexes, and a woeful lack of accessible open space to which it would be possible to evacuate the population (Nakamura and White, 1988:143).

EASTERN EUROPE

Following a brutal revolution and civil war at the end of World War I, the area of the former Russian Empire was governed by a centralized, authoritarian "Marxist-Leninist" political party. This "Soviet Union" survived until it was dissolved in 1991 to create a number of independent states. The largest successor state is Russia, followed by the Republic of the Ukraine. These new states have all, to a greater or lesser extent, replaced centralized authoritarian rule with some degree of popular, "democratic rule" and reduced the role of state ownership and control in their economies.

The rest of Eastern Europe was ruled by puppet regimes, forcibly established and maintained by the Soviet Union, from the 1940s until the late 1980s. These states were also characterized by a high degree of centralization of power in state and party apparatus and systematic repression of their populations. Government ownership of most productive enterprises (except for small peasant farms in some of the Eastern European countries outside of the Soviet Union) and centralized state planning of economic activity prevailed in all these countries. With the partial exceptions of East Germany and parts of Czechoslovakia, these were only partially industrialized and urbanized societies in 1950.

The Soviet Union and the rest of the states under its control all attempted rapid industrialization (or reconstruction of industry in the case of East Germany). Overall levels of industrialization and urbanization did rise rapidly between 1950 and 1980. Still, levels of output per worker, total industrial output, and the level of technological sophistication remained significantly below that of the advanced capitalist countries. In pursuit of rapid industrialization, centralized control of the economy was used to maintain a high level of capital investment in new manufacturing facilities at the expense of private consumption and many public services. Especially in the case of the Soviet Union, a very high level of military expenditures was a further economic drain. On the other hand, economic inequality was much less than in the advanced capitalist societies, and the population enjoyed relative employment security and (except for top government officials) shared equally in a wide range of free or heavily subsidized services (Chirot, 1986:263–75).

By the 1980s these countries were experiencing growing economic difficulties and political unrest. Their huge centralized state bureaucracies were inefficient, inept, and frequently riddled with corruption.

Inadequate work incentives, overstaffing, and backward technology kept worker productivity low. The standard of living stagnated or declined as their economies began to flounder. Attempts at economic and political reform, begun in the Soviet Union, set off a series of dramatic political changes, which eliminated Soviet-controlled, one-party rule in Eastern Europe and led to the political collapse of the Soviet state. The new governments attempted to reform their economies by relying more on privately owned enterprises and market mechanisms in place of centralized state planning.

The "post-Soviet" period has proven difficult for all these countries. Best off has been the former East Germany, which is in the process of being fully integrated politically and economically with wealthy, democratic West Germany. Reconstruction of East Germany has been more difficult than initially expected, however. Even the very ample resources of the German state have been strained by the effort to close antiquated industries, absorb displaced workers, and undertake urban reconstruction. The Czech Republic, freed of the burden of less-developed Slovakia, has enjoyed heavy Western European investment in what was already the most efficient and modern of the Eastern European economies, and may be making the transition to a fairly advanced, capitalist economy.

Most of the rest of Eastern Europe, including the former Soviet Union, has experienced severe economic and political difficulties. The economies are burdened with an old, state-owned industrial sector that is technologically backward, poorly managed, inefficient, and short on investment capital to modernize. Some of these industries have been allowed to collapse and others limp along at low levels of output as private or state enterprises. Overall industrial output declined drastically. The total economic output of Russia shrank more in the 1990s than the U.S. economy did during the Great Depression, before appearing to stabilize at the new low levels. A long period of inflation, declining wages, growing poverty, increasing indebtedness to Western lenders, and other indications of economic distress and decline characterized all the Eastern European economies during the 1990s (Aron, 1999; Lynch, 1999). Their future in a competitive global economy does not seem to be that of advanced industrial economies like the United States or Western Europe. Rather, a different role for these countries in the world economy seems increasingly apparent. They offer, especially to Western European investors, a place to locate lower technology, labor-intensive industrial processes to take advantage of the drastically lower wage levels. They also are, or potentially could be, important sources of raw materials (e.g., timber), cheap agricultural products (e.g., from Poland and the Ukraine), and oil and natural gas from Russia and other states of the former Soviet Union. Thus, over the near-term future, their role for Western Europe (the emerging "European Union") seems likely to be similar to that served by the more industrialized and urbanized countries of Latin America (e.g., Mexico, Brazil, Chile) for the United States and the rapidly industrializing countries of Asia for Japan (Shannon, 1996:122; McMichael, 2000; Lynch, 1999; Synder, 1999).

Such an economic role in the world economy would have clear implications for social and political conditions in these countries that are consistent with current trends. Average annual income per person would be "intermediate" by world standards (somewhere around $3000–$4000 compared to over $20,000 in advanced industrial countries), similar to Mexico or Brazil. The class system would be marked by extreme economic inequality. The large mass of the urban working class would be extremely poor. Most wealth would be in the hands of a small, business (and political) elite. In between would be a relatively small (by U.S. or Western European standards) middle class of managers and professionals. By the end of the 1990s most of the available economic and social indicators suggest that this is the scenario that these countries are following (McMichael, 2000: 160–61). Such conditions appear likely to foster considerable political discontent (in fact, by the end of the 1990s they already had). The tremendous economic inequality and the failure to achieve the generally high living standards of Western Europe and the United States are likely to threaten regime stability. If other countries in a similar situation (e.g., Mexico, Brazil) are any guide, the economic elite will attempt to protect their interests through a combination of control of the electoral process, actual or threatened state repression of the opposition, and governmental corruption (Shannon, 1996: 122–23, 115–17; Andrusz, 1996; Holmstrom and Smith, 2000; Solnick, 1998: 240–53).

However, what will happen depends also on the legacy of a half-century (longer in the Soviet Union) of "state socialism." That legacy conditions both the resources these countries will have to deal with their problems and defines the nature of many of those problems. Hence, we need to start our examination of urban conditions with a discussion of that legacy. We can then turn to the beginnings of urban change brought about by the last decade's political and economic reorganization.

Urban Legacy of State Socialism

Despite fundamental differences in the basic system of political economy between the United States and Eastern Europe, there were some general similarities in their urban development. As in Western Europe, the United States, and Japan, the driving force behind Eastern European urbanization was industrialization. Jurgen Friedrichs points out:

> . . . there are no specific socialist types of land use, distribution of new housing, internal organization of residential blocks, or location of companies. Even the principal goal of socialist city plan-

ning—to locate new residential areas close to working areas—has been pursued in Western planning too, and failed, since most residents did not have jobs in the adjacent working areas. (1988:128)

Faced with relatively rapid urbanization and industrialization, limited resources, and the overriding obligation to facilitate industrialization, state planners found themselves approving land-use patterns with many similarities to those in the West.

As in Western Europe, during the 1970s and 1980s central areas of Eastern European cities became more and more specialized as centers of administration and, secondarily, cultural and retail centers. At the same time, inner districts lost population while outer districts, suburbs, and more distant satellite cities grew rapidly. A growing separation between places of residence and work increased commuting distances and time. Central cities gained employment in the service sector, and manufacturing employment became a smaller percentage of total city employment. New manufacturing enterprises were constructed in suburban locations (Friedrichs, 1988).

Residential patterns changed as these urban areas grew. Initially, luxury housing for the political leadership (often upper-class housing left over from prerevolutionary or prewar days) was located conveniently near government administrative offices. Hence, the existing good housing was nearer the center of the city, and the least privileged workers were relegated to peripheral (often self-built) slums on the outskirts. That pattern was reinforced in those cities in which workers needed government permits to live inside the city limits. New migrants, often with the lowest status jobs, could not get such permits and so had to live outside city limits. These "peripheral slums" are still much in evidence in most cities. However, beginning in the 1960s, most of the newer and better housing was built on the outskirts of the cities. The reason was simple—such a location provided the open land which made possible the inexpensive construction of large-scale housing projects. Exclusive housing compounds or weekend retreats also were constructed in exurban areas for the political elite, while they retained their exclusive, centrally located apartments. Older buildings outside of the exclusive residential district (often drastically subdivided into tiny apartments with communal kitchens and bathrooms) became the least desirable housing. Consequently, a pattern of better quality housing in the suburbs emerged that is roughly analogous to that in advanced capitalist countries (Friedrichs, 1988; Palen, 1987:301–2).

As of 1990, one fundamental difference in urban conditions between Eastern Europe and the United States was based on the simple fact that these are substantially poorer countries. In the late 1980s overall economic production per person still remained in a range of from less than one-fifth to not quite two-fifths as high as that in the United States (World Bank, 1987). Such a huge difference meant not just comparatively low living standards in relation to the United States, but also much more limited resources available to government to deliver services.

In principle, the state socialist version of Eastern European urban development occurred according to centrally controlled government plans which were to assure coordinated and rational land use, adequate provision of services, and geographically balanced urbanization. State control of industrial investment decisions, ownership of most urban land, and control of urban housing construction gave it the ability to implement the central plan.

However, in practice the planning process did not yield many of its expected benefits. In general, the concerns of the economic planners for rapid industrial development took precedence and the lion's share of the available resources. This emphasis almost guaranteed that the efforts of urban planning authorities would be frustrated. Factories came first; housing, services, and concerns about geographical balance came in a distant second. Economic and urban planning also were poorly coordinated. For example, until 1976 in the Soviet Union each industrial department developed its plans independently of each other and of urban governmental agencies. One problem this created was that the location of new housing and industry was often poorly coordinated, creating unanticipated demands for transportation. Urban planning agencies were equally uncoordinated. Huge apartment complexes were constructed on the outskirts of the cities without adequate preparation to provide services and transportation systems. Around Moscow these new complexes were often occupied for years before basic retail outlets, medical facilities, and transportation links were put into place. Inflexible national guidelines often were inappropriate to local conditions. For instance, new complexes were provided with hospital accommodations of a certain capacity relative to the size of the complex, without any consideration of the age distribution of the residents.

At the local level, urban government officials often had very limited authority to make decisions and respond to citizen complaints. Especially in smaller cities, the major industrial enterprises actually had more control over local conditions and services than did local officials. Soviet factories often built their own housing complexes and provided their own services (e.g., water, power, medical care, and retail stores). The managers of the factories consequently had more control over local urban conditions than did municipal government. Failure to anticipate changing conditions also meant that plans were out-of-date before they were fully implemented. Soviet planners consistently underestimated the rate of growth around Moscow, for example. More generally, the attempt to control regional urbanization had only a limited impact. It did have some impact and led to urban development in some undeveloped regions (e.g., Soviet Siberia). Nonetheless, it never created the sort of balance that the urban planning authorities sought to achieve (Friedrichs, 1988; Palen, 1987: 298–301; Hall, 1977).

In the 1980s housing remained perhaps the greatest problem for Eastern European urban areas. There was a severe absolute shortage of housing units, the units were extremely small, and their quality was low. Several factors contributed to the housing crisis: (1) the poor quality and deteriorating condition of the pre-1940 housing stock, (2) the devastation of urban areas during World War II, (3) extremely rapid urbanization requiring new housing units, and (4) inadequate resources available to construct housing. The latter factor in part reflected the policy of neglecting urban housing needs to concentrate investment resources on industry. However, in the last decades of Soviet rule more resources were released for housing, and the overall rate of construction was quite high. Beginning in the late 1950s, construction of housing in the Soviet Union averaged over two million units annually, although the economic crisis of the late 1980s probably reduced that rate. The problem was that even such a relatively high construction rate (the Soviet rate was comparable to that of the United States) was insufficient to make up for past deficiencies and meet the needs of a rapidly growing urban population. The result of the continuing shortage of units was that there were long waiting lists for apartments, adult children (even if they married) often had to double-up with parents in already cramped apartments for years, and people had to accept grossly inadequate accommodations (e.g., single rooms with communal bathrooms and kitchens) because nothing else was available (Friedrichs, 1988; Palen, 1987:299–300; Light, 1983:409–12).

In the Soviet Union almost all urban housing was state-owned by a housing authority or an industrial enterprise. In the rest of Eastern Europe there was a mixture of state-owned buildings, independent housing cooperatives (tenant or factory controlled, but with construction money borrowed from the state), and private ownership. In the past, private housing was often the worst. It was constructed by low-status workers who had been unable to obtain state-provided housing. It was often located on the periphery of urban areas in places poorly provided with physical infrastructure and transportation. More recently, private construction by the more affluent (especially outside of the Soviet Union) created better-than-average quality private housing.

By Western standards, even new state-owned housing was incredibly cramped: in the Soviet Union the goal of urban planners was ninety-seven square feet of living area per person, and in the 1980s about half the population still lived in units that did not meet that standard. In older buildings shared kitchens and bathrooms remained common. In the Soviet Union, most new housing consisted of large, high-rise apartment buildings built from standardized components made in factories and assembled on the site. The buildings were drab, utilitarian, poorly constructed, and prone to deterioration. As already mentioned, the new complexes were often built prior to completion of planned service facilities (e.g., schools, medical centers), transportation links, and even such basic physical infrastructure as road paving. This made living in them difficult, involving long trips on inadequate public transportation to work, shop, go to school, or seek medical attention. On the other hand, despite these flaws and despite continuing shortages, housing conditions improved relative to those in the grim decade following World War II. Moreover, housing was heavily state-subsidized. Apartments rented for very low rents, and the average family paid only a small fraction of its income for housing (Friedrichs, 1988; Palen, 1987; Light, 1983; Hall, 1977).

Eastern European planners consistently favored public transportation over accommodating the automobile. Until the 1980s, automobiles were in extremely limited supply and priced at intentionally prohibitive prices. Little attention was given to providing automotive services, and limited numbers of automobiles meant that urban expressways did not need to be built. Only since the 1980s did street congestion from private automobiles become noticeable in most Eastern European cities. Hence, the bulk of the urban population had no choice but to rely on public transit facilities. The reason for this policy was simple: mass transit provided the cheapest way to provide urban transportation.

Considerable resources were devoted to expanding and improving the urban-transit system, and heavy state subsidies kept fares low. In many cities (e.g., Moscow) a rapid and efficient transit system (including subways) provided high quality service to central-city areas. However, expansion of these systems did not keep up with demand due to rapid urbanization and the decentralization of housing and industry. Also, more workers ended up needing to commute from the urban outskirts to the central city than was anticipated. Hence, residents in outlying residential areas faced limited, crowded, and inconvenient transportation facilities (usually buses) and long commuting times (Friedrichs, 1988; Hall, 1977).

Consistent with their socialist ideology, these countries attempted to provide a wide range of basic health, educational, and recreational facilities to urban residents, available to all at little or no cost. (Until recently, these governments also attempted to guarantee employment to all citizens.) Given the economic limitations imposed by their relatively backward economies, the range of basic services accessible to average citizens was impressive. On the other hand, the quality of those services was generally low and inadequate facilities led to "rationing by waiting in line." For example, medical facilities were crowded, ill-equipped, and often poorly supplied with even basic medicines. Hence, general living conditions were more equal, but at a uniformly low level by Western standards. At the same time, government and party leaders had access to a wide range of specially reserved service facilities, housing, and consumer goods stores, which allowed them a much better living standard than that of the general population.

Government emphasis on increasing production above all else led to another serious problem. Pollution reached levels much worse than in the advanced capitalist countries. Air pollution from industry, toxic dumping, careless deforestation, unsafe work environments, and the like received little or no attention from the authorities. Air pollution-related respiratory illness became a major health problem in many cities. Toxic chemicals or bacterial contaminants were found in the water supplies of many Polish cities. Forest death due to industrial pollution and acid rain was widespread in East Germany, Poland, and Czechoslovakia. Contamination of agricultural areas and fisheries was widely reported in the 1980s. Only limited and belated remedial action was taken in the 1980s (Brown and Flavin, 1988:7; *Roanoke Times,* 1990:Fl).

Recent Urban Trends

The existing "built environment" of any large urban area is so huge it would be unrealistic to expect major changes in a period of ten years, regardless of the rate of social, economic, political, or cultural change. Nonetheless, urban areas of the previously state socialist countries have begun to reflect some of the societal changes that they are undergoing.

Certainly the central districts have undergone dramatic, if superficial, change as tourism restrictions have eased. A few Western hotels have been built; private retailing, restaurants, and night spots have flourished; the number of foreign cars on the streets has grown; and more affluent consumers display their new-found prosperity. A new middle class of small business owners, managers, and business professionals has sprung up. In Russia, following the financial "crash" of 1998, industrial production stabilized, agricultural production finally reached the level of self-sufficiency, some kinds of industrial production found export markets, and government tax receipts began to approach the level of expenditures (Aron, 1999).

At the same time, the growth of extreme poverty is evident in the growing numbers of homeless, street peddlers, and small flea markets, as well as the increasing threat of street crime. In the still-drab residential districts, most workers have experienced dramatic declines in wages and living standards. As inefficient state enterprises have been closed or struggle along at reduced rates of output and smaller number of workers (either as private or state enterprises), high levels of chronic urban unemployment have come to characterize these countries. Overall, the success of some smaller private retail and service enterprises has not counter-balanced the severe contraction in output, wages, and employment in the old, state-owned industrial sector. State construction of massive, austere housing complexes has mostly ground to a halt. Private construction is limited to a small amount of housing for the more affluent. The already severe urban housing shortage has gotten worse. Budgetary crisis and pressures to reduce government expenditures have meant visible reductions in the maintenance of the urban infrastructure and the delivery of most public services. In Russia, the combination of a rapid deterioration in the public health system, growing mass poverty and malnutrition, and rampant alcoholism has meant a decline in average male life expectancy to levels below that of many Third World countries (59 years on average in 1995). Russia also faces a "brain drain" of some of its most skilled engineers and scientists as wage levels and employment opportunities have deteriorated. Both street crime and large-scale organized crime (reaching to the highest levels of government) have become serious problems (Andrusz, 1996; Hersh, 1994; Lynch, 1999).

Overall, it is hard to paint an optimistic picture of the urban future in most of Eastern Europe. The apparent evolution of their economies toward something like the more industrialized countries of the Third World suggests that urban conditions are likely to become more like Mexico City or São Paulo, Brazil. Why that kind of urban development is so troubling is an issue to which we now must turn.

THE THIRD WORLD

The most extraordinary urban trend of the last half century has been the historically unprecedented rate of urbanization in the Third World (sometimes called the *periphery* in relation to the "core" of North America and Western Europe). These are the relatively poor and less industrialized countries of South America, Africa, the Middle East, and Asia. Because of the increasing diversity of conditions in these countries, it is now common to distinguish between those in the periphery proper and those in the *semi-periphery*. The poorest countries are those in the periphery. They include most of sub-Saharan Africa and South and East Asia (including India and China.) They are extremely poor: average income per person (GDP per capita in 1998) was about $500 per year, compared to over $20,000 per year in the United States (World Bank, 2000). Their economies are still primarily agricultural and more than two-thirds of their populations are rural. However, compared to the past, many of these countries (most importantly, China and India) now have significant industrial facilities. China had an especially high rate of growth in the 1990s although its per capita income of about $700 still means it is an extremely poor country. The countries of the semi-periphery include most of the countries of Latin America, North Africa, the Middle East, and a few smaller countries in Southeast Asia. They are more affluent than the periphery: average income per person averaged about $3000 per year in 1998 (World Bank, 2000). These countries are "partially industrialized," with about one-half to two-thirds of their populations living in urban areas. A few of these countries (e.g., South Korea, Taiwan, Singapore) achieved such rapid rates of industrialization in the last three decades that they have been called the "Newly Industrialized Countries" or NICs (Shannon, 1996:102, 109; World Bank, 1993:238–39). Even after a severe economic downturn in 1998, South Korea, for example, had a per capita income level of $8600 (World Bank, 2000).

Despite immense diversity, it is possible to identify one general common problem of Third World countries: their rapid rate of population growth. Beginning about five decades ago, their mortality rates (the probability of dying at a given age) fell dramatically. This drop was primarily in response to improvements in such public health measures as vaccination, pest control, and antibiotic use. Until recently (when it began to decline slowly), the fertility rate (the number of children a woman has on average) remained high. The result was explosive population growth. Total population more than doubled from 1960 to 1995 (to around 4.5 billion). The most rapidly growing countries have been doubling their populations in less than 20 years. Most countries are actively seeking to encourage smaller families. China has the most successful fertility control program (but also the most coercive one). It has already cut fertility down to about two children per woman. Most observers are now hopeful that fertility will decline to the point at which population will actually stop growing in about half a century. However, that means that massive population growth will continue (especially for the next quarter century), and even the most optimistic projections are for there to be at least 8 billion people in the Third World by the middle of the twenty-first century (Weeks, 1999).

All of the countries of the Third World have been attempting to *modernize:* they are seeking to raise their average standard of living through industrialization and agricultural improvements and create "modern" social institutions such as educational systems. Most have achieved some modest degree of success. Average levels of production per person, life expectancy, literacy, industrial output, and the like have risen at least slowly in most of these countries (except sub-Saharan Africa, where declines occurred in the 1980s and 1990s) and rapidly in a few. However, most remain dismally poor by U.S. standards. The World Bank estimated that more than one-fourth of the population of the Third World (more than one billion people) was living in "absolute poverty" in 1990; that is, they lacked the economic means to sustain a healthy life (World Bank, 1990:1–2). While the percentage in absolute poverty declined somewhat (from 28 to 24 percent), the number of poor remained essentially unchanged in the

1990s. The World Bank estimates that if the world pattern of slow economic growth and rising inequality that characterized the 1990s continues, the number of people in absolute poverty will remain essentially unchanged through 2015 (World Bank, 2000: 4–5). In addition, the majority of the rest of the population lives under conditions that would qualify as abject poverty in the United States. At current rates of improvement, only a few countries can hope to achieve living conditions for most of their people even remotely comparable to those now enjoyed in the advanced capitalist countries within the lifetime of anyone reading this book. Indeed, because incomes in the advanced capitalist countries have also been increasing, the absolute gap between the average incomes in the Third World countries and those of the advanced capitalist countries has been increasing since 1950 (Passe-Smith, 1993; Durning, 1990:136). The World Bank estimates that the poorest two-thirds of the world's countries have lost ground economically relative to the richest one-third in the last few decades (World Bank, 2000:4)

The reasons for this disappointing rate of improvement are complex and a matter of some controversy. Most observers agree that the rapid increases in population have had and will continue to have major negative effects on these countries' efforts to modernize, and even threaten the most crowded of them with the inability to feed themselves (Weeks, 1999). On the other hand, few sociologists would argue that population growth by itself explains the continued poverty of most of the Third World. Some sociologists (called modernization theorists) have emphasized the problems caused by the continued social and cultural "traditionalism" of these societies, which has made them slow to adopt necessary social, political, and economic reforms. Other sociologists (called world-system theorists) argue that Third World countries have been relegated to a disadvantaged position in the international economy. World trading and investment patterns benefit the advanced capitalist countries at the expense of those in the Third World. Only those countries that have been able to achieve a high degree of political autonomy from the advanced capitalist countries (e.g., Japan) have been able to avoid or break out of this disadvantageous position in the world economy and achieve rapid modernization (Shannon, 1996).

It is in this context of extreme poverty, rapid population growth, and frustratingly slow attempts to modernize that Third World urbanization has been occurring. The overall rates vary, and there are major differences in the overall levels of urbanization that Third World countries have achieved (see table 9.1). However, what is striking for most of these countries is the very rapid rate at which they are urbanizing. The rate of urbanization in the Third World has been much higher than that which has occurred elsewhere. Moreover, when combined

Table 9.1
Urbanization in the Third World and Selected Countries

	Urban Population as Percentage of Total Population		Percent of Population in Urban Agglomerations of More than One Million		
	1980	1998	1980	1995	2015
All Third World	32	41	10	14	16
Low Income[1]	22	30	7	10	13
Middle Income[2]	56	65	18	22	23
Brazil	66	80	27	33	34
China	20	31	8	11	14
Egypt	44	45	23	23	25
Indonesia	22	39	7	13	16
Kenya	16	31	5	8	14
Mexico	66	74	27	28	26
Nigeria	27	42	6	11	15
Pakistan	28	36	11	19	25
Zambia	40	39	9	15	23

[1]Mostly Peripheral Countries
[2]Mostly Semi-Peripheral Countries

SOURCE: World Bank. 2000. *World Development Report*. Washington, DC: World Bank: 150–152.

with population growth, the total numbers of people being added to urban areas in the Third World are immense. In 1950 about 280 million people lived in urban areas out of a total Third World population of 1.6 billion. Today there are about 2.2 billion urban dwellers out of a population of about 5 billion (Weeks, 1999). In the recent past the rate of urbanization has been slowing somewhat. Nonetheless, even this slower growth rate will still result in a huge increase in the urban population. Current projections call for a doubling of the urban population in the periphery and semi-periphery between 2000 and 2030 (an increase of almost two billion people). During 2000–2030 urban growth will account for almost all of the total population growth in poor countries. In a reversal of the trend of the last few decades, it appears that the rate of growth of the largest cities in the periphery and semi-periphery is moderating, and future urbanization will be more evenly distributed among a larger number of smaller cities (United Nations Population Division, 1999).

Causes of Rapid Urbanization

Part of the growth of urban areas in the Third World is simply due to the high fertility and low mortality rates of the people living in them, causing a high rate of natural increase in their populations. However, the extreme rapidity of the recent growth reflects massive migration of rural residents to urban areas. This large-scale migration will not continue indefinitely. Eventually, the populations will be predominantly urban, and (like the United States) migration will cease to be a major cause of growth. Completion of the "urban transition" (having 70–80 percent of the population in urban areas) is one reason (besides slowing overall population growth) that rates of urban growth are expected to begin to decline significantly in the most urbanized countries of the Third World in the twenty-first century (Kelley and Williamson, 1984:179). The already high urbanization levels in some semiperipheral countries in Latin America means that these countries have already reached the end of massive rural to urban migration. Yet, for the time being, migration is expected to continue in most poor countries. What accounts for this massive shift?

In part, the answer is—as it was for the United States in the nineteenth century—that workers have been attracted by the development of large-scale industry, corporate and government offices, large retail establishments, and the like (the so-called *formal sector* of the urban economy). However, the number of workers being added to the labor force in Third World cities greatly exceeds that needed to work in the formal sector. Hence, the cause of rural-to-urban migration has not been simply conventional industrialization by itself. Indeed, early observers of Third World urbanization argued that those workers not in the formal sector constituted "excess urbanization," and as a result, Third World countries were experiencing "overurbanization." This nonfunctional urbanization was occurring simply because of rapid population growth in general and excess population in the countryside in particular (Gibbs and Schnore, 1960). However, more recent research and theorizing calls this view into question.

It is true that rural conditions are generally appalling and provide a strong motivation to look for better opportunity in the cities. Income levels are extraordinarily low, and the growth in opportunities for employment have not been keeping pace with population growth. In some cases rural population densities (especially in Asia) are such that peasant landholdings are an acre or less, and consequently, can neither support a household adequately nor be further subdivided for the next generation. In many countries the situation is made worse by the fact the much of the land is held by large landowners (the native aristocracy or foreign corporations), leaving large numbers of peasants impoverished tenant farmers or landless day laborers. The development of commercial agriculture (often for export) using modern mechanized methods has also reduced the demand for rural labor in some countries. In addition, many Third World governments have favored urban areas at the expense of people in the countryside. Price controls on agricultural products have kept rural incomes low to assure cheap food for the cities. Government investment in infrastructure, industrial facilities, education, and other services has tended to favor the cities—especially capital cities (Firebaugh, 1979; Geisse and Sabatini, 1988; Rondinelli, 1988; Sachs, 1988; Dogan and Kasarda, 1988).

Nonetheless, most recent research indicates that it is the relative attractiveness of the cities, not the problems of the countryside, which primarily accounts for rural-to-urban migration (Gugler, 1996). While the formal sector of the urban economy has been unable to absorb the growing urban labor force, a larger (and more rapidly growing) *informal* sector has provided most of the employment opportunities. The informal sector consists of small enterprises and self-employed workers who provide a wide range of services and small-scale production of goods. Women who sew garments in their homes, scavengers, shopkeepers of tiny stores, water carriers, manual day-laborers, pedicab pullers, and self-employed carpenters are all members of the informal sector. Incomes of most workers in this sector are as low or lower than those in the formal sector, and usually several members of the family must work even to assure the minimum subsistence needs of the household.

Early observers of the informal sector argued that it represented a form of "underemployment" in which workers engaged in relatively unproductive labor simply as a means of survival because of inadequate employment opportunities in the formal sector and the countryside. More recently, the informal sector has come to be viewed as an integral part of the urban economy in the Third World:

> [The] . . . informal sector has several functions. It absorbs labor that cannot be employed in agriculture or large-scale manufacturing; subsidizes export manufacturing by providing the factories with production inputs at low prices and cheap goods and services to poorly paid workers; and helps make possible wages below that necessary for the subsistence of manufacturing workers' households. Workers in manufacturing enterprises supplement their pay by "moonlighting" in the informal sector or by having other family members work in that sector. (Shannon, 1996: 100)

In societies where capital for modern, large-scale production is inadequate, the informal sector thus represents a means of employing labor and obtaining necessary goods and services with minimal capital investment. It is "labor-intensive" production, but it is as productive as labor-intensive agriculture (or even more productive where agriculture is especially backward or land is scarce). It is part of a larger economic system that is based on the exploitation of extremely cheap labor to produce inexpensive goods and agricultural commodities for the national and world market. Such production has been the traditional role of peripheral and semi-peripheral countries in the world economic system. The informal structure simply represents, therefore, a new urban form of the kind of economic activity that has characterized these countries for a long time. As such, it is a reflection of the disappointing progress these countries have made toward full economic modernization and their continued subordination and exploitation in the world division of labor (Shannon, 1996:89–90; Geisse and Sabatini, 1988:323–24; Smith, 1996:19–25).

Low income levels in both the formal and informal sectors mean massive urban poverty and squalid living conditions. As we will see, general conditions in these cities are extremely unpleasant. Why then do workers come from the countryside? Wage levels may be higher in the cities, but it is likely that higher living costs wipe out any benefit. Hence, part of the reason people continue to come is simply that the lack of any opportunity for many in the countryside makes even the limited opportunities in the cities look attractive. In addition, even if the probability of real economic success is low, urban areas are also attractive because they provide at least the possibility of success:

> Third World cities . . . act like a giant Las Vegas in the sense that the bulk of their populations are gamblers, though the games are different. . . . The rewards [of city life] may look insignificant when compared to the excessively high price . . . in terms of daily life difficulties . . . [but] the important thing is that there are rewards for some. The large cities are places of hope, while the drudgery of rural life looks hopeless. (Sachs, 1988:337–39)

In short, whatever their problems, these cities offer the best real chance (however slim) for social mobility (Kasarda and Parnell, 1993: xi).

Special Characteristics and Problems

Not only has urbanization proceeded with extraordinary rapidity in the Third World, until recently it has tended to concentrate in a limited number of very large cities. Small and medium-sized cities are fewer and have grown more slowly than one would expect (based on the U.S. experience) given overall levels of urbanization. Instead, one very large city (or a few large cities in the bigger countries) has been the primary focus of urbanization. The resulting giant cities are called *primate cities*. For example, Mexico City contained about 18 million people in 2000 (up from 14 million in 1980), representing 20 percent of the total population of the country. It also dominates the Mexican economy. It accounts for over half of national nonagricultural economic activity, 35 percent of government employees, and almost 70 percent of national financial assets (United Nations Population Division, 1999; Schteingart, 1988:270–89). Similarly, Bangkok generates

86 percent of the national product in banking, real estate, and insurance and 74 percent of Thailand's manufacturing production (Kasarda and Parnell, 1993: xi).

In part, primate cities are a legacy of the colonial past. During the colonial period each colony developed a single administrative center that also functioned as the center from which to collect production from the countryside for export and to import manufactured goods. Modern infrastructure was concentrated in the colonial capital to serve the needs of the import-export enterprises, colonial administrators, and the consumption needs of European colonists and native elites. The export facilities and internal transportation and communication systems were all oriented toward this city.

Once one city had this overwhelming advantage, it continued to be the most attractive location for new activities. It had the best infrastructure, the largest market for manufactured goods, the best living amenities for foreign business executives and native elites, a large pool of available labor, the best transportation and communication links, and the most developed business services. The primate city simply became the best place to locate manufacturing activities and other business enterprises. In many cases, the primate city is the seat of national government, and the concerns of government officials for good conditions for themselves and to maintain urban civil peace lead them to further focus expenditures for services on the capital city (Palen, 1987:344–45).

There has been a debate about the effect of primate cities on economic development in Third World countries. On the one hand, many critics argue that concentration of economic activities in one city occurs at the expense of the rest of the country. The development of agriculture, the provision of services, and the creation of nonagricultural employment opportunities in outlying areas are retarded (Rondinelli, 1988:307–9). On the other hand, others have argued that primate cities represent the most efficient location for modern industrial activity, and hence, investment in those cities will provide the highest rate of return and the most rapid growth of the economy (Stark, 1980). The current consensus view is represented by Harry Richardson's conclusion:

> The most important conclusion . . . is that mega-city size is not a critical policy variable. . . . The size of a mega-city is not closely correlated with its economic efficiency or the severity of its negative externalities. . . . Even the growth rate of the mega-city need not be a problem unless it is so high that it impedes economic growth, fiscal stability, provision of public services, and implementation capacity. Such growth management costs are triggered at different rates in different cities. . . . [N]o mega-city appears to be experiencing growth rates in the dangerous range. (1993:52)

Although it is too early to tell for sure, data from the last decade suggest that the largest of the primate cities (e.g., Mexico City) are no longer growing as fast as they did in previous decades. Instead, small or mid-sized cities are growing faster. The growing problems of the "mega-cities" may have made them less attractive to both rural migrants and investors. Many smaller cities have enjoyed recent success as centers of export industries. However, these cities seem to be reproducing, on a smaller scale, most of the conditions of their larger brethren as they grow (United Nations, 1996).

The rapid growth of most Third World cities does mean that those cities have a number of serious problems relating to overall living conditions and quality of life. Growth has been so rapid, the population is so overwhelmingly poor, and the ultimate size of the populations is so huge that Third World cities are confronted with serious problems and urban policy challenges (Gugler, 1997; Brennan, 1993; Gilbert, 1994; Palen, 1987:333–431; Yeung, 1988; Nagpaul, 1988; Rondinelli, 1988; Geisse and Sabatini, 1988; Sachs, 1988; Teune, 1988; Flanagan, 1999:160–63; Bartone, 1993; UN Environment Program and World Health Organization, 1994; World Bank, 2000: 134–37, 162–63).

Housing supply has not even approximately kept up with demand. That has meant escalating land and rental housing costs. For more affluent segments of the population, the tight, expensive housing situation severely limits the size and quality of housing. For the great bulk of the population with extremely low incomes, it has meant being housed in squalid, crowded slums and even worse squatters' shantytowns. Government attempts to build even the most basic, low-income housing have not even made a dent in the need for such housing. These governments are themselves very poor, and the size of the population in need and its rate of growth greatly exceed the ability to commit adequate resources. The more fortunate find accommodations in tiny, rundown apartments or subdivided houses, often one family per room, without indoor water or sanitary facilities. The rest of the population (one-third or more in most cities) reside in flimsy shacks on tiny parcels of land for which they may pay rent to an owner or on which they squat (illegally occupy the site). In turn, they may own the shack (often built out of scavenged materials, sheets of tin, cardboard, and lumber scrap) or rent it from a slightly better-off "landlord" who owns several structures or rents out part of his or her own residence. Structures are crowded closely together along narrow dirt pathways with a limited number of narrow streets.

Slum areas, especially the newer squatter settlements, usually lack even the most basic physical services: paved streets, piped water, sewers, garbage collection, and electricity. Illegal squatters are in no position to demand physical infrastructure or police, fire, or educational services (even if the government could afford to provide them).

Open latrines and sewage ditches, lack of weather-tight and insect-proof housing, accumulating garbage, rat and insect infestations, contaminated and inadequate water supplies, and virtually no public health facilities make the slums and squatters' settlements squalid, fetid, unhealthy places to live. In some instances squatter settlements "mature" into more permanent communities, with better housing, services, and infrastructure. However, new squatter settlements continue to form at the same time.

Rapid urbanization has also contributed to grossly inadequate and overutilized public physical and social services. Most of these cities have public service systems that would be minimally adequate (by even the most generous criteria) for populations only a fraction of their current size. Water, sewage, and garbage collection facilities are available for only the more affluent part of the population. Public transportation systems carry two and three times their engineered capacities and still do not meet the need for transportation. Streets and main thoroughfares are hopelessly congested. Construction of schools and the provision of teachers rarely have kept up with the growing population. Public medical facilities are of poor quality, massively overcrowded, and limited in number.

Pollution problems are also severe, getting rapidly worse, and represent immediate threats to urban health and general environmental quality. Third World cities have the worst pollution problems in the world. Industrial air and water pollution, smoke from cooking fires, growing automobile use, toxic waste dumping, lack of adequate sewage treatment and garbage disposal, and unsafe industrial practices all contribute to massive urban pollution problems. Many Third World cities already have pollution levels that harm the health of their populations. For example, pollution-caused respiratory disease is common, as is exposure to air and water-borne carcinogens and other toxins. Desperate to attract foreign investment, Third World governments have been hesitant to impose any pollution restrictions on foreign corporations. Indeed, some countries have been accepting waste from the advanced capitalist countries to earn desperately needed foreign exchange. Anxious to encourage domestic industry, lacking much capital for industrialization (let alone pollution control equipment), and faced with the need to increase production as fast as possible, Third World governments have emphasized industrialization at the expense of environmental damage.

Faced with these problems created by the rapid growth of giant cities, many governments in the Third World have made some attempts to encourage more decentralized urbanization and/or development of nonagricultural employment opportunities in rural areas. For the most part, these efforts have been limited in scope and have not had much effect on the pattern of urbanization (Todaro, 1984).

Perhaps the most ambitious efforts were those in China prior to the mid-1980s. The Chinese government made decentralized urbanization a cornerstone of its economic modernization program. The effort does appear to have limited big city growth in the period. However, the overall strategy of modernization, of which they were part, yielded only mixed results (Goldstein, 1988; Yeung, 1988; Chen, 1988).

During the 1980s and 1990s the Chinese government gradually moved away from state control of the economy and restrictions on large city growth. The "responsibility" system in agriculture replaced most collective farms. Peasant families leased land from the collective and were free to farm as they pleased and sell most of their production on the open market. The hope was that this would increase rural incomes and encourage production of consumer goods for the farmers in towns and smaller cities. At the same time, private enterprise, foreign investment in manufacturing facilities, and increased reliance on markets to control prices and production decisions were introduced (Mok, 2000; Murphey, 1988).

The result has been rapid economic growth, but that growth has been accompanied by urban development more similar to the rest of the Third World. Allowing free movement of peasants, the creation of private enterprises providing unrestricted urban employment, and the elimination of other economic controls have meant fewer restrictions on the growth of China's large cities. The result has been a huge wave of migration to the large cities on the coast. The explosion of small enterprises in Chinese cities closely resembles the growth of the informal sector in other Third World cities. The fact that the state no longer guarantees employment has left increasing numbers of young workers looking for a means to support themselves. Foreign investment also tends to be concentrated in a few large cities, especially the special "free zones" around cities on the coast. Hence, there are indications that large-scale industrialization is going to remain concentrated in a small number of large cities. The most extreme example of this tendency is Shanghai. Already China's largest port and biggest industrial center, it continues to grow very rapidly. By the late 1990s conditions and problems in Shanghai were similar in many respects to those in the largest of the primate cities in the rest of the Third World (Mok, 2000; Li Minqi, 1996; So and Chiu, 1995:243–50; Gottdiener, 1994: 264–65; Goldstein, 1993; Murphey, 1988).

The overall trend seems clear. Third World governments have simply been overwhelmed by the rapid pace of urbanization and possess very limited financial resources to deal with the problem. Continued rapid urbanization and even more austere government budgets as the result of increasing economic difficulties in most of these countries (including a huge foreign debt in many countries) since the 1980s have meant that service levels continue to deteriorate. The short-term prospects for general improvements appear to be poor. Long-term improvements would depend upon much more rapid economic development, stabilizing overall population growth, and the end of massive rural-to-urban migration. Under such circumstances, urban governments in Third World countries might begin to marshall the resources to deal with their accumulating problems.

MAIN POINTS

1. Western European countries are economically advanced capitalist societies that experienced processes of industrialization and urbanization relatively similar to those in the United States. Currently, their urban areas continue to display significant similarities to those in the United States: suburbanization of population and industry, some decline of traditional industries, the continued success of central downtown districts as administrative centers, and growing reliance on the automobile.

2. Besides often having developed around a "historic core" of a preindustrial city, Western European urban areas display differences from those in the United States which primarily reflect the greater intervention of government into the urban development process: green belts; new towns; tighter control on urban land use; attempts to decentralize urban development geographically; more government-subsidized, multifamily housing; high levels of public services; and greater reliance on mass transit. Housing, traffic congestion, and pollution continue to be serious problems in these urban areas.

3. Tokyo shares with other advanced capitalist cities certain basic features: an administratively oriented downtown, growing suburbanization of population and industry, decline of older industries in the central city, and growing automobile use.

4. The land available for urban use is severely limited in Japan by topography and government policy. High-rise construction has been limited until recently because of the threat of earthquakes. The result is intense competition for the available land and very high prices. In turn, these high land costs have severely limited the size and quality of urban housing (almost all privately provided) and forced workers to look for housing far from their places of work.

5. Limited street capacity and government policy in Japan have meant extremely heavy reliance on public transportation,

which is of good quality but has not expanded rapidly enough to accommodate the growing population and increasing amount of commuting. Japan has been slow to invest in urban infrastructure and services, which are inadequate and of low quality (except for education). Until recently, extremely high levels of pollution had not prompted any effective control measures by government.

6. Eastern European urbanization took place in the context of state ownership of the economy, centralized economic planning, and the attempt to achieve maximum investment in industry by limiting consumption. Yet, overall levels of production and national wealth remained much lower than in the advanced capitalist countries. The result were cities where the requirements of industry took precedence over other considerations, and the resources available to meet the needs of the urban population were limited.

7. In principle, urbanization in Eastern Europe was centrally planned. In practice, the planning mechanisms worked poorly and the pressures to minimize costs resulted in an emerging urban ecology roughly analogous to that in capitalist countries. Despite efforts to increase the housing stock, housing remained cramped, of low quality, and in extremely short supply. Limited purchasing power and state policy meant people had to rely on an extensive system of mass transit; however, this system did not expand fast enough to meet growing populations and increasing suburbanization. Many urban services, food, housing, transportation, medical care, and the like were state-subsidized at nearly uniform low prices or provided free. That guaranteed less inequality in living standards for the population, but state-provided goods and services were of low quality and in chronic short supply. Pollution problems were severe and there was almost total neglect of pollution control.

8. Most of Eastern Europe has been undergoing a process of at least partial "democratization" and the creation of market-based economies. However, the weakness of their economies seems likely to relegate most countries to the status of relatively poor, partially industrialized societies—similar to the large countries of Latin America. If so, urban conditions seem unlikely to improve any time soon.

9. The most rapid urbanization in the recent past has been in the Third World. Populations there are growing rapidly and also migrating from rural to urban areas. Migration is the result of a combination of the lack of real opportunity in the countryside and at least some prospects for employment in the cities. Most workers in the cities work in the very low-wage informal sector

of the urban economy, which helps to subsidize the operation of the modern industrial sector. The resulting rapid urbanization has tended to concentrate in a limited number of cities which are quickly achieving gigantic size. These urban populations are extremely impoverished. The majority live in cramped, squalid slums or squatters' shanties. Modern urban services reach only a more affluent minority of the urban population, and water, garbage, sewage, electrical, and communications systems are hopelessly overloaded and inadequate. Pollution levels are dangerously high and rising.

KEY TERMS

Formal Sector   The most "modernized" sectors of the economy in Third World countries, including such activities as large industrial plants, corporate and government offices, and large retail establishments.

Green Belts   Areas adjoining cities in which urban development is prohibited.

Informal Sector   The sector of the economy in urban areas of the Third World which consists of small enterprises or self-employed workers producing a wide range of services and simple, often handicraft, goods.

Modernization   The process by which Third World countries are attempting to develop more productive and technologically sophisticated economies and the social and political institutions appropriate to such an economy.

New Towns   Planned satellite communities in suburban or exurban areas, often designed to provide places of residence, employment, shopping, and services.

Periphery   The poorest and least industrialized countries in the world. They include China, India, sub-Saharan Africa, and a few of the poorest countries in Latin America.

Primate Cities   The "giant" cities that are the result of the concentration of Third World urbanization in a limited number of very large cities.

Semi-periphery   Those countries which have achieved partial industrialization, but continue to have substantial rural populations and relatively low per capita incomes—a third or less of those in advanced industrial countries. The semi-periphery includes most of the countries of Latin America, the Middle East, a few of the smaller countries of Southeast and East Asia, and probably most of the countries of Eastern Europe.

SUGGESTED READING

Gilbert, Alan. 1994. *The Latin American City*. London: Latin American Bureau. A readable overview of urban conditions in Latin America.

Sassen, Saskia. 1994. *Cities in a World Economy*. Thousand Oaks, CA: Pine Forge. A brief statement of Saskia's view of the emerging world division of labor among cities with a focus on global "command and control" centers.

10

Urban Problems in Perspective

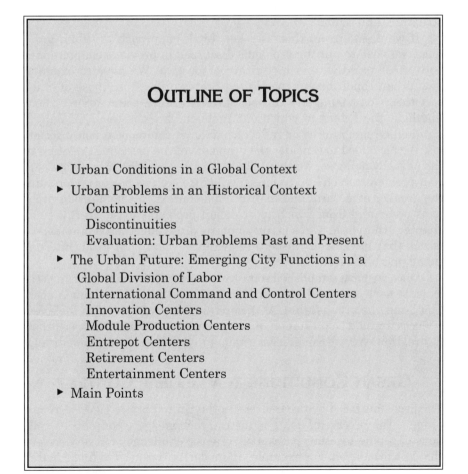

The previous chapters have painted a fairly dismal picture of urban woe. That is because the urban problems of the United States really are quite serious. However, we need to put these problems into better perspective. Otherwise, we run the risk of falling into a common intellectual trap: there is a persistent tendency for observers of the American urban scene to see urban problems in a parochial and historically unconnected fashion. Each problem is viewed independently of the others and its seriousness is evaluated by a set of contemporary expectations or standards (which usually change even faster than the conditions being described). The result of this kind of thinking is a "crisis" mentality in which alarms are raised and dire predictions are made, only to have the problem forgotten when attention is drawn to yet another "crisis." Thus the public (or at least the media) focus shifts from crime, to homelessness, to welfare mothers, to decaying infrastructure, and so on.

If we are to avoid this "Chicken Little" approach to urban problems, we need to put the problems discussed in previous chapters into both a comparative and historical perspective. We have to examine how urban conditions in the United States differ from those of other societies. Comparing the United States to other countries will help highlight the extent to which our problems are the result of unique national circumstances or reflect tendencies common to many societies. We also need to consider the problems of the present in relation to the past. By doing so, we should be in a better position to evaluate current problems. Such an attempt should also help us better understand the broader structural and institutional context in which urban problems occur and from which most urban problems arise. In this final chapter, therefore, we will attempt to draw together a number of issues that have been raised and evaluate them both in an international and historical context.

Once we have established some sort of perspective on the urban problems we have discussed, we will be in a position to address a final important issue: the urban future. At the present "state of the art" in the social sciences it would be presumptuous to claim to be able to predict the urban future. However, we can at least attempt to think about it systematically.

URBAN CONDITIONS IN A GLOBAL CONTEXT

The problems faced by urban areas in the United States clearly are not unique. The process of using industrial technology to concentrate millions of people together poses a set of basic challenges to every society that has urbanized. For example, all modern cities need to find a better way to deal with the wastes generated by industrial processes. However, the specific conditions under which urbanization has occurred have shaped both the ability of societies to confront those challenges and the specific methods that they have employed.

Not surprisingly, urban conditions in the United States are most similar to those in countries that share our basic level of wealth and system of political economy. The wealthy, capitalist, electoral democracies of Western Europe and Japan experienced an urbanization process roughly similar to our own. Resource allocation and land-use patterns basically reflect the operation of the market, in the context of economies dominated by large private corporations with considerable political power. All these countries now enjoy a level of wealth that allows a high standard of living and provides the resources for a high level of public services. They also confront many of the same problems that we do: what to do with automobile congestion; how to reduce pollution levels; how to assist those whom the private economy does not adequately support; how to meet the demand for affordable, good quality housing; and what to do about the decline of traditional manufacturing industries. All face the challenge of finding a place in a rapidly changing global economy in which the location of economic activities is changing with unprecedented speed.

The key difference between the advanced capitalist countries in the last few decades has been the extent to which government has actively intervened to deal with urban problems and control the urbanization process. In general, Western European countries have relied the most on government action and Japan the least. The approach of the United States has been somewhere in between. However, in the last two decades, the role of the federal government in dealing with urban problems in the United States has been reduced. Similarly, concerned for their competitiveness in the international economy and facing slower economic growth, many Western European countries also have scaled back some of their more generous social programs. Indeed, the advanced industrial countries, struggling for world market share and international corporate investment, may be in a process of "leveling down" their social welfare systems to a common lower level to cut both labor costs and corporate taxation. As of this writing, the United States clearly has proceeded the farthest down this path.

Other than variations in average income (now narrowing) and the relative scarcity of urban land, these differences in government involvement go a long way toward explaining differences in urban conditions among the advanced capitalist countries. Western European cities have done the best in regard to those things that government can provide most effectively: social services, mass transit, and subsidized housing for the poor. The cost, of course, has been a greater diversion of private income to public purposes. In contrast, while the middle classes in the United States also enjoy very good conditions and even enjoy relatively good public amenities where those are provided by local government (in the affluent suburbs), many publicly provided urban services are more limited and the conditions faced by the economically disadvantaged are much worse. In other words, living conditions vary more in the United States, depending upon a family's private income. Moreover, progressive neglect and deterioration of the publicly provided physical infrastructure threatens even the suburban middle classes. Japan has been extremely slow in providing services not directly related to the success of its giant corporations. As a consequence, Japanese urban dwellers face the least desirable general living conditions among the advanced capitalist countries.

Overall, people in the formerly "state socialist" countries of Eastern Europe endure substantial hardship in comparison to urban residents in the advanced capitalist countries. The most important reason for this difference is economic. These are simply much poorer countries. However, the lack of economic resources was compounded by authoritarian governments that sought national power through a single-minded pursuit of rapid industrialization. Centrally planned economies based on state-owned enterprises gave these governments almost complete control over the allocation of economic resources. Both private consumption and public services were limited so that investment could be concentrated in heavy industry. For example, limited funds devoted to housing meant that urban housing was of poor quality and in chronic short supply. On the other hand, there was a commitment to provide universal employment security, subsidized housing and basic necessities, and universal access to a wide range of (often low-quality) services. After initial success, the industrialization drive foundered, and these countries entered a period of economic stagnation and political unrest that finally resulted in political collapse. The new, generally more democratic governments of Eastern Europe are now struggling to convert their economies to more market-based ones and open themselves fully to world trade and investment. In most cases they appear to be taking a role in the world economy more similar to semi-industrialized Third World countries than to wealthy advanced industrial countries. If that is so, improvements in basic urban conditions for all but a favored few will not come soon.

Urban problems are most daunting of all in the Third World. A number of factors make this urbanization different from that which occurred in the advanced industrial countries: (1) the extreme poverty of these countries, (2) unprecedented rates of population growth, (3) very high rates of urbanization, (4) inadequate supplies of capital to invest in modern industrial production, (5) economies based on the exploitation of low-wage labor, and (6) the tendency to develop primate cities. The resulting giant cities, teeming with desperately poor people, have simply been overwhelmed with problems. Despite some countries that have achieved rapid rates of industrialization, especially in Asia, the likelihood of even fairly successful development substantially improving urban conditions in these countries still appears to be mostly a distant hope. In comparison, urban problems in the United States look benign indeed.

URBAN PROBLEMS IN AN HISTORICAL CONTEXT

American urban areas have always faced serious problems. As we saw in chapter 1, many of the problems these areas now face are either continuations of problems that arose in the past or are the consequences of trends that developed over a long period of time. In other words, there is a significant degree of historical continuity to American urban problems. However, that is not true in all cases. Some problems are either new or significantly different from those of the past. So there are historical discontinuities as well as continuities in urban conditions.

Continuities

One persistent historical theme in American urban conditions and problems has been their connection to various kinds of socioeconomic inequality. Throughout this book we have referred repeatedly to various kinds of inequality in terms of income, education, opportunities for employment, housing, treatment by government, access to transportation, and political influence. There is nothing new about this pervasive inequality. Inequality has been a persistent fact of life in American society from the very beginning. To be sure, in some ways and to some degree (there is considerable debate on just how much), inequality may be less than it was a century ago. Such things as changing opportunities for employment, the extension of legal rights and guarantees to minorities and women, and government "transfer payments" (taxation of the affluent to help the less affluent) probably have had some moderating influence on the extent of inequality in American society when examined over the long term.

However, as we have seen, very significant inequality continues to exist in American society. Moreover, in the last few decades, there have been indications that certain kinds of inequalities have been increasing. For example, the percentage of the population below the poverty line has been rising, homelessness became a serious urban problem, budgetary cutbacks at all levels of government disproportionately affected the poor, and the general level of income and wealth inequality increased.

Overall, the bottom 80 percent of households have seen their share of national income decline compared to the early 1970s, while the top 20 percent have enjoyed an increase. The greatest decreases and increases have been at the extremes of the income distribution. In other words, the lower your income in 1970, the more it has declined, and among high-income households the richest have experienced the greatest increase in income (U.S. Bureau of the Census, 1996d).

The problem this inequality creates is not "merely" that some people are deprived relative to others in society. There are very few urban problems we have discussed that are not at least intensified by continued and/or growing inequality. For instance, many of these problems can be directly linked to the continued existence of large numbers of the poor and near-poor in our urban areas. Some kinds of crime, the difficulties faced by urban school systems, the persistence of slums and urban decay, the financial crisis of the central cities, the heavy burdens on the social-welfare system, the movement of the more affluent from the central cities, and more generally, the continued debate over the appropriate allocation of limited governmental resources can all be linked to the persistence of large pockets of low-income people in urban areas.

A second recurrent theme in American urban history has been how we, as a culture, perceive cities and urban life. As was pointed out in chapter 3, Americans have a long tradition of being uneasy about urban life and longing for a mythological rural past of simplicity and close community ties. This "anti-urban bias" and romantic quest for community has repeatedly colored the American response to urban conditions and contributed directly and indirectly to the problems we have examined.

One consequence of the negative perception of urban life is that Americans have spent considerable effort trying to run away from or ignore cities. At least in part, the various waves of suburbanization that characterized the twentieth century (and the more recent non-metropolitan growth) may be seen as a manifestation of this tendency. Of course, only the more affluent segments of the population have been able to indulge in the luxury of this sort of escapism. And part of the basis for dislike of cities is that they have always been seen as centers of lower-class residence. Once established in our suburban enclaves, we have tried to insulate ourselves from the "evils" and problems of the cities by erecting zoning barriers, supporting discriminatory real estate practices, resisting annexation and regional government, and opposing those policies and programs which would help the cities deal with their problems.

More generally, rural nostalgia and resentment of things urban have repeatedly provided an ideological basis and justification for sociopolitical movements seeking to reverse social or cultural trends of which they disapprove. The evils of modern society are contrasted with the "simple virtues" of the rural past, and these movements call for the reestablishment of cultural or social patterns presumed to have existed in rural America. Again, the first targets (or victims) of these movements often have been efforts to deal with the problems of the cities and the needs of urban population groups (such as foreign immigrants or the poor).

On a more sophisticated level, this distrust or ambivalence felt toward cities has often extended even to intellectual observers of American cities. For instance, we saw that what has been called the "classical view" of urban society among American social scientists (and some of their European predecessors) primarily focused on the negative aspects of urban life. At the very least, these theories have reinforced popular biases against the cities. In some cases, they may also have led to an incorrect identification of the problems and needs of urban communities (e.g., the view that the real problem of the urban poor was their "social disorganization") and hence to the misdirection of public policy and resources.

Of course, this anti-urban bias has not meant a total refusal to collectively address urban problems. There have been several waves of urban reform. Programs adopted during the Great Society period (1960s), the New Deal (1930s), and the Progressive Era (1900s) all included major elements intended to ameliorate urban conditions. More recently, public opinion polls in the 1980s showed high levels of public concern for such problems as pollution and homelessness. Although some of the reforms proposed were biased by anti-urbanism (e.g., attempts to weaken the power of immigrant-based political machines in the early part of this century), others represented sincere attempts to deal with urban problems. Private, volunteer efforts to deal with such issues as urban poverty or homelessness also have been a recurrent feature of the urban scene. Some of these efforts had a real impact on improving urban conditions. Still, one cannot help but be struck by the limited nature of these efforts and the fact that the impulse toward reform was quickly dissipated.

On a more general level, the fact that we are a highly individualistic culture has created a constant tension between meeting collective needs, including those of our urban communities, and maintaining maximum individual autonomy over the pursuit of individual goals. As a culture, we have always had trouble acknowledging the need for taxes, government programs, and regulations that reduce individual freedom and personal income to provide for the "collective good." If anything, the last twenty years have been a period where that tension between individual and societal needs has become more pronounced in our political life (Bellah et al., 1985; Nisbet, 1970; Slater, 1970; Monti, 1999).

The constraints imposed by our particular system of "political economy" is another historical continuity. Despite an immense increase in the size and scope of governmental activities, the U.S. political system has continued to operate within a particular institutional context. That framework consists of a capitalist economic system and a social-class system in which there is considerable economic inequality and a system of political influence that favors the affluent. Within a capitalist society, there is, almost by definition, considerable tension between the demands that government solve problems and the desire of private interests to make decisions in their own self-interest, dispose of property as they please, and allocate resources as they choose. Moreover, not all groups have equal political power. While there is considerable room for debate on how centralized political power is, it seems clear that some groups are disproportionately influential in the political system. They may not get their way all the time, but they have more say than others. Generally speaking, these more influential groups consist of the more affluent and the large corporations that dominate the private economy. As a result, the tension between the private sector and the government has always been most acute when government has attempted to tax or regulate the activities of the more affluent and (especially in the last century) the large corporations. Conversely, these powerful groups have also been in a better position to make demands on government for services and resources which benefit them.

We have observed the consequences of this situation repeatedly in our examination of urban problems and trends. The basic direction of urban development has depended on corporations' decisions regarding the nature and location of their investments. We have seen that this power to direct the location of investment severely constrains the actions of local governments. They feel that they must please corporate interests to maintain the local economy. We also have seen that the role of government has frequently been limited to a "reactive" role concerning corporate investment decisions. When these decisions have created problems for various groups or localities or generated the need for government services, government has then stepped in to provide additional services and repair the social or physical damage. Hence, much of the focus of government effort has been on responding to, rather than controlling or preventing, the problems created by private economic decisions.

Even when the government has taken a more "activist" role in attempts to deal with urban problems, it has remained especially sensitive to the interests and concerns of the more affluent and the large corporations. We saw this, for example, in the apparently greater tolerance of the criminal justice system in dealing with white-collar crime, as well as in the way urban renewal turned into displacement of the poor from areas adjacent to business districts. Similarly, we saw that when the government intervened in the urban housing market, the bulk of the available resources was employed to provide subsidies for more affluent home buyers, protect the interests of the banks, and expand the market for private building contractors.

This bias in government policy does not mean that various programs have not benefited the less affluent and less powerful. Nor should we conclude that corporations and the wealthy always have received everything they wanted. However, government policy has displayed a clear tendency to consider the interests and respond to the demands of some groups more than others.

Discontinuities

It should also be obvious that not all the problems urban areas face today are the same as those of the past. In some very important ways, both the specific problems urban areas now face and the circumstances under which they are occurring are different from the past.

One clear difference is simply that many urban areas now face the problems of age rather than the problems of newness and growth. (The obvious exceptions to this pattern are the newer urban growth areas.) For the first time in our history, we have a significant number of large, old cities. Their problems are not those of the past: rapid population growth, the construction of service and physical infrastructures, and rapid land-use conversions. Instead, they now face the problems of maturity: economic bases consisting of old factories and stagnant industries, a rapidly aging housing stock, population losses or stagnation, limited ability to increase tax revenues, and worn-out, antiquated physical infrastructures.

The large concentration of African Americans in many central cities represents another new problem. It would be a mistake to assume that the problems African Americans now face are the same as those that European immigrants faced in the past. Granted, there are obvious similarities. There are also fundamental differences. The immigrants of a century ago came to the central cities when employment opportunities for unskilled, uneducated workers were growing rapidly. Educational requirements for occupational advancement were less, and changes in the nature of employment opportunities favored upward social mobility. African Americans in the cities now face a decline in the absolute numbers of jobs, even more rapid declines in unskilled jobs, greater educational barriers to employment, and increasing competition for jobs in middle-class occupations. At the same time, the nature of the racial prejudice and discrimination that African Americans have faced has been more pervasive, deeply held, and harder to avoid (because of skin color) than the ethnic prejudice and discrimination faced by immigrant ethnic groups. On balance, it thus appears likely that African Americans have faced more obstacles and problems than the urban migrants who preceded them.

The relatively high level of recent immigration from Third World countries has added yet another new dimension to urban ethnic relations. Both visibly and culturally more distinctive than immigrants from Europe in the past, they have raised public fears about cultural homogeneity and ethnic diversity to the highest level since the last great wave of European immigration in the early twentieth century. We seem to be in for a period of cultural adjustment to a large, diverse immigrant population that already has witnessed an increase in hostility toward the new immigrant groups. "Ethnic group" politics (ethnic group voting and political issues viewed in ethnic terms) seem likely to be part of the political landscape for at least the next generation.

Public awareness of and tolerance for certain conditions and problems also has changed. As a consequence, what people consider an "urban problem" in which government should become involved has changed. We are much less tolerant of abusive or corrupt behavior on the part of the police and public officials. Awareness of the potential seriousness of environmental pollution has increased immensely in the last three decades. Despite continued manifestations of prejudice and discrimination, tolerance for visible racism and its consequences certainly is much less than before. In general, our ideas of "acceptable" conditions of life have undergone considerable upgrading, and our expectations about the responsibility of government in guaranteeing certain minimum conditions have increased immensely. The huge increase in public concern about crime reflects both changing perceptions of its threat and real increases in the commission of some kinds of crime.

American urban areas face both these new problems and the problems inherited from the past under rapidly changing conditions that influence both the nature of the problems and our response to them. Despite the relative prosperity of the 1980s and the long economic expansion of the 1990s, some long-term economic trends remain troublesome. Whole industries that were once the basis of much of our economic success and the primary support of our older industrial regions are either stagnant or in decline. Even many of the industries that relocated to the South in the 1970s have begun to experience difficulty dealing with foreign competition. This has been only partially balanced by the growth of the newer high-technology industries. In addition, as we have seen, the economic benefits of this new industrial growth have not been distributed equally between the regions or among categories of workers. The overall national loss of better-paying industrial work and the rapid growth of lower-paying service employment has been an especially disturbing trend. Much of the past improvement in urban conditions was simply a reflection of the growing affluence of the urban population. The uneven growth of personal income and growing economic inequality mean that parts of our urban areas (or even whole cities) are inhabited by those who have lost out in the "new economy," even as other areas display the extraordinary wealth generated in the economic expansion of the 1990s.

Long-term structural changes in the economy have increasingly created another limitation on local, state, and even federal efforts to deal with urban problems. Large, often multinational, corporations have come to dominate more and more of the economy. One thing this means is that industry is more than ever before both willing and able to transfer operations to those places it regards as most favorable to profitable operations. If government in a particular locality, region, or country attempts to increase taxes, impose regulations, or protect efforts at unionization, it runs the risk of having its economic base undermined by industrial flight. Such flight carries with it the prospect both of increasing the problems faced by government because of economic decline and reducing the ability to raise revenues to deal with the problems. Thus, government at all levels—local, state, and federal—is constrained to act to meet corporate demands in return for corporate investment in the economy.

We remain the most automobile-dependent society in the world. Our entire urban landscape is a testament to the almost universal use of the automobile, based on abundant cheap gasoline. Ample petroleum supplies in the 1980s and 1990s should not blind us to our growing dependence on foreign supplies of petroleum. Uncertain supply and prices may finally provide the motivation to at least try new methods of powering our vehicles, although the process is likely to be a long and costly one. In addition, the need to deal with the increasingly complex and dangerous environmental problems caused by fossil-fuel burning are becoming very pressing. The need to do something about these environmental issues will further complicate our energy problems and certainly will entail higher costs. These increasing costs will directly affect such things as transportation and industrial production and also limit the resources available to deal with other urban problems.

Of course, the story of the last generation has not been simply one of industrial decline. Business and financial services have flourished. Some major cities in the United States have shifted in the direction of functioning as "command and control centers" for the management of enterprises and the provision of capital and technological expertise for an increasingly integrated world market. This trend has had highly visible consequences for a few of our large cities. Their central business districts have continued to function as centers of administration, finance, and communication activities. These districts have retained their economic importance despite the loss of some white-collar office operations and the frequent failure of attempts to maintain these districts as centers of mass-market retailing. As will be discussed later, this resilience seems to be especially marked in a few large central cities, and may portend a new economic role for these cities.

At the same time, computers and the internet are rapidly transforming business operations, retail marketing, and leisure activities.

Much of the dynamism of the economy in the 1990s reflected the rapid growth of this technology. Besides the direct effect "telematics" are having in those places that are centers of computer design, production, and software generation, the new technologies are making it more and more possible to conduct business and make financial transactions on a global scale. So far at least, this development has favored a few cities that are financial and corporate headquarters (Sassen, 2000).

Certain recent social trends also represent relatively new developments with at least a potential effect on future urban conditions. For example, the nature of the households that make up the urban population have changed markedly since the 1950s. The number of children per family is down to around two. The proportion of married women (including those with young children) who work has risen substantially. The majority of married-couple households now have two wage earners. The marriage rate has fallen slightly, and the number of people who never marry has increased. The number of single-parent households has risen substantially. As the baby-boom generation ages in the next two decades, there will be a bulge in the population of middle-aged couples who have completed their child-rearing years. When this group retires (after 2015), a very rapidly growing proportion of households will consist of the elderly.

Associated with these family composition changes have been trends in the economic circumstances of households over the last three decades. Perhaps the most important of these trends have been the declining availability of good-paying industrial jobs (which has meant declines in real wages for less educated workers) and virtually stagnant purchasing power for all workers except those at the top of the occupational structure. These trends account for the pressure on even middle-class households to have two wage earners. In turn, women's participation in the labor force has been a major motivation to have few or no children. Only better educated, married-couple, dual-income households have seen significant increases in income (per family member), and those who have remained childless have fared best of all. Conversely, single-earner families have lost ground, and single-earner families (especially those headed by women) with children have fared very badly indeed. As we have seen, the growth of the latter type of household contributed to the growth of poverty in the 1980s (Albeda and Tilly, 1990).

These household composition and income trends also have had, and probably will continue to have, other major impacts on urban conditions. For example, better-educated, childless households provided the major market for housing in gentrified neighborhoods. Out in the suburbs, better-educated, dual-income households have also contributed to the boom in ever-larger, more elaborate homes (so-called "pocket mansions") and the elaborate array of services demanded by time-stressed, affluent households. On the other hand, single-earner households with children are those who are most at risk from rising housing costs and make up a growing proportion of those who are homeless (see chapter 5).

Another fundamental change which we now confront in regard to our urban problems has to do with the extent of the role of government. Compared to the early 1900s, we depend much more on the services government provides. Large numbers of people in our urban areas depend on government for income as employees, pensioners, and recipients of various transfer payments (e.g., welfare, food stamps, Medicare). Government absorbs a major portion of our total national income and is a major purchaser in our economy. Tax policies, economic policies, and regulations have a major impact on business operations. We have seen repeatedly what this means in terms of urban developments and problems. Much of what occurs in urban areas is either caused by or strongly influenced by government policies. Indeed, what we have seen is that government is not only an agency for solving urban problems, it also has been a source of them. For example, in the last few decades the political trend has been to move away from the social services and programs that serve the poor. As we have seen, this has had a major impact on the budgets of large central cities with significant concentrations of poor residents.

In fact, the importance of government has provoked a counter trend. There has been a growing resistance to government activities and interventions. Some groups and individuals have been increasingly unwilling to pay the taxes necessary to support existing levels of public services or to provide the resources for additional government initiatives. At the same time, there has been growing distrust of government and increased skepticism about the ability and effectiveness of government to deal with problems. The more affluent have become more concerned with holding on to their existing standard of living and less sympathetic toward the problems of the less fortunate. If, as some believe, we are moving into a "neo-Victorian age" in which the social welfare system is progressively dismantled, social conditions among both the poor and the less affluent of the working class are likely to deteriorate markedly. Such a major shift in public policy would have widespread, obvious consequences for urban trends and conditions in the United States.

Evaluation: Urban Problems Past and Present

Where do all these considerations leave us? How do our present problems stack up against those of the past?

On the positive side, there clearly are good reasons to have a sense of urban progress. Judged by a set of absolute standards based on conditions in the past, many of the "old" problems of the urban past are now less severe. This is especially true of those which were linked to economic conditions and the standard of living. Certainly, general living conditions are immensely better than they were in our early industrial cities. We are much safer, healthier, and more comfortable than were our urban forbearers. In addition, many of the other problems of the urban past are at least not much worse today (e.g., relative inequality and deprivation). Some are probably less severe (e.g., racism, ease of transportation). Many of our "new" problems are simply the result of rapidly rising expectations (e.g., housing) or higher standards and better knowledge (e.g., pollution). In the light of the past then, these problems are not nearly as severe as they appear to us. Finally, some of the things that observers in the past considered as fundamental problems of urban areas now appear to be less severe than they feared (e.g., "social disorganization"). On balance, general conditions in our urban areas are much better than they were at the end of the nineteenth century.

On the negative side, however, urban problems remain serious. Even a partial list of some of the issues that have been addressed in previous chapters is sobering. While we have made progress in improving our general standard of living, many urban dwellers live under conditions which, given our general affluence, are offensive, demeaning, demoralizing, and debilitating. Relative deprivation is real deprivation. Urban poverty has not only persisted, it has increased. That we were ignorant of the effects of pollution a century ago does not make it any less of a threat now. Moreover, we are now facing the effects of worldwide environmental disruption with potential consequences that we are just beginning to grasp. The threat of service retrenchment or breakdown and governmental insolvency in the central cities is a problem that affects millions of urban residents. Our failure to maintain the basic physical infrastructure of our metropolitan areas threatens not only to impact the quality of life but also the efficiency and competitiveness of our industry. The unmet social and physical needs of the disadvantaged even in our growing urban areas is a time bomb ticking behind the glittering facades of those cities. The energy inefficiency of our transportation system represents a potential "Achilles heel" of our sprawling, low-density urban complexes. Water supply, pollution, and waste removal represent problems that will require very expensive solutions during a time of limited governmental resources. Economic trends may create new problems and limit our ability to respond to them.

Thus, there are valid historical grounds to be concerned about both current urban conditions and future trends. The next generation of urban dwellers is not likely to be sympathetic to our complacent argument that things are better now than they were in the past if we allow our problems to accumulate and conditions to deteriorate in the future.

THE URBAN FUTURE: EMERGING CITY FUNCTIONS IN A GLOBAL DIVISION OF LABOR

It is not possible to predict the precise nature of urban development in the next quarter century. There are simply too many unpredictable factors. Nonetheless, it is possible to examine what would happen if current trends were to continue. This "projection" cannot hope to be more than a crude approximation of what will, in fact, happen. It is a useful exercise primarily because it addresses the possible implications of current trends and is, thereby, another way of evaluating those trends.

There has always been considerable variation in United States urban areas in terms not only of size, but also economic activities. John Logan and Harvey Molotch (1987) argue that, as a result, the trends we have discussed will have different impacts on each urban area. They contend that five general types of cities will emerge, reflecting an emphasis on a particular kind of economic activity. Saskia Sassen (2000) has also suggested a similar emerging "division of labor" between different kinds of cities. Of course, most urban areas will combine some or all of these activities. Indeed, one of the reasons for the unusually rapid growth of the Los Angeles basin has been that it has combined most of these activities (Davis, 1990). Hence, we will limit the present discussion to the main functional activities that seem likely to emerge and suggest some cities that seem to illustrate these functions. Whether it is actually possible to clearly categorize a specific city as one or the other "type" is not something we will try to address. In addition to those activities suggested by Logan and Molotch, we will also discuss an additional activity proposed by E. Barbara Phillips (1996) and identify by citation some of the other researchers, besides Logan and Molotch, who have explored these possibilities.

International Command and Control Centers

A few of our largest cities have traditionally been the location for the headquarters of a large percentage of our national corporations and also have functioned as national or regional financial centers. Certain trends in the national and world economy suggest that these cities will continue to experience similar growth, along with the growth of the business services necessary to those operations (e.g., corporate law firms, investment houses, marketing firms, engineering consultants, and accountants). Corporate consolidation (through mergers and acquisitions) is further concentrating the administration of corporations in the hands of a few giant companies. Expansion of overseas operations, given modern transportation and communication, allow even multinational companies to administer their operations from one main administrative center. As we saw in chapter 2, there is less and less connection between the location of productive facilities and corporate headquarters. The growing integration of the world economy into a single world market (or at least a few giant regional ones) and electronic communications and computing capabilities have also created a single vast financial system. This system has a small number of central financial markets operated by a relatively select group of increasingly large financial institutions located in a few major cities (e.g., Zurich, London, New York, and Tokyo). The result is that these cities are becoming headquarters for the administration and finance of corporations whose scope of operations is global. In addition, these same centers are the logical locations for branch offices of foreign corporations doing business in a particular country (Logan and Molotch, 1987; Phillips, 1996:107; Sassen, 2000:1–31).

In these cities, central business districts have continued to experience rapid expansion. The concentration of high-status managers and professionals also provides markets for luxury retail goods, restaurants, hotels, and cultural activities. It is in these cities that centrally located residential districts have experienced the most gentrification. Not surprisingly, the cost of housing has skyrocketed, and the market for luxury housing experienced a boom in the 1980s. (Like most booms in the housing market, the result was overbuilding and overpricing, which led to a slowdown in many of these housing markets in the early 1990s.) In most of these cities, government, anxious to encourage the boom, poured resources into these central office districts and gentrifying neighborhoods to fund such things as cultural facilities, convention centers, and slum removal. The result of these trends has been cities with glittering cores of prosperous business districts, affluent neighborhoods, restored parks, and upgraded recreational and leisure activities. Journalistic observers of these developments have proclaimed that an "urban renaissance" is underway (Sassen, 2000:1–31).

Such a judgment may be premature. In most such cities, economic development has been uneven. The cores may glitter, but slums continue to fester. Headquarters cities do provide employment for large numbers of high-status managers and professionals. Other employment trends in most of them are less hopeful. The largest percentage of new jobs created by headquarters operations and financial institutions are low-paid clerical positions. The other growth area is retail trade and services, again dominated by low-paid workers. At the same time, in most of these cities the better paid manufacturing jobs—held by less educated and skilled workers—continue to disappear. Unemployment (especially among African-American males) remains high. "Booming" New York and Los Angeles both had almost one-fourth of their households below the poverty line in the mid-1980s, and neither poverty nor unemployment declined significantly in major metropolitan areas in the 1990s until the last two years of the decade's economic "boom" (U.S. Census Bureau, 1996c; 2001b). It is hardly coincidental that homelessness became a visible and serious problem in our largest cities in the last two decades. What appears to be emerging in these cities is a bipolar class system composed of an affluent managerial and professional class at one end and an impoverished class of working poor and unemployed at the other. Some observers of these cities even argue that what is emerging in the poor neighborhoods of those cities resembles conditions in the Third World, in that there has been a rapid growth of the informal sector of the economy (Sassen-Koob, 1984, 1987; Sassen, 2000; Fainstein and Harloe, 1992).

Hence, even in these cities, economic revival does not appear to be enough to provide the tax base necessary to reverse the decline in city services. (New York started the 1990s with another financial crisis.) City governments have concentrated on providing high-quality services to prosperous areas. It appears likely that they will be forced to allow continued deterioration of such things as streets, schools, police protection, transportation, and fire protection outside those areas. Continued poverty, low service levels, and the displacement of the poor from central areas of the city will result in spreading urban decay. Eventually, this urban decay will spill over in a major way (some already has) into the inner ring of suburbs. Many of the problems discussed in earlier chapters therefore will continue in these cities, although their location will have shifted away from city centers (Logan, 1987).

The suburban areas (except for the older working class and industrial suburbs) of these cities continued to prosper in the 1980s and 1990s. To the extent that their prosperity is not tied to traditional manufacturing industry, that trend seems likely to continue. More suburban office complexes, often adjacent to malls, are creating mini-downtowns. Routine, clerical operations involving large numbers of workers are less costly in the suburbs (because of lower rental costs and an ample supply of trained workers). Some kinds of corporate headquarters operations, such as trucking firms and wholesale distributors, do not require a downtown location and have been moving to the suburbs. In some cities (e.g., Boston, Los Angeles) various kinds of high-tech manufacturing are concentrated in suburban locations. The trend in the growing suburban areas is thus one in which there will be even more "city" activities (e.g., offices, factories, and central shopping areas). The central city consequently will be even more irrelevant to most suburban workers, except in the bedroom communities of high-status managers and professionals who mostly will continue their downtown employment. Increasing numbers of clerical workers, rising land costs, and the economic and social trends discussed earlier may also lead to further increases in the amount of multifamily housing in the suburban areas of larger cities (Fishman, 1987; Garreau, 1991; Gottdiener and Hutchinson, 2000: 85–92).

Innovation Centers

The American economy has become increasingly dependent on research and development activity to maintain its competitiveness. Most of our newer industry has been spawned by that activity. In addition, a major source of technical innovation in the last few decades has been military research. Certain types of research and development—carried on by a combination of government agencies, private firms, and nonprofit institutions—do not need to be near either production facilities or corporate headquarters. Rather, they are most dependent upon the ability to attract and/or interact with highly trained technical professionals. Consequently, research and development facilities have tended to concentrate in the same locale to take advantage of existing labor pools of needed professionals. Often they have been consciously planned and subsidized by government and have tended to be located near major research universities. Examples of innovation centers include Austin, Texas; Cambridge, Massachusetts; the Silicon Valley in Northern California; and the Research Triangle area of North Carolina.

These innovation centers tend to dominate the smaller cities where they are usually located. The professionals who work in them expect high-quality services (e.g., education) and numerous cultural and recreational facilities. Housing costs (due to rapid growth and an affluent population) and taxes (to pay for services) usually are relatively high. That often causes difficulties for the large number of low-paid service workers employed in most universities and in the research facilities. High-tech firms that are the spin-off of research activities provide some industrial employment. However, once a production process becomes large-scale and routine, the search for lower wages and land costs is likely to mean relocation of the production facilities, as has already happened in the computer industry in Silicon Valley (Logan and Molotch, 1987; Phillips, 1996: 107).

Module Production Centers

As we have seen, traditional forms of industrial production have become increasingly flexible in terms of where they are located. They need not be near corporate headquarters, or even in the same country. They are located where overall costs are lowest and the degree of labor control is greatest. For most industries, there is a large number of places that will meet their basic production requirements. Hence, these locations are expendable, virtually interchangeable production "modules." If the relative advantage of a place declines, corporations have little long-term commitment to remaining and will seek newer, more attractive locations. That means cities (and their workers) are in competition with one another for large-scale industrial investment. With increasing global competition among corporations, the competition for industrial investment also has become global. United States steel workers not only compete with those in Japan and Europe but also those in South Korea and Brazil.

Those cities that cannot offer what is required to specialize in non-industrial activities appear to be relegated to "production modules": more or less interchangeable components of industrial production processes. To attract investment they will have to offer a mix of cheap land, low taxes, trained workers, docile labor forces (i.e., weak unions), low wages, minimal regulation, and good transportation links. That does not necessarily mean that each place has to have the lowest wages or taxes compared to its competitors. Rather, it has to have the most attractive combination of factors relative to the needs of particular industries (Gappert, 1995; Phillips, 1996:107). For some industries (e.g., garment making) where the primary concern is labor costs, cities in the Third World appear to be winning. Producers of toxic chemicals have been fleeing the United States across the border to Northern Mexico, where environmental regulation is virtually nonexistent. In other cases, locations in the United States remain the most attractive. Witness, for example, the Japanese auto industry's substantial investment in final assembly plants in the United States, though not in the big cities.

Even those metropolitan areas which are relatively successful in this competition for corporate investment face an uncertain future. Success will always be contingent upon maintaining attractiveness in a rapidly changing world economy. For example, attracting enough investment to achieve full employment will tend to drive up labor costs and decrease competitiveness. Many communities in the South, which attracted industry with low wages, now find themselves losing out to low-wage areas in the Third World. Hence, industrially oriented metropolitan areas will be locked into a permanently dependent relationship with corporate investors. Whether that will allow them to raise taxes, provide services, or control development in order to benefit their areas seems doubtful. Consequently, most of the urban problems we have discussed here, especially those relating to poverty and low service levels, seem likely to persist even in industrial growth centers. The experience of the Sunbelt cities during the 1970s seems to be instructive. Even though they enjoyed rapid growth, relatively high levels of poverty persisted and service levels remained low. In similar areas, attempts to revive city centers will enjoy only limited success, since their ability to function as corporate headquarters will be limited. The experience of Akron-Canton, Ohio is suggestive. All but one of the giant tire companies centered there is now owned by foreign corporations with headquarters elsewhere, although a number of tire plants still remain.

In addition, not all metropolitan areas are likely to be competitive. Some of our older industrial cities have been only marginally successful in attracting new industry. For example, David Perry (1987) argues that the Buffalo, New York region is a good example of a declining, old industrial center. Buffalo's experience suggests an ominous future for such metropolitan areas. These cities persist as regional marketing and financial centers and attempt to market themselves as places with a large pool of unemployed or low-wage workers. As industrial jobs have declined, most job creation has been in the low-wage service sector. Out-migration is high, and those who remain are the old and least skilled. An increasing percentage of the population is poor (if they are young) or dependent on social security (if they are old). Long-term unemployment means expansion of the informal economy among discouraged workers. Declining income levels and growing poverty imply increasing decay of the oldest part of the housing stock. Central business districts are increasingly moribund and more dependent on such things as government office buildings. Central-city governments have been especially hard hit. Rapid declines in their tax bases have had devastating impacts on their ability to deliver services and repair infrastructure. Their declining populations are increasingly poor. These cities are coming to function as reservations of the unemployed or subemployed poor. In short, what appears to be emerging are a number of chronically depressed metropolitan areas in which urban conditions appear likely to continue to deteriorate. A similar situation, only with the process of stagnation and decline more advanced, now prevails in most of the old industrial centers of Great Britain outside of the greater London area.

Entrepot Centers

Another kind of emerging city is also tied to global economic trends: the "entrepot" or intermediary city. Examples of cities that have this function as a major aspect of their economy include Miami, El Paso, Brownsville, and San Diego. They have large numbers of legal and illegal immigrants (mostly Hispanic). These "new immigrants" have tended to concentrate disproportionately in a few areas. Limited skills and/or their illegal status make these workers willing to accept very low wages and unpleasant working conditions. Hence, urban production and many services in these areas are increasingly based on the exploitation of low-wage labor. These workers are employed in service work (e.g., the tourist industry in Miami), illegal sweatshops (e.g., garment making), and even high-tech industries that require low-wage, semi-skilled workers. What appears to be emerging in the United States are areas of some cities which function economically much like cities in the Third World. Their basic economic activities are those based on the exploitation of low-wage labor. Hence, some industries, instead of relocating their plants in the Third World, are taking advantage of the emerging "internal periphery" of some of our urban areas.

These border cities are also trade and financial centers for importing, marketing, and distributing imports (including illegal drugs) and exports, especially to Latin America and/or Asia. San Diego is a major import-export port city for Asia. Miami has become a city essentially tied to Latin America. It functions as a regional banking center, port, air transportation hub, and even a favored recreational and shopping center for the Latin American wealthy (Sassen, 2000: 88–92). Cities along the border with Mexico are increasingly integrated into a "Rio Grande Valley" economy operating on both sides of the border (see Bloomberg and Martinez-Sandoval, 1982).

Retirement Centers

In another two decades, more than one-fifth of the U.S. population will be elderly. In addition, more workers are retiring early. Increasingly, this growing elderly population is migrating to cities whose climate and other amenities make them attractive places to retire.

Some of these retirement centers contain relatively high-income residents. These "leisure cities" (e.g., Sarasota and Fort Myers in Florida) are in a position to offer high levels of services and support for the elderly because they have local tax resources similar to affluent suburbs (Gladstone, 1998). However, other communities, while most are not officially poor, are lower income. Their income is heavily dependent on Social Security payments. At the same time, especially among those of more advanced age, their service needs are relatively great. Hence, what will happen in these communities depends on future developments in the federal provision of services for the elderly. If the federal government leaves service provision to the elderly primarily in the hands of the private sector or local government, these retirement centers will be faced with service demands that will outstrip local tax resources. The result could be "retirement slums" in which the local support networks are inadequate. Since women live longer and tend to have much lower retirement incomes if they are divorced or widowed than do married couples or men, it may mean that we can anticipate the development of ". . . old people's slum cities, disproportionately female, dependent, and empty of resources" (Logan and Molotch, 1987:277).

Entertainment Centers

Some urban areas have been successful in developing entertainment attractions that draw large numbers of tourists and play a major role in the regional metropolitan economy. Both south Florida and central Florida (around Disney World and the other large tourist attractions that have developed there) are examples. Other examples would be Tahoe City, Las Vegas, Atlantic City, and Williamsburg (Virginia). Workers at the large corporate-owned attractions are often unionized and relatively well paid (Gladstone, 1998:20). On the other hand, smaller retail service business (e.g., motels and restaurants) require low-wage, often seasonal workers, including illegal immigrants (Phillips, 1996:106–7). Overall, areas that cater to large-scale tourism have higher per capita incomes and lower levels of poverty than the average U.S. metropolitan area (Gladstone, 1998:20).

MAIN POINTS

1. Urban conditions must be evaluated in relation to those of other countries and in the past.

2. United States urban conditions are similar to those of other advanced capitalist countries. However, the extent of government intervention varies and has some effect on urban conditions in those countries. Urban conditions in the rest of the world are substantially worse than those in the United States.

3. Some problems urban areas face arose in the past or are the consequence of trends that developed over time. Some of the continuities with the urban past include: continued inequality and the problems associated with inequality, the quest for community, and the relative success of powerful economic interests to either limit government actions or use government for their own benefit.

4. Other urban problems or the context in which they develop differ from those in the past: the aging of older cities, the problems faced by African Americans, public awareness of and tolerance for certain urban problems, the growing importance of relative rather than absolute deprivation, the effects of a changing economy, our changing ability and/or willingness to deal with urban problems, the dilemmas raised by continued reliance on fossil fuels, the effects of changing family composition and income levels, and the extent to which urban conditions are shaped by government actions.

5. If current trends continue, six major kinds of urban functional centers seem likely to emerge: international command and control centers, innovation centers, module production centers, entrepot centers, retirement centers, and entertainment centers. While the central economic activities and relative economic prosperity of these centers is likely to vary substantially, most of them will continue to encounter the same problems currently being faced by various urban areas in the United States.

SUGGESTED READING

Logan, John, and Harvey Molotch. 1987. "The Dependent Future."
Chapter Seven in *Urban Fortunes*. Berkeley: University of California. This discussion will amplify the urban scenarios addressed in
this chapter.

Garreau, Joel. 1991. *Edge City: Life on the New Frontier*. New York:
Doubleday. A readable account of the emergence of suburbs as the
new urban form in the United States.

Davis, Mike. 1990. *City of Quartz*. London: Verso. Describes what Los
Angeles has become and how it got that way, with suggestions on the
direction of urban change in the future. This is an engrossing book.

Bibliography

Abu-Lughod, Janet L. 1991. *Changing Cities*. New York: HarperCollins.

Adams, James. 1989. *The Big Fix: Inside the S & L Scandal*. New York: Wiley.

Albelda, Randy. 1996. "Farewell to Welfare but not to Poverty." *Dollars and Sense* 208:16–19.

Albelda, Randy, and Chris Tilly. 1990. "What's Work Got to Do With It?" *Dollars and Sense* 154:16–18.

Alford, Robert, and Roger Friedland. 1975. "Political Participation and Public Power." In *Annual Review of Sociology*, edited by A. Inkles. Palo Alto, CA: Annual Reviews.

American Plastics Council, 2001. *1998 Recycling Rate Study*. www.plasticsresource.com

Anderson, Charles H. 1974. "The Poor." In *Toward a New Sociology*. 2d ed. Homewood, IL: Dorsey Press.

Andrusz, Gregory. 1996. "Structural Change and Boundary Instability." In *Cities after Socialism,* edited by G. Andrusz, M. Harloe, and I. Szeelenyi. Cambridge, MA: Blackwell.

Applebaum, Richard P., and William J. Chambliss. 1997. *Sociology*. 2d ed. New York: Addison Wesley.

Arnott, Richard, and Kenneth Small. 1994. "The Economics of Traffic Congestion." *American Scientist* (September/October): 451–55.

Aron, Leon. 1999. "Is Russia Really 'Lost'?" *American Enterprise Institute Russian Outlook* (Fall).

Bahl, Roy. 1984. *Financing State and Local Government in the 1980s*. New York: Oxford University Press.

Bahl, Roy, and Larry Schroeder. 1978. "The Outlook for City Fiscal Performance in Declining Regions." In *The Fiscal Outlook for Cities*, edited by R. Bahl. Syracuse, NY: Syracuse University.

Bakalis, Michael. 1987. "City's Schools Need Emergency Surgery: Decentralization Urged As a First Step." *Chicago Sun Times,* 17 June.

Baldassare, Mark. 1978. *Crowding in Urban America.* Berkeley: University of California.

———. 1989. "Public Support for Regional Government in New Suburbia." *Urban Affairs Quarterly* 24:460–69.

———. 1994. "Regional Variations in Support for Regional Governance." *Urban Affairs Quarterly* 30:275–84.

Ballantine, Jeanne. 1989. *Sociology of Education.* Englewood Cliffs, NJ: Prentice-Hall.

Banfield, Edward, and James Wilson. 1966. *City Politics.* New York: Vintage.

Bankston, Carl, and Stephan Caldas. 1997. "The American School Dilemma: Race and Scholastic Performance." *Sociological Quarterly* 38(3):423–29.

Barlow, Hugh. 1990. *Introduction to Criminology.* Glenview, IL: Scott, Foresman.

Barry, Patrick. 1989. "Downtown Transit: Lessons from Other Cities." *Transit Brief.* Chicago: Metropolitan Planning Council.

Bartone, Charles. 1993. "Environmental Challenge in Third World Cities." *Journal of the American Planning Association* 57(4): 411–15.

Bell, Derrick. 1989. "The Case for a Separate Black School System." In *Black Education: A Quest for Equity and Excellence,* edited by W. D. Smith and E. W. Chunn. New Brunswick, NJ: Transaction Publishers.

Bell, Terell. 1983. *A Nation at Risk: The Imperative for Educational Reform.* National Commission on Excellence in Education.

Bell, Wendell. 1958. "Social Choice, Life Styles and Suburban Residence." In *The Suburban Community,* edited by W. Dobriner. New York: Putnam.

Bellah, Robert, Richard Madson, Ann Swidler, William Sullivan, and Steven Tipton. 1985. *Habits of the Heart.* Berkeley: University of California.

Bendick, Marc, and David Rasmussen. 1986. "Enterprise Zones and Inner-City Economic Revitalization." In *Reagan and the Cities,* edited by G. Peterson and C. Lewis. Washington, DC: The Urban Institute.

Bendix, Reinhard. 1960. *Max Weber: An Intellectual Portrait.* Garden City, NY: Doubleday.

Berry, Brian. 1973. *The Human Consequences of Urbanization.* New York: St. Martin's Press.

Berry, Brian, and Donald Dahlman. 1978. "Population Redistribution in the United States." *Population and Development Review* 3:468.

Berry, Brian, and Phillip Rees. 1969. "The Factorial Ecology of Calcutta." *American Journal of Sociology* 74:445–91.

Beyond Gridlock: The Future of Mobility As the Public Sees It. 1988. Washington, DC: Advisory Committee on Highway Policy, 2020 Transportation Program.

"Big City Metro." 1990. Series presented by KETC-TV, St. Louis.

Bish, Robert, and Elinor Ostrom. 1973. *Understanding Urban Government.* Washington, DC: American Enterprise Institute.

Bixby, Ann. 1988. "Overview of Public Social Welfare Expenditures Fiscal Year 1986." *Social Security Bulletin* 51:27.

Blauner, Robert. 1964. *Alienation and Freedom: The Factory Worker and His Industry.* Chicago: University of Chicago Press.

Block, Fred. 1980. "Beyond Relative Autonomy: State Managers as Historical Subjects." *Socialist Register, 1980*:227–42.

Bloomberg, Warner, and Rodrigo Martinez-Sandoval. 1982. "The Hispanic-American Urban Order: A Border Perspective." In *Cities in the 21st Century,* edited by G. Gappert and R. Knight. Beverly Hills: Sage.

Bobo, Lawrence, and Camille Zubrinsky. 1996. "Attitudes on Residential Integration." *Social Forces* 74(3): 883–927.

Bogdon, Amy, and Zhong Yi Tong. 1999. "Minority and Low-Income Neighborhoods Benefit Most from Mortgage Lending Increases." *Housing Facts and Findings* 1(2): 12–15.

Bolton, Dan. 1989. Interview by author. Danville, Illinois.

Bourgeois, Philippe. 1995. *In Search of Respect: Selling Crack in El Barrio.* New York: Cambridge University Press.

Bradbury, Katharine, and Yolanda Kodrzycki. 1992. "What Past Recoveries Say about the Outlook for New England." *New England Economic Review* (September/October): 15–32.

Bradford, Calvin, and Gale Cincotta. 1992. "The Legacy, the Promise, and the Unfinished Agenda." In *From Redlining to Reinvestment,* edited by G. Squires. Philadelphia: Temple University Press.

Bratt, Rachel. 1986. "Public Housing: The Controversy and Contribution." In *Critical Perspectives on Housing,* edited by R. Bratt, C. Hartman, and A. Meyerson. Philadelphia: Temple University Press.

Braun, Denny. 1991. *The Rich Get Richer.* Chicago: Nelson Hall.

Brennan, Ellen. 1993. "Urban Land and Housing Issues Facing the Third World." In *Third World Cities: Problems, Policies, and Prospects,* edited by J. Kasarda and A. Parnell. Newbury Park, CA: Sage.

Broder, David. 1990a. "Skinner's 'Moving America': A Cop-Out." *Chicago Tribune,* 11 March.

———. 1990b. "Pure Hearts and Gimmickry Aren't Enough." *Chicago Tribune,* 22 April.

Brown, Deborah. 1979. "Off the Track." *The Progressive* (July): 17.

Brown, James. 1972. "A Look at the 1970 Census." In *Appalachia in the Sixties.* Lexington: University of Kentucky.

Brown, Lester, and Christopher Flavin. 1988. "The Earth's Vital Signs." In *State of the World 1988,* edited by L. Brown. New York: W. W. Norton.

Browne, Lynne. 1989. "Shifting Regional Fortunes: The Wheel Turns." *New England Economic Review* (May/June): 27–40.

Bukro, Casey. 1975. "Garbage Dumps Fill Up at a Crisis Rate." *Chicago Tribune,* 18 December.

———. 1988. "Incinerating Trash Gains Popularity, but Pollution Concerns Persist." *Chicago Tribune,* 14 August.

———. 1989. "To 'Garbologists', Study of Landfills Isn't All Rot." *Chicago Tribune,* 15 October.

Burgess, Ernest. 1924. "The Growth of the American City: An Introduction to a Research Project." *Publications of the American Sociological Society* 18:88–97.

Butler, Edgar. 1977. *The Urban Crisis: Problems and Prospects in America.* Santa Monica, CA: Goodyear.

Byerly, Edwin. 1995. *State Population Trends.* U.S. Bureau of the Census. Washington, DC: GPO.

Byerly, Edwin, and Kevin Deardorff. 1995. *National and State Population Estimates: 1990 to 1994.* U.S. Bureau of the Census, Current Population Reports. Washington, DC: GPO.

Calhoun, John B. 1960. "Population Density and Social Pathology." *Scientific American* 206:139–48.

Califano, Joseph A. 1993. "Overview: Welfare Reform, Introduction." *Yale Law School Review* 11: 109–12.

Campbell, Karen. 1990. "Networks Past: A 1939 Bloomington Neighborhood." *Social Forces* 69:39–55.

Campbell, Karen, and Barrett A. Lee. 1990. "Gender Differences in Urban Neighborhoods." *Sociological Quarterly* 31:495–512.

Caplow, T., H. M. Bahr, J. Modell, and B. A. Chadwick. 1991. *Recent Social Trends in the United States 1960–1990.* Montreal: McGill-Queen's University Press.

CBS. 1989. "New York Is Falling Apart." *60 Minutes,* 19 February.

Chen, Xiangming. 1988. "Giant Cities and the Urban Hierarchy in China." In *The Metropolis Era,* vol. 1, edited by M. Dogan and J. Kasarda. Beverly Hills: Sage.

Cherlin, Andrew. 1999. *Public and Private Families.* 2d ed. New York: McGraw-Hill.

Cheshire, Paul. 1993. "Some Causes of Western European Patterns of Urban Change, 1971–88." In *Urban Change in the United States and Western Europe,* edited by A. Summers, P. Cheshire, and L. Senn. Washington, DC: Urban Institute Press.

Chicago Tribune. 2/27/1989. "Metra's Promising Track to the Future."

———. 3/22/1989. "Keeping Pace with Transportation."

———. 8/14/1989. "Taking the Bus to Opportunity."

———. 7/16/1994. "Lessons in How to Build a Railroad."

———. 6/5/1995. "Planting the Seeds for Rail's Future."

———. 7/9/1995. "A Winning People-to-Jobs Strategy."

———. 12/27/1995. "California Softens Rule on Electric Cars."

———. 3/15/1996. "Schools That Make a Difference."

Chirot, Daniel. 1986. *Social Change in the Modern Era.* New York: Harcourt Brace Jovanovich.

Choldin, Harvey. 1985. *Cities and Suburbs: An Introduction to Urban Sociology.* New York: McGraw-Hill.

Christian Science Monitor. 1996. "The Puzzling Decline in Urban Homicide Rates." 2 January: 9.

Citro, Constance, and Robert Michaels, eds. 1995. *Measuring Poverty: A New Approach.* Washington, DC: National Academy Press.

City of Schaumburg. 2001. Telephone conversation with author, 15 October.

Clark, Terry. 1968. "Community Structure, Decision-Making, Budget Expenditure and Urban Renewal in 51 American Communities." *American Sociological Review* 33:576–93.

Cohn, Bob. 1989. "Looking Beyond the HUD Scandal." *Newsweek,* 21 August: 19.

Coleman, James, and Sara Kelly. 1976. "Education." In *The Urban Predicament,* edited by W. Gorham and N. Glazer. Washington, DC: The Urban Institute.

The Condition of Teaching: A State-by-State Analysis. 1988. Princeton, NJ: The Carnegie Foundation for the Advancement of Teaching.

Congressional Quarterly. 1978. "Mass Transit Legislation." In *Urban America: Policies and Programs.* Washington, DC: Congressional Quarterly.

The Congressional Record. 1983. 5 May: S6097–6101.

Cooley, Charles. 1930. "The Theory of Transportation." In *Sociological Theory and Research.* New York: Henry Holt.

Coontz, Stephanie. 1992. *The Way We Never Were: American Families and the Nostalgia Trap.* New York: Basic Books.

Cordova, Teresa. 1991. "Community Intervention Efforts to Oppose Gentrification." In *Challenging Uneven Development: An Urban Agenda for the 1990s,* edited by P. Nyden and W. Wiewel. New Brunswick, NJ: Rutgers University Press.

Crain, Robert L., and Jack Strauss. 1985. "School Desegregation and Black Occupational Attainment." Johns Hopkins University Center for the Social Organization of Schools, Report 359.

Cressey, Donald. 1969. *Theft of the Nation.* New York: Harper and Row.

Curtis, James, Edward G. Grabb, and Douglass Baer. 1992. "Voluntary Association Membership in 15 Nations." *American Sociological Review* 57(2): 39–52.

Dahl, Robert. 1961. *Who Governs? Power and Democracy in an American City.* New Haven, CT: Yale University.

Danziger, Sheldon, and Peter Gottschalk. 1995. *America Unequal.* Cambridge: Harvard University Press.

Darden, Joe T. 1987. "Choosing Neighbors and Neighborhoods." In *Divided Neighborhoods,* edited by G. Tobin. Newbury Park, CA: Sage.

Darden, Joe, Richard Hill, June Thomas, and Richard Thomas. 1987. *Detroit: Race, Class and Uneven Development.* Philadelphia: Temple University Press.

Davis, Kingsley. 1975. "The American Family in Relation to Demographic Change." In *U.S. Commission on Population Growth and the American Future,* vol. 1, edited by C. Westhopp and R. Parker. Washington, DC: GPO.

Davis, Mike. 1990. *City of Quartz.* London: Verso.

Dawkins, Marvin, and Jomills Braddock. 1994. "The Continuing Significance of Desegregation." *Journal of Negro Education* 63(3): 394–412.

Dear, Michael, and Jennifer Wolch. 1987. *Landscapes of Despair: From Deinstitutionalization to Homelessness.* Princeton: Princeton University Press.

DeLeeuw, Frank, Ann Schnare, and Raymond Struyk. 1976. "Housing." In *The Urban Predicament,* edited by W. Gorham and N. Glazer. Washington, DC: The Urban Institute.

Demaris, Ovid. 1974. *Dirty Business.* New York: Avon Books.

Dentler, Robert. 1977. *Urban Problems: Perspectives and Solutions.* Chicago: Rand McNally.

DeSena, Judith. 1994. "Local Gatekeeping Practices and Residential Segregation." *Sociological Inquiry* 64(3): 307–15.

Deutsch, Claudia H. 1999. "Letting Little Go to Waste." *New York Times,* 17 March: C1, 8.

Devine, Joel, and James Wright. 1993. *The Greatest of Evils.* New York: Aldine de Gruyter.

DiGaetano, Alan. 1997. "Urban Governing Alignments and Realignments in Comparative Perspective." *Urban Affairs Review* 32(6):844–70.

DiGaetano, Alan, and Paul Lawless. 1999. "Urban Governance and Industrial Decline." *Urban Affairs Review* 34(4):546–77.

Dogan, Mattei, and John Kasarda. 1988. "Introduction: How Giant Cities Will Multiply and Grow." In *The Metropolis Era,* vol. 1, edited by M. Dogan and J. Kasarda. Beverly Hills: Sage.

Donahue, John. 1989. *The Privatization Decision: Public Ends, Private Means.* New York: Basic Books.

Downs, Anthony. 1973. *Opening Up the Suburbs: An Urban Strategy for America.* New Haven: Yale University.

———. 1998. "How America's Cities Are Growing." *Brookings Review* (Fall): 8–12.

Dreier, Peter. 1997. "The New Politics of Housing: How to Rebuild the Constituency for a Progressive Federal Housing Policy." *Journal of the American Planning Association* 63(1): 5–29.

Dreier, Peter, and John Atlas. 1994. "Reforming the Mansion Subsidy: Tax Break for the Rich." *The Nation* 258(17): 592–96.

Dreier, Peter, and J. David Hulchanski. 1993. "The Role of Nonprofit Housing in Canada and the U.S.: Some Comparisons." *Housing Policy Debate* 4(1): 43–80.

Ducharme, Donna. 1991. "Planned Manufacturing Districts: How a Community Initiative Became City Policy." In *Harold Washington and the Neighborhoods,* edited by P. Clavel and W. Wiewel. New Brunswick, NJ: Rutgers University Press.

Duncan, Greg. 1984. *Years of Poverty, Years of Plenty.* Ann Arbor: University of Michigan Institute for Survey Research.

Durkheim, Émile. 1947. *Division of Labor in Society.* Translated by G. Simpson. Glencoe, IL: Free Press.

———. 1951. *Suicide.* Translated by J. Spaulding and G. Simpson. Glencoe, IL: Free Press.

Durning, Alan. 1990. "Ending Poverty." In *State of the World 1990,* edited by L. Brown. New York: Norton.

Duster, Troy. 1987. "Crime, Youth Unemployment, and the Black Urban Underclass." *Crime and Delinquency* 33: 300–316.

Easterbrook, Gregg. 1990. "Everything You Know about the Environment Is Wrong." *New Republic,* 30 April.

Economist. 1996. "Will Crime Wave Goodbye?" 6 January: 19–20.

Edin, Kathryn, and Laura Lein. 1997. *Making Ends Meet: How Single Mothers Survive Welfare and Low-Wage Work.* New York: Russell Sage Foundation.

Edmondson, Brad. 1994. "Alone in the Driver's Seat." *American Demographics* (June): 44–57.

Eisinger, Peter. 1998. "City Politics in an Era of Devolution." *Urban Affairs Review* 33(3):308–25.

———. 2000. "The Politics of Bread and Circuses." *Urban Affairs Review* 35(3):316–33.

Eller, T. J. 1996. "Who Stays Poor? Who Doesn't?" U.S. Bureau of the Census, Household Economic Studies Series (June): 50–55.

Ellis, Mark, Richard Barff, and Ann Markusen. 1993. "Defense Spending and Interregional Labor Migration." *Professional Geographer* 45(3): 286–96.

Ellwood, David. 1988. *Poor Support: Poverty in the American Family.* New York: Basic Books.

European Environmental Protection Agency. 1997. "Air Pollution in Europe 1997." Monograph no. 4. http://reports.eea.eu/92-9167-059/en.

Fainstein, Susan S. 1996. "The Changing World-Economy and Urban Restructuring." In *Readings in Urban Theory,* edited by S. Fainstein and S. Campbell. Cambridge, MA: Blackwell.

Fainstein, Susan, and Norman Fainstein. 1989. "The Ambivalent State: Economic Development Policy Under the Reagan Administration." *Urban Affairs Quarterly* 25: 41–62.

Fainstein, Susan, and Michael Harloe. 1992. "Introduction: New York and London in the Contemporary World." In *Divided Cities: New York and London in the Contemporary World,* edited by S. Fainstein, I. Gordon, and M. Harloe. Cambridge, MA: Blackwell.

Fainstein, Susan S., and C. Hirst. 1995. "Urban Social Movements." In *Theories of Urban Politics,* edited by D. Judge, G. Stoker, and H. Wolman. Thousand Oaks, CA: Sage.

Fallows, James. 1986. "East Asia: Letter from Tokyo." *Atlantic Monthly* 258(2): 14–19.

———. 1989. "Tokyo: The Hard Life." *Atlantic Monthly* 263(3): 16–19.

Farley, Reynolds. 1964. "Suburban Persistence." *American Sociological Review* 29:38–47.

———. 1984. *Blacks and Whites: Narrowing the Gap?* Cambridge: Harvard University Press.

Farley, Reynolds, and William Frey. 1994. "Changes in the Segregation of Whites from Blacks during the 1980s." *American Sociological Review* 59(1): 23–45.

Farley, Reynolds, Howard Schuman, Suzanne Bianchi, Diane Colasanto, and Shirley Hatchett. 1978. "Chocolate City, Vanilla Suburbs." *Social Science Research* 7:319–44.

Farley, Reynolds, C. Stech, T. Jackson, M. Krysen, and K. Reeves. 1993. "Continued Racial Residential Segregation in Detroit: 'Chocolate City, Vanilla Suburbs' Revisited." *Journal of Housing Research* 4(1): 1–38.

Farley, R., C. Stech, M. Krysen, and T. Jackson. 1994. "Stereotypes and Segregation: Neighborhoods in the Detroit Area." *American Journal of Sociology* 100(3): 750–80.

Fava, Sylvia. 1975. "Beyond Suburbia." *Annals of the American Society of Political and Social Science* 422:10–24.

Feagin, Joe. 1988a. "Urban Real Estate Speculation in the United States." In *Critical Perspectives on Housing,* edited by R. Bratt, C. Hartman, and A. Meyerson. Philadelphia: Temple University Press.

———. 1988b. *Free Enterprise City: Houston in Political and Economic Perspective.* New Brunswick: Rutgers University Press.

Feldman, Robert. 1998. "Sputter, Cough, Choke: Japan Misfires as the Engine of Asia." *Brookings Review* (Summer):18–22.

Fine, Michelle. 1991. *Framing Dropouts: Notes on the Politics of an Urban Public High School.* Albany: SUNY Press.

Firebaugh, Glenn. 1979. "Structural Determinants of Urbanization in Asia and Africa." *American Sociological Review* 44:199–215.

Fischer, Claude. 1976. *The Urban Experience.* New York: Harcourt Brace Jovanovich.

———. 1981. "The Public and Private Worlds of City Life." *American Sociological Review* 46:306–16.

———. 1982. *To Dwell Among Friends.* Chicago: University of Chicago Press.

Fischer, Claude, Mark Baldassare, and Richard Ofshe. 1975. "Crowding Studies and Urban Life: A Critical Review." *Journal of the American Institute of Planners* 41: 406–18.

Fishman, Robert. 1987. *Bourgeois Utopias: The Rise and Fall of Suburbia.* New York: Basic.

Flanagan, William. 1990. *Urban Sociology: Images and Structures.* Needham Heights, MA: Allyn and Bacon.

———. 1993. "The Structural Roots of Action and the Questions of Convergence." In *Research in Urban Sociology: Urban Sociology in Transition,* edited by R. Hutchinson. Greenwich, OH: Jai Press.

———. 1995. *Urban Sociology.* 2d ed. Needham Heights, MA: Allyn and Bacon.

———. 1999. *Urban Sociology.* 3d ed. Needham Heights, MA: Allyn and Bacon.

Fordham, Signithia. 1988. "Racelessness as a Factor in Black Students' School Success." *Harvard Educational Review* 58(1): 54–84.

Francis, Diana. 1988. "Business as Usual in the Greed Game." *Maclean's,* 7 November.

Fremon, Charlotte. 1970. "The Occupational Pattern in Urban Employment Change, 1945–67." In Paper 114–31: 11. Washington, DC: Urban Institute.

French, Hilary. 1990. "Clearing the Air." In *State of the World: 1990,* edited by L. Brown. Washington, DC: Worldwatch Institute.

Frey, William. 1998. "The Diversity Myth." *American Demographics* 20(6):38–43.

Fried, Marc. 1969. "Grieving for a Lost Home." In *The Urban Condition,* edited by Leonard Duhl. New York: Simon and Schuster.

———. 1973. *The World of the Urban Working Class.* Cambridge: Harvard University.

Friedman, F. G. 1953. "The World of 'La Miseria'." *Partisan Review* 20:218–31.

Friedrichs, Jurgen. 1988. "Large Cities in Eastern Europe." In *The Metropolis Era,* vol. 1, edited by M. Dogan and J. Kasarda. Beverly Hills: Sage.

Galle, Omer, and Walter Gove. 1978. "Overcrowding, Isolation and Human Behavior: The Extremes in the Population Distribution." In *Social Demography,* edited by K. Tauber and F. Sweet. New York: Academic Press.

Gallup, George. 1976–77. "Human Needs and Satisfaction: A Global Survey." *Public Opinion Quarterly* 40:465–67.

Gandy, Matthew. 1994. *Recycling and the Politics of Urban Waste.* New York: St. Martin's.

Gans, Herbert J. 1962. *The Urban Villagers.* New York: Free Press.

Ganz, Alexander. 1985. "Where Has the Urban Crisis Gone?" *Urban Affairs Quarterly* 20:449–68.

Gappert, Gary. 1995. "Conclusion and Epilogue: The Future of Cities and Their Policies in the Global Economy." In *North American Cities and the Global Economy*, edited by Peter Kresl and Gary Gappert. Thousand Oaks, CA: Sage.

Garreau, Joel. 1991. *Edge City: Life on the New Frontier*. New York: Doubleday.

Geisse, Guillermo, and Francisco Sabatini. 1988. "Latin American Cities." In *The Metropolis Era*, vol. 1, edited by M. Dogan and J. Kasarda. Beverly Hills: Sage.

Gelles, Richard J., and Ann Levine. 1995. *Sociology: An Introduction*. New York: McGraw-Hill.

Gibbs, Jack, and Leo Schnore. 1960. "Metropolitan Growth: An International Study." *American Journal of Sociology* 66:160–70.

Gilbert, Alan. 1994. *The Latin American City*. London: Latin American Bureau.

Gilderbloom, John, and Richard Applebaum. 1988. *Rethinking Rental Housing*. Philadelphia: Temple University Press.

Gist, Noel, and Sylvia Fava. 1974. *Urban Society*. New York: Crowell.

Gittel, Marilyn. 1980. "The Impact of Community Organization on Urban School Systems." Address at the Sixth Annual Conference on the Urban South. Norfolk, VA.

Gladstone, David. 1998. "Tourism Urbanization in the United States." *Urban Affairs Review* 34(1):3–27.

Gleick, Elizabeth. 1995. "Segregation Anxiety." *Time* 145(17): 63–64.

Glenn, Jim. 1999. "The State of Garbage in America." *BioCycle* 40(4): 60–71.

Gluck, Peter, and Richard Meister. 1979. *Cities in Transition*. New York: Vintage.

Goldstein, Sidney. 1988. "Levels of Urbanization in China." In *The Metropolis Era*, vol. 1, edited by M. Dogan and J. Kasarda. Beverly Hills: Sage.

———. 1993. "The Impact of Temporary Migration on Urban Places: Thailand and China as Case Studies." In *Third World Cities, Problems, Policies, and Prospects*, edited by J. Kasarda and A. Parnell. Newbury Park, CA: Sage.

Goode, William. 1963. *World Revolution and Family Patterns*. New York: Free Press.

Goozner, Merrill. 1988. "Industrial Assignment for Colleges." *Chicago Tribune*, 11 September.

Gordon, David M. 1977. "Class Struggle and the Stages of American Urban Development." In *The Rise of the Sunbelt Cities*, edited by D. Perry and A. Watkins. Beverly Hills: Sage.

Gordon, Peter, and Harry Richardson. 2000. "Critiquing Sprawl's Critics." Cato Institute Policy Analysis no. 365.

Gorham, William, and Nathan Glazer, eds. 1976. *The Urban Predicament*. Washington, DC: The Urban Institute.

Gorov, Lynda. 1997. "A West Coast Comeback." *Boston Globe*, 8 June: E1, E7.

Gottdiener, Mark. 1977. *Planned Sprawl: Public and Private Interests in Suburbia*. Beverly Hills: Sage.

———. 1987. *The Decline of Urban Politics*. Newbury Park, CA: Sage.

———. 1994. *The New Urban Sociology*. New York: McGraw-Hill.

Gottdiener, Mark, and Ray Hutchison. 2000. *The New Urban Sociology.* 2d ed. New York: McGraw-Hill.

Gottman, Jean. 1964. *Megalopolis.* Cambridge: Massachusetts Institute of Technology.

Gove, Walter, Michael Hughes, and Omer Galle. 1979. "Overcrowding the Home: An Empirical Investigation of Its Possible Consequences." *American Sociological Review* 44: 59–80.

Greenwald, Gerald. 1990. "This Week with David Brinkley." *WAND-TV,* 4 March. Decatur, IL.

Greenwald, John. 1996. "A No-Win War Between the States." *Time,* 8 April: 44–45.

Greer, Scott. 1962. *Governing the Metropolis.* New York: John Wiley.

Greve, Frank. 1996. "Americans Demand More of Poor." *Rochester Democrat and Chronicle,* 4 August.

Griffith, Jeanne, Mary Frase, and John Ralph. 1989. "American Education: The Challenge of Change." *Population Bulletin* 44: 1–4.

Gueron, Judith M. 1993. "Welfare and Poverty: The Elements of Reform." *Yale Law and Policy Review* 11:113–125.

Guest, Avery. 1978. "Suburban Social Status: Persistence or Evolution?" *American Sociological Review* 43: 251–64.

Gugler, Josef. 1996. "Regional Trajectories in the Urban Transformation: Convergences and Divergences." In *The Urban Transformation of the Developing World,* edited by J. Gugler. Oxford: Oxford University.

———, ed. 1997. *Cities in the Developing World.* Oxford: Oxford University.

Habermas, Jurgen. 1975. *Legitimation Crisis.* Boston: Beacon.

Haggerty, Lee. 1971. "Another Look at the Burgess Hypothesis: Time As an Important Variable." *American Journal of Sociology* 76: 1084–93.

Hall, Peter. 1977. *World Cities.* 2d ed. New York: McGraw-Hill.

———. 1988. "Urban Growth and Decline in Western Europe." In *The Metropolis Era,* vol. 1, edited by M. Dogan and J. Kasarda. Beverly Hills: Sage.

Hannerz, Ulf. 1980. *Exploring the City: Inquiries Toward an Urban Anthropology.* New York: Columbia University.

Harding, Alan. 1995. "Elite Theory and Growth Machines." In *Theories of Urban Politics,* edited by D. Judge, G. Stoker, and H. Wolman. Thousand Oaks, CA: Sage.

Harris, Chauncey, and Edward Ullman. 1945. "The Nature of Cities." *Annals of the American Academy of Political and Social Science* 242: 7–17.

Harris, Marvin. 1981. *America Now.* New York: Simon and Schuster.

Hartley, Shirley. 1972. *Population Quantity vs. Quality.* Englewood Cliffs, NJ: Prentice-Hall.

Harvey, David. 1973. *Social Justice and the City.* Baltimore: Johns Hopkins University Press.

Hatfield, Larry. 1989. "Nation's Youth Ill-Prepared for Employment: Job Skills Scarce as Competition Rises." *San Francisco Examiner,* 6 August.

Hawley, Amos. 1950. *Human Ecology.* New York: Ronald Press.

———. 1971. *Urban Society.* New York: Ronald Press.

Haynes, Norris, and James Comer. 1990. "Helping Black Children Succeed: The Significance of Some Social Factors." In *Going to School: The African-American Experience,* edited by K. Lomotey. Albany: SUNY Press.

Hays, R. Allen. 1995. *The Federal Government and Urban Housing.* Albany: SUNY Press.

Henderson, Keith. 1993. "In Many States, Lawsuits Contest the Fairness of School Funding." *Christian Science Monitor,* 23 March: 1, 4.

Henderson, Yolanda. 1990. "Defense Cutbacks and the New England Economy." *New England Economic Review* (July-August): 3–24.

Hersh, Seymour. 1994. "The Wild East." *Atlantic Monthly* 273(8): 61–86.

Heumann, Leonard. 1979. "Housing Needs and Housing Solutions: Changes in Perspectives from 1968 to 1978." In *The Changing Structure of the City,* edited by G. Tobin. Beverly Hills: Sage.

Hogan, Dennis P., Ling-Xin Hao, and William L. Parrish. 1990. "Race, Kin Networks, and Assistance to Mother-Headed Families." *Social Forces* 68: 797–812.

Holmstrom, Nancy, and Richard Smith. 2000. "The Necessity of Gangster Capitalism: Primitive Accumulation in Russia and China." *Monthly Review* 51(9):1–15.

Houston, Jack. 1989. "It's All Aboard for Disabled as Metra OKs Lifts for Its Trains." *Chicago Tribune,* 16 September.

Hoxby, Caroline. 1995. Cited in *Business Week,* 17 April.

Hoyt, Homer. 1939. *The Structure and Growth of Residential Neighborhoods in American Cities.* Washington, DC: GPO.

Hughes, James. 1974. *Suburban Dynamics and the Future of the City.* New Brunswick, NJ: Center for Urban Policy Research.

———. 1996. "Economic Shifts and the Changing Homeownership Trajectory." *Housing Policy Debate* 7(2): 293–325.

Hundley, Tom. 1988. "Colleges Going to High Schools to Help Minorities Get Prepared." *Chicago Tribune,* 4 December.

Hunter, Floyd. 1952. *Community Power Structure.* Chapel Hill: University of North Carolina.

Ihlanfeldt, Keith, and David Sjoquist. 1998. "The Spatial Mismatch Hypothesis: A Review of Recent Studies and their Implications for Welfare Reform." *Housing Policy Debate* 9(4):849–92.

Irvine, Jacqueline. 1985. "Teacher Communication Patterns as Related to the Race and Sex of the Student." *Journal of Educational Research* 78(6): 338–45.

Jackson, Kenneth. 1985. *Crabgrass Frontier: The Suburbanization of the United States.* New York: Oxford University.

Jackson, Maggie. 1993. "All Fall Down." *Jacksonville Journal-Courier,* 27 December.

Jaffe, Greg, and Douglas Blackmon. 1998. "When UPS Demanded Workers, Louisville Did the Delivering." *Wall Street Journal,* 24 April.

James, Frank. 1996. "Clinton Proposes Major Fix Up for Schools." *Chicago Tribune,* 12 July.

Japan Institute of Policy Research. 2000. "Where Is Japan's Conservative Influence Headed?" <http://www.jipr.org/digest45.html>

Jargowsky, Paul. 1994. "Ghetto Poverty Among Blacks in the 1980s." *Journal of Policy Analysis and Management* 13: 288–310.

Jencks, Christopher. 1978. "What's Behind the Drop in Test Scores." *Working Papers for a New Society* (July/August): 29–41.

Jencks, Christopher, M. Smith, H. Acland, M. J. Bane, D. Cohen, H. Gintis, B. Heyns, and S. Michelson. 1972. *Inequality.* New York: Basic Books.

Jiminez, Gilbert. 1996. "U.S. Highways in Poor Shape, AAA Report Says." *Chicago Tribune,* 12 June.

Johnson, Dirk. 1996. "Wisconsin Welfare Effort on Schools Is a Failure, Study Says." *New York Times,* 19 May.

Johnson, Norman. 1987. *The Welfare State in Transition.* Amherst: University of Massachusetts.

Jones, Emrys. 1988. "London." In *The Metropolis Era,* vol. 2, edited by M. Dogan and J. Kasarda. Beverly Hills: Sage.

Jones-Wilson, N. Arnez, and C. Asbury. 1992. "Why Not Public Schools?" *Journal of Negro Education* 61(2): 125–37.

Judge, David. 1995. "Pluralism." In *Theories of Urban Politics,* edited by D. Judge, G. Stoker, and H. Wolman. Thousand Oaks, CA: Sage.

Judge, David, Gerry Stoker, and Harold Wolman, eds. 1995. *Theories of Urban Politics.* Thousand Oaks, CA: Sage.

Kain, John, and Kraig Singleton. 1996. "Equality of Educational Opportunity Revisited." *New England Economic Review* (May/June): 87–114.

Kamin, Blair, and David Ibata. 1990a. "Gridlock Finds Home in Suburbs." *Chicago Tribune,* 18 February.

———. 1990b. "Tollway Paves Suburbs' Road to Congestion. *Chicago Tribune,* 19 February.

———. 1990c. "Long Commutes Make Roads Work Overtime." *Chicago Tribune,* 20 February.

———. 1990d. "Mass Transit Mostly Runs on Empty." *Chicago Tribune,* 21 February.

Kantor, Paul. 1987. "The Dependent City: The Changing Political Economy of Urban Development in the United States." *Urban Affairs Quarterly* 22: 493–520.

Kantor, Paul, H.V. Savitch, and Serean Haddock. 1997. "The Political Economy of Urban Regimes." *Urban Affairs Review* 32(3):348–77.

Kapinos, Thomas. 1989. "Attitudes Toward Mass Transit." *Mass Transit* (April): 10–15.

Kaplan, Marshall. 1995. "Urban Policy: An Uneven Past, An Uncertain Future." *Urban Affairs Review* 30: 662–80.

Kasarda, John. 1989. "Urban Industrial Transition and the Underclass." *Annals of the American Academy of Political and Social Sciences* 501: 26–47.

———. 1993. "Inner-City Concentrated Poverty and Neighborhood Distress: 1970 to 1990." *Housing Policy Debate* 4(3): 253–302.

Kasarda, John, and Morris Janowitz. 1974. "Community Attachment in Mass Society." *American Sociological Review* 39: 328–39.

Kasarda, John, and Allan Parnell. 1993. "Introduction: Third World Development Issues." In *Third World Cities: Problems, Policies, and Prospects,* edited by J. Kasarda and A. Parnell. Newbury Park, CA: Sage.

Keating, Michael. 1995. "Size, Efficiency, and Democracy: Consolidation, Fragmentation and Public Choice." In *Theories of Urban Politics,* edited by D. Judge, G. Stoker, and H. Wolman. Thousand Oaks, CA: Sage.

Keating, W. Dennis. 1994. *The Suburban Racial Dilemma: Housing and Neighborhoods.* Philadelphia: Temple University Press.

Keith, Timothy, and Ellis Page. 1985. "Do Catholic High Schools Improve Minority Student Achievement?" *American Educational Research Journal* 22(3): 337–49.

Kelley, Allen, and Jeffrey Williamson. 1984. *What Drives Third World City Growth?* Princeton, NJ: Princeton University.

Kemp, Michael, and Melvyn Cheslow. 1976. "Transportation." In *The Urban Predicament,* edited by W. Gorham and N. Glazer. Washington, DC: Urban Institute.

Kendall, Peter, and Gary Washburn. 1996. "Gas-guzzling–1996 Style." *Chicago Tribune,* 6 July.

Kennedy, Randy, and John Sullivan. 1998. "Collapses of Buildings Prompt Flaws in City Inspections." *New York Times,* 23 September: A27.

Kerns, Wilmer, and Milton Glanz. 1988. "Private Social Welfare Expenditures, 1972–1985." *Social Security Bulletin* 51:4.

Keyser, Sheldon. 1999. "Stimulation of Rural Transit Connections: Effects of the St. Louis Light Rail Metro Expansion."

Kilborn, Peter T. 1995. "Michigan's Welfare System: Praise Amid Warning Signs." *New York Times,* 24 October.

Kim, Illsoo. 1981. *The New Urban Immigrants: The Korean Community in New York.* Princeton, NJ: Princeton University.

King, Sabrina. 1993. "The Limited Presence of African-American Teachers." *Review of Educational Research* 63(2): 115–49.

Kirby, Andrew. 1985. "Nine Fallacies of Local Economic Change." *Urban Affairs Quarterly* 21: 207–20.

Kirby, Joseph A. 1996. "Hartford Failure Raises Doubts About School Privatization." *Chicago Tribune,* 28 January.

Kleniewski, Nancy. 1984. "From Industrial to Corporate City: The Role of Urban Renewal." In *Marxism and the Metropolis,* edited by W. Tabb and L. Sawers. New York: Oxford University.

Knaap, Gerrit, Lewis D. Hopkins, and Chengri Ding. 1999. "Do Plans Matter? Effects of Light Rail Plans on Land Values in Station Areas." Lincoln Institute of Land Policy, working paper.

Koepp, Stephen. 1988. "Gridlock!" *Time,* 12 September: 52–60.

Kotler, Milton. 1969. *Neighborhood Government: The Local Foundations of Political Life.* Indianapolis, IN: Bobbs-Merrill.

Kozol, Jonathan. 1991. *Savage Inequalities.* New York: HarperCollins.

Kraar, Louis. 1988. "The Drug Trade." *Fortune,* 20 June: 27–38.

Kuczka, Susan. 1996. "Wisconsin Welfare Recipients Skeptical of Reform." *Chicago Tribune,* 25 May.

Lacayo, Richard. 1996. "Law and Order." *Time,* 15 January: 48, 50–53.

Larsen, Calvin, and Stan Nikkel. 1979. *Urban Problems.* Boston: Allyn and Bacon.

Lauria, Mickey, ed. 1997. *Reconstructing Urban Regime Theory.* Thousand Oaks, CA: Sage.

Lave, Charles A. 1979. "The Mass Transit Panacea." *The Atlantic Monthly* (October): 39–52.

Layton, Lyndsey. 2001. "And, You Don't Have to Look for Parking." *Washington Post National Weekly Edition*, April 23–29.

Lee, Sharon. 1998. "Asian Americans: Diverse and Growing." *Population Bulletin* 53(2): 1–40.

Lemann, Nicholas. 1988. "The Unfinished War." *Atlantic Monthly* (December): 37–56.

Leo, Christopher, with Mary Beavis, Andrew Carpenter, and Robyne Turner. 1998. "Is Suburban Sprawl Back on the Political Agenda?" *Urban Affairs Review* 34(2):179–212.

Levine, Daniel, and Eugene Eubanks. 1990. "Achievement Disparities Between Minority and Nonminority Students in Suburban Schools." *Journal of Negro Education* 59(2): 186–94.

Lewis, Dan A., and Kathryn Nakagawa. 1995. *Race and Educational Reform in the American Metropolis: A Study of School Decentralization.* Albany: SUNY Press.

Lewis, Oscar. 1966. "The Culture of Poverty." *Scientific American* 215: 3–9.

Li Minqi. 1996. "China: Six Years After Tiananmen." *Monthly Review* 47(8): 1–13.

Liebow, Elliot. 1993. *Tell Them Who I Am: The Lives of Homeless Women.* New York: Free Press.

Light, Ivan. 1972. *Ethnic Enterprise in America.* Berkeley: University of California Press.

———. 1983. *Cities in World Perspective.* New York: Macmillan.

Lineberry, Robert. 1970. "Reforming Metropolitan Governance: Requiem or Reality?" *Georgetown Law Journal* (March-May): 675–718.

Lipsky, Michael. 1976. "Toward a Theory of Street-Level Bureaucracy." In *Theoretical Perspectives on Urban Politics,* edited by W. Hawley et al. Englewood Cliffs, NJ: Prentice-Hall.

Logan, John. 1988. "Fiscal and Developmental Crises in Black Suburbs." In *Business Elites and Urban Development,* edited by S. Cummings. Albany: SUNY Press.

Logan, John, Richard Alba, and Thomas McNulty. 1996. "Ethnic Economics in Metropolitan Regions: Miami and Beyond." *Social Forces* 72(3): 691–724.

Logan, John, and Harvey Molotch. 1987. *Urban Fortunes: The Political Economy of Place.* Berkeley: University of California.

Logan, John, and Mark Schneider. 1981. "The Stratification of Metropolitan Suburbs, 1960–1970." *American Sociological Review* 46: 175–86.

Logan, John, Rachel Whaley, and Kyle Crowder. 1997. "The Character and Consequences of Growth Regimes." *Urban Affairs Review* 32(5):603–30.

Lowe, Marcia. 1993. "Rediscovering Rail." In *State of the World 1993,* edited by L. Brown. New York: W. W. Norton.

———. 1994. "The Global Rail Revival." *Society* (July/August): 54.

Lupsha, Peter, and William Siembieda. 1977. "The Poverty of Public Services in a Land of Plenty." In *The Rise of the Sunbelt Cities,* edited by D. Perry and A. Watkins. Beverly Hills: Sage.

Lynch, Peter. 1999. "Russia: Report Card on Survival." *Great Decisions 2000.* Washington, DC: Foreign Policy Association.

Lyon, Larry. 1987. *The Community in Urban Society.* Homewood, IL: Dorsey Press.

Macionis, John J. 1997. *Sociology.* 6th ed. Upper Saddle, NJ: Prentice-Hall.

Mackensen, Rainer. 1999. "Urban Decentralization Processes in Western Europe." In *Urban Change in the United States and Western Europe,* 2nd ed. Washington, DC: Urban Institute.

Maclennan, Duncan. 1993. "Decentralization and Residential Choices in European Cities: The Role of State and Market." In *Urban Change in the United States and Western Europe,* edited by A. Summers, P. Cheshire, and L. Senn. Washington, DC: Urban Institute.

MacLeod, Jay. 1995. *Ain't No Making It.* Boulder, CO: Westview Press.

Mallach, Alan. 1988. "Opening the Suburbs: New Jersey's Mt. Laurel Experience." *Shelterforce* (August/September): 12–15.

Mandel, Michael J., et al. 1995. "Will Schools Ever Get Better?" *Business Week,* 17 April: 65.

Marcuse, Peter. 1982. "Determinants of State Housing Policies: West Germany and the United States." In *Urban Policy Under Capitalism,* edited by N. Fainstein and S. Fainstein. Beverly Hills: Sage.

Marger, Martin. 1987. *Elites and Masses: An Introduction to Political Sociology.* Belmont, CA: Wadsworth.

Markusen, Ann, and Joel Yudken. 1991. *Dismantling the Cold War Economy.* New York: Basic Books.

Marsden, Peter. 1987. "Core Discussion Networks of Americans." *American Sociological Review* 52: 122–31.

Marshall, Alex. 1994. "The Quiet Integration of Suburbia." *American Demographics* 16(8): 9–13.

Marshall, Harvey. 1979. "White Movement to the Suburbs." *American Sociological Review* 44: 975–94.

Massey, Douglas S. 1996. "Concentrating Poverty Breeds Violence." *Population Today* (June/July): 5.

Massey, Douglas, and Nancy Denton. 1993. *American Apartheid: Segregation and the Making of the Underclass.* Cambridge: Harvard University Press.

Mayer, Harold, and Richard Wade. 1969. *Chicago: Growth of a Metropolis.* Chicago: University of Chicago.

Mayer, Susan, and Christopher Jencks. 1989. "Growing Up in Poor Neighborhoods: How Much Does It Matter?" *Science* 243: 1441–45.

McAneny, Leslie, and Lydia Saad. 1994. "America's Public Schools: Still Separate? Still Unequal?" *Gallup Poll Monthly* (May): 23–33.

McConnaughey, Janet. 1994. "Retreads: Some New Ideas for Old Tires." *Chicago Tribune,* 26 June.

McGahey, Richard. 1986. "Economic Conditions, Neighborhood Organization, and Urban Crime." In *Communities and Crime,* edited by A. J. Reiss and M. Tonry. Chicago: University of Chicago.

McLanahan, Sara, Irwin Garfinkel, and Dorothy Watson. 1988. "Family Structure, Poverty and the Underclass." In *Urban Change and Poverty,* edited by M. McGreary and L. Lynn. Washington, DC: National Academy Press.

McMichael, Philip. 2000. *Development and Social Change.* 2d ed. Thousand Oaks, CA: Pine Forge.

Mendell, David. 2000. "Daley Following in Footsteps of Father." *Chicago Tribune,* 20 July:1, 14.

Milgram, Stanley. 1970. "The Experience of Living in Cities." *Science* 167: 1461–68.

Miller, Randi. 1990. "Beyond Contact Theory." *Youth and Society* 22(l): 12–34.

Mishel, Lawrence, Jared Bernstein, and John Schmitt. 1996. *State of Working America, 1996–97.* Washington, DC: Economic Policy Institute.

Mishel, Lawrence, Jared Bernstein, and John Schmitt. 1999. *State of Working America, 1998–99.* Washington, DC: Economic Policy Institute.

Mok, Ka-ho. 2000. *Social and Political Development in Post-Reform China.* New York: St. Martin's.

Molotch, Harvey. 1988. "Strategies and Constraints on Growth Elites." In *Business Elites and Urban Development,* edited by S. Cummings. Albany: SUNY Press.

Monti, Daniel. 1999. *The American City: A Social and Cultural History.* Malden, MA: Blackwell.

Moore, Taylor. 1996. "Load Monitoring." *EPRI Journal* (March/April): 13–15.

Morgan, David, and Michael Hirlinger. 1993. "The Dependent City and Intergovernmental Aid." *Urban Affairs Quarterly* 29: 256–75.

Muller, Peter. 1981. *Contemporary Suburban America.* Englewood Cliffs, NJ: Prentice-Hall.

Muller, Peter O. 1997. "The Suburban Transformation of the Globalizing American City." *Annals of the American Academy of Political and Social Science* 551 (May):234–47.

Muller, Thomas. 1993. *Immigrants and the American City.* New York: NYU Press.

Murphey, Rhoads. 1988. "Shanghai." In *The Metropolis Era,* vol. 2, edited by M. Dogan and J. Kasarda. Beverly Hills: Sage.

Murray, Charles. 1984. *Losing Ground: American Social Policy 1950–1980.* New York: Basic Books.

Myers, Linnet. 1995. "Cultural Divide over Crime and Punishment." *Chicago Tribune,* 13 October.

Nadakavukaren, Anne. 2000. *Our Global Environment.* 5th ed. Prospect Heights, IL: Waveland Press.

Nagpaul, Hans. 1988. "India's Great Cities." In *The Metropolis Era,* vol. 2, edited by M. Dogan and J. Kasarda. Beverly Hills: Sage.

Nakamura, Hachiro, and James White. 1988. "Tokyo." In *The Metropolis Era,* vol. 2, edited by M. Dogan and J. Kasarda. Beverly Hills: Sage.

National Center for Education Statistics. 1989. *Digest of Education Statistics.* Washington, DC: U.S. Department of Education.

———. 2001. *Digest of Education Statistics, 2000.* Washington, DC: U.S. Department of Education, NCES-2001-034.

New York Times. 1996. "Spelling the End of Welfare as We Know It." 4 August.

Newman, Sandra, and Ann Schnare. 1993. "Last in a Line: Housing Assistance for Households with Children." *Housing Policy Debate* 4(3): 417–56.

Newton, Kenneth. 1976. "Feeble Governments and Private Power: Urban Politics and Policies in the United States." In *The New Urban Politics,* edited by L. Masotti and R. Lineberry. Cambridge, MA: Ballinger.

———. 1978. "Conflict Avoidance and Conflict Suppression: The Case of the United States." In *Urbanization and Conflict Market Societies,* edited by K. Cox. Chicago, IL: Maaroufa.

Nifong, Christina. 1996. "School Privatization Heads to Remedial-Education Class." *Christian Science Monitor,* 2 February: 12.

Nisbet, Robert. 1970. *The Social Bond.* New York: Knopf.

Nivola, Pietro. 1998. "Fat City: Understanding American Urban Form from a Transatlantic Perspective." *Brookings Review* (Fall): 17–19.

Numbers News. Published by American Demographics. Ithaca, NY. Various dates.

Oakes, Jeannie. 1985. *Keeping Track: How Schools Structure Inequality.* New Haven: Yale University Press.

O'Connor, James. 1973. *The Fiscal Crisis of the State.* New York: St. Martin's Press.

Ogbu, John. 1990. "Literacy and Schooling in Subordinate Cultures: The Case of Black Americans." In *Going to School: The African-American Experience,* edited by K. Lomotey. Albany: SUNY Press.

———. 1991. "Minority Coping Responses and School Experience." *Journal of Psychohistory* 18(4): 433–56.

Ogintz, Eileen. 1989a. "'Adopting the Future: Millionaire Shares a Dream So Kids Can Make College Come True." *Chicago Tribune,* 2 November.

———. 1989b. "Education Inc.: Business and Community Leaders Merge So Inner-City Kids Can Profit." *Chicago Tribune,* 4 December.

Oliver, Melvin, and Thomas Shapiro. 1995. *Black Wealth / White Wealth: New Perspectives on Racial Inequality.* New York: Routledge.

Orfield, Gary. 1994. "Housing and the Justification of School Segregation." *University of Pennsylvania Law Review* 143(5): 1397–1406.

Orfield, Myron. 1997. *Metropolitics.* Rev. ed. Washington, DC: Brookings Institution.

———. 1998. "Conflict or Consensus." *Brookings Review* (Fall): 31–34.

Orleans, Peter, and Miriam Orleans. 1976. *Urban Life: Diversity and Inequality.* Dubuque, IA: Brown.

Ornstein, Allan, and Daniel Levine. 1985. *Introduction to the Foundations of Education.* Boston: Houghton Mifflin.

Ostrom, Elinor. 1983. "The Social Stratification-Government Inequality Thesis Explored." *Urban Affairs Quarterly* 19:91–112.

Our Nation's Highways: Selected Facts and Figures. 1995. Washington, DC: U.S. Department of Transportation.

Our Nation's Highways: Selected Facts and Figures. 1998. Washington, DC: Federal Highway Administration, U.S. Department of Transportation.

Overholser, Geneva. 2000. "Mass Transit Making a Comeback." *Chicago Tribune,* 21 June:1, 11.

PACE. 2001. Personal communication.

Page, Clarence. 1996. "Reality Check on School Vouchers." *Chicago Tribune,* 13 March.

Pahl, Raymond. 1977. "Managers, Technical Experts and the State." In *Captive Cities,* edited by M. Harloe. New York: John Wiley.

Palen, John. 1987 (1975). *The Urban World.* New York: McGraw-Hill.

Pammer, J. 1990. *Managing Fiscal Stress in Major Cities.* New York: Greenwood.

Park, Kee Ok. 1994. "Expenditure Patterns and Interactions among Local Governments in Metropolitan Areas." *Urban Affairs Review* 29:535–64.

Parker, R. Andrew. 1995. "Patterns of Federal Urban Spending: Central Cities and Their Suburbs, 1983–1992." *Urban Affairs Review* 31:184–205.

Parkinson, Michael. 1979. "Dilemmas for the City Schools: Racial Isolation and Fiscal Stress." In *The Changing Structure of the City,* edited by G. Tobin. Beverly Hills: Sage.

Parks, Roger, and Ronald Oakerson. 1989. "Metropolitan Organization and Governance: A Local Public Economy Approach." *Urban Affairs Quarterly* 25:18–29.

Parsons, Talcott. 1969. *Societies in Evolutionary and Comparative Perspective.* Englewood Cliffs, NJ: Prentice-Hall.

Passel, Jeffrey. 1994. "Immigrants and Taxes: A Reappraisal of Huddle's 'The Cost of Immigrants'." Washington, DC: Urban Institute.

Passell, Peter. 1995. "With Cheap Fixes Completed, the Cost of Clean Air May Exceed the Benefits." *New York Times,* 19 December.

Passe-Smith, John. 1993. "The Persistence of the Gap: Taking Stock of Economic Growth in the Post-World War II Era." In *Development and Underdevelopment: The Political-Economy of Inequality,* edited by M. Seligson and J. Passe-Smith. Boulder, CO: Lynne Rienner.

Pearce, Diana. 1990. "Women and Housing." Washington, DC: Wider Opportunities for Women (mimeo).

Pempel, T.J. 1999. "Unsteady Anticipation: Reflections on the Future of Japan's Political-Economy." In *International Order and the Future of World Politics,* edited by T.V. Paul and J. Hall. Cambridge: Cambridge University.

Penner, Rudolf. 1998. *A Brief History of State and Local Fiscal Policy.* The Urban Institute.

Perrucci, C., R. Perrucci, D. Targ, and H. Targ. 1988. *Plant Closings.* Boston: Aldine de Gruyter.

Perry, David. 1987. "The Politics of Dependency in Deindustrializing America: The Case of Buffalo, New York." In *The Capitalist City,* edited by M. Smith and J. Feagin. New York: Basil Blackwell.

Petersen, George. 1976. "Finance." In *The Urban Predicament,* edited by W. Gorham and N. Glazer. Washington, DC: The Urban Institute.

Peterson, Paul. 1985. *The New Urban Reality.* Washington, DC: Brookings.

Phillips, E. Barbara. 1996. *City Lights: Urban-Suburban Life in the Global Society.* 2d ed. New York: Oxford University.

Pilzer, Paul. 1989. *Other People's Money: The Inside Story of the S & L Mess.* New York: Simon and Schuster.

Piven, Frances, and Richard Cloward. 1971. *Regulating the Poor: The Functions of Public Welfare.* New York: Vintage.

Polsby, Nelson. 1963. *Community Power and Political Theory.* New Haven: Yale University.

Popenoe, David. 1985. *Private Pleasure, Public Plight: American Metropolitan Community Life in Comparative Perspective.* New Brunswick, NJ: Transaction Books.

Popkin, Susan, Larry Buron, Diane Levy, and Mary Cunningham. 2000. "The Gautreaux Legacy: What Might Mixed-Income and Dispersed Strategies Mean for the Poorest Public Housing Tenants?" *Housing Policy Debate* 11(4): 911–42.

Poplin, Dennis. 1979. *Communities: A Survey of Theories and Methods of Research.* New York: Macmillan.

Popple, Philip, and Leslie Leighninger. 1990. *Social Work, Social Welfare, and American Society.* Needham Heights, MA: Allyn and Bacon.

Population Today. Various dates.

Portes, Alejandro, and Ruben Rumbaut. 1996. *Immigrant America: A Portrait.* 2d ed. Berkeley: University of California Press.

Postel, Sandra. 1985. "Managing Fresh Water Supplies." In *State of the World: 1985,* edited by L. Brown. Washington, DC: Worldwatch Institute.

———. 1990. "Saving Water for Agriculture." In *State of the World: 1990,* edited by L. Brown. Washington, DC: Worldwatch Institute.

———. 1992. *Last Oasis: Facing Water Scarcity.* New York: W. W. Norton.

———. 1996. "Forging a Sustainable Water Strategy." In *State of the World: 1996,* edited by L. Brown. New York: W. W. Norton.

President's Commission on Law Enforcement and the Administration of Justice. 1967. *Task Force Report: Organized Crime.* Washington, DC: GPO.

Prewda, Bob. 1989. "Effectively Marketing Community Transportation." *Community Transportation Reporter* 7:8–9.

Pucher, John, and Christian Lefevre. 1996. *The Urban Transport Crisis in Europe and North America.* London: Macmillan.

Pucher, John, and Fred Williams. 1992. "Socioeconomic Characteristics of Urban Travelers: Evidence from the 1990–91 NPTS." *Transportation Quarterly* (October): 561–81.

Puma, Michael. 1997. "The Prospects Study and Desegregation." *Journal of Negro Education* 66(3): 330–35.

Putnam, Robert D. 1995. "Bowling Alone: America's Declining Social Capital." *Journal of Democracy* 6:65–78.

Quintanilla, Ray. 2000a. "Vallas Backs Night High Schools." *Chicago Tribune,* 3 March:1,12.

———. 2000b. "Truant Solution Still Often Absent." *Chicago Tribune,* 22 April:1,15.

Rank, Mark. 1994. *Living on the Edge: The Realities of Welfare in America.* New York: Columbia University Press. Reviewed by Katherine S. Newman in *Social Service Review* (March 1996): 159–61.

Raspberry, William. 1996. "Welfare Reform, Wisconsin Style." *Washington Post,* 22–28 July.

Reardon, Kenneth M. 1997. "State and Local Revitalization Efforts in East St. Louis, Illinois." *Annals of the American Academy of Political and Social Science* 551(May):234–47.

Redfield, Robert. 1947. "The Folk Society." *American Journal of Sociology* 52:293–308.

Reich, Robert. 1991. *The Work of Nations.* New York: Alfred A. Knopf.

Reid, Sue. 1988. *Crime and Criminology.* New York: Holt, Rinehart and Winston.

Reischauer, Robert. 1978. "The Economy, the Federal Budget and Urban Aid." In *The Fiscal Outlook for Cities,* edited by R. Bahl. Syracuse, NY: Syracuse University.

Reisner, Marc. 1989. "The Emerald Desert." *Greenpeace* (July/August): 6–10.

Renner, Michael. 1988. *Rethinking the Role of the Automobile.* Worldwatch Paper 84. Washington, DC: Worldwatch Institute.

———. 1989. "Rethinking Transportation." In *State of the World: 1989,* edited by L. Brown. Washington, DC: Worldwatch Institute.

Reuss, Alejandro. 1996. "Scapegoating Immigrants." *Dollars and Sense* 208:22.

Richardson, Harry. 1993. "Efficiency and Welfare in LDC Mega-Cities." In *Third World Cities: Problems, Policies, and Prospects,* edited by J. Kasarda and A. Parnell. Newbury Park, CA: Sage.

Rimer, Sara. 1996. "Upheaval and Calm as Big Dig Transforms Boston." *New York Times,* 28 April.

Ritter, John. 1996. "Public Housing Is Making an About-Face." *USA Today,* 15 November.

Rivkin, Steven. 1994. "Residential Segregation and School Integration." *Sociology of Education* 67(4): 279–95.

Roanoke Times and World News. 1990. "Pollution in the Wake of Stalinism." 28 January.

Robinson, Tracey. 1987. "Dropouts Get New Chances at School, Success." *Chicago Sun-Times,* 15 June.

Roethlisberger, Fritz, and William Dickson. 1939. *Management and the Worker.* Cambridge: Harvard University.

Rondinelli, Dennis. 1988. "Giant City Growth in Africa." In *The Metropolis Era,* vol. 1, edited by M. Dogan and J. Kasarda. Beverly Hills: Sage.

Rosenbaum, James E. 1995. "Changing the Geography of Opportunity by Expanding Residential Choice: Lessons from the Gautreaux Program." *Housing Policy Debate* 6(l): 231–69.

Rossell, Christine. 1995. "Controlled-Choice Desegregation Plans: Not Enough Choice, Too Much Control?" *Urban Affairs Review* 31(l): 43–54.

Rossell, Christine, and David Armor. 1996. "The Effectiveness of School Desegregation Plans, 1968–1991." *American Politics Quarterly* 24(3): 227–36.

Rubin, Beth A. 1996. *Shifts in the Social Contract. Understanding Change in American Society.* Thousand Oaks, CA: Pine Forge Press.

Rubin, Irene, and Herbert Rubin. 1987. "Economic Development Incentives." *Urban Affairs Quarterly* 23:37–62.

Rubin, Lillian B. 1994. *Families on the Fault Line.* New York: HarperCollins.

Rumbaut, Ruben. 1996. "Origins and Destinies: Immigrants, Race, and Ethnicity in Contemporary America." In *Origins and Destinies,* edited by Sylvia Pedraza and Ruben Rumbaut. Belmont, CA: Wadsworth.

Rusk, David. 1993. *Cities Without Suburbs.* Washington, DC: Woodrow Wilson Center.

Sachs, Ignacy. 1988. "Vulnerability of Giant Cities and the Life Lottery." In *The Metropolis Era,* vol. 1, edited by M. Dogan and J. Kasarda. Beverly Hills: Sage.

Salama, Jerry. 1999. "The Redevelopment of Distressed Public Housing: Early Results from HOPE VI Projects in Atlanta, Chicago, and San Antonio." *Housing Policy Debate* 10(1):95–142.

Salholz, E., M. Reese, and L. Buckley. 1988. "California's Slow Growth Spurt." *Newsweek,* 26 September: 26.

Saltman, Juliet. 1989. *A Fragile Movement: The Struggle for Neighborhood Stabilization.* Westport, CT: Greenwood Press.

Sassen, Saskia. 1990. "Economic Restructuring and the American City." *Annual Review of Sociology* 16:465–90.

———. 1994. *Cities in a World Economy.* Thousand Oaks, CA: Pine Forge.

———. 1996. *Losing Control? Sovereignty in an Age of Globalization.* New York: Columbia University.

———. 2000. *Cities in a World Economy.* 2d ed. Thousand Oaks, CA: Pine Forge.

Sassen-Koob, Saskia. 1984. "The New Labor Demand in Global Cities." In *Cities in Transformation,* edited by M. P. Smith. Beverly Hills: Sage.

Sassen-Koob, Saskia. 1987. "Growth and Informalization at the Core." In *The Capitalist City,* edited by J. Feagin and M. P. Smith. New York: Basil Blackwell.

Schevitz, Tanya. 2000. "Closing the Faculty Housing Gap." *San Francisco Chronicle,* 7 July. <http://www.sfgate.com>

Schnore, Leo. 1972. *Class and Race in Cities.* Chicago: Markham.

Schteingart, Martha. 1988. "Mexico City." In *The Metropolis Era,* vol. 2, edited by M. Dogan and J. Kasarda. Beverly Hills: Sage.

Seeman, Melvin. 1958. "On the Meaning of Alienation." *American Sociological Review* 24:783–91.

Shannon, Thomas R. 1980. "Traditional Mass Transit in Southern Cities: A Mistaken Priority." *The Sixth Annual Conference on the Urban South.* Norfolk, VA: Norfolk State University.

———. 1996. *An Introduction to the World-System Perspective.* 2d ed. Boulder, CO: Westview.

Sharff, Jagna. 1987. "The Underground Economy of a Poor Neighborhood." In *Cities of the United States,* edited by L. Mullings. New York: Columbia University.

Shepard, Jon M. 1996. *Sociology.* 6th ed. St. Paul: West Publishing.

Shevky, Eshrev, and Wendell Bell. 1955. *Social Area Analysis.* Stanford, CA: Stanford University.

Shorter, Edward. 1975. *The Making of the Modern Family.* New York: Basic Books.

Shujaa, Mwalimu. 1992. "Afrocentric Transformation and Parental Choice in African American Independent Schools." *Journal of Negro Education* 61(2): 148–59.

Sites, William. 1997. "The Limits of Urban Regime Theory." *Urban Affairs Review* 32(4):536–71.

Sjoberg, Gideon. 1960. *The Pre-Industrial City: Past and Present.* New York: Free Press.

Skolnick, A. S. 1992. *The Intimate Environment.* New York: HarperCollins.

Slater, Phillip. 1970. *The Pursuit of Loneliness.* 1970. Boston: Allyn and Bacon.

Smelser, Neil. 1967. "Process of Social Change." In *Sociology: An Introduction,* edited by N. Smelser. New York: John Wiley.

Smith, David. 1996. *Third World Cities in Global Perspective: The Political Economy of Uneven Urbanization.* Boulder, CO: Westview.

Smith, Joel. 1970. "Another Look at Socioeconomic Status Distributions in Urbanized Areas." *Urban Affairs Quarterly* 5:423–53.

Smith, Neil. 1984. *Uneven Development.* New York: Basil Blackwell.

So, Alvin, and Stephen Chiu. 1995. *East Asia and the World Economy.* Thousand Oaks, CA: Sage.

Solnick, Steven. 1998. *Stealing the State.* Cambridge: Harvard University.

Spates, James, and John Macionis. 1987. *Sociology of Cities.* Belmont, CA: Wadsworth.

Squires, Gregory. 1994. *Capital and Communities in Black and White.* Albany: SUNY Press.

Stahura, John. 1979. "Suburban Status Evolution and Persistence." *American Sociological Review* 44:937–47.

Stark, Oded. 1980. "On Slowing Metropolitan City Growth." *Population and Development Review* 6:95–102.

Steglich, W. G., and Margaret Snooks. 1980. *American Social Problems*. Santa Monica, CA: Goodyear.

Stein, David. 1994. "Chicago Commuters: Increasing the Traffic Blues." *Streetwise* (May): 12.

Stein, Robert. 1989. "Market Maximization of Individual Preferences and Metropolitan Service Responsibility." *Urban Affairs Quarterly* 25: 86–116.

Stern, Richard, and Claire Poole. 1989. "Like a Slaughter-House for Hogs." *Forbes,* 25 December: 42–44.

Sterngold, James. 1994. "Life in a Box: Japanese Question Fruits of Success." *New York Times,* 2 January.

Stoker, Jerry. 1995. "Regime Theory and Urban Politics." In *Theories of Urban Politics,* edited by D. Judge, G. Stoker, and H. Wolman. Thousand Oaks, CA: Sage.

Stoll, Clifford. 1989. *The Cuckoo's Egg: Tracking a Spy Through the Maze of Computer Espionage*. New York: Doubleday.

Stone, Clarence. 1989. *Regime Politics: Governing Atlanta, 1946–1988*. University Press of Kansas.

———. 1993. "Urban Regimes and the Capacity to Govern." *Journal of Urban Affairs* 15:1–28.

———. 1995. "Political Leadership in Urban Politics." In *Theories of Urban Politics,* edited by D. Judge, G. Stoker, and H. Wolman. Thousand Oaks, CA: Sage.

Stone, Michael. 1986. "Housing and the Dynamics of U.S. Capitalism." In *Critical Perspectives on Housing,* edited by R. Bratt, C. Hartman, and A. Meyerson. Philadelphia: Temple University.

Sullivan, Kathleen. 2000. "Paving Our Way to L.A." *Seattle Post-Intelligencer,* 6 January:A13.

Sutherland, Edwin. 1949. *White Collar Crime*. New York: Holt, Rinehart and Winston.

Swinton, David. 1993. "The Economic Status of African Americans During the Reagan-Bush Era: Withered Opportunities, Limited Outcomes, Uncertain Outlook." In *The State of Black America,* edited by B. J. Tidwell. Washington, DC: National Urban League.

Synder, Jack. 1999. "Russia: Responses to Relative Decline." In *International Order and the Future of World Politics,* edited by T. V. Paul and J. Hall. Cambridge: Cambridge University.

Szabo, Joan. 1989. "Our Crumbling Infrastructure." *Nation's Business* (August): 16-17, 22–24.

Taeuber, Karl, and Alma Taeuber. 1965. *Negroes in Cities*. New York: Atheneum.

Teune, Henry. 1988. "Growth and Pathologies of Giant Cities." In *The Metropolis Era,* vol. 1, edited by M. Dogan and J. Kasarda. Beverly Hills: Sage.

Thomas, Clayton, and H. V. Savitch. 1991. "Introduction: Big City Politics Then and Now" and "Conclusion: End of the Millennium Big City Politics." In *Big City Politics in Transition,* edited by H. V. Savitch and J. Thomas. Newbury Park, CA: Sage.

Thomas, Melvin. 1993. "Race, Class, and Personal Income: An Empirical Test of the Declining Significance of Race Thesis, 1968–1988." *Social Problems* 40(3): 328–42.

Thomas, Melvin, Cedric Herring, and H. D. Horton. 1994. "Discrimination over the Life Course: A Synthetic Cohort Analysis of Earnings Differences

Between Black and White Males, 1940–1990." *Social Problems* 41(4): 608–28.

Thomas, Pierre. 1995. "Bias and the Badge." *Washington Post,* 18–24 December.

Tilly, Chris. 1996. *Half a Job: Bad and Good Part-Time Jobs in a Changing Labor Market.* Philadelphia: Temple University Press.

Timmer, Doug, D. Stanley Eitzen, and Kathryn Tulley. 1994. *Paths to Homelessness: Extreme Poverty and the Urban Housing Crisis.* Boulder, CO: Westview Press.

Todaro, Michael. 1984. "Urbanization in Developing Nations: Trends, Prospects, and Policies." In *Urban Development in the Third World,* edited by P. Ghosh. Westport, CT: Greenwood Press.

Tönnies, Ferdinand. 1957. *Community and Society.* East Lansing: Michigan State University.

Transit in Toronto. 1987. Toronto: Toronto Transit Commission.

Uehara, Edwina. 1990. "Dual Exchange Theory, Social Networks, and Informal Support." *American Journal of Sociology* 96:521–57.

Ungar, Sanford J. 1995. *Fresh Blood: The New American Immigrants.* New York: Simon and Schuster.

United Nations. 1996. *Survival in the Cities: Urban Poverty and Economic Development.* New York: United Nations Department of Public Information. <http://www.un.org/esa/socdev/iyephab/html>

United Nations Environment and World Health Organization. 1994. "Air Pollution in the World's Megacities." *Environment* 36(2):4–37.

United Nations Population Division. 1999. *World Urbanization Prospects: The 1999 Revision.* New York: United Nations.

U.S. Bureau of Labor Statistics. 1996. "Displaced Workers Who Lost Full-Time Wage and Salary Jobs." *Labor Force Statistics from the Current Population Survey,* table 7. Washington, DC: U.S. Bureau of Labor Statistics.

———. 2001. *Labor Force Statistics from the Current Population Survey.* Washington, DC: GPO.

U.S. Census Bureau. 1973. *Census of the Population, 1970.* Vol. 1: Characteristics of the Population. Washington, DC: GPO.

———. 1979. *The Journey to Work.* Washington, DC: GPO.

———. 1990. *1990 Census of the Population, General Population Characteristics.* Washington, DC: GPO.

———. 1994. *Population Distribution and Population Estimates.* PPL-27, table 3. Washington, DC: GPO.

———. 1995. *Statistical Abstract of the U.S. 1995.* Washington, DC: GPO.

———. 1996a. "Sociodemographic Data: Population." Table 3, Distribution of Population by Region, Residence, Age, Sex, and Race. Washington, DC: GPO.

———. 1996b. "Sociodemographic Data: School." Table A-5, Persons 14 to 24 Years Old By High School, Graduate School, College Enrollment, Attainment, Gender, Race, and Hispanic Origin. Washington, DC: GPO.

———. 1996c. "How We're Changing: Demographic State of the Nation: 1996." Current Population Reports, Special Studies Series P-23-191. Washington, DC: GPO.

———. 1996d. "A Brief Look at Post-War U.S. Income Inequality." Current Population Reports, Series P-60-19 1. Washington, DC: GPO.

———. 1999a. *Statistical Abstract of the U.S. 1999.* Washington, DC: GPO.

U.S. Census Bureau. 1999b. *American Housing Survey*. Washington, DC: GPO.

————. 2000a. "Population Trends in Metropolitan Areas and Central Cities, 1990 to 1998." Current Population Reports P25–1133. Washington, DC: GPO.

————. 2000b. "Poverty in the United States, 1999." Current Population Reports P60–210. Washington, DC: GPO.

————. 2000c. "The Foreign-Born Population in the United States, March 1999." Current Population Reports P20–519. Washington, DC: GPO.

————. 2000d. "Resident Population of the 50 States, the District of Columbia, and Puerto Rico: Census 2000." <www.census.gov/population/www.cen2000>

————. 2000e. *Current Population Survey* (March, table 21). Washington, DC: GPO.

————. 2000f. *American Housing Survey, 1999*. Washington, DC: GPO.

————. 2001a. *Poverty in the United States, 2000*. Washington, DC: GPO.

————. 2001b. *Statistical Abstract of the United States, 2000*. Washington, DC: GPO.

————. 2001c. *Household Net Worth and Asset Ownership, 1995*. Washington, DC: GPO.

————. 2001d. *Money Income in the United States, 2000*. Washington, DC: GPO.

U.S. Department of Housing and Urban Development (HUD). 1995. *Empowerment: A New Covenant with America's Communities*. President Clinton's National Urban Policy Report. Washington, DC: GPO.

————. 1998. *State of the Cities, 1998*. Washington, DC: GPO.

————. 1999. *State of the Cities, 1999*. Washington, DC: GPO.

————. 2000. *State of the Cities, 2000*. Washington, DC: GPO.

U.S. Department of Labor. 2001. *The Value of the Federal Minimum Wage, 1938–2000*. Washington, DC: GPO.

U.S. Department of Transportation. 1992. "Commuter Rail State of the Art: A Study of Current Systems." Washington, DC: GPO.

————. 1994a. "Commuting Alternatives in the United States: Recent Trends and a Look to the Future." Washington, DC: GPO.

————. 1994b. "Selected Highway Statistics and Charts." Federal Highway Administration, FHWA-IL-96-005. Washington, DC: GPO.

————. 1999. *Conditions and Performance Report: Highway, Bridge, and Transit Finance*. Washington, DC: GPO.

U.S. Environmental Protection Agency. 2001a. *Latest Findings on National Air Quality: 2000 Status and Trends*. Office of Air Quality Planning and Standards, EPA 454/K-01-002.

————. 2001b. www.epa.gov/air/urbanair/ozone/hlth.html. Accessed 11-6-2001.

————. 2001c. *Progress Report on the EPA Acid Rain Program*. www.epa.gov/airmarkt/arp/overview.html. Accessed 11-5-2001.

————. 2001d. Office of Solid Waste. www.epa.gov/epaswer/non-hw/muncpl/facts.html. Accessed 11-7-01.

U.S. Federal Bureau of Investigation. Various years. *Crime in the United States*. Washington, DC: GPO.

U.S. Immigration and Naturalization Service. 1999. *Statistical Yearbook of the INS, 1997*. Washington, DC: GPO.

Verhovek, Sam Howe. 1993. "Rich Schools, Poor Schools, Never-Ending Litigation." *New York Times*, 30 May.

"A Vision for Regional Public Transportation." 1994. Issue Brief, Metropolitan Planning Council (October): 2–4.

vonHoffman, Alexander. 1996. "High Ambitions: The Past and Future of American Low-Income Housing Policy." *Housing Policy Debate* 7(3): 423–46.

Wacquant, Lois, and William J. Wilson. 1989. "The Cost of Racial and Class Exclusion in the Inner City." *Annals of the American Academy of Political and Social Science* 501:8–25.

Walberer, Julie. 1989. "Metra, Disabled Must Keep Harmony." *Chicago Tribune*, 14 October.

Waldman, Steve. 1989. "The HUD Ripoff." *Newsweek*, 7 August: 16–22.

Waley, Paul. 2000. "Tokyo: Patterns Familiarity and Partitions of Difference." In *Globalizing Cities*, edited by P. Marcuse and R. van Kempen. Oxford: Blackwell.

Wall Street Journal. 1989. "Busing in Higher Costs." 20 November.

Wallace, Samuel E. 1980. *The Urban Environment.* Homewood, IL: Dorsey.

Walters, Laurel Shaper. 1996. "Charter Schools Get A's from Many Reformers." *Christian Science Monitor,* 16 February: 5.

Walton, John. 1966. "Discipline, Method, and Community Power." *American Sociological Review* 33:576–93.

Warf, Barney, and Brian Holly. 1997. "The Rise and Fall and Rise of Cleveland." *Annals of the American Academy of Political and Social Science* 551(May):208–21.

Warner, Sam. 1962. *Streetcar Suburbs.* Cambridge: Harvard and Massachusetts Institute of Technology.

Washburn, Gary. 1989. "CTA Riders Face New Challenge." *Chicago Tribune,* 29 October.

———. 2001. Telephone conversation with author, October 15.

Washington Post. 6/15/1975.

Watkins, Alfred J., and David C. Perry. 1977. "Regional Change and the Impact of Uneven Urban Development." In *The Rise of the Sunbelt Cities,* edited by D. Perry and A. Watkins. Beverly Hills: Sage.

Watson, Keith, and Steven Gold. 1999. *The Other Side of Devolution: Shifting Relationships between State and Local Governments.* The Urban Institute.

Wattenberg, Ben. 1999. "The Sprawl Brawl." *On the Issues.* American Enterprise Institute.

Weeks, John. 1999. *Population.* 7th ed. Belmont, CA: Wadsworth.

Weinberg, Daniel H. 1995. "Measuring Poverty: Issues and Approaches." Washington, DC: U.S. Bureau of the Census, Poverty Measurement Working Papers Series.

Weiner, Edward. 1988. *Urban Transportation Planning in the United States: An Historical Overview.* Washington, DC: U.S. Department of Transportation.

Weir, Margaret. 1996. "Central Cities' Loss of Power in State Politics." *Cityscape* 2(2):23–40.

Weisman, Alan. 1989. "L.A. Fights for Breath." *This World,* 6 August: 19.

"Welfare Reform's Good Report Card." 1999. *Chicago Tribune* editorial, 14 June:1,12.

Wellman, Barry, and S. D. Berkowitz. 1988. *Social Structures: A Network Approach.* Cambridge: Cambridge University.

Wellman, Barry, and Scot Wortley. 1990. "Different Strokes for Different Folks: Community Ties and Social Support." *American Journal of Sociology* 96:558–88.

White, Morton, and Lucia White. 1962. *The Intellectual Versus the City.* Cambridge: Harvard and Massachusetts Institute of Technology.

Whyte, William. 1956. *The Organization Man.* Garden City, NY: Doubleday Anchor.

Widrow, Woody. 1987. "Dispelling the Myths of Housing Vouchers." *Shelterforce* (September/October): 15.

Wilder, Margaret, and Barry Rubin. 1988. "Targeted Redevelopment Through Urban Enterprise Zones." *Journal of Urban Affairs* 10(l): 1–17.

Wilensky, Harold, and Charles LeBeau. 1965. *Industrial Society and Social Welfare.* New York: Free Press.

Wilson, James. 1983 (1975). *Thinking About Crime.* New York: Vintage.

Wilson, Robert, and David Schulz. 1978. *Urban Sociology.* Englewood Cliffs, NJ: Prentice-Hall.

Wilson, William J. 1987. *The Truly Disadvantaged.* Chicago: University of Chicago.

Wilson-Sadberry, Karen. 1995. "Impact of the School Environment: Desegregation to Resegregation." In *Race and Ethnicity in America,* edited by G. Thomas. Washington, DC: Taylor and Francis.

Wirth, Louis. 1938. "Urbanism as a Way of Life." *American Journal of Sociology* 44:1–24.

Wolff, Kurt. 1950. *The Sociology of Georg Simmel.* New York: Free Press.

Wolman, Harold, and Michael Goldsmith. 1992. *Urban Politics and Policy.* Cambridge, MA: Blackwell.

Wood, Robert. 1964. *1400 Governments: The Political Economy of the New York Metropolitan Region.* Garden City, NY: Doubleday.

Woolbright, Louie, and David Hartmann. 1987. "The New Segregation: Asians and Hispanics." In *Divided Neighborhoods,* edited by G. Tobin. Newbury Park, CA: Sage.

Work, Clemens. 1987. "Jam Sessions." *U.S. News and World Report,* 7 September: 20–26.

Working Group on Housing. 1989. *The Right to Housing: A Blueprint for Housing the Nation.* Washington, DC: Institute for Policy Studies.

World Bank. 1987, 1989, 1990, 1993, 2000. *World Development Report.* New York: Oxford University. <http://www.worldbank.org/data/countrydata/countrydata/html>

Wuthnow, Robert. 1994. *Sharing the Journey.* New York: Free Press.

Wyly, Elvin, and Steven Holloway. 1999. "The Color of Money Revisited: Racial Lending Patterns in Atlanta's Neighborhoods." *Housing Policy Debate* 10(3): 555–600.

Yeung, Yue-Man. 1988. "Great Cities in Eastern Asia." In *The Metropolis Era,* vol. 1, edited by M. Dogan and J. Kasarda. Beverly Hills: Sage.

Yinger, John. 1987. "The Racial Dimension of Urban Housing Markets in the 1980s." In *Divided Neighborhoods,* edited by G. Tobin. Newbury Park, CA: Sage.

———. 1995. *Closed Doors, Opportunities Lost: The Continuing Costs of Housing Discrimination.* New York: Russell Sage Foundation.

Zhou, Min. 1992. *Chinatown: The Socioeconomic Potential of an Urban Enclave*. Philadelphia: Temple University Press.

Zito, Jacqueline. 1974. "Anonymity and Neighboring in an Urban High-Rise Complex." *Urban Life and Culture* 3:243–63.

Zukin, Sharon. 1982. *Loft Living: Culture and Capital in Urban Change*. Baltimore: Johns Hopkins University Press.

Index